TRADITION AND CRISIS

TRADITION AND CRISIS

Jewish Society at the End of the Middle Ages

Jacob Katz

TRANSLATED AND WITH AN
AFTERWORD AND BIBLIOGRAPHY BY

Bernard Dov Cooperman

Syracuse University Press

First Syracuse University Press Edition 2000
00 01 02 03 04 05 6 5 4 3 2 1

Originally published in Hebrew as *Masoret u-Mashber* in 1958.
Previously published in 1993 by New York University Press.

The paper used in this publication meets the minimum requirements of American National Standard for Informational Sciences—Permanence of Paper for Printed Library Materials, ANSI Z39.48-1984.∞™

Library of Congress Cataloging-in-Publication Data

Katz, Jacob, 1904–
[Masoret u-mashber. English]
Tradition and crisis: Jewish society at the end of the Middle Ages / Jacob Katz: translated and with an afterword and bibliography by Bernard Dov Cooperman.
p. cm. — (Medieval studies)
Previously published: 1st pbk. ed. New York : Schocken Books, c1993.
Includes bibliographical references and index.
ISBN 0-8156-2827-7 (pbk. : alk. paper)
1. Jews—Social life and customs. 2. Jews—History—70-1789. I. Cooperman, Bernard Dov, 1946– II. Title. III. Medieval studies (Syracuse, N.Y.)

DS112 .K373 2000
909'.04924—dc21 99-089432

Manufactured in the United States of America

To the memory of my brothers,
may their memory be for a blessing:
Chaim David
who fell in the Land of Israel
during the bloody riots of
Wednesday, 4 Shvat, 5698
and
Israel
who was murdered together with his family
in the Holocaust of Hungarian Jewry
in the month of Sivan, 5714.
—J.K.

To the memory of my mother
עליה השלום:
Bella Nurenberg Cooperman
1905–1988
—B.D.C.

Contents

Translator's Foreword

When I first began teaching college-level courses in Jewish history, I regularly assigned Professor Jacob Katz's well-known study *Tradition and Crisis* as required reading. In the original Hebrew (Jerusalem: 1957–58; second edition, 1963), the work had had a profound effect on my own approach to the Jewish past, and I was eager to share my enthusiasm with my students. To my chagrin, however, I discovered that students often found the English translation difficult to read and hard to follow. Occasional paragraphs and sentences had been dropped, thoughts were left unclear, and all of the footnotes had been omitted from the English version.

I mentioned my frustration to Professor Katz and, in what may have been a rash moment, offered to "fix up" the text should a new English edition be contemplated. I must admit that when, several years later, Professor Katz approached me with the news that a publisher was willing to issue such a new edition, I agreed without realizing just how much work would be involved. In fact, the present work is a totally new translation of the original. When an occasional ambiguity or stylistic issue required modifying the text, I have checked directly with Professor Katz. In adding the footnotes, I have modified the citation style to fit the needs of the English reader; I have rechecked many of the references and corrected typographical errors or added to citations where necessary. I have also added references to English translations of cited works where these exist. Finally, I have added two appendices that I hope will be useful to both the beginner and the specialist: a list of Professor Katz's primary and secondary sources (with new editions noted) and an afterword evaluating the impact of this book on the field in the years since it was first published. If the footnotes and appendices encourage English-speaking historians to make more extensive use of rabbinic sources in their work, a major goal of this new edition will have been accomplished. In accordance with the audience at which this translation is aimed, I have for the most part limited my survey to works available in English.

The main part of this translation was done during a year's stay at the Institute for Advanced Studies in Jerusalem, and I should like to thank the director and staff of the Institute for the congenial and supportive atmosphere that they provided. Thanks also to our family in Israel, Nathan and Lily Silver and their children, whose generosity and warmth have meant so much to us over the years. Dr. Michael Grunberger and the staff in the Hebrew Division of the Library of Congress were always gracious in helping with the seemingly endless task of chasing down footnotes. I also want to thank Bonny Fetterman, senior editor of Schocken Books, who, because of her admiration for Professor Katz's work, devoted enormous effort to making this publication possible. Finally, I acknowledge with love my wife, Dianne Elisheva, and our children, Hillel, Aliya, Avital, and Yael, who agreed to forgo even further their just claims on my time so that this project could be finished. In dedicating this translation to the memory of my mother, Bella Nurenberg Cooperman, I would like to honor a woman who devoted her life to maintaining tradition in the face of constant crisis.

Bernard Dov Cooperman
College Park, Maryland
November 1990

Preface

It is unusual that a book translated more than two decades ago should be thought in need of, and worthy of, a new rendering. The present translation of my *Tradition and Crisis* is, however, not merely an improved version of the previous one but, rather, the first complete English version of the Hebrew original, which includes for the first time its extensive footnotes. These were omitted from the earlier translation because it was judged that the prospective American reader would be content with the basic text and would not be interested in the scholarly apparatus with its references to the historical sources. This may indeed have been the case in the early 1960s. In the meantime, however, due to the tremendous—and unexpected—expansion of Jewish studies in American universities, Jewish history has become a part of the curriculum of hundreds of academic courses. Probably by virtue of its theme—the description of traditional society prior to its dissolution on the threshold of modernity—*Tradition and Crisis* was found to be a useful introduction to the problematics of Jewish history. In this context, the lack of documentation in the English translation was often criticized and regretted.

Professor Bernard Dov Cooperman, then of Harvard University, appreciating the book's merits in the original Hebrew but critical of the deficiencies of the English version, came up with the suggestion of a new and complete translation and generously volunteered to undertake the task. He not only added the missing notes but made the text itself much more readable, taking care at the same time that the author's original intention continued to be reflected in the new translation. At times he suggested changes from the original Hebrew, most of which I gladly accepted. He also added an afterword of recent publications by various authors, including the author himself. This bibliographical essay will bring the interested reader up-to-date on research related to the subject of this book that has appeared in the intervening years. To include these new findings in the text itself would have meant disrupting the book's structure. The book does not pretend, therefore, to be of the latest vintage. Rather, it recommends itself as having stood the test of time, and it is hoped that this new rendering will increase its usability as an introduction to this crucial era in Jewish history.

Jacob Katz
The Hebrew University
Jerusalem
October 1988

Preface to the First Edition

This book is historical in subject and sociological in approach. It focuses on the sixteenth through eighteenth centuries, a period that is considered part of the modern era in general European history but the end of the Middle Ages in the context of Jewish history. In order to address my subject—Jewish society—I had to draw upon the analytical tools of sociology, the science of society. My desire to present all aspects, institutions, and functions of that society forced me to deal with many topics: political and social conditions, economic problems, forms of organization, the structure of the family, the methods of education, and the efforts at renewal in both religious and social spheres.

I am well aware that many, and perhaps most, of the topics under consideration deserve a separate, detailed treatment of their own. Nevertheless, it is wrong to assume that there is only one form of progress in historical research: from the particular to the general. We also test the particular and determine its value and meaning by placing it within a properly constructed framework. Only by viewing the particular within a comprehensive overview can we see what is missing and what remains to be done.

My description is derived from the various primary sources of the period: communal and provincial *pinkasim* [registers], ethical and polemical works, and the like. I have drawn on the halakhic literature of the period—*responsa*, codes, and commentaries—more than is common among historians. Moreover, I have not restricted myself to noting historical *realia* incidentally recorded in these works. I have focused on the laws themselves, which, after all, formed an obligatory religious norm for the Jews of that era. For me these laws stand out as evidence of the life and spirit of the time, and bear witness to the many theoretical and practical conflicts that affected both the individual and the community. I have drawn upon the religious training of my youth in order not to treat as dead letters that which was, for our subjects, a philosophy of life.

I had already arrived at some of the conclusions suggested here during my early studies abroad, and I have been able to include sections of my doctoral dissertation[1] in the last two chapters. Similarly, the chapters dealing with the family are based on my article "Marriage and Sexual Life at the End of the Middle Ages," which appeared in *Zion* 10 (1944–45).

It goes without saying that I have depended heavily on studies of this period by earlier and current scholars. It is doubtful whether several of the chapters in this book could have been written without the prior work of my friend Professor Israel Halperin, who edited *Pinkas Vaad Arba Araẓot* and *Takanot Medinat Mehrin*. The informed reader will also notice that in several fundamental issues of Jewish history in the Diaspora, I have relied on the views of Professor Yitzhak Baer. Even though most of Professor Baer's studies deal with a period earlier than mine, his insights remain illuminating. I was forced to rely on the research of others especially in the area of Kabbala and the movements that stemmed from it. Though these are very obscure areas, historians can now easily rely on the research of Professor Gershom Scholem and his followers. I readily admit to having drawn upon this fountain of knowledge, both in conversations and through his writings.

Three members of the Department of Sociology have given freely of their time and effort to this project. Professor S. N. Eisenstadt, Dr. Yonina Talmon-Gerber, and Dr. Joseph Ben-David each read the manuscript at different stages. Their comments and criticism encouraged me to perfect the content and improve the structure insofar as I was able to do so. If anything distinguishes my book from similar works, it is the fact that I have benefited from the friendship of people in two fields, history and sociology.

In writing this book I was aided by a Metz Foundation research fellowship granted me by the Faculty of the Humanities at Hebrew University for the year 1954–55.

I did not write this book in order to advocate any specific current policy. As its title indicates, however, the book describes a stage in the development of the Jewish people in which cracks began to appear in the unifying conceptualization that had informed Judaism almost from the very start. The entire Jewish past is implicit in this transition from "tradition" to "crisis," and the tension between these two forces continues to be a major problem in our own day. I do not believe that any historical investigation can provide answers to contemporary problems, but history can help us to understand the background to the situation we face today. If my book contributes to this process of understanding, I will be gratified by this incidental benefit.

Jacob Katz
Jerusalem
1st of Shvat, 5718 [*1957*]

A Note on Transliteration

In order to make the text as readable as possible, I have simplified the transliteration of Hebrew texts. Even though it is anachronistic, I have chosen to imitate the modern pronunciation of Israeli Hebrew —the most familiar form of the language today. *Alef* and *ayin* are marked (′) only when the English reader might otherwise be confused (e.g., *yoẓ'ei* for **יוצאי**; *de'a* for **דעה**; and note *loke'aḥ* for **לוקח**). *Chet* is denoted by *ḥ* and *tzaddik* by *ẓ*, except in names and terms with familiar spellings in English, such as Yitzhak and Bar Mitzva. Names are generally transcribed as they appear in the *Encyclopedia Judaica* (1972), and accepted English equivalents have been substituted where they exist. Hebrew acronyms are represented by uppercase letters, with vowels added in lower case to make the words readable in English (e.g., RaMBaM for *R*abbi *M*oses *B*en *M*aimon; RaSHI for *R*abbi *SH*lomo [Solomon] ben *I*saac; but note ReMA′ for Rabbi Moses Isserles, to correspond with the common pronunciation of the Hebrew **רמ״א**). Cross-references to acronyms are included in the list of sources at the end of this volume. Finally, references to passages in standard halakhic codes and their commentaries have been systematized as follows: §123.4.5 would refer to the annotation **ה** that is appended to paragraph **ד** in chapter **קכ״ג** of the text.

B.D.C.

PART I

THE BASIS OF EXISTENCE

1

Definition of Our Subject

This book is intended as a description of a "traditional society"—that is, a society that saw itself as based upon a body of knowledge and a set of values handed down to it from the past. World Jewry was such a "traditional society" at least from the Talmudic era until the age of the European Emancipation. Indeed, segments of Jewish society may be referred to in this way even in more recent times. We shall confine our discussion to one particular period: We are interested in presenting a socio-historical analysis of traditional Jewish society specifically in the period immediately prior to its dissolution—that is, from the end of the sixteenth to the second half of the eighteenth century. The dissolution of this society—the transition to Hasidism in the East and to Haskala (Enlightenment) and civil rights in the West—will form an integral part of our subject. We shall deal with earlier periods only insofar as they serve as sources for the ideas and values that were passed down to this period; we shall not treat them as subjects in themselves.

The sixteenth, seventeenth, and eighteenth centuries form a particularly eventful period in Jewish history. From a demographic point of view, we see Polish Jewry rising to far greater prominence than it had ever had prior to the mid-sixteenth century. About a century later, German Jewry likewise regained some of its earlier vitality. During this period Jews established communities in Holland and England, countries that had been closed to them for many centuries. The Jewish resettlement of Palestine, despite its uneven pace, may also be seen as a characteristic aspect of the period.

This period was also important in the cultural history of the Jewish people. In the area of literature, we can point to prolific output in the fields of Halakha, Kabbala, and homiletics. Whatever we may think of the content and lasting importance of this literature, its very quantity bears witness to the intensity of contemporary spiritual activity. Reactions to current events, most notably the Polish pogroms of 1648–49 and the messianic activities of Sabbetai Ẓvi in Turkey in 1665–66, provide further evidence of this spiritual enthusiasm. And about a century later, two more movements—Hasidism and Haskala—would likewise create major turning points in the social history of the community.

The Nature of Social History. We will not treat each of these subjects and processes individually. Unlike the purely chronological approach to history, which treats each event as a separate topic, the methodology of the social historian imposes certain limits on its practitioner and demands a more organic approach. First, we are circumscribed geographically. Since we will also be dealing with the breakdown of traditional society in our description, we are limited to the countries where this process of dissolution took place. These are Lithuania, Poland, Hungary, and the Germanic lands from Moravia and Bohemia in the East to Alsace in the West. In short, we shall be concerned with the area of settlement of Ashkenazic Jewry in the most extended sense of this term. The Jewries of these countries were affected by the transition to Hasidism on the one hand, and the social disintegration that followed emancipation on the other. In other countries—France, Italy, England, the Balkans, North Africa, and elsewhere—different factors and circumstances applied.

Geographic self-limitation is demanded not only by our desire to portray the society's dissolution. It is also necessitated by the very nature of our methodology. Unlike narrative history, social history concerns itself with the social reality prevailing at a given time rather than with the individual event. Social history describes and analyzes not what happened at a specific time and place but what *typically* occurred within a society. No sphere is outside its frame of reference. Economic, political, cultural, social, and religious activities must all be described and analyzed. Data from all these spheres must be assembled, but only in order to provide clues as to the behavioral *norms* prevailing in each field during the period. In other words, social history is concerned not with particular events but with the institutions within which those events took place.[1]

Accordingly, when we come to describe economic activity, in-group and out-group social relations, community administration, family life, and the like, we do not ask: How did a particular individual conduct himself in any one of these areas? Instead, we pose the questions: What was customary? How did the *average* member of society act? Our approach is based on the assumption that members of a society do not conduct themselves in an accidental or arbitrary manner. Rather, people's conduct follows fixed patterns, and the sum total of these accepted patterns in each sphere is the institutionalized norm of behavior for that sphere within that society. To the extent that more than one parallel pattern is accepted as within the norm, the individual is free to choose among them. But if he chooses a pattern of behavior that is not accepted in this way, he will be considered deviant, a result that in itself guarantees the rarity of such a choice. The accepted pattern represents not only the average or mean; it is also the norm that determines the behavior of contemporaries.

The first task of social history is therefore to discover what is the typical and accepted pattern embodied within the framework of various social institutions. This aim can be achieved so long as we confine our study to institutions such as the family, of which many exist simultaneously within a single society. It is widely accepted that there is room, alongside the study of specific family histories (i.e., genealogy), for the social history of the family in general. This social history seeks to describe the traits characteristic of most families in a society and then to trace the variations in the archetypal pattern. Admittedly, the family described by the social historian has no actual reality; it is merely an abstraction conjured up by the scholar, who constructs it from the records of the many families he investigates. Nevertheless, this generalizing approach constitutes the most rewarding method of describing the nature and evolution of the family in its social context.

Scholars do not agree quite as unanimously that this method applies also to the study of larger and more formal social institutions, such as the *kehila* (Jewish community) and supra-*kehila* organizations. With regard to these, scholars have traditionally opted for a different approach; they have described the history of each *kehila* and supra-*kehila* unit individually. In fact, however, there is no essential difference between the family and the community. Both lend themselves equally well to investigation and description as specific one-time events and as examples of more general phenomena. Everything depends on the aim in mind. While the history of any *kehila* may be presented as an individual, specific case, that of the *kehila* per se has to be reconstructed through a process of abstract generalization.

Geographic Divisions of History. Our aim and methodological objective require us to limit the geographical extent of our description. Even though, as we shall see, the Jewish people throughout the Diaspora were united by the sense of a common past, this historical consciousness did not forge the Jews into a single society. All Jews, whether in Poland or Yemen, Holland or Palestine, saw themselves as members of a single nation. Moreover, they all maintained some social institutions—for example, those devoted to education and religious worship—that articulated their common tradition. But even these institutions varied from country to country. How much greater, then, were the local variations in institutions devoted to economic, administrative, familial, or other social concerns. These social institutions cannot be lumped together and treated as a single unit.

In order to describe Jewish society in depth, we must divide the Jewish world territorially into a number of "centers." Each center or territory thus gains a sort of historiographical independence that accurately reflects its real-life independence from all the others. The more clearly we can see a common normative standard that determines life-style, the more justified we are in declaring a region a single historical entity that must be treated as a unit by social historians. Similarly, the existence of a common normative standard in several geographic regions can be taken as proof of a living connection between them, for it is difficult to believe that the same normative standards would rule public and private behavior in diverse areas unless there was such a real link between them.

There are a number of criteria by which we can determine the extent of contact between geographic regions for any period: To what other areas was a region linked economically? Where was a given dialect spoken? (The latter usually determined the range of internal migration within a single center.) How large was the area within which marriages were commonly arranged? How far did students usually travel in order to study Torah? From where did communities usually draw their rabbinical scholars? And so forth. These are the type of criteria that we can use in order to establish the extent of mutual influence among centers otherwise divided by both distance and political boundaries. All of the countries that we have included in the present discussion—Poland, Bohemia, Moravia, Germany, and western Hungary—form a single unit from all of these points of view. This is the fundamental justification for the geographic boundaries that we used in our research. The breakdown of this unity and the emergence of self-consciously diverse communities is in itself one of the indications of the historic turning point that we shall observe in our study.

Indications of National Unity. It goes without saying that in subdividing Jewish history regionally we are following the dictates of our methodology and do not in any way mean to question the underlying national unity of the Jewish people in the Diaspora. Quite the contrary; it is because we accept that essential unity that we must carefully define the extent to which it can serve as a basis for a unified historical portrait. Jewish communities everywhere shared a common faith, national tradition, and hope for future redemption, and these shared values marked the Jews off clearly from their gentile neighbors. But the fact that each Jewish community stood apart from its environment does not of itself prove that these widely scattered communities formed a single social unit in any real sense. Only to the extent that their shared values actively and effectively led to real mutual contact can we conclude that there was also a social unity behind the national identity.

Were there extensive contacts between Jewish communities? There can be no question that the answer to this question is in the affirmative. The widely scattered communities were linked in every way possible. There was ongoing concern for each other's fate, effective responses to crisis, and mutual aid when possible.[2] Indeed, compared with other periods in Jewish history, the sixteenth through eighteenth centuries witnessed a marked strengthening of the real bonds between the various sections of the people. Contacts between various parts of the people were probably more intense during our period than they had ever been since the declining days of the Roman Empire, when world Jewry was still united within a single organizational framework.

The Jewish people was especially dependent on long-distance travel and communication to maintain contacts between its various communities. Inevitably, therefore, Jewish life benefited in particular from the improved means of transportation and the intensified commercial links generally characteristic of Europe and the Mediterranean region in this era. Intensified contact is evident in various spheres—for example, in the area of mutual aid. When the Jews of Prague were in trouble in 1745, the leading Jews of all central Europe lent a helping hand.[3] Communities from Istanbul to Amsterdam likewise took it upon themselves to help ransom Jewish captives after the pogroms of 1648–49 in eastern Europe.[4]

Jewish pilgrimage and, even more so, migration to the Holy Land also increased markedly during this period, and served to strengthen the Jews' sense of a common origin and to reinforce their hope for a shared, messianic future. The links between Diaspora communities were also strengthened by the pilgrims' memories of their meetings in Palestine with Jews from all over the world and by the common cause of supporting the communities in Palestine. During our period special emissaries of those communities traveled throughout the Diaspora seeking funds and, at the same time, helping to link and unite the various communities they visited.[5]

Increased mobility in the Jewish community also facilitated the dissemination of culture and helped to spread the new ideas currently emerging in various centers of learning. Law codes, new methods of Talmudic study, and kabbalistic and hermeneutic concepts were spread much more rapidly and reached a much greater audience than had been true in earlier periods. The success of the Sabbatean movement can be understood only on the basis of the wide circulation of the Lurianic concepts of redemption and their deep penetration into the Jewish consciousness.[6] That Sabbetai Ẓvi could convince a widely scattered people to expect redemption on a single day bears eloquent testimony to the unity of the Jewish people during this period.

To the extent that it is ever legitimate to speak of the history of nations in organic terms, it is certainly legitimate to do so with regard to the Jewish people in the Diaspora. The Jews formed a "national body" that reacted to external stimuli as well as to internal developments. Although that national body would begin to dissolve imminently and lose its capacity for unified action, it had reached the height of its potential for action specifically in this period.

Granted this "organic" unity, we certainly seem to have sufficient justification for writing a *national* history of the Jewish people. But as we have tried to explain, such a study would necessarily be limited to those aspects of Jewish history that were truly common to the entire people—that is, to those processes and events that determined its common religious, historical, and messianic values. As soon as we try to include the other aspects of life—political, economic, institutional, and the like—in our study, we are forced to limit ourselves to historical units smaller than the entire people. Obviously, the two types of studies—the national and the regionally defined—will overlap to a degree. The regional treatment must mention elements common to the entire nation, since the fate of each Jewish community in every place and at every time was determined by the shared fact of Jewishness. To a certain degree Jewish history repeats itself not just in chronological terms but in geographical terms as well, and the history of each Jewish community is merely a variation on the common theme. But this does not contradict the individuality of these smaller units. It is the historian's task to uncover the particularist nuances and to set them against the more general background. One can also argue that all of human history is nothing but a set of variations on a few common motifs, and yet no two historical units are completely identical.[7]

Thus, in describing a particular example of traditional Jewish society we aim simultaneously at two goals. We hope to describe that society in its unique, historical singularity and at the same time present the historical picture as an example of traditional Jewish society in general. It might be argued that in the concluding part of our study the transition to Hasidism and Haskala presents us with historical developments so singular that they have no echo in the broader history of Jewish society and therefore cannot be regarded as typical phenomena. What parallels are there, after all, to Hasidism or Haskala? But in fact even these two apparently unique movements can be seen as examples of broader phenomena. Hasidism and Haskala exemplify the two forces that typically cause the disintegration of traditional social institutions: religious charisma and rationalism. Religious charisma springs from a sense of immediate religious mission, whereas rationalism is grounded upon a belief in the unlimited power of reason and logic. Religious charisma and rationalism are essentially opposites, and are likely to come into conflict when they exist in the same historical framework. But they share a common attitude toward traditionalism: Both find the source of their authority in themselves, and tend to minimize any authority that rests solely on the force of tradition.[8] Both of these types of challenges can be found in Jewish history even in earlier periods. More than once, traditional Jewish society has faced the real threat that rationalist criticism or the demands made by a sense of religious mission could harm or destroy it completely.[9] This is not the place to deal with the question of how or why traditional society escaped this danger prior to the first half of the eighteenth century. But the fact that both of these powerful challenges emerged simultaneously on the historical stage at the end of our period serves as double testimony to the historic watershed at which traditional society had arrived.

2

Jewish Society and Its Environment

While it is true that the Jewish people can be treated by historians as a single social unit, its dispersal inevitably implies that each section of this social unity was simultaneously a part of a broader gentile society. Of course, Jewish communities participated in this broader society in a different way than they did in the Jewish totality. The Jewish community belonged to the local non-Jewish society primarily in an ecological sense. Still, there is more than mere physical proximity involved here. There was also the fundamental social interdependence that must exist wherever people maintain any type of contact to fulfill mutual needs. In this sense the Jews were certainly a part of their surrounding society everywhere. They provided certain functions for that society, and many of their needs were supplied by it. In sociological terminology we can call the Jews a "subgroup" of the surrounding society. Though isolated in many respects, the Jewish subgroup was also integrated into surrounding society and dependent on it for survival. In subsequent chapters we shall explore the nature of this interdependence, just as we must describe the ways in which the two societies were separate from each other.

Logically speaking, we should begin our description with the economic functions that Jews fulfilled in the surrounding society. After all, it was the economic sphere that served as a common ground for Jewish-gentile interdependence. But the nature of Jewish economic activity was itself determined by other factors: the Jews' religious and social separateness from society and the political status that resulted from that separateness. Therefore, before we treat Jewish economic life we must first describe the demographic, ecological, religio-cultural, and political facts that ultimately determined the Jews' place within the surrounding society.

Demographic Factors. Demographers estimate that there were some three-quarters of a million Ashkenazic Jews at the beginning of this period (1648), a third in central Europe and two-thirds farther east, in Poland and Lithuania. They represented about one-half of the world

Jewish population. By the end of this period, European Jewry had doubled in size: at the end of the eighteenth century its numbers stood at approximately a million and a half. Despite growth, it seems that Jews never formed more than 2 or 3 percent of the total population in Poland, Lithuania, Germany, and Austro-Hungary, except perhaps in seventeenth-century Poland, where they may have amounted to as much as 6 or 7 percent.[1] Neither Jews nor their leaders had any clear idea of these numbers, either in absolute terms or relative to the size of the general population. But we can be sure that everywhere, even in Poland, the Jews always perceived of themselves as a tiny minority.

Presumably, the Jews' sense of minority status varied with the size of their own community and with the frequency of contact with members of other, nearby communities. We know that both the size of Jewish communities and the overall density of Jewish population varied enormously in this period. Jewish settlements ranged from isolated individuals living among gentiles to the ten thousand and more in the Prague community of the seventeenth and eighteenth centuries.[2] As for density, in western and central Germany communities were widely separated, so that direct contact was maintained only between members of the more mobile upper strata. In other regions—for example, in Poland, Moravia, and Alsace—Jews lived in cities and villages that were quite close to each other, so that continuous and ongoing contacts created the impression of a mass Jewish reality beyond the communal level. As we shall see, even the greatest isolation never broke down the Jews' sense of community. On the other hand, even in areas where the Jews might by chance form the majority of the population, they always accepted their minority status as natural and permanent, an expression of the qualitative distinctions between themselves and the indigenous population.

Special Characteristics. The special status of the Jewish community found its ecological expression in the fact that the Jews lived in neighborhoods separate from those of the general population. In our period, the ghetto (or ghettolike) system was in use in almost the entire Ashkenazi-Polish region. The Jews were restricted to certain streets by government ordinance, except in those hamlets and villages where the Jewish population was too small to warrant the establishment of a special quarter. Similarly, several German cities, such as Hanover and Dresden, did not insist on separate neighborhoods to keep Jews and Christians apart because Jews first settled there when the segregationist policy was already in decline. Even in such places, however, the Jews tended to congregate in one quarter near communal institutions such as the synagogue and house of study. Though these Jewish neighborhoods certainly provided better living conditions than the closed, narrow ghettos, their spontaneous emergence demonstrates again the tendency toward separateness that characterized Jewish life.

A further sign of Jewish social segregation lay in the Jew's outward appearance. In this period, it was no longer felt necessary to mark the Jewish population off with a special "Jew badge," as had been the practice during the Middle Ages. In most regions such laws had totally disappeared.[3] But many other factors still distinguished the Jew from the population at large, a population that was itself variegated in appearance along lines of profession and class. The Jews differed to a greater or lesser extent from the rest of the population in their clothing as well as in other aspects of their outward appearance—in the sidelocks and beards of men, the covered hair of married women, and perhaps also in their general physiognomy, which was more clearly distinct than in periods of greater social contact between the populations.

Language represented a third sign of Jewish separateness. As is well known, the Jews of the Ashkenazi-Polish region spoke Yiddish during this period. Though Yiddish varied from country to country and region to region, the important fact from our point of view is that Jews spoke a different language among themselves than the one used by the surrounding population. The gap between the languages varied from region to region. In eastern Europe—that is, in Poland and Lithuania—Yiddish was totally different from the local vernacular. The local population did not understand Yiddish at all—except for those few individuals who made it their business to learn the language or who came to understand it through their contacts with Jews in much the same manner that Jews learned to speak the vernacular to meet their own immediate needs.[4] On the other hand, in Germany and in those Polish cities settled by Germans, the two languages shared a common origin and root, and it was relatively easy for members of each group to understand the language of the other. But the linguistic closeness of Yiddish to German is essentially irrelevant to our point. Even within a nation speaking a common language, slight differences of accent and idiomatic usage suffice to create social barriers between members of different classes. How much more so was this true for speakers of Yiddish, who were distinguished from their neighbors not only by linguistic usage but also by nationality and religion. Even the *Jüdisch-Deutsch* dialect of German Jews, though historically close to spoken German, differed from it in pronunciation, syntax, and especially vocabulary. Like the Yiddish of eastern Europe, *Jüdisch-Deutsch* had absorbed hundreds of words and expressions from Hebrew and

Aramaic, and especially from the literary texts that provided the mainstay of popular education. This absorption of idioms and concepts from the world of traditional thought gave Yiddish and *Jüdisch-Deutsch* an essentially Jewish character despite their Germanic linguistic roots. And indeed, both Jews and non-Jews saw *Jüdisch-Deutsch* as a sign of cultural separation. So long as the Jews maintained their religio-cultural autonomy and exclusiveness, Yiddish and *Jüdisch-Deutsch* remained the appropriate means of expression for that inner Jewish world.[5]

The Religious Difference and Civil Status. The differences that we have listed so far all stem ultimately from the fundamental differences over religious principles that had separated Christianity and Judaism since ancient times. Each faith had its own set of beliefs and opinions, institutions for prayer, sacred mores, and customs. It was these that determined distinct Jewish and Christian ways of life. As we shall see, contact between the two communities was maintained despite this confessional barrier. Still, the strong attachment of the faithful to two opposing faiths remained the most important and conspicuous barrier separating two groups in constant physical proximity to one another.

Or so it would appear. Our study reveals that the special status of the Jew in the Diaspora was not a direct result of the religious difference. Members of other religions that were no less opposed and hostile to each other than Judaism and Christianity lived together in several areas of the world without either group being assigned a status similar to that of the Jews. The major feature of this status was that the Jew did not have the *right* to reside even in the place where he was born, unless this right was granted to him by a special judicial-legislative act. It was not religion per se that determined the Jew's place in the Christian world but the political and social conclusions that, from the second half of the Middle Ages on, society derived from the Jew's status. The teachings of the Church, to which were added complex political and juridical factors, eventually led to a situation in which the Jew's status gradually changed from that of a citizen to that of a foreigner whose residence depended on a special privilege from the ruler. This approach was concretized in the generally accepted term *servi camerae*—servants of the king. The only debate was over to which "king" the Jews belonged—in Germany it was the emperor or the burghers, and in Poland it was the king or the lords of giant estates. About the "servant" status of the Jew—that is, about the Jew's dependence on whoever had power to grant the right of residence—there was no debate.[6]

Nor did the Jews themselves question this assumption. Their status was not merely something imposed upon them by an external reality reinforced by centuries-long custom. Judaism also taught that the Jews' only right in the Diaspora was purchased from, and granted by, the rulers' kindness. Even when there was no apparent danger that the ruler would remove his favor and cancel the settlement privilege, the Jews privately saw themselves as merely waiting until God, in His mercy, would send the Messiah to redeem them and restore them to their homeland. This hope for future redemption reinforced the Jews' self-image as "temporary settlers," and thus they appeared to gentiles. Christians also made use of the Jews' spiritual attachment to the land of their historical origin as a further justification for not considering the Jews a part of the native population.[7] Thus was completed the ideological structure that considered the Jew a tolerated stranger rather than an accepted member of society.

The characterization of Jews as "temporary residents" was sometimes taken quite literally. The Jews were often required to negotiate with the local authorities for settlement rights. Even already-established Jews would sometimes have to negotiate their continued right of residency. In both cases we are speaking about a formal agreement between two parties—an agreement that fixed the Jews' rights as well as their obligations: on the one hand, their legal status, the types of professions permitted them, and so forth, and on the other hand, the taxes and other duties incumbent upon them. In fact, it is difficult to treat these as free agreements reached between equal parties. The Jewish side in the negotiation can be termed "free" only when we are speaking of a substantially wealthy individual Jew who had the option of migrating to other lands. One cannot speak of the two sides to the negotiations being equal in cases where an entire Jewish population was seeking a place to live, much less when the negotiations were over the extension of a residence permit that if not granted would mean the expulsion of the local Jews.

The authorities had not only the power but also the unquestioned legal right to expel the Jews. If we do not find many expulsions in this period, and indeed, if we sometimes find governments inviting Jews to settle in regions where they had not formerly lived, this was a result of the concrete role that the Jews played in the economic life of the state. But even in these places, Jews settled only on the basis of a negotiated agreement, one that could be revoked, at least in theory, at any time. And there were some expulsions even during this era—for instance, the expulsion from Vienna in 1670 and that from Prague in 1745. The negotiations that went on to try to revoke these decrees and the responses of Jews to them clearly show that even the Jews themselves did not see expulsion per se as an infringement of their rights. The Jews argued that there was no reason to expel them—that is, that the expulsion was based on a false accusation, or that expulsion was economically unwise, or that it was religiously or morally improper for the rulers to expel them. But we never find the Jews claiming that an injustice had been done them, or claiming rights under some legal principle,[8] as they had even in the Middle Ages and as they would begin to do again at the end of our period. For brief periods, such as in Poland before 1648–49 and in Germany among the Court Jews, we note that the consciousness of exile lessened in the sense that the Jews developed a certain sense of local security. But even at these times, the feeling of relative security was not so much the result of a reliance on law as it was the psychological by-product of the real influence and power that certain classes of Jews had at that time. If that power diminished and that status declined, the Jews' feeling of security—never based on a sense of absolute belonging—also eroded. The Jews understood their troubles and suffering, such as the pogroms of 1648–49, not merely in political and social terms but as part of the broader punishment of exile. They were confirmed in this view by the extra measure of suffering that was theirs even during a general catastrophe and, particularly, by the redoubled efforts to convert them at such times.

The conceptions and opinions described above formed the ideational basis that fixed the status of the Jewish populace in each place. The objective economic conditions, the value that the rulers placed upon the profit that might derive from Jewish settlement within their territories, the degree of pressure that rival factors placed upon the Jews in the economic sphere, and finally, the power of religious fanatics to whom the Jews appeared as a thorn in the side—these are the major factors that determined whether Jews would be allowed to enter and settle in a state, and whether those Jews already resident would be allowed to continue living there. Of course, once Jews had been given residence rights in an area, the very fact of their residence also became a factor—but only because it is harder to remove something *post facto* than to establish it in the first place. Prior Jewish residence never became a legal precedent *per se*.

The Area of Jewish Settlement. There was clearly significant migration during our period within the Ashkenazi-Polish center. During the first half of the seventeenth century, Jews migrated to Volhynia, Podolia, and the Ukraine. The Polish estate owners' need for investors and administrators opened the gates to Jewish settlers. Similar needs, though operating in a different economic environment, led to the creation of new communities and the expansion of older ones in Germany during the second half of the seventeenth century. The principles of mercantilism that sought to increase the state's supplies of money made rulers more willing to accept Jewish settlers. But negative factors were also evident. The Jews competed with their economic counterparts within the general population, the craftsmen and guild merchants, and there was not always an economic or political force present to support the Jews. Until the end of our period, and even afterward, not a few cities and regions—such as the Mazovia region, the Polish city of Drogobych (Drohobycz), Munich in Germany, and Strasbourg in France—remained totally closed to Jews. Other cities, such as Warsaw and Leipzig (until the beginning of the eighteenth century), allowed Jews to enter only for business purposes on market days and the like, but prevented them from settling permanently.[9] The combination of three factors—the expectation of profit, the fear of competition, and the power of religious fanaticism—determined the fate of the Jews and decided whether or not they would receive permission to settle in a given place. These factors operated within the public-legal context described above, which denied to the Jews any claim to a *right* of residence. From a legal point of view, a Jew seeking a residence privilege in a given place had first to prove his case. Hence, any description of the characteristics of this period must not content itself with simply listing expulsions. Rather, we must realize that all Jews lived their lives under the shadow of possible expulsion to one degree or another. As we shall see, one of the primary tasks of the communal and supra-communal organizations during this period was to watch for any possible threat of expulsion and, should one arise, to try to allay it.

3

Barriers against the Outside

The demographic, ecological, religio-cultural, and political facts described in the previous chapter are the objective realities that determined the existential framework of the Jewish community as a whole. Each individual member of this community related to the non-Jewish world in thought and deed in accordance with these realities. But thoughts and behavior are not simply the results of an individual's particular reaction to a situation. In this area, as in all others, thoughts and actions are directed by a traditional set of received concepts and norms. It is now our task to describe this tradition.

Laws that Separated. How did Jews define their own position in the gentile world? What, in other words, did they see as the major factor differentiating them from the rest of the world? The answer would appear to lie in Jewish tradition's claim to exclusive religious truth, all other religions being seen as false and illusory.[1] Talmudic tradition labeled all religions aside from Judaism with the same negative term, *avoda zara* (literally: alien worship; idolatry), and in the normal usage of halakhic (Jewish legal) debate, in the diatribes of ethical works, and in sermonic formulations, this term was unselfconsciously assumed to apply to Christianity as well. As we shall see below in our chapter on the foundations of education, this absolute distinction between Israel and the nations was inculcated in Jews from their earliest youth.

The traditional sources include an entire network of laws and rules intended to control every aspect of contact with the non-Jew, from matters of food and drink to the give-and-take of commerce. We might assume, therefore, that the Jew of our period had a clear set of guidelines by which to determine his conduct in the surrounding world. In fact, however, there was an enormous gap between the principles laid down in the tradition and the practical legal decisions arrived at by the interpreters of tradition in this regard. In theory, the Talmudic legislation that intended to create a social barrier as divisive and distancing as possible between members of the Jewish community and their gentile neighbors remained in force. But this was true only on a formalistic level.

Law and Reality. Already during the Middle Ages the Jews' situation had fundamentally changed from what it had been during the Talmudic period. Medieval Jewry no longer comprised a local majority that could provide most of its basic needs for itself. The community was now everywhere a minority, no more than an appendage to the economic structure of an alien society. Under such circumstances there was no longer any possibility of maintaining the segregationist rules whose intent had been to distance Jews from idolatry and idolators. And thus already during the Middle Ages we see the effective revocation of segregationist laws that had forbidden Jews to trade with non-Jews in certain products (*Avoda Zara,* fol. 14b) or on certain days (*ibid.,* fol. 2a). During the Middle Ages authorities were still called upon to justify such license.[2] By our period, sanction was simply assumed on the authority of the Jewish medieval legislators. Only trade in obvious objects of worship, such as incense, remained forbidden, for the medieval commentators had not found a casuistic means of allowing this. Indeed, the tendency now was to extend the commercial license to all other areas of contact with the gentiles.[3]

There were several reasons for this tendency. The most important factor was to be found in the economic conditions of Jewish life in this period. As we shall see, in this period the Jews came to be much more integrated into the economies of the lands in which they lived. The economic activities that this entailed came into conflict with restrictive religious rulings. We shall see below how the general problem of conflicts between religious imperative and economic need were resolved; for now it suffices to note that with regard to religious laws intended to segregate Jews from gentiles, economic pressure led to the revocation even of those laws that had still been observed during the Middle Ages. The clearest example of this is provided by the trade in *stam yeinam* —wine made by gentiles. It is forbidden for a Jew to drink and, theoretically, even to trade in, a gentile's wine. In the Middle Ages this restriction was still observed. The rabbis had found it quite difficult to find a way to permit trade even in a Jew's wine if it had been touched by a non-Jew and thus rendered forbidden for Jews to drink. Similar difficulties had been encountered in trying to allow Jews to accept gentile wine in payment for a debt.[4] In this period, on the other hand, license to engage in this trade gradually spread, especially in areas such as the Polish cities near the Hungarian border and in the Moravian communities, where the wine trade was an important part of the Jews' livelihood. At first the more stringent among the rabbis objected to this development, but they were not able to prevail in the face of increased economic pressure.[5] With time, this proscription gradually disappeared altogether, and the wine trade became a typical Jewish occupation in many regions of eastern and western Europe.[6]

Economic pressures, however, were not enough automatically to allow deviation from established religious norms. The suspension of any stricture required justification in halakhic terms as well, and there were already medieval halakhic precedents available for breaking down the restrictive segregationist rules. The great halakhists of the eleventh and twelfth centuries had allowed certain forbidden practices in the Talmud on the grounds that contemporary gentiles (i.e., Christians) were different from the idolators of Talmudic times. On the grounds that "gentiles in our time do not understand the essential nature of idolatry," it was allowed, for example, to trade with Christians on their holy days, and to accept the oath of a Christian as legal evidence in a Jewish court.[7] This distinction between contemporary Christians and idolators of the past was originally offered only in formalistic terms as one of several halakhic arguments to resolve a specific question.[8] The intense competitive tension between Christianity and Judaism that characterized the Middle Ages had not allowed for anything more.

But now, a changing relation between the two faiths allowed for interpreting this distinction as a broad statement of principle. In this period, the tension of religious competition had died down. Christians were less interested in converting the Jews, and the Jews, for their part, had virtually abandoned any such ambitions. There were isolated incidents of conversion to Judaism even in our period, but the emotional ardor tied up in the act, still present during the Middle Ages, was now gone.[9] The declining tension did not derive from any rapprochement or blurring of the distinctions between the two faiths, nor can it be attributed to a general decline in the importance of religion in defining society (as would be the case later, during the period of traditional society's collapse). To the contrary, declining tension in our period derived from social, environmental, and cultural barriers that had become so strong that the members of the two faiths were almost completely separated from each other. As we shall see, such separation would find ideological expression in contemporary views of the place of Israel among the nations. But this separation also fostered a certain tranquility vis-à-vis Christianity. No longer a threatening enemy, it was simply the religion of the nations among whom the Jews had settled. Formal statements intended only to remove the label of idolatry from Christianity were now enhanced by positive statements about the nature of the faith: "The nations in whose shelter the Jews live while in exile . . . believe in the doctrine of Creation, in the exodus from Egypt, and in the principles of faith, and they direct themselves toward Him who created the heaven and the earth."[10] Such statements are now repeated in various contexts. And the tolerant attitude toward Christianity further strengthened the original halakhic arguments. On the basis of the extended interpretation of the original distinction, halakhists became much more lenient with regard to *stam yeinam.*[11] On similar grounds, R. Moses Isserles allowed trading in Christian ritual objects such as "strings of knots called *Ptor Havalim.*"[12] Even where the Halakha continued to view the Christian ritual as idolatrous—as, for instance, when R. Ephraim Kohen treated the question of whether one might lend a Christian elegant clothes in which to go to Church[13]—it is clear that there was no desire to draw the most stringent conclusions from this position. The *heter* (halakhic dispensation) was easily derived from casuistic distinctions or given, as the Halakha put it, "because of enmity" and "the ways of peace"—that is, out of a desire to foster good neighborly relations.

Social Distancing. Of course, statements about the need for good relations with one's neighbors should not be equated with a desire to increase the level of social contact between Christians and Jews. Similar statements had been made already in medieval, and even Talmudic, times: Jewish doctors and, even more so, midwives were allowed to treat non-Jews, for example, "in order [to avoid] enmity."[14] But the intent had been only to foster an atmosphere of goodwill in circumstances where mutual relations were absolutely essential. It was always assumed that any such contact between Jew and non-Jew would remain utilitarian in purpose. The intention was not to encourage spending time together engaged in social amusements.[15] In this respect, the strict sanctions were never abrogated; indeed, they may have become more stringent in this period. Any kind of ongoing social contact between Jew and non-Jew was prevented in the first place by the regulations concerning forbidden food and drink. These sanctions did not prohibit a gentile from eating at a Jew's table, but they did prevent any kind of reciprocity, a necessary prerequisite for social relations based on equality. Visits and invitations involving meals between Jews and gentiles could occur only by happenstance,[16] and contemporary halakhists criticized even these. Halakhists and moralists were constantly on guard to see that neither contemporary social conditions nor the precedent of the licenses given in the economic sphere sanctioned breaking down the barriers to social rapprochement.

Day-to-day conditions required Jews occasionally to enter the houses of gentiles. It was never suggested that spending time in a gentile's house was forbidden in itself. Halakhic and ethical questions were raised only as peddling became more widespread and led to Jewish women entering Christian houses in order to sell their wares. Here we see a sharp conflict between religious and social forces. On the one hand, traditional ethical concepts saw the Jewish woman's taking to the road alone as an abandonment of her assigned role in society. Her staying in a gentile's house also raised formal halakhic issues, since it was forbidden for her to be alone with a male (*yiḥud*). On the other hand, the professional differentiation of the period, as we shall see, made it necessary to involve women in the making of a living. The halakhic sources clearly reveal the gradual economic integration of women, and the ways in which varying local social pressures led to different solutions. The initial tendency was to forbid women to engage in peddling or to allow this only if they were accompanied by a man, a condition so impractical as to make women's peddling impossible. In eighteenth-century Lithuania, there were still powerful social classes who saw their interests threatened by peddling, and they made use of religio-ethical arguments in their struggle against it.[17] In western Germany, on the other hand, where peddling became a primary source of Jewish livelihood, the halakhists moderated their opposition and even found a way to allow women to peddle, albeit with the caveat that they were merely justifying what had already become customary and that their license should be relied upon only when absolutely necessary.[18]

There were no parallel principles concerning the entry of Jewish males into Christian houses.[19] But halakhists had still to establish guidelines for Jews' behavior at prayer, for observance of the dietary laws, and the like. The intention of all this was clear: The Jew was directed to maintain the socioreligious barrier even when he was forced to be in the company of gentiles. The problem was a delicate one: How could one avoid insulting the gentile host while maintaining the socio-religious differentiation?

The conflict between these two goals—allowing necessary economic integration on the one hand, and maintaining a vital degree of social-religious differentiation on the other—is evident in many of the halakhists' and ethicists' discussions. They were not merely bothered by the increased level of economic contact. They were worried that the arguments by which such contacts were justified might be taken further and applied in unintended ways—that "a stricture relaxed in part was a stricture relaxed completely." This is once again clearly illustrated by the case of *stam yeinam*, or gentile wine. As we have noted, the practice of trading in gentile wine became quite widespread. At the same time, in many circles of Jewish society it became quite common to consume such wine. Presumably the practice was especially common in those countries, such as Italy and Moravia, where wine was the national drink, and where abstinence was especially difficult.[20]

But it was not the difficulty involved in observing a stricture that led people to ignore it. After all, other dietary restrictions also caused problems, and their observance required equally great effort and considerable self-denial on the part of the Jew. Laxity of practice spread in this case because the logic by which permission had been given to trade in wine could be extended to drinking it. Already in the Middle Ages, RaSHI and the Tosafists had worried about this possibility and debated whether to allow commerce in gentile wine. They ruled against this trade for fear that Jews would also ignore the prohibition against drinking the wine.[21] In our period, when the legitimacy of trading in gentile wine was broadly accepted, the demands of logical consistency had the expected effect. It seems clear that drinking *stam yeinam* was not limited to the unlettered masses. It was sanctioned even by halakhists who relied on the Tosafists' line of thinking. The lenient in this regard included even the greatest halakhist of his time, R. Moses Isserles.[22] He did not try to allow totally what was, in some regions, regarded as forbidden, but he did establish grounds for being lenient in this regard, and he provided strong enough justification that it was henceforth impossible to excommunicate those who engaged in the practice. The logical argument was made that if it was permitted to trade in the wine of contemporary gentiles because they were not considered idolators, then neither should it be forbidden to drink their wine.

While social pressure and the force of logic combined to form a potent argument for relaxing the traditional stricture, there was another, equally powerful factor that worked in the opposite direction: namely, the fear of social intimacy that might result from any relaxation of the rules against drinking gentile wine. This concern was already mentioned in the Talmud as one of the reasons for forbidding *stam yeinam*: "Their wine is forbidden because of their daughters" (*Avoda Zara*, fol. 36b). So long as it had been deemed forbidden to derive any pleasure from such wine, i.e., to trade in it, the legists had not had to fall back on this argument, which applied only to actual consumption of the wine. But once the sanction against trading in such wine fell into abeyance, those opposed to the drinking of *stam yeinam* fell back on this argument—or, rather, upon expressions of concern about the possibility that social barriers to intimacy and friendship might fall.[23] It is interesting to see how these thinkers managed to reinforce the stricture by using a totally new rationale.

The leading figure in this effort was R. Judah Loew of Prague, the MaHaRaL, the most important authority in the generation following R. Moses Isserles. MaHaRaL publicized a ban on drinking *stam yeinam* and used every available means of public censure to reinforce this ruling.[24] For him, the ban on drinking gentile wine was a method of maintaining the social division between Jews and non-Jews, and he used a new conceptual formulation to justify its enforcement. His line of reasoning was quite similar to those of the kabbalists: for him, wine prepared properly by Jews became a symbol of the metaphysical essence of Judaism, while wine that had been touched by a gentile came to represent its opposite. Thus, drinking *stam yeinam* ceased to be merely a ritual infraction of a secondary rank—an *isur de-rabanan*, or rabbinic stricture not derived directly from the Bible. Now the issue was raised to metaphysical status, and anyone drinking *stam yeinam* was seen as having withdrawn from the heavenly community of Israel.[25] This sort of argument derives from MaHaRaL's view that all human actions, and especially man's ritual acts, in effect initiate chain reactions in higher worlds, an approach very close to the views of the *Zohar*. It is no wonder, therefore, that contemporary kabbalists seized upon MaHaRaL's argumentation and supported the ban on *stam yeinam*.[26]

Judaism and Christianity. The changed rationalization for the stricture on *stam yeinam* provides a good illustration of a more general point: The distinction between Judaism and Christianity now shifted from the contents of faith to the realm of metaphysics. Once Christianity was no longer to be considered idolatry, the basis for forbidding gentile wine had eroded. The new rationale therefore focused on the symbolic meaning of wine drinking. This shift of focus from differences in faith to differences in essence was typical of contemporary thought and of the effort to define attitudes toward the outside world.

Both views, that which saw Jew and gentile as divided by the contents of their faiths, and that which saw them as different in essence, exist together in the midrashic and philosophic traditions of ancient and medieval Judaism.[27] The authors of the Midrash and philosophers like R. Judah ha-Levi had to distinguish between the natures of Jew and gentile as a basis for the distinction in faith and fate. They might see this distinction as stemming from a biological-racial factor (Jews were descended from Abraham, Isaac, and Jacob, while gentiles were descended from Esau, etc.). Alternatively, they might see it as deriving from some differing reaction to a historical-metaphysical event (Jews accepted the Torah and gentiles refused it). The origin of the distinction was irrelevant; in the end, the distinction was perceived as a difference in essence for which the individual was not responsible and over which he had no control. The difference in creed thus lost its fundamental importance. Differences in belief were now seen only as the product of the deeper division in the biological-metaphysical or historical-metaphysical natures of the two camps. This approach, which stressed the "underlying nature" of the two groups, became quite popular in our period, especially because of the influence of the Kabbala, and in particular of the *Zohar*. The *Zohar* very much follows this line of argument in distinguishing Israel from the nations, and sees the uniqueness of Israel as a function of the nation's link to the sacred spheres in the divine system, while gentiles were linked by their essence to the impure spheres.[28]

Versions of these concepts were popularized in different forms in this period through the ethical and homiletical literature, and became virtual principles of contemporary faith. Kabbala was not the only factor that contributed to the acceptance of these notions. The idea that Jews and gentiles differed in metaphysical essence mirrored the deep sociological division between the two groups. Despite the high level of utilitarian economic contact and the limited positive appreciation of Christianity as a religion for the gentiles, Christianity remained a dark and forbidding world for Jews, perhaps even more than in the Middle Ages. Christianity was no longer merely a rival religion seeking to capture the soul of the Jew and divert him from the true faith. Now Christianity was feared as the expression of an alien world and the embodiment on earth of the demonic "other side." Jewish martyrs during the First Crusade (1096) had resisted conversion, according to contemporary accounts, in order to bear witness to the truth of their faith in the face of those who came in the name of false gods. The martyrs of this era, on the other hand, sought to save themselves from a gaping pit of impurity that threatened to engulf them. The chronicles that recorded the Chmielnicki massacres in eastern Poland (1648–49) do not suggest that the martyrs hated Christianity or desired to disprove it, as had been the case in the Middle Ages. Now, the issue was perceived as a divine trial whose purpose could not be fathomed by man. *Kidush ha-shem*, the sanctification of God's name through martyrdom, became associated with a stoic acceptance of one's fate, no longer enriched by a sense that one was personally choosing and willingly opting for one's faith. In 1096 conversion had been an insidious temptation. For the martyrs of 1648–49, conversion to Christianity could not possibly have led to salvation; it was nothing more than a way to save one's life, and a way that they spurned.[29]

While contemporary thinkers acknowledged that Christianity at least approximated belief in the one God, this view never penetrated deeply into the public consciousness, and it is questionable whether it was even integrated into the philosophies of these thinkers themselves. We have seen in our discussion of *stam yeinam* that a new symbol arose to mark the alienness of the gentile world. All the more so was this true with the traditional symbols of Christianity: These never lost their frightening and alien character. Though Christian religious objects might, for business purposes, lose their status as instruments of idolatry, their ritual function was never given positive value. The rules intended to keep Jews away from the Christian ritual continued to be fully enforced.[30] We no longer find the conscious hatred of Christian religious symbols current in the Middle Ages. In place of hatred and contempt, we find a deeply rooted fear and abhorrence in the public mind. It is not by chance that even members of the Frankist sect, however alienated from Judaism they had become as a result of the revolutionary religious experience that they had undergone, nevertheless recoiled at using Catholic religious symbols.[31] In this we can see the results of the Jews' age-old historical experience, which inculcated a sense of the alienness of these symbols even while, on a rational level, they were tending to adopt a more restrained, even tolerant, attitude.

4

Contact with the Surrounding Society

We have seen that the Jews simultaneously formed both a subgroup within the general society and a close-knit, insular separate society, a veritable "world unto itself." This was the paradox of Jewish communal existence: a separate society that existed only through the constant contact of its inhabitants with the outside. The nature and extent of such contacts varied with the locale and the personalities involved.

The Isolated Individual. To clarify the matter, let us examine the two extreme forms of contact with the non-Jewish world. On the one hand, we have a Jew and his family living apart from other Jews in a gentile village, a fortress, or sometimes even a city. He might earn his living by leasing the estate, running an inn, trading, moneylending, or tax collection. Whatever his profession, this individual could provide very few of his daily needs by himself, and he relied, for the most part, on the surrounding society, bartering for or buying what he needed. He would generally maintain good relations with his neighbors; gentile and Jew would help each other as need arose in everyday matters and, of course, during emergencies. Regardless of the fact that the Jew saw himself—and was seen—as an outsider, without such relations he could not have survived. And there is no doubt that, in the absence of special tensions, close ties really did exist everywhere between these isolated Jews and their neighbors. They helped each other at times of natural disaster and other crises.[1] In sociological terminology, one might say that such Jews were part of gentile society insofar as it was their "survival group."

On the other hand, this individual also had social, religious, and cultural needs that he could not fulfill through his "survival group." The isolated Jew would satisfy such needs in a manner that varied with circumstances and with the nature of his own attachment to Judaism. Accommodation to the surrounding environment ranged from total assimilation into the survival group to absolute maintenance of ties to his Jewish "reference group": from the extreme of conversion to the dominant faith on the one hand, to the strictest observance of all Jewish rules aimed at religious and social separation on the other, despite the enormous self-denial this entailed.

In practice, both the individual and the Jewish communal and supra-communal institutions generally tried to break down the isolation of such persons.[2] A Jew who did well financially in a new region tended to attract other settlers, not always to his own delight. If he could, he would engage a teacher for his children, and if his business was an extensive one, he would hire assistants and household help. Entire communities sometimes grew up in this way as a result of an individual's decision to settle in a given locale.[3] But even if the Jew remained isolated, he would occasionally travel to a Jewish center on business or in order to celebrate the religious holidays.[4] In addition, the Jew's home provided hospitality for Jewish travelers. Jewish beggars, itinerant preachers (*magidim*), and sometimes even the rabbi of a nearby town would call upon the Jew. The visitor might have come on some personal errand, or he might have come specifically to instruct the local Jew in aspects of his religion.[5] Either way, such a visit inevitably strengthened the ties between the individual and the values of the broader Jewish community.

The Isolated Community. The polar opposite to our isolated individual was a Jew who lived in a large Jewish community and earned his living exclusively from his co-religionists: for instance, the preacher (*magid*) of a particular synagogue—as opposed to his itinerant counterpart—or a *melamed* (children's teacher). Theoretically, even this person was economically linked to the non-Jewish farmers whose produce he consumed. But there were intermediaries between the two—the merchant, the craftsman, and the peddler, for example—and these freed him from direct contact with the alien world. Such individuals would appear to have been immune to the conflict faced by the isolated Jew—the conflict between the need to survive and the need to maintain one's Jewish values. For them, the survival group and the reference group were virtually identical.

Degrees of Closeness. Most members of Jewish society existed somewhere between the two extremes that we have described. They came into contact with non-Jews in the course of their business dealings. The frequency of such contact and its social character varied with their occupation. The moneylender who waited at home for his gentile clients to borrow or repay, to pawn or redeem a pledge, had only a formal contact with the outside. The terms of the loan were more or less fixed according to the value of the pledge, were subject to exact calculation, and involved no extended bargaining. The merchant who kept a store and, all the more so, the merchant who took his goods to market had to solicit his customers, often bargaining with them for some time. Agreement on a price was in effect a reconciliation between adversaries who, up to that point, had sought to outbargain and outwit each other. And despite their mutually opposed interests, the circumstances exerted a certain pressure toward socializing. Peddling, which became very prevalent during this period, brought the Jew and Jewess right into gentile homes.[6] Traveling merchants joined the caravans and rode in the wagons of non-Jews and often had no choice but to lodge in their homes.[7] Individuals, especially communal representatives, leaders, and *shtadlanim* (intercessors at court), often traveled to cities where there were no Jews, and they would lodge in the homes of gentiles. In sixteenth-century Germany we find that many Jews, among them the greatest of Torah sages, frequented health spas and spent extended periods in a gentile environment.[8]

Other professions and occupations brought the Jew into almost constant contact with individual gentiles. Take, for example, the Jewish farmer, who paid part of the yield to the owner of the estate, or the "Court Jew," who served his ruler in a variety of ways.[9] And there was also the converse social relationship, as in the case of a Jew who leased an estate or owned some other business and had non-Jewish employees who were socially dependent upon him. In those regions where the government did not forbid it, there were non-Jewish servants in the homes of wealthy Jews.[10]

The tie between the doctor and his patient, whichever was the Jew and whichever the gentile, constituted a unique form of social relationship. This was also true of the relation between teacher and student. Jews sometimes studied languages or the sciences with gentile teachers, and Christians, especially theologians, needed Jews for their Hebrew studies.[11] Medicine was usually studied through apprenticeship to an experienced physician, although Jews also studied medicine at universities, either locally, as in Germany from the seventeenth century, or abroad, as did Jews from Poland who attended Italian universities.[12] Sometimes, though admittedly not often, Jews studied a craft with a Christian master.[13]

In short, Jewish social separateness and residential segregation did not imply total lack of contact between members of Jewish society and the non-Jewish world. The major importance of segregation lay in the fact that it expressed a theoretical value: It was in effect a declaration that absolute separation between Jew and gentile was desirable, were it only feasible. Moreover, even if not absolute, self-separation also helped to define a separate area of exclusively Jewish activity. The Jewish neighborhood lived a public life and a private life in which gentiles had no part. Gentiles visited here only on business; they were absolutely excluded from social life and, of course, from ceremonies of a religious or ritual character.[14] What happened on the outside was judged, moreover, according to the values of the Jewish quarter. Even isolated Jews who resided permanently outside the closed Jewish environment still evaluated their lives by its standards. Because of their distance from the centers of Jewish life, they saw themselves as living in a heightened *galut* (exile). Many of these Jewish villagers had experienced an intensive Jewish life during their youth, when they had studied at one of the Torah centers, only ending up in an outlying settlement after they had failed in business in those centers. Even Jews who were born and educated in the outlying settlements and hence were socialized into the local non-Jewish environment shared this ideologically based recognition of the superiority of life in the larger Jewish communities. Never during this period do we find an intellectual stream that found positive value in the dispersion of the Jews among the gentiles. Dispersion was seen as an economic or political necessity, to be neither praised nor condemned. The existence of Jewish centers emphasized the possibility, and the desirability, of a complete separation from the gentiles.

Different Attitudes toward Separation. In principle, therefore, the entire Jewish community lived according to a tradition that demanded separation from the outside. Of course, there were differences between the masses of Jews who depended upon the tradition to guide their everyday lives and the scholars authorized to interpret that tradition and apply it to an ever-changing reality. Most, if not all, of the latter lived in the large Jewish centers and usually were among those who had only indirect contact with the gentile world. It is no wonder, therefore, that there was a certain measure of tension between the demands of the halakhic and ethical leadership and the masses who had to live by those demands. Jewish burghers and, even more so, the villagers who lived in far-flung settlements developed certain *heterim* (rationalizations for halakhic license) with regard to contact with the non-Jewish world. They claimed that these *heterim* were local custom and therefore halakhically valid. The halakhic leadership either fought against these *heterim* or tried to justify them ex post facto, all in accordance with the severity of the infraction, the pressure of circumstances, and the personal inclinations of the rabbi involved.[15] Be that as it may, however, the very need to present these *heterim* as more or less legitimate customs proves that those who made use of them did not intend any basic reform of tradition. There was no intention here to make fundamental changes in it. Whatever the degree of their observance, the masses who lived by the tradition shared a uniform reverence for it with the textual scholars. All agreed that an act could be justified, whether before or after the fact, only on the basis of precedents or principles implicit in the tradition itself.

5

The Attitude toward the Environment

So far we have seen how Jewish society, while protecting its religious character through a set of strong cultural barriers, still managed to find dispensations for its members to engage in economic activities with the outside world. But this did not exhaust the problem. Jews needed more than permission to deal with non-Jews; they also needed a set of judicial and ethical norms to guide them in their business dealings.

We might have assumed that such norms would derive from the gentile court systems of the lands in which Jews lived. After all, by the terms of the Jews' charters and privileges (*kiyumim*), legal problems between Jews and non-Jews almost always fell within the jurisdiction of the state, or *malkhut* as it was called in the Hebrew sources.[1] But courts serve to decide only matters that have already become problematic. Maintaining economic contact and cooperation on a daily basis between Jewish and non-Jewish society required an ongoing institutional arrangement, a sort of unwritten and perhaps even unstated agreement, concerning the norms proper to this mutual relationship. The problem was sociological rather than legal, and courts could help only indirectly by fixing norms or publicizing legal decisions. In a case such as this, where society was divided along very clear socio-religious lines, the courts, imposed upon the Jews from the outside, could not effectively promulgate unified norms of practice. Indeed, Jews tended to regard the non-Jewish courts with scorn. They saw them only as extrinsic mechanisms for establishing order to which they—the Jews—resorted only when compelled to do so (*bi-sh'at ha-dḥak*). Jews did not believe that these courts would rule justly in cases between Jews and Christians.[2] Hence, it is almost impossible to believe that the Jewish public sought a guide to proper behavior in these non-Jewish courts. To the extent that Jews' behavior vis-à-vis non-Jews was guided by ethical conceptions, these conceptions were drawn exclusively from internal Jewish sources.

Duality in Jewish Law and Ethics. The traditional Jewish texts presented a dualistic system of ethics and justice; that is, there was one law and ethic for the Jew and another for the gentile. This did not necessarily imply an advantage for the Jew over the non-Jew. For instance, the Talmudic authorities disagreed over what type of act (*kinyan*) was necessary to effect a legal transfer of ownership: the giving of money or the symbolic pulling (*meshikha*) of the object by the new owner. But all agreed that the type of act required for a Jew was different from that required for a gentile: if money effected transfer for the one, then pulling was necessary for the other, and vice versa.[3] The main point was, as one contemporary halakhic sage put it, that "the Torah, in its totality and in its minutiae, was given exclusively to Israel"[4]—that is, it concerned only the internal affairs of Jews. Relations between Jews and gentiles had to be handled under a sort of auxiliary legislation. This attitude had always been accepted without question, and continued to be so even now, when only a part of Jewish law was actually applied in practice. The notion that a single system of justice could control relations between human beings without regard to ethnic and religious origins never occurred to anyone. It is important to understand that this duality of justice and ethics was not a *reservatio mentalis*—that is, a mental reservation that Jews hid when doing business with non-Jews. Rather, it was a fundamental assumption shared by all sectors of society. No universal system of justice could have applied in this period. Both Jews and gentiles of necessity required a special moral and legal code for dealing with outsiders. The only question was what the nature and content of this code would be.

The problem for Jewish society was that those judicial and ethical norms that had governed relations with gentiles since Talmudic times were no longer appropriate to the realities of this period. The Talmud conceived of the Jews as a people living in its own land. Alongside the Jews lived a number of undesirable, pagan gentiles. Contact with these pagans could lead to sin, and it was consequently a positive duty (*mitzva*) to distance them from the community, to dislodge them, or at times even to destroy them. Such circumstances provided the background for disputes in the Talmud among the *Tana'im* and *Amora'im* as to whether one should be consistent, permit theft from a gentile and even refrain from saving his life if in danger, or whether such severity toward gentiles should be conditioned by religious and humanitarian considerations, by the desire for converts, or by consideration of non-Jewish public opinion ("In order to sanctify God's name, one should never cheat a gentile"), etc.[5]

By our period, however, under the ghetto conditions of the sixteenth through eighteenth centuries, and to a large extent already during the early Middle Ages, circumstances had changed considerably. The gentiles were no longer a minority subject to Jewish control. Quite the opposite was the case. Moreover, the gentiles were no longer true pagans. They believed in the Christian notion of monotheism, which, as we have seen, was not identical for Jews with the paganism of antiquity. Similarly, the religious competition between the two groups had weakened. The Jews no longer strove to convert the gentiles, and the Christians no longer tried to force the Jews to renounce their faith.

One might have supposed that such radical changes in circumstances would have been sufficient to render the received Jewish tradition obsolete. But as we have seen, one of the essential characteristics of Jewish society was that, at least in theory, it maintained the tradition in its entirety. Moreover, even in practice these ancient rules did not completely fall into disuse. Certain matters of ritual law, for instance, continued to depend upon the nature of a gentile's act of acquisition. These included the selling of leavened goods to a non-Jew before Passover and other matters of ritual cancellation of ownership (*hafka'a*).[6] Halakha demanded that the transfer be done in accordance with that type of acquisition which applied to gentiles. Similarly, the status of the gentile in Jewish law affected monetary dealings between Jews—as, for instance, when a Jew empowered a gentile to collect a debt owed him by another Jew.[7] In all such questions the Jews of our period saw neither the necessity nor the right to change the tradition.

Conflict between law and reality occurred at those points where the law affected direct relations between Jews and gentiles. The conditions under which Jewish society lived necessitated the cancellation of those laws concerning relations with gentiles that, if followed, could have brought tragedy down upon the community. Questions of ethics aside, utilitarian considerations forbade the Jews of the Middle Ages and of the sixteenth through eighteenth centuries to rule that theft from a gentile was permissible. But such rules could not simply be arbitrarily revoked. Rather, traditional methods of exegesis, the twisting of the legal ruling in the desired direction, were used to negate the tradition. In this manner, already in the Middle Ages it was declared that theft from a gentile was forbidden.[8] Indeed, if the matter might become known to gentiles and thus result in the "desecration of God's name," even misleading a gentile was forbidden. Under similar circumstances one was obliged to return something that a gentile had lost.[9] Still, the fact that these two rulings, returning the lost article and not misleading the gentile, depended on whether or not the matter might become known bears witness to the fact that the older rule was not negated on principle. Profiting from a gentile's error when the Jew had had no part in that error was not forbidden, and the Jew could do so with no pangs of conscience. During the Middle Ages and into the modern era we continue to find halakhic authorities deciding which of two Jews had the right to profit from a gentile's mistake when there was some doubt as to who had held the property in question first.[10] Such rulings reveal that exegesis could not negate these rules totally, and that there was a limit to how much their impact could be softened.[11]

Are Christians Idolators? There were also attempts to bring about a fundamental revision in the halakhic status of gentiles along the same lines as the attempts to allow increased social contact between Jews and gentiles, which we discussed in chapter 3. Halakhic reasoning tended, as we have noted, to distinguish between the ancient pagans, contact with whom the Mishna and Talmud had restricted severely, and the Christian nations among whom Jews now lived. Possibly under the influence of early-sixteenth-century humanism, Jewish scholars of a philosophical-theological bent took this distinction to its logical conclusion, arguing even that traditional terms such as *goyim* ([non-Jewish] nations) and *umot ha-olam* (nations of the world) should no longer be applied to Christians. Was it reasonable, after all, to equate nations that accepted the truth of Moses' Torah, of the prophets' words, and of the ancient miracles with pagans who had rejected those beliefs?[12] This approach, espoused by individual thinkers from the sixteenth through the eighteenth centuries, would ultimately pave the way for recognition of a common core to Christianity and Judaism. Meanwhile, Christians could at least be exempted from the harsh laws that the Talmud and later Jewish authorities had applied to the pagans of antiquity. The Tosafists had effectively revoked the pagan status of their contemporaries by ruling that gentiles no longer understood the nature of idolatry. This essentially negative argument was now strengthened by positive statements that stressed the Christians' link to fundamental Jewish tenets. Thus a distinction that had initially been intended only to permit trade in Christian religious objects now served as a basis upon which Christians might be granted a positive status in the judicial and ethical realms. Several important halakhic scholars championed this idea, and the obligation to act ethically with gentiles was thus elevated to the rank of principle and based upon those religious values shared by both Judaism and Christianity.[13]

In this context we might also consider the statements appearing on title pages of many books published in central Europe from the eighteenth century on, statements that explicitly differentiated between the gentiles of antiquity and contemporary Christians.[14] On the one hand, these generalized declarations may be seen as merely attempts to evade the censors, who forbade the publication of anti-Christian materials. And in fact, the books themselves did not draw any practical conclusions from these declarations. Christians continued to be included in the traditional categories, for instance in discussions of whether they might serve as agents in the performance of certain rituals, whether food they had prepared could be eaten by Jews, and so forth. On the other hand, we should not conclude that the title-page declarations were consciously dishonest. The distinction between Christians and pagans was applied in full when it came to practical questions of business ethics. These thinkers, because of their casuistic approach to legal problems, simply felt no logical necessity to apply their statements to all possible cases.[15] There was also a social dimension involved. The implications of the distinction between Christians and pagans were perceived only by a limited class of scholars, and even here only marginally. Such statements had little influence on the thinking of the broader classes of Jewish society. The depressing conditions of the Diaspora on the one hand, and the strong hold of tradition on the other, militated against the emergence of an ethical system based upon a moral identification with the outside world, whether derived from general humanistic values or from the notion of a common faith.

In the end, therefore, a serious question of social education remained—one vital to the security of the community. How could Jewish leaders guarantee the desired high standards of conduct when the conditions of Jewish existence fostered an attitude of scorn toward the demands of propriety and ethics? The institutions of Jewish self-government, the *kehila* and the supra-communal organizations, kept an ever-watchful eye on the actions of the individual in every area. They warned Jews to obey the law of the land and recommended honest and trustworthy behavior in business. Anyone who transgressed in these matters was punished with every means available at the time: fines, corporal punishment, and excommunication. The community could also threaten not to come to the aid of transgressors arrested by the gentile authorities. Sometimes Jewish leaders tried to avert problems in advance by warning gentiles not to deal with suspect Jews.[16] In extreme cases, when a Jew had been caught red-handed, the communal leaders could go so far as actually to hand their co-religionist over to gentile justice. As we shall see, this was the most severe punishment that Jewish society could impose.[17]

But such legal and disciplinary measures did not, in and of themselves, solve the problem. The question remained how to encourage the desired behavior toward gentiles not out of fear of retribution but as part of an overall, autonomous religious and spiritual system. There were, after all, many factors that could serve to assuage the conscience of the Jew who failed to act correctly toward gentiles: the mutual instrumentality of the relationship between Jews and the outside world; gentile hatred of Jews, something repeatedly proven by experience; the assumption that Jews were better than other peoples; and the dualistic notions of justice implicit in the tradition. Under these circumstances, only the most powerful moral considerations could be expected to lead Jews to behave ethically toward gentiles rather than to justify opportunism.

Preserving the Community's Good Name. The decisive argument for ethical behavior was, ultimately, the very status of Jews within the surrounding society. It was universally understood that the actions of an individual Jew could place the entire community in danger. Communal institutions and leaders warned repeatedly that the individual was responsible for the fate of the whole.[18] The security of the community, originally merely a utilitarian consideration, came to be seen as a supreme ethical value in itself. The individual was expected to forgo personal profit for the sake of the public good even if he himself might escape the direct consequences of his actions.

The demand for ethical behavior on the part of the individual was also based upon another principle: the need to preserve the Jews' good name, and hence that of the religion they espoused. In order to achieve this goal Jews would have to behave in a fashion exemplary even according to the standards of the non-Jewish world. The Talmudic expressions *kidush ha-shem* and *ḥilul ha-shem* ("sanctification" and "desecration of the divine Name") were adopted to express this concern. Over the course of the Middle Ages, the meaning and connotation of these terms had expanded continuously, in part because of Jewish missionary ambitions. Medieval rabbis had called for exemplary behavior on the part of Jews for the sake of attracting gentiles into the Jewish camp. In our period, though the expressions still occur quite frequently, it is clear that their positive undertones had faded. This was inevitable granted the contemporary indifference of Jews to the religious fate of the surrounding gentile world.[19] *Ḥilul ha-shem* and *kidush ha-shem* were now understood in a passive rather than an active sense: as warnings against defaming Judaism's good name rather than as positive demands for the defense of the purity of Judaism in the eyes of the nations. Sometimes these phrases amount to nothing more than a warning about the real danger facing the community because of individual misconduct.

There was yet one other approach that Jewish thinkers used in trying to establish the moral necessity for proper behavior toward gentiles. These thinkers relied not on the shared Judaeo-Christian religious heritage (which implied the moral worthiness of Christians), but on autonomous, purely Jewish, considerations. In this approach, stealing from gentiles or defrauding them was forbidden because of the impact such evil actions had on the Jew himself, regardless of their victim.[20] But note that even such arguments ultimately rested upon the assumption that there was a deep division between Jewish and gentile society, and that ethical imperatives basically applied only to members of the Jewish group. Jewish isolation left its mark even when ethical thought sought to free itself from utilitarian considerations. There was evidently no other solution for this society but to show its realistic appraisal of its situation by imposing self-enforced legal curbs prompted by considerations of security and the need to preserve the community's good name. These goals were now raised to the level of abstract ethical principle.

6

Economic Structures

In this chapter we shall outline some of the fundamental structural changes that occurred in Jewish economic life from the sixteenth to eighteenth centuries. The implications of these changes went far beyond the merely economic—the premodern state, after all, tolerated Jewish settlement only because it perceived Jewish economic activities as valuable. Hence, the charters (*kiyumim*) that legitimized the Jewish presence within the state invariably included permission for economic activity, and specified, explicitly or implicitly, which occupations Jews might pursue.[1] As we shall see, which professions Jews were allowed to pursue was governed by fixed traditions quite as much as were the definitions of Jewish rights and privileges in all other areas of life.[2] Thus, any change in the economic role of the Jews implied a change in an essential foundation of their legal status. Of course, our analysis will not limit itself to the Jewish economy as defined in the charters; we shall try to describe the historical reality of the Jewish economy, a reality that often exceeded the charters' limits, with or without the knowledge and acquiescence of government officials.

Jewish Economic Differentiation. The sixteenth through eighteenth centuries witnessed a shift in the Jewish economy from relative uniformity to occupational diversification. During the Middle Ages the Jews of Poland and Ashkenaz had been engaged primarily in international trade and loanbanking.[3] While these occupations remained important sources of income during our period as well, we now see Jewish financiers expanding their sphere of activity in new directions. Along with loans at interest, in which the lender's concern was only the likelihood of the debt being repaid, we begin to find Jewish investments of capital in productive enterprises under direct Jewish management. Tax and customs farming, coin minting to government order, the exploitation of mines, the operation of distilleries, and the production of potash were all regarded as attractive forms of investment. Similar opportunities for profit were available in the field of agriculture. The landed gentry in Poland and Lithuania would lease out whole estates together with their tenant farmers to Jews, offering opportunities for unlimited economic exploitation. Commerce, too, became more diversified—primarily through the increased variety of commodities in which Jews traded. In addition to luxury items imported from distant lands, the Jews began to participate in the marketing of rural produce in the city and abroad. The methods of Jewish trading also became more varied. In addition to the older type of merchant who came directly to the large homes of his wealthy clients or traded at the large fairs, we now find the Jewish storekeeper whose shop was open to clients all year long. We also see Jews offering their goods to the less wealthy strata of society. The Jewish peddler wandering from village to village with his stock on his back became a familiar sight in almost every area. This is also the era in which we see the emergence among Jews of contractors purveying to royalty. These merchants specialized above all in military goods. The most important could provide for an entire army and, de facto, financed the military campaigns of their sovereigns.

To complete the picture we must also note the increasing incidence of Jewish craftsmen in this period. In Poland and Lithuania of the seventeenth and eighteenth centuries, Jewish artisans formed a broad class and made a substantial contribution to the Jewish economy.

The forms of diversification that we have described did not occur in all regions simultaneously or to the same extent. The most extensive examples are provided by Poland and Lithuania of the seventeenth century. In the Germanic lands, in Alsace, and in western Hungary the leasing of estates was not common. On the other hand, these regions saw the rise of the royal purveyor. The *Hofjude*, or Court Jew, had no real parallel in Poland and Lithuania. While such regional variations in the patterns of economic activity are important for local history, they are not very significant for a broad overview of the society as a whole.[4]

It is important to understand that the new diversity in the Jewish economic base did not derive from any change in the political status of the Jews. The Jews remained, as before, legal aliens who had been conditionally granted certain privileges of residence. The new economic diversification stemmed rather from broad changes in the political and economic life of European society as a whole. We will outline here those changes that most directly affected Jewish economic life. First of all, the geographic *range* of trade expanded. This tended to stimulate local production, both to supply distant markets and to trade for increased imports of foreign goods. The *content* of trade also expanded: We now find surplus agricultural products and raw materials moving from country to country alongside the traditional luxury items. The expanding possibilities for marketing served to encourage acquisition of those surplus goods that were not absolutely necessary for local consumption. The tempo of *manufacturing* likewise picked up, using technologies both old and new, and the marketplace developed. This essentially describes the intensive economic life of sixteenth- through eighteenth-century Europe.[5] Of course, economic advance was neither continuous nor universal. Regions enjoyed progress for a time and then retrogressed, usually because of political factors, wars, and the like. But on the whole, development led to a widening of the marketplace and the range of trade, to increased manufacturing, and to greater quantity and variety in production.

Development depends on the coincidence of a number of factors: improved technical equipment and means of transportation, innovation in marketing and storage techniques, and increases in both the efficiency of labor and the entrepreneurial aggressiveness of investors, estate owners, and merchants. The Jews, as active participants in the economy, could take some credit for progress in these fields. On the whole, however, their role was not especially innovative or conspicuous, and certainly should not lead us to attribute overall economic development to Jewish initiative.[6] There was only one area vital to economic development in which the Jews did have a particularly important role—namely, the mobilization of monetary reserves. Increased efficiency of production and the exchange of surplus goods through long-distance trade would not have been possible without the development of financial instruments that allowed for the long-term advancement of moneys in expectation of delayed profits. In this area the role of Jews was far greater than was warranted by their relative size within the general population. This situation continued logically from the earlier period, when loanbanking and international commerce were the main sources of Jewish livelihood. These activities had depended upon the availability of liquid assets, and now Jews simply directed their capital toward the new types of investments. The common denominator in the two periods was the fact that the Jews' livelihood, and hence also their right of residence, depended on the assumption that they controlled financial reserves necessary to promote economic activity.

The Role of Jews in Finance. The increasing role of capital in the economy also meant a corresponding rise in the prestige of capitalists, including those Jews with money and the reputation of being able and willing to raise money when necessary for economic development. The more that money was recognized as vital to the state's economy, the more bargaining power the Jew had, and the greater was his real influence—provided, of course, that he lived up to his reputation. Obviously, not all Jews were wealthy. Everywhere we find a significant class of poor, even destitute, Jews. But at the same time, the Jewish community as a whole—and outsiders saw the Jews as a single community—included a number of individuals of substantial means who could undertake what were increasingly recognized as decisively important financial functions. In general, therefore, our period is marked by an increase in the real social status of Jews and an enhanced social appreciation of their role.

The Jews of our period inherited their capital from the Middle Ages. As previously noted, even then loanbanking had required capital. Despite the frequent expulsions, special levies, and confiscations to which they were subjected, medieval Jews had managed to pass on a capital reserve from generation to generation. This is not to imply that money necessarily remained in the hands of the same families. The rise and fall of families formed a sort of continuous cycle in which capital changed hands among members of the community.[7] But within Jewish society as a whole and within each individual community there were a number of enormously wealthy individuals, and at least a part of their capital passed from one generation to the next, if not always directly from father to son.

The Jews' economic potential stemmed from more than their possession of liquid assets. Their chief economic virtue lay in the fact that they actively employed these funds, and therefore served as an economic catalyst at times without parallel in Christian society. The emphasis on keeping money active tended, first of all, to preclude investment in real estate. Local laws generally prevented Jews from acquiring land, but these were not a significantly harsher deterrent than the regulations that limited Jewish enjoyment of other privileges, such as customs farming, coin minting, etc.[8] In fact, the Jews tended not to invest in land because they had no real desire to do so. The attraction of landownership lies largely in the economic stability and social prestige it confers on the newly wealthy. But the Jew saw himself as a temporary, rather than a permanent, resident of the state. Promises of stability and status therefore had no real attraction for him. He had no hope of perpetuating his wealth in a given locale, nor could he expect to gain a recognized place within the social-economic hierarchy of the dominant society. He viewed the outside world in instrumental terms: he sought only to gain his livelihood from that world. Hence the Jew tended to focus specifically on those forms of investment that offered returns within his own lifetime: commerce, leaseholds, minting, mining, and so forth, as opposed to investment in real estate.

The focus on keeping money active inevitably led to a second characteristic of Jewish economic endeavor: investment of other people's money in addition to one's own. So long as one's goal is long-term ownership of a field or vineyard, it is best, where possible, to purchase the land with one's own money. On the other hand, stocking up for a trading venture or purchasing a manufacturing concession for a limited period of time can be done with anyone's money, so long as the expected revenues are sufficient to satisfy all the investors. Thus, the nature of Jewish economic activity fostered the creation of credit, i.e., the supply of loan capital from which a fund for commercial and industrial development could be established. The use of credit was not, of course, a uniquely Jewish invention; it was a basic feature of the new economy of the time. Extensive use of credit, however, was undoubtedly one of the characteristics marking Jewish economic activity during this period. Jews borrowed from Jew and non-Jew alike, and combined various artificial instruments of credit such as the endorsable bill of credit known as *MaMRaMe* (see below) in order to finance their operations. The creation of credit became profitable because money now bore fruit not only through direct loans but also through capitalist investment in business, leaseholding, and productive enterprise.[9] It appears that old-style moneylending by Jews gradually declined in importance vis-à-vis the Middle Ages in both relative and absolute terms.

Jewish society was therefore "capitalist" in the sense that it derived its livelihood from investment in enterprises in which the necessary manual labor was performed primarily by members of the surrounding population. Of course, the entire Jewish community did not support itself directly through this type of capital investment. First, various groups within Jewish society had no income. These were paupers, beggars, and other "nonproductive" elements, such as the scholars who nourished and cultivated the society's traditional values and whom the society felt obligated to support in return. Second, there was a not inconsiderable group within Jewish society engaged in rendering internal services: teachers, rabbis, synagogue beadles, and preachers (*magidim*), each of whom we shall meet below when we analyze communal institutions. Third, there was the Jewish working class: servants, laborers, and artisans who engaged in production, transport, and management of enterprises financed by Jewish capitalists. There were also self-employed artisans who worked independently of these Jewish investors.

Such was the physiognomy of Jewish society. As we shall see when we analyze social stratification, ours was a period of increasing occupational diversification. But growing diversity had little impact on the essential structure of the Jewish economy. Everyone, with the possible exception of craftsmen, continued to depend directly on the capitalistic enterprises of the Jewish financier for his livelihood. Even the craftsman was often *de facto* tied to the financier who ordered products for shipment to distant markets; this was true irrespective of whether the artisans provided their own raw materials or got these from the entrepreneur on credit.[10] Moreover, artisans were apparently dependent on the capitalists even for their right of residence. Nowhere were Jewish artisans granted residence privileges of their own.[11] Rather, they were forced to fight continually for the right to settle and work in a given place, and it seems that even when they won such privileges from the authorities, it was only because they were lumped together with the Jewish capitalists, whose usefulness was more readily apparent.

7

Sociological Aspects of Jewish Capitalism

There is a social as well as an economic side to capitalism, and the external structure of society affects the growth of invested wealth as much as the terms of investment do. In order truly to understand the relation between capitalism and the Jews, therefore, we must also investigate this sociological aspect. Upon reflection, we find that there are, in this sociological sense, three different types of capitalism: state, protected, and free-market.[1]

In pure state capitalism, the opportunity for investment is provided through participation in the revenues that the government collects from its subjects. The primary example of such participation is provided by tax- and customs-farming. The financier simply advances the anticipated revenue to the ruler and profits from the difference between what he has advanced and what he will later collect. He collects these revenues by the authority, and through the coercive power, of the government.

The obverse of state capitalism is free-market capitalism. Here the capitalist does not depend upon the power of the state in any way. He simply calculates his production and marketing costs and balances these against an estimate of the profits to be expected from the sale of the product in the free market—a much more complicated basis for investment than what is called for under state capitalism. In abstract sociological terms, free-market capitalism requires the total withdrawal of government from the economy—a precondition that may never have been fully met although there were attempts in this direction during the era of liberalism.

Between these two extremes lies protected capitalism—in effect, a mixture of the two. Economic activity is market oriented, as in free capitalism, but it is also controlled by the government, which determines the goods to be sold and who may sell them. The law both limits the nature of economic activity and allocates what is allowed to favored groups and individuals. In return for these concessions, the government takes a share of the profits, either through direct levies or through the general increase in wealth resulting from the business activity.

Jews and State Capitalism. With these basic distinctions in mind, we can now properly examine the oft-repeated claim that the Jews made a significant, or even a primary, contribution to the development of the two most characteristic economic forms of the seventeenth and eighteenth centuries: state and protected capitalism. In fact, this development was motivated primarily by the desire of all secular rulers, whatever the size of their states, to convert part or all of their feudal dues from payments in kind and in personal service into monetary revenues. The state developed the rationalized bureaucracy and system needed to generate such tax revenues only slowly. Hence, rulers were only too happy to turn over the power to tax to private individuals in return for a fixed or variable payment in cash.

It was nothing but a historical accident that in eastern and central Europe—in Poland, Lithuania, and the German Empire—Jews were the most able to provide the necessary financial services. Capital and commercial experience were concentrated in their hands more than in those of any other group. In eastern Europe no local burgher class had ever emerged that would have been capable of ejecting the Jews from capitalist activity; in Germany such a class had existed but it was impoverished and had practically disappeared during the Thirty Years War and its aftermath.[2] Significantly, France, the classic land of absolutism combined with state capitalism, accomplished the transition from feudal to monetary revenues without the participation of Jewish capitalists.

On the other hand, even if the Jews did not create the new forms of capitalism, they were remarkably successful at adopting them, because of certain characteristic features of Jewish society and status. First, Jews' international ties helped in the transmission of goods and the creation of credit. Jews of various lands traded with each other and lent each other money on a basis of mutual trust.[3]

Second, since Jewish society was religiously and socially segregated, it tended to relate to other classes along largely instrumental lines. This attitude served as an unparalleled stimulus for growth in the economic sphere. Jews had no social aspirations in the outside world, nor were they restricted in their business activities by family commitments. Jews were therefore free to see the surrounding society as nothing but an arena for their economic endeavor. This is a classic example of a social minority whose separateness and isolation prepare it for, and direct it toward, economic activity—and nothing else.[4] Business acumen eventually came to be considered a uniquely Jewish characteristic, and this assumption itself gave the Jews a certain advantage over their Christian competitors.

The Jews' special political status gave them yet another, ultimately more significant, economic advantage. In state and protected capitalism political power is exploited to achieve economic aims. If the ruler needs a partner in this endeavor, he will obviously prefer someone without political rights and ambitions of his own. Jews were the ideal economic partner because there was no fear that they would take a partisan stand in the struggle between the ruler and his subjects. Even after Jews had achieved economic power of their own, they would never try to gain comparable political strength. The Jews' political powerlessness and their exclusive focus on economic activity made them the ideal instrument for state and protected capitalism in the eyes of those who held political power.[5]

Of course, there can be no question as to why the Jews were eager for financial links with the rulers; they simply had no choice. Their personal security, their right of residence, and their right to engage in business all depended on the ruler. This state of affairs had evolved already in the Middle Ages, as the right of the Jews to live in a given place ceased to be taken for granted. The Jews were thus forced to depend on the government, and they knew that their own opportunities grew as the government increased its direct and indirect participation in, and dependence upon, such revenue-generating activities. The Jew, because of the very nature of things, saw his status and security as dependent upon a strong relationship with the rulers; he prided himself on having acquired royal protection and labeled it "closeness to the king."

Court Jews. The Court Jew provides us with the prime example in western Europe of the individual Jew who was dependent on a ruler. He served kings and princes who were gradually converting their feudal domains into absolutist states. The rulers needed monetary income and had to free themselves from dependence on the feudally privileged noble classes. The Jews who were connected to the rulers were able to take advantage of these conditions, and their financial activities expanded and became more varied and dynamic.[6]

It is important to remember that there is no essential difference between the activity of the Court Jews and that of a large part of Jewish society, which operated on a more modest scale but under similar arrangements. The unique identifying characteristic of this partnership between Jew and ruler was the fact that profits depended upon state sponsorship. This was not affected either by the relative power of the ruler and the size of his domain on the one hand, or by the amount of invested capital on the other. We find the same desire for the conversion of feudal revenues into cash at all levels of government—among petty rulers, princelings, nobles, and estate owners everywhere, even in areas where centralized control had not yet been achieved or, for that matter, where, as in Poland from the second half of the seventeenth century, there had actually been a tendency toward decentralization. These petty rulers would maintain one or more Jews on their estates and use them to market produce locally, regionally, and even internationally, in order to generate cash. The Jewish lessee who rented an inn on a nobleman's estate, produced potash or processed hides and other local raw materials, and even the Jew who merely bought up surplus produce and marketed it elsewhere—each of these was a Court Jew in miniature. The Jew depended on the franchise obtained from the ruler for his profits, and the ruler granted this franchise because the Jew possessed the necessary investment capital as well as the desire and ability to use that capital for the sake of profit. Any description of Jewish society in this period must emphasize the role of the petty financiers tied to minor rulers just as much as that of the major capitalists who operated under the protection of the central rulers. Both enjoyed the new economic conditions under which marginal Jewish moneylenders became fully integrated into the spheres of exchange and even direct production.[7]

Jewish Artisans. As our period advanced, other, secondary forms of Jewish economic activity emerged parallel to the primary activities that had originally justified toleration of Jews in the eyes of the authorities. Sometimes the rulers agreed to these new activities *ex post facto*, and sometimes they remained ignorant, or chose to remain ignorant, of them. Once Jews settled in an area, and especially if their number came to exceed that originally estimated or fixed, they needed additional sources of livelihood and they took advantage of every economic opportunity that arose. The most instructive example is the emergence of artisans in Poland and Moravia during the seventeenth century, something that came about purely under the pressure of economic circumstances.[8] Jews had no strong tradition of craft labor, nor did they view it as a professional ideal.[9] Nor did the authorities promote Jewish crafts; there is no example anywhere of Jewish craftsmen being invited or even being accepted as the primary Jewish settlers in a region. At best the authorities tolerated such craftsmen ex post facto. The craftsmen were nothing but an appendage to the main social body of merchants, lessees, and moneylenders, and were tolerated, more or less gracefully as the case might be, because of the right of the main social body to exist.[10]

Forbidden Trade. The same tendency to economic expansionism held true with regard to various sorts of commercial activity. Jews did not limit themselves to that branch of the economy for the advancement of which they had first been invited into the area; rather, they engaged in any form of economic activity that became available. They exchanged local surpluses for foreign goods, not always in a manner, or within the limits, that the government had approved. Interregional and international trade were not always viewed positively by the authorities; imports were sometimes considered threatening to the local economy.[11] Similarly in the case of moneylending—even if it was not usually forbidden the Jews, it was certainly no longer the reason for their being invited to settle in a region, as it had been during the Middle Ages (and, indeed, as it continued to be in lands outside our frame of reference.)[12] And there were also forms of Jewish economic activity that were actually forbidden outright, such as smuggling, money changing, and the melting down of coinage. There is no way of knowing how extensive Jewish participation was in such illegalities. Their enemies assumed a priori that Jews were guilty of this type of illegal activity. And since these irregularities were, in fact, marginal aspects of professions in which Jews engaged legally, the temptation was much greater for Jews than for other sectors of the populace. Jewish society tried to prevent its members from breaking the law of the land,[13] but illegal activities such as smuggling and coin melting were common phenomena everywhere in Europe. On the other hand, we must remember that the lower classes of Jewish society were struggling for their very existence, and sanctions, whether internal or external, had little chance of preventing them from taking advantage of any potential source of livelihood.

Jews and Free Capitalism. Jews tended to make the most of economic opportunities even under adverse circumstances; certainly they were not restrained by any commitment to established methods of production and marketing. If a Jew discovered a new method of increasing his profits, he was not deterred by its very novelty. But the new methods for maximizing profits that characterized this innovative period in the development of capitalist production and marketing were just as unfamiliar to the Jews as they were to the other citizens of the state. Jews had almost no part in the rationalization of methods of production, since Jewish contact with production processes was so limited.[14] The notion that the government withdraw from the economic sector, later a fundamental principle of economic liberalism, was even less likely to occur to a Jew than to others since the Jew was so heavily reliant on the government for both his security and his livelihood.

Competition and Monopoly. The question that occupied Jewish society was rather how to regulate competition among Jews for government contracts. Different objective conditions had determined the halakhic views of earlier generations, and the halakhic sources presented mutually contradictory traditions about the legality of earlier settlers maintaining a monopoly and keeping later arrivals from competing with them. Even at the beginning of our period legists had not yet decided this issue.[15] However, with the rise in the power of the communities and the supra-communal institutions at the end of the sixteenth century, the tendency to limit competition increased. From this point on we find communal ordinances that forbade competitors to make contact with the non-Jewish lessor so long as the original lease remained in force and even for a certain length of time thereafter.[16] Communal ordinances similarly accepted the principle of *ḥezkat ha-yishuv*—that is, the right of members of a community to prevent strangers from settling in their locale without prior permission—even though it had never been completely accepted by legists.[17] The notion that strangers could be prevented from coming and trading in a place had its roots in Talmudic law, and in our period there was a tendency to expand this right of exclusion and to insist on applying it in practice.[18] The right to limit new settlement was justified on the grounds that the existing community members had paid the authorities for their right of trade, and no one who had not contributed to the expenses had the right to profit from the opportunity. Thus, it is clear that the notion of free trade and unrestricted competition did not hold, in theory or practice, within Jewish society, nor were there individuals or groups in favor of completely unrestricted competition. Competition occurred only within the framework of these restraints. In other words, the debate was not over the principle of *ḥazaka*, or monopoly, but rather over who had the right to enjoy it.

Unrestricted competition existed, if at all, only between Jews and their non-Jewish business rivals. First of all, Jewish institutions had no control over the surrounding society and had no way of enforcing any arrangement binding on both sides. Equally important, the Jews were little involved with the broad problems of the national or regional economy, and did not decide what was forbidden or permitted for themselves out of concern for the general welfare.[19] Here we find the most decisive expression of the negative impact of Jewish society's total political dependence. Since Jews controlled at best only their own small part of the economy, they were capable of examining economic data only from their own narrow point of view. They perceived of gentile society and its economy as a fixed, unchanging entity with which they had to develop some sort of modus vivendi—one that would satisfy the authorities and the general population and at the same time guarantee maximum protection to the interests of Jewish society. It could never have occurred to Jews that they should attempt to change or influence matters for the sake of the common good. Jewish organizations did sometimes restrict their members from competing even with non-Jews to the extent that this might involve fraud, instill jealousy, or endanger Jews as individuals or as a group.[20] On the other hand, many communal ordinances were intended to protect the economic interests of Jewish society from external competition,[21] and this consideration provided a convincing argument, or at least a rationalization, for maintaining monopolies among members of Jewish society: Unrestrained competition was ultimately to the benefit of the non-Jews upon whom the Jews depended for their livelihood. In order "not to lose Jewish money," it was necessary for Jews to limit competition among themselves.[22]

Thus Sombart erred when he concluded from the unrestrained competition of Jews with their non-Jewish business rivals that Jews were committed to principles of free trade and eventually managed to impose this view on non-Jewish society. Sombart did not understand the phenomena he was describing. Jews did, in fact, quickly adopt and actively promote the spread of free capitalism once it had been developed by others. But the intensity of Jewish participation in the new economy was not the product of any internal tendency attuned to the "spirit" of capitalism; rather, it was first and foremost the result of the Jews' status in society. As we have already seen, the status of the Jew within the state led him to relate to his business dealings in a totally instrumental fashion. It was this attitude that led the Jew to evaluate every business deal solely on the basis of short-term profit. Once free capitalism had proven to be a source of profits, Jews had no inhibitions about switching from the prevailing pattern of investment to the new mode.

Social Tensions. An additional factor in the rapid transition of Jews to the new forms of investment was the social tension that existed within Jewish society itself. There had always been a broad class of Jews who depended for their existence on the crumbs that fell from the tables of those who controlled the so-to-speak "official" sources of Jewish livelihood, or who eked out a desperate, and sometimes only questionably legal, livelihood. As we shall see from an analysis of the structure of Jewish society, these excluded Jews did not have any alternative means of establishing themselves economically; rather, they always remained candidates for the positions occupied by the wealthier. This was their only possible escape from poverty.[23] Thus, when new economic opportunities opened up in the surrounding society, there were members of Jewish society who stood ready to take advantage of them. Those who controlled the Jewish sources of livelihood had no interest in political or economic change—and this is what gave the impression that the Jewish community was committed to preserving the status quo. But once political or economic changes had occurred, Jews adapted to them quite quickly. Such changes were the longed-for, golden opportunity for those depressed elements within Jewish society to realize their dreams of economic and social advancement. Both conservatism and the enthusiasm for change and novelty are simultaneous expressions of the political status of Jewish society and of the competitive tension that was characteristic of the community.

8

Religion and Economic Activity

At this point we can turn our attention to the question of the relation between Judaism as a religion and the special economic role played by Jews within European society during the sixteenth through eighteenth centuries. So far, our analysis has not revealed any special characteristic, whether innate or historically acquired, that prepared the Jews for the role they assumed. Objective data—the Jews' political status, the fact that they possessed liquid capital, and the unity of their group over a broad geographic dispersion—would appear to provide a sufficient explanation for the extent and nature of Jewish economic activity. But this does not mean that we are entitled to ignore the Jews' religion. This, too, was one of the "objective criteria" that distinguished the Jews from their neighbors. At least indirectly, the Jews' religious distinctiveness influenced their economic behavior, and we must now ask how much their religion itself, or, perhaps better, their world view and mentality, either encouraged or discouraged their economic activity. Our analysis of the influence of religion on economic life will deal with four aspects of Judaism: its ritual prescriptions, its social teachings, the educational and psychological influence that it has on its adherents, and the manner in which its fundamental beliefs define virtue and the ultimate goals of human existence.

Religious Limitations. During our period, as Jews engaged in an increasing range of economic activities, questions arose concerning the religious legitimacy of some of these new endeavors. Greater integration into the economic life around them meant that Jews were forced to deal, directly or indirectly, in trades that had not been permitted in the halakhic literature. The question of trade in gentile wine, which we treated in chapter 3, is only one example of such a problem. Jewish merchants also bought and sold meat that had not been slaughtered in accordance with Jewish law. Leaseholders fed their gentile workers such meat, and if they leased entire villages or towns, they often found that pigs were being raised under their aegis.[1] All of these activities were apparently forbidden by tradition. Tax-farming and estate leasing, the retail trade in liquor, and, above all, the transporting of goods from place to place all presented problems for the Jew trying to observe the traditional, halakhically defined Sabbath. This was also true for activities like the leasing of flour mills, fish ponds, and distilleries, and the production of potash. Many questions arose concerning the Jew's right to profit from *ḥameẓ* (leavened products) on Passover.[2] In western Europe, where the Jews' integration into the economy was not as far-reaching, only a portion of these problems arose. But toward the end of our period, increased Jewish participation in industrial development raised the problem of Sabbath observance in a new form.[3]

Popular and Halakhic License. Two factors—the nature of Jewish participation in the economy and the relative flexibility of halakhic reasoning—allowed Jews to resolve the conflict between religious requirements and new economic realities. The fact that Jews did not operate within a totally self-contained, Jewish economy meant that they often had gentile partners or assistants in the management of estates and factories. The Jews could simply ask these gentiles to substitute for them on the Sabbath and other religious festivals. This did not completely resolve the halakhic problem, since it was still forbidden for the Jew to profit from the gentile's work, have the gentile carry out his instructions, or even allow the gentile to work in a Jewish-owned business on the Sabbath.[4] But these objections were essentially formal, and hence could be resolved through essentially formal mechanisms, such as fictional contracts or making the gentiles partners with the Jews.

The individual Jew and, in the final analysis, the halakhists were primarily concerned with keeping the Jew physically away from the area where the work was being performed on the holy day,[5] but even this was not always possible in practice. The popular imagination therefore devised a method of maintaining at least a symbolic distance from the workaday. The practice was widely accepted of selling liquor and the like to gentiles even on holy days but of not touching the money![6] Halakhists could not, of course, rely on such weak distinctions, but even they—assuming that the business would not formally belong to the Jew—sometimes allowed him to be present on the side (as, for instance, during the collection of tolls from travelers) in order to supervise a gentile worker.[7] It must be stressed, however, that all such *heterim* (special licenses)—popular and halakhic alike—assumed that the Jew actually kept the Sabbath, refrained from working, and spent most of the day in the special atmosphere appropriate to a holy day. The rabbis absolutely refused to countenance occupations, such as the long-distance transporting of merchandise by Jewish teamsters, that would likely prevent the Jew from observing the distinctive aspects of the Sabbath on a regular and ongoing basis.[8]

Halakhists used a similar principle—namely, the distinction between direct, personal contact on the one hand, and activities in which the Jew had only a financial interest on the other—to develop theories by which Jews might trade in foods that they were unquestionably forbidden to eat. *Stam yeinam* (gentile wine—see chapter 3) was forbidden primarily because of its potential use by Christians in their ritual; on the other hand, Jews saw meat that had not been ritually slaughtered as taboo per se and felt qualms about dealing in it. The halakhists articulated this attitude in rationalistic terms when they worried lest the merchant himself come to eat these foods.[9] Rules against such trade, therefore, made sense only in cases where the Jew would have direct personal contact with the product. When, however, the Jew would have only indirect contact with the forbidden foods from which he profited—as in cases of managing leased estates or large-scale trade—these qualms tended to disappear. One can legitimately see this development as a reflection of the new rationalist economic outlook, within which commercial goods lost their individuality and came to be treated as mere objects from which to derive profit. Be that as it may, trade in such items came to be accepted, at first almost incidentally—something that could never have happened with regard to eating them. The halakhists then tried to justify these practices ex post facto.[10]

The greatest hesitations were expressed with regard to profiting from pig breeding, an occupation that Jews had always shunned as somehow "un-Jewish" and that, according to tradition, was cursed. The rulings against this practice always included strong emotional appeals.[11] There is evidence that some leaseholders did try to end pig breeding on the estates they controlled,[12] but in Volhynia and Galicia, the major regions of such leasing, the first half of the seventeenth century witnessed general acceptance of the practice. Finally a major jurist, Rabbi David ha-Levi, author of *Turei Zahav* and rabbi of Ostrog, actually defended the Jews of his region with the characteristic argument that pig breeding was, after all, only a part of the total farm economy: "It is not associated with the Jew, nor does the Jew have anything to do with it. . . ."[13]

Rules against Usury and the Heter Iska. Beyond the problems created by Jewish participation in the non-Jewish economy, even more significant halakhic questions were raised by the development, in our period, of intense internal commercial networks linking Jews one to another in a fashion unknown in the Middle Ages. Extended trading networks over long distances required the creation of instruments of internal credit. Jews had to be able to borrow from, and make use of, financial and commercial services offered by other Jews. Such relations between Jews presented legal and moral problems for which the sources provided no ready solutions. The primary example of this kind of problem was posed by the question of lending money at interest. In fact, the problem also arose with regard to trade in forbidden foods: The original *heter*, or license, was actually limited to cases in which a Jew happened to come into possession of such foods and then sold them to a gentile. Now the exigencies of trade were forcing Jews to sell such products to each other.[14]

Talmudic Law Adjusts to New Conditions. The halakhic problem of lending at interest was not, per se, new. Even in the Middle Ages, when the bulk of the Jewish money trade involved loans to gentiles, there were also cases of loans between Jews that required halakhic justification. Already then, various devices had been invented in order to save the borrower and lender from formally transgressing the serious laws against lending at interest. But in the Middle Ages it had been relatively easy to find a solution to this problem, not only because such transactions were relatively rare, but also because the loans resulted from direct contact between the interested parties, either through the drawing up of a contract or through the depositing of a pawn with the lender. From the halakhic point of view, such loans involved *ribit kẓuẓa*—that is, interest whose rate was fixed by the lender in advance—and as such were most problematic. But at least the personal contact between the parties allowed for phrasing the terms of the loan in such a manner as to satisfy the halakhic authorities. One could write the contract in such a way that the loan became, in formal terms, a joint business venture, even though the lender's profits were assured and his capital was never at risk. In the case of loans against a pledge, the authorities involved a gentile in the transaction, having him borrow from the one Jew with the pawn of the other.[15]

In our period, these formal halakhic mechanisms were no longer sufficient to meet the needs of changing conditions. In many cases the medieval pure loan had given way to business investments in factories, credit advanced against the purchase of goods, and the like.[16] On the one hand, the legal fictions of the Middle Ages had become reality, and the halakhic problems were actually eased. On the other hand, however, the very concreteness of the transactions created new halakhic problems. The prohibition against charging interest applied in its broadest sense to any financial dealings or investments in which the chances of profit were greater than the risk of loss. Profits under such conditions were termed *avak ribit* (literally: the dust of interest) and were prohibited, if not by biblical law, then at least by later rabbinic injunction (*mi-de-rabanan*). Precise distinctions between interest proper, even if only *avak ribit,* and permissible profits involved many problematic issues that even the halakhists found difficult to resolve or agree upon.[17] Third, the direct contact between borrower and lender that had characterized medieval transactions was now replaced by borrowers who owed money in an anonymous credit market. Bills of credit passed from creditor to creditor, and the negotiability of such notes only made the halakhic problems more complicated.[18] Only a few specialized experts could deal with these complex and difficult problems, and simple merchants—even if they were familiar with fundamental halakhic principles—were soon lost in the maze. Authorities were genuinely concerned lest Jews grow cynical and come to mock the entire prohibition against taking interest.[19]

This situation, which had certainly developed by the end of the sixteenth century, caused great concern among halakhists. Solutions to the problem were sought in two broad directions, one educational-administrative and the other legislative-reformist. The educational approach was associated with the name of Rabbi Joshua Falk, author of the *Sefer Me'irat Einayim,* who recorded the decisions of the leading Talmudic scholars gathered at Lublin for the Grominice fair of 1607. These decisions were accepted by the leaders of the Council of the Four Lands and recorded in the Council's minutes. The intent of these decisions was to impose expert halakhic supervision on all transactions involving the prohibition of interest. The experts would ensure that the participants observed all the practices and used all the legal devices required in order to avoid transgressing. They were also to explain "the logic of the matter to the participants in such a way that it will not be an object of derision in their eyes and thus lead to their treating other things lightly as well." Falk wrote his pamphlet for the benefit of both the expert and the ordinary businessman. Hence, rules were presented in a dual version, once in apodictic form without halakhic explanation, and then again with full explanations drawn from the sources.[20]

In fact, these rulings of the Council of the Four Lands had no real chance of being accepted in practice. Even those who instituted these rules realized that merchants might well hesitate to reveal their business affairs to local experts, and the Council therefore suggested that an expert be appointed in every family, such that everyone would be able to turn to a relative for advice.[21] Obviously such an arrangement could not be maintained for long, and the Council's warning that any contract written without the authorization of an appointed expert would not be accepted by the courts was undoubtedly an empty threat.

A quite different approach to the problem of interest grew up, not under the aegis of the Council of the Four Lands, the supreme institution of the largest of Jewish communities, but, so to speak, of itself. Hence, when we refer to this approach as "legislative-reformist" we do not mean to imply that an institutionalized declaration of intent to change the law was ever issued, although in essence that is exactly what occurred. In fact, already during his lifetime and even after the appearance of his pamphlet, methods not strictly in accord with Rabbi Falk's instructions were being used to circumvent the law. These *heterim* (licenses) based themselves on differing halakhic principles, but they all waived the need for detailing the terms of the contract and obviated the need for asking a scholar's opinion about each and every transaction.[22]

The most popular of these *heterim* was the so-called *heter iska ke-tikun MaHaRaM*, or *MuRaM* (business license developed by R. Menaḥem—i.e., R. Isaiah Menaḥem, also known after his father-in-law as Menaḥem Mendel Avigdor's, died 1599). While rabbi of Cracow, and even before the meeting at Lublin that led to Falk's pamphlet, Rabbi Menaḥem published a model business contract (*shtar iska*) that allowed for circumventing the prohibition of interest under certain circumstances.[23] Copies of this contract were widely distributed, and eventually people contented themselves with noting on their own contracts and agreements that these were to be understood in accordance with "the ruling instituted by our teacher, Rabbi Mendel." Some objections were raised to the use of this abbreviated formula, and ethicists, in particular, were not happy with the entire approach.[24] But it seems that the strictest halakhists actually preferred this abbreviated formula to the writing of new contracts for each business deal, since there was less chance of error in the complicated wording otherwise necessary. The abbreviated formula, on the other hand, simply indicated that the parties had intended that their contract be in accord with the authorized formula.[25] The rules against lending at interest had long ago been circumvented; we now see how the last halakhic reservations concerning the dynamic forces of the contemporary economic scene were neutralized.

The development of the *heter iska* is only one example, albeit the most prominent, of the process of adaptation called for by the increased economic ties between members of the Jewish community. The issue of interest was particularly problematic, since, at least in later Halakha, it was given ritualistic significance over and above its economic importance.[26] Other halakhic questions that were regarded in more purely financial terms could be resolved without such elaborate rulings and halakhic justifications. The major economic change in our period was the development and intensification of credit between Jews. The financial mechanism developed to provide this credit was the *MaMRaME,* a negotiable promissory note payable to the bearer on demand. The institution of the *MaMRaMe,* and perhaps even its essential legal character, was known as early as the thirteenth century.[27] But only from the sixteenth century on does it become the major instrument of debt for the internal Jewish credit market.[28] The use of this instrument necessitated courts capable of quick action that could enforce immediate payment of the note on presentation. As we shall see, such courts existed within the Jewish community.[29] But from our point of view, it is important to note that the use of *MaMRaMe* was a significant deviation from the halakhic traditions of the Talmud, which saw indebtedness as applying only to a specific named individual. By Talmudic law, the transfer of debt (i.e., the selling of promissory notes) could be accomplished only through very complicated formal procedures, and these were simply insufficient for the needs of the new, dynamic economy. Once again we see the Talmudic tradition abrogated almost unintentionally, and a totally new understanding of contracts integrated unconsciously into halakhic jurisprudence.[30] The same process also applied in other areas of law: for instance, the question of indemnification (*asmakhta*),[31] and the establishment of the relative order of creditors' claims in cases of bankruptcy.[32] The emergence of a public credit market demanded halakhic guarantees for the security of investments; the Halakha responded to this demand through flexible and far-reaching adaptation.

Attitudes about Wealth. Even if their religious and legal traditions did not prevent Jews from participating in the emerging monetary and credit economy, did these traditions *encourage* such participation? As we have already noted, it is entirely possible to explain the readiness of Jews to adopt the new economic methods as the political and social results of their status as a tolerated religious minority. But it is of course possible that the content of the religion itself also had some direct influence, either through its social teachings or through some psychological impact of its essential tenets.

There is certainly no question that in this period Judaism approved wholeheartedly of the desire to amass capital. The ethicists were not unaware of the dangers implicit in wealth: both the temptation to acquire it illicitly and the ethical failings to which money often led. But the ethicists merely concluded that it was necessary to emphasize and to re-emphasize these dangers. They constantly stressed the importance of trading honestly—that is, of avoiding illegitimate methods in the acquisition of wealth.[33] They similarly emphasized the need to use wealth properly, and stressed that charity should be given in the proper amounts and in such a manner that it not insult the recipient or lead to haughtiness on the part of the donor.[34] Opinions varied on whether the very possession of wealth was proof of divine approval. There were those who tended to see material success as an indication of a blessing from "Him who controls all wealth," and this view was supported from the traditional texts. Others rejected this view, either because of some personal idiosyncrasy or because of their experience or social status.[35] The religious tradition did not allow for any decisive ruling in this regard. Still, even those who doubted that wealth proved anything about religious rectitude never denigrated the possession of wealth per se. Neither the desire for wealth nor its possession was ever labeled as unethical on principle. Poverty, on the other hand, was always regarded as a trial that one should be willing to endure. It never became an ideal to which man should aspire, even for the strictest moralists. Though obviously familiar with the traditional sources that idealized poverty in this manner, the halakhists and ethical teachers either ignored them or explained them away through pilpulistic and homiletic devices. Jewish society depended for its very existence on income-producing capital, and this fact forced Jewish ethical teachings unhesitatingly to legitimize the possession of wealth at least as no evil. Anyone growing up in the Jewish society of the sixteenth through eighteenth centuries would therefore have encountered attitudinal patterns that encouraged and favored his desire for money and wealth far more than they restricted it—of course, after establishing suitable preconditions and restrictions as to acquisition and use. Hence, from the point of view of its social teachings, Judaism took a completely positive attitude toward economic activity.

Religious Justifications for Human Existence. We can further see in the Jewish religion, or, more correctly, in the Jewish way of life built upon that religion, an educational and psychological preparation for what is called "rational" economic activity—that is, for activity in which the means is evaluated purely in terms of its efficiency in achieving the desired end. The religious life trains the Jew to evaluate his actions in light of their ultimate purpose by discouraging affective reactions and directing him toward the calculated use of time. In short, the religious life prepares the Jew for a planned and rational way of life. Several scholars have argued that the well-known commercial abilities of Jews are a result of this religious education.

Still, the importance of this kind of spiritual preparedness is actually limited. Sociology teaches us that the main key to an understanding of the relation between religion and economic activity does not really lie in the social teachings of a given religion, or in the way in which it prepares people psychologically.[36] As we have seen, Judaism clearly adapted to economic need in its social teachings and in the ritual prescriptions derived from those teachings. There is similarly a limit to how far we can attribute rational behavior in one sphere to the psychological influence of rational behavior in another. As Max Weber has shown in his fundamental studies, the main influence of religion in the social sphere stems specifically from the central religious issues of faith and the justification of man before his Maker, issues that appear to have no relevance to anything outside the sphere of pure religion.

Thus, what we must investigate is Judaism in its purely religious sense, the Judaism that assigns a place to man in this world, that defines his function, and that guides him toward salvation. We must decide whether this essence of Judaism was a factor that encouraged the type of economic activity upon which Jewish survival was based. To put the question in another way: Did the Jewish religion ascribe a positive role to economic activity in justifying man before his Maker and, in a psychological sense, before himself? This is the question that Max Weber asked about Protestantism of that same period. But whereas Weber answered his question in the positive, we must answer absolutely in the negative with regard to Judaism. The acquisition of wealth was tolerated and sometimes even praised, but Judaism never saw economic success as a sign of man's rectitude before man or God. To be considered virtuous, one had at least to obey the religious injunctions and aspire to the religious ideal classically defined as "Torah, commandments, and good deeds." In the sense that it enlarged one's possibilities, wealth might serve as a means, albeit not a necessary means, toward accomplishing this religious end. The study of the Torah, the fulfillment of the commandments, and, of course, the performance of good deeds were all made possible in accordance with one's means. Wealth facilitated study of the Torah, for instance, by freeing the individual from concern over his livelihood, although one had to be careful lest management of wealth itself steal time from study. To the extent that specific commandments involved financial expenditures, wealth enabled one to perform them, and in a more munificent and elegant manner. And finally, the extent of one's ability to give charity and, to some extent, to perform other acts of *gmilut ḥesed* (loving-kindness) depended directly on one's financial means.[37] But the very fact that wealth was seen merely as the *means* by which the commandments might be accomplished proves that wealth occupied a subordinate place in the scale of values of the society defined by Judaism. The acquisition of wealth and its use were not likely to replace the original means of religious justification and become ends in themselves. At most, success in the economic sphere might be considered as supporting evidence for a man's righteousness, but the primary proof had to come from the religious sphere itself: that is, from rigorous fulfillment of the letter and the spirit of the commandments, which included the proper use of the wealth entrusted to him. To say that Judaism encouraged economic activity would require that actions within the purely religious sphere lose their value and make way for, or even lend authority to, unrestricted activity in the economic sphere, science, and art. It goes almost without saying that such a development never occurred within Judaism itself. Judaism developed a tolerant attitude toward activities in these spheres only ex post facto, and even then it only allowed these activities; it never sanctified them as ends in themselves.

Torah Study and the Allocation of Time. The factor that, above all, prevented such a development in Judaism was the obligation to study Torah (*talmud tora*). Were it not for this, one can imagine Jews continuing to fulfill all the practical commandments and dedicating—in a secondarily religious sense—the rest of their time to economic activity. But study of the Torah laid claim to all of the Jew's free time once he had provided for his physical needs and fulfilled his religious duties. In theory the Jew was obliged to study the Torah during every free moment.[38] Of course, this ideal was achieved only by a few exceptional scholars who gave themselves over completely to this task. Most Jews contented themselves with establishing fixed times for study or even by reading the relevant passages included in prayer books. Thus, in actual fact the average Jew was free to devote himself completely to his business. But such a course of action had always to justify itself in the face of the fundamental demand that he devote all of his time to the study of the Torah. In principle no one was exempted from this demand, and no distinction was made between the scholar and the layman. The ethical literature constantly re-emphasized that even those not capable of deep understanding were nevertheless obligated to use their time to study according to their own ability. Anyone who devoted more time than seemed necessary to making a living was required to account for this "waste of time." Of course, there were ways to justify such secular preoccupations. It was impossible, for instance, precisely to limit the extent of what was "necessary" for one's daily existence. There were also methods of fulfilling the commandment of Torah study indirectly, through a proxy. Anyone who contributed to the support of scholars, and certainly anyone who maintained them on his own, was considered as having participated in their study. He was considered a "partner" in the performance of the commandment, for it could not have been accomplished without him, and the patron was promised the same reward as the scholar.[39]

Hence, although the obligation to study Torah did not in fact prevent engaging in business or following any occupation whatsoever, it did prevent such a course of action from gaining religious legitimacy in its own right. It was legitimate to engage in a profession, but such activity remained essentially secular. There was no way to sanctify such economic activity without totally distorting Judaism.

PART II

COMMUNAL INSTITUTIONS AND STRUCTURE

9

The Form and Structure of the Kehila

The fact that Jews were segregated from the rest of society—both by state law and of their own volition—meant that the majority of their individual and group needs had to be provided from within their own community. The Jews were forced to create institutions with the ability and authority to carry out the various necessary social functions. The most common and most basic of these institutions was the *kehila* (plural: *kehilot;* communal organization), which united within itself and bound together all of the permanent residents of a given locale. In the present chapter we shall examine the basis of the *kehila*'s authority and its various institutions and offices. We shall ask to what extent the institutions of Jewish self-government approached the rationalized forms of contemporary government in which a given office was defined and existed without reference to the individual incumbent and to those who used its service. Finally, we shall look at the balance between lay and rabbinic leadership and the link between the rabbinate and the *kehila*.

The *kehila* was more than a reflection of the demographic growth of a group of Jews to some critical number at which communal activity was possible. The formation of a *kehila* was a social act intended to articulate the religious and cultural ties that linked individual Jews to one another. Organization was, in the first place, imposed on the Jews by their common and parallel needs. But the *kehila* that they created was based upon Talmudic law and implied explicit or implicit acceptance of the validity of that law. In this sense, the *kehila* derived from the attachment of its members to the shared Jewish tradition.

Ashkenazic and Local Custom. Of course, conditions had changed enormously since the Talmudic period. Hence, even though the norms of Jewish society theoretically derived from Talmudic law, the halakhists were forced more than once to admit that in questions of election procedure, tax assessment, and other matters of communal governance, it was difficult to issue a pure *din tora*, a decision derived directly from earlier rabbinic sources.[1] The extent to which the community might impose its will on the individual was questioned repeatedly in our period, and jurists tried to decide cases on the basis of precedents drawn from the halakhic literature. The Mishna and Tosefta had ruled that the inhabitants of a city could require each other to share in the building of the city wall, the establishment of a synagogue, and the purchase of a Torah scroll. The jurists now tried to expand upon these few examples and rule on other, quite different matters, ranging from the communal purchase of an *etrog* (citron) for Tabernacles or hiring of a children's teacher to sharing in the cost of negotiating government recognition of the *kehila*'s autonomy.[2] The general tendency was toward obligating the individual to share in the public burden even in cases where he would derive no personal benefit from his contribution. But the halakhists never articulated the individual's obligation and status vis-à-vis the *kehila* in abstract and generalized terms.[3]

The *kehila* could draw on two authoritative sources for its procedural norms: the Talmud and *minhag*, or customary usage. There are two different notions implied in *minhag*. First, *minhag* includes everything that had been accepted as binding by Ashkenazic Jewry as a whole; these customs had, for the most part, been recorded formally in halakhic works that were regarded as almost as authoritative as the Talmud.[4] But *minhag* also includes specific local usages for which there was some evidence—and not necessarily in writing. Usually such local customs did not totally contradict the more general Ashkenazic *minhag*; rather, they introduced slight variations or dealt with issues for which there was no clear-cut ruling in the general tradition. This is not surprising when we remember that the *minhag* of each area reflected a branching out of the common Ashkenazic legal tradition rather than a totally independent development. (This, incidentally, provides yet a further proof for our view of Ashkenazic Jewry as a single social unit.)

Takanot. One of the characteristics of communal government in our period was the commitment of such local usages to writing. Every *kehila* of standing had a comprehensive system of bylaws, or *takanot*.[5] It is safe to assume that these *takanot* represented the accumulated decisions taken at meetings of community members or their representatives. Although in the Middle Ages there was still debate between major halakhists (*Rabenu* Tam and Rabbi Eliezer ben Joel ha-Levi [Ra'AViYaH]) as to whether the community had the right to impose its will on the individual, by our period the supremacy of the community had long been recognized. By the end of the sixteenth century at the very latest, we find that communities had special committees of *baalei takanot* to formulate their bylaws. Once the *kehila* —and, in some places, the *av bet din* (communal rabbi)—had approved their wording, the *takanot* became binding on both the members and the leaders of the community.[6]

Halakha and Kehila Governance. In summary, we may say that Jewish communal government exhibited aspects of both a traditional and a rationalized system: On the one hand, the *takanot* were perceived as based on traditional values; on the other, the very fact that the *takanot* were committed to writing lent them the more rationalized character of a fixed system of obligatory norms. In the end, the rationalized system of governance would always be based on the emotional appeal of traditional values. The *takanot,* and the authority of the leadership generally, were based on concepts that linked the individual to the collective Jewish fate and claimed an intrinsic value for the *kehila.* Emotional terminology drawn from the Talmudic lexicon—we hear of "the needs of the community" or "the need of the majority" as well as concern for the "status" and "standing" of the *kehila*—served as both guidelines and legitimation for the leaders.[7] In those areas where it was customary for communal ordinances to be submitted to halakhic scholars for approval, the link between the *takana* and the religious law theoretically binding on all Jews was a direct one. But even where halakhists did not have the power to decide on issues of public policy, this does not imply that Jewish public life was deaf to halakhic norms. For one thing, the local customary law of the *kehila* was an integral part of Halakha. Moreover, it was assumed that the communities would limit any arbitrary actions in accordance with halakhic notions of justice and righteousness, which could be clarified by referring to local customs. It was this link to the Halakha and past custom that limited, at least in theory, the possibility of arbitrary rule based on intimidation.[8] Moreover, at least in theory, the halakhists were assumed to be the ones to rule on unclear or doubtful issues in the interpretation of the written *takanot.*[9]

The Ashkenazic-Polish *kehila* of the sixteenth through eighteenth centuries was not the small, structurally unified institution of the Middle Ages, which could be governed by its members and scholars through a form of almost continuous participatory democracy. This *kehila* differed as well from the transitional format of the thirteenth through fifteenth centuries, when the institutionalized *kehila* declined in strength and Jews depended upon local scholarly individuals for leadership.[10] For one thing, at least the leading *kehilot* of our period were far larger than before, numbering now in the hundreds, sometimes in the thousands, and, in a few cases at the end of the period, even in the tens of thousands and more.[11] Moreover, as we shall see, these *kehilot* were not homogeneous as to wealth, occupation, or educational achievement. Of necessity the large *kehilot* required a hierarchically organized and directed leadership, with decision making assigned to a small number of individuals. Structural stratification and the occasional need to impose disciplinary measures are the telltale signs that the *kehila* had outgrown the primary group stage in which the governing officials and the governed were linked by an immediate and intimate relationship. And once this system of differentiation had spread among the large *kehilot*, smaller *kehilot* inevitably followed suit, even though their numbers did not necessitate abandoning the medieval norms of government.

Sephardic Influence. These changes in the size and structure of the Polish-Ashkenazic communities made it difficult to apply traditional Ashkenazic norms of government in practice. Though differences remained, in structural terms these *kehilot* were now closer to the medieval Sephardic model than to the Ashkenazic, and it was easier for halakhists to resolve problems according to precedents found in the Sephardic tradition than in the Ashkenazic. In other words, these communities were confronted by a contradiction between concrete reality and their ideological frame of reference. On the one hand, the halakhists of Poland and their contemporaries in the *kehilot* of Germany consciously and emphatically sought to preserve their Ashkenazic tradition and opposed the increasing penetration of Sephardic halakhic influence through Sephardic halakhic manuals such as the *Shulḥan Arukh*. On the other hand, when it came to governance of the *kehila* these same scholars in fact abandoned much of their Ashkenazic tradition and almost unknowingly absorbed principles and details of communal governance and organization from Sephardic halakhic works.[12] This tendency in the field of Halakha was unquestionably the product of the real changes in *kehila* size that we have described.[13]

The Parnasim and Other Functionaries. The concentration of communal leadership in the hands of a limited group of from three to six (or sometimes more) *parnasim* or *rashim* (heads) is a clear indication of the *kehila*'s stratified structure. Next in the hierarchy of offices stood the *tovim* (*viri buoni*; good men), *gaba'im* (treasurers), and *memunim* (overseers). Each of these had his own specific field of activity. The *tovim* assisted and advised the *parnasim*; the charity *gaba'im* administered the *hekdesh* (i.e., the poorhouse) or the synagogue; and the other officials supervised prices and weights and measures at the market, as well as *kashrut*.[14] All of these officers served by appointment as a public service. Though personal interests and satisfactions presumably affected whether the individual accepted an appointment and how he fulfilled it, these were essentially unpaid positions, a fact that in itself lent them a political-governmental aspect not shared by the offices of the functionaries.

The factor that most influenced the character of a specific *kehila* administration was not the number of *parnasim* on the administrative body, but the division of labor among them. One *parnas* was declared the *parnas ha-ḥodesh*—warden of the month—and he was considered superior to his fellows. As its title indicates, this office rotated on a monthly basis. But the significance of this rotation varied tremendously with the particular style of administration. In the communities of Germany, Moravia, and western Hungary, the *parnas ha-ḥodesh* was the chairman of the council of *parnasim*. He had the right to call a meeting and had other clearly defined functions. Authority, however, remained ultimately lodged in the hands of the council, and all actions of the *parnas ha-ḥodesh* were based upon its authority.[15] On the other hand, in the communities of Poland and Lithuania, during his month the *parnas ha-ḥodesh* was the only authority; he initiated actions, made decisions, and directed the executive apparatus, while the other *parnasim* became merely his assistants.[16]

The appointed officers were regularly called upon to make decisions as to whether, for instance, a given *minhag* or *takana* applied to a certain situation, or when and where to enforce the law. Thus, these communal leaders—unlike the paid clerks—really functioned as rulers. These leaders were never forced to account for their actions, since there was no public watchdog institution along the lines of a modern parliament. The only guarantee, therefore, that they would discharge their office faithfully lay in their own identification with the social values that they represented. The communal *takanot* that outlined their official duties and functions took this into consideration. Sometimes the *takanot* devised mechanisms by which to force the leaders to supervise each other, as by requiring a large quorum for certain decisions or by insisting on a final accounting, especially with regard to financial revenues and expenditures. At times fines were levied on delinquent *parnasim*, although such fines were intended less as penalties than as a method of encouraging desirable behavior.[17] In the final analysis, the *takanot* had to rely upon the assumption that the officials respected the values of society. They therefore reminded the *parnasim* of their obligation to attend faithfully to communal needs, and warned them that any infraction was tantamount to incurring a punishment of *ḥerem* (excommunication).[18] In cases of particularly heavy responsibilities, officials were sometimes required to take a formal oath that they would properly perform their task. This was true for those who selected candidates for office, tax assessors, and the *parnasim* themselves upon first taking office, or if there was some special problem, as when a *parnas* was suspected of using the influence of the gentile authorities in order to gain his office.[19] The resort to the *ḥerem* and oath point to the religious character of their responsibilities. Ultimately, it was only piety that could guarantee that officeholders would adhere to society's values when no human power could force them to do so. And piety—in Hebrew, *yir'at shamayim*, or "fear of heaven"—ranged all the way from its most primitive sense of fear of the magical power of the words of the oath to its pure religious meaning as the desire to imitate the qualities of the omniscient God.

Although there was a clear hierarchy of offices within the *kehila*—*parnasim* above *tovim* above *gaba'im* and *memunim*—each level was, to a large extent, independent of those above. Hierarchy was a function of the relative importance of the specific task and the competence of the office; it did not involve subordination of one official to another.[20] On an operational level, the only small expression of hierarchy among the officers occurred when the *parnasim* delegated someone to perform a specific task, such as fixing food prices.[21]

To the extent that officeholders needed help in carrying out their duties, they would make use of assistants, or *shamashim*, paid by the *kahal*. The number of such paid functionaries varied with the size of the community. In some places, one functionary could handle all of the tasks, whereas in other places a considerable number of functionaries—town scribes, court messengers, town witnesses (*edim de-mata*), watchmen, prison guards, and street cleaners—amounted to a structured system. In the largest communities we find an entire bureaucratic apparatus.[22] Of course, these positions were salaried rather than honorary, although the bulk of the salary came not directly from the *kehila* but from fees charged to those to whom the service was rendered. It made no difference whether the service was to the individual's benefit or not. The functionary was entitled to collect a fee as much from someone who was excommunicated or jailed as from someone who requested a notarized document, sought the attachment of property, or the like.[23] The size of the fee for each service was generally specified in the communal *takanot*. The fact that the communal leadership fixed these fees indicates that a partial rationalization of communal service had been achieved. But this was only a partial rationalization. It is almost certain that at least some of the communal functionaries did not devote full time to their office, and had other sources of income.

The typological distinction between officials who actually held authority and functionaries who merely executed orders was not absolute, since the functionaries were sometimes authorized to initiate proceedings on their own. Sometimes, for instance, the *takanot* specified that the *shamash,* without waiting for instructions from the communal officers, was to excommunicate anyone who acted in a certain manner. In other places, he was ordered to attach property or arrange payments on his own authority.[24] In this we see expressed a tendency to free the communal executive apparatus from its dependence upon the legislative authority. But even if authority thus passed, to some extent, to the executive staff, we must remember that the responsibility and accountability of the two branches remained quite different. Whereas the officeholder was ultimately responsible only to his own conscience as to whether his decisions were consonant with the values of society, the paid functionary was liable to suffer real sanctions, such as "loss of his position" (a repeated threat), for failing to obey the officers or to implement instructions spelled out in the *takanot.* On the other hand, there were cases in which the *takanot* made the functionary responsible for enforcing the *takanot* themselves and freed him from the obligation of obeying the officeholders, if the latter demanded something contradictory to the *takanot.*[25] It is, in fact, difficult to imagine a case of such clear confrontation between a functionary and a communal officer. In any case, the expertise of the functionary (who was in continuous service to the community) with regard to customary procedures normally prevented any more or less intentional deviations from the norms of the *takanot.*

The Shtadlan. There was one functionary in the large *kehilot* and the supra-communal organizations who formed a complete exception to all the rules we have laid down regarding public servants. This was the *shtadlan* (intercessor), who was obliged to devote all his time to cultivating contacts with the outside, gentile world, or at least to be always ready to make such contacts. Sometimes this would require that he travel far from home. The *shtadlan* of a community, and all the more so of an entire province, was called upon to deal with the secular authorities, who often were located some distance away. Moreover, unlike all other communal functionaries, the *shtadlan* required specialized knowledge not always found in other members of the community: command of the vernacular and legal terminology, familiarity with the local legal and political systems, and aggressiveness and flexibility in negotiations. These talents and skills could hardly be learned in either Jewish or non-Jewish schools. They could be acquired only by unusually talented people who were prepared to devote enormous personal effort and intense individual study to them and to adopt a life-style that was accessible to only a very few, special families.[26] Because of his uniqueness, the *shtadlan* was granted much more liberal working conditions; because of the importance of his function, the communities and supra-communal organizations were ready to share in the special expenses of maintaining him.[27]

The Jewish community viewed contact with the gentile world as the exclusive prerogative of the organized *kahal* and province. The individual was forced to rely upon the *kehila* officers to act as his representatives vis-à-vis the outside world even if the matter involved his private affairs. Usually, in fact, the great effort and expertise required made it necessary for all to rely on the *shtadlan*.[28]

Even in private cases, the *shtadlan* acted in the name of the community and it was therefore preferable that he not become the agent of any one individual. At least in one place, Cracow, the logical step was taken of forbidding the *shtadlan* from receiving any reward from the individual on whose behalf he had acted. In other places, the *shtadlan* was allowed to ask for a fee but could not make his help conditional on being paid.[29] In other words, special circumstances created a type of functionary closely corresponding to the modern rationalized version of the public official, who serves the community without any personal relation to those who need him, and who receives the bulk of his salary out of public funds. One of the signs of the decline of the *kehila* and of the supra-communal organizations in the eighteenth century was that they were no longer able to pay the *shtadlanim* a fixed salary. The *shtadlanim* were now given a percentage of the community's current income and presumably were not prevented from taking a fee for their services from those who made use of them.[30]

The Communal Rabbi. Our description of those who participated in the governance of the community would not be complete without mentioning the communal rabbi—even though there were aspects of the rabbinical office that had nothing to do with communal government. The rabbi's functions as halakhic authority in ritual and civil matters, as teacher, and as preacher were of long standing and did not depend on his holding formal communal office. Anyone who had been ordained a rabbi by his teacher or another recognized authority was entitled to rule on halakhic questions. Whether he chose to do so, especially with regard to difficult matters such as divorce and levirate marriage, was up to him and those who chose to seek him out.[31] In our period, scholars who held no communal office were still sometimes asked to serve as judges. Similarly, the authority to teach the Torah derived only from the willingness of students to be taught. Again, in some places in our period, there were heads of Talmudic academies who held no other communal office. Even so, there was a clear tendency in our period not to allow halakhic authority to be exercised spontaneously but rather to concentrate it in the hands of individuals formally recognized by the community as rabbis.

The rabbi was usually chosen from among a number of candidates at a meeting of the townspeople or by a more limited body functioning as their representatives.[32] Of course, the candidate had to have been ordained as a qualified halakhic judge in the fashion mentioned above, but the rabbi's particular authority vis-à-vis the members of his community derived exclusively from this act of appointment, which was formally noted in the *kehila* record book and spelled out in a formal "letter of rabbinical appointment" (*ktav rabanut*). This letter detailed the conditions of the appointment.[33] The rabbi was hired for a fixed period of time, usually three years.[34] His base salary was fixed, as were his other sources of income. These latter included, aside from spontaneous gifts, fees for services such as supervising the writing of a marriage or divorce contract, or acting as a judge. The honors owing to the rabbi, such as when he would be called to the Torah in the synagogue, were similarly specified. In those places where the rabbi was also to serve as the head of a *yeshiva*, the letter would mention this obligation as well as the community's commitment to support a given number of nonlocal students.[35] The rabbi would assume his post amid much formal and festive ceremony, through which the congregation accepted the rabbi's religious authority,[36] and from that point on, he was considered the *mara de-atra* (literally: master of the place)—in effect, possessed of a monopoly over the "rabbinic" duties we have outlined. From this point on, no one else could decide halakhic questions or judge cases, or preach or teach in public, without his permission or at least tacit consent. Some of the rabbinic duties might be passed on to secondary officeholders—halakhists, preachers, and the like—but these latter were subject to the rabbi's supervision. It was considered a serious breach of discipline for them, or anyone else, to disobey the rabbi or, much worse, to insult him, and the institutions of the *kehila* were obliged to suppress such actions with whatever means were available.[37]

The Communal Rabbi and the Parnasim. The development of this communal rabbinate was linked to the strengthening of the organized *kehila* typical of our period. It was only the existence of a permanent apparatus for levying taxes that gave the *kehila* the ability to promise the rabbi a fixed salary sufficient to provide him with a significant part of his livelihood. In earlier periods, up through the first half of the sixteenth century, the rabbi had derived his entire livelihood from fees for service. Similarly, it was the creation of a method of enforcement of communal discipline that made it possible to allocate all rabbinic tasks to a single individual and to eliminate his potential rivals. This again had not been the case in earlier eras, when competition between rabbis was very extensive.[38] The rabbi's new dependence on the strength of the organized community could have a negative effect: In many cases, especially in Poland and Lithuania, rabbinical posts were now bought. The candidate or his family would pay the *kehila* or those designated to choose the rabbi a one-time fee in return for the appointment. We shall deal with the sociological implications of this phenomenon below.[39] Here, it is sufficient to point out that anyone who had purchased his rabbinical position considered it, and all the prestige, honor, and income that went with it, as his own personal office for the duration of his term. Had there been no *kehila* organization that could guarantee the "buyer" a return on his "investment," such a "sale" of the rabbinical office could never have taken place.

Just as the contemporary rabbi depended upon the *kehila*, the organized *kehila* depended upon him. Here we return to the point from which we began our analysis: the *kehila*'s power rested in principle on the holiness of the tradition. To contemporaries, the preservation of the *kehila* was tantamount to preservation of the religion, or, as the highly emotive current expression had it, "the Torah." It was no wonder, therefore, that the Jews sought some sort of institutional expression for their understanding by installing the bearer of the tradition as the head of the community. We have already noted that in most places the rabbi was asked to authorize the *takanot*, even if he had no role in formulating them. There were even places where the rabbi was given the authority to supervise the enforcement of the basic *takanot*, such as ensuring that all bylaws were observed during an election.[40] It goes without saying that the communal leadership was forced to rely upon the rabbi to provide a religious imprimatur for its decisions, to warn against infractions of the *takanot*, and to authorize especially severe punishments—for instance, the great *ḥerem* (decree of excommunication).[41] The rabbi was even more crucial as representative, in his religious-halakhic role, of the community vis-à-vis other communities—as, for instance, when he was asked to debate with other halakhists who had issued judgments or decrees of excommunication against members or leaders of the community.[42]

Thus, the two forms of communal leadership—that of the *parnasim* and that of the rabbis—were closely linked and dependent upon each other, and neither could exist or function without the aid of the other. Of course, such mutual dependence also led to frictions and disputes over prestige, jurisdiction, and the division of labor. The balance of power varied from place to place, and monographic studies of various communities or regions reflect different equilibria arrived at by these two forms of authority within the *kehila*. On the whole, however, it is possible to see the rabbinate gradually gaining a more secure role for itself in communal life, and the rabbi himself becomes a more clearly defined type. Communities change their rabbis less often. The initial appointment was for at least three years, and in some places for longer.[43] And the rabbi was occupied primarily with his official duties. Even though there still were rabbis who engaged in commerce and moneylending through the end of our period, the more the rabbinate became a guaranteed source of livelihood and prestige, the more it became the rabbi's sole profession and occupation.[44] The increasing signs of respect accorded the rabbi attest to the rising social status of the office. In the synagogue, the congregation waited for him before starting the service, and the reader would not begin the repetition of the *amida* until the rabbi had finished his prayers.[45] It seems that much of the prestige that, during the first half of our period, and especially in Poland, was accorded to the head of the *yeshiva* (who was not always a communal rabbi) now devolved onto the city rabbi, whether or not he functioned as a *rosh yeshiva*. The rising social status of the rabbinate inevitably brought with it a corresponding rise in expectations of the incumbent and increased emphasis on his responsibility for what went on in his community. Often he was blamed for the ills of Jewish society, and he was held responsible for the perfection of public life. It is no wonder, therefore, that the crisis that affected traditional society at the end of our period seemed to many to be primarily a crisis in the rabbinate.

10

The Kehila's Range of Activities

The *kehila* leadership was generally responsible for the workings of all communal institutions, and no aspect of group life lay outside its sphere of authority. Economic activity, relations with non-Jews, family and social matters, religion, and education were all subject to its control to a greater or lesser extent. But without question the principal task of the communal leadership was to represent the *kehila* to the outside world and to maintain relations with the non-Jewish authorities. In some regions the link between the Jewish and non-Jewish authorities was officially formalized, either in that the election of the *parnasim* required prior government approval or in that the *parnasim* were required to swear or attest allegiance to the authorities.[1] But even in those areas where the election appeared to be a merely internal Jewish matter, both the members of the community and the authorities assumed that the elected leaders were the ones intended and authorized to maintain contact with the government. The leaders were held responsible by the authorities for raising taxes, tributes, and any special, or emergency, levies from the community. To a not-insignificant degree, they were also held responsible by the authorities for the actions of individual Jews. Not infrequently they would be called upon to discipline individual violators of the law or even to hand over such individuals for trial by the secular authorities.[2]

The Enforcement Powers of the Parnasim. In return for these services, the heads of the Jewish community could rely on government backing and support whenever they had to enforce their own decisions. As we have demonstrated, in the final analysis the *kehila* depended for its existence on the internal cohesion of the community. But this cohesion was, after all, a function of Jewish ideals and moral values, and idealism could not always control conflicts of personal interest, nor could it prevent individuals from deviating from accepted norms. For the Jewish community, as for any other society, therefore, it was vital to have available an appropriate means of enforcement. And since the physical means of enforcement were concentrated in the hands of the state, the Jewish community had access to them only insofar as the government would allow. Hence, the Jewish charters regularly included authorization from the government for the community to enforce its decisions, sometimes even specifying how the authorities would aid in implementing this. For example, it might be specified that a certain percentage of any fine imposed by the Jewish communal leadership would go to the general fisc.[3] This allocation of a certain amount of enforcement power to the *kehila* is the basis for the well-known "autonomy" of the Jewish community. This autonomy, in theory given to the Jewish community as a whole, was in practice at the disposal only of the official leadership. For all that it was based on powerful elements within the Jewish consciousness and ethic, the authority of the communal leaders would have been impossible without government backing and enforcement of compliance. To a great extent, justifying the communal leaders' rule in traditional and religious terms was a means of covering up the real source of their authority. The members of the community were requested to be loyal to their group because of internal values alone, and the emotion-laden terminology of tradition hid the external factor that was the true basis of the community's authority. The paradox implicit in this internalized rationalization of external power is seen clearly when the independence of the *kehila* was guaranteed by a *takana* that fined any Jew who went to the secular authorities to appeal a sentence imposed by the Jewish leaders, and that assigned part of this fine to the secular fisc.[4]

Types and Division of Taxes. The community leadership needed the authority and power to enforce its decisions primarily when allocating the tax burden, the largest part of which went to pay fees owed to the government.[5] The method of allocating taxes was based on accepted custom, a mixture of traditionalism and semi-rationalization. The amount of the property tax was calculated on the basis of a sworn declaration of worth by the taxpayer, or through an estimate by assessors sworn to issue fair appraisals.[6] The assessment did not fix an absolute amount for the individual to pay within the assessment period; rather, it determined the percentage of the total communal obligation that the individual was required to cover. Owing to the frequent fluctuations in the level of the *kehila*'s expenses and the absence of an accounting system for forecasting budgetary needs, the leadership could not determine the absolute amount of the individual's tax obligation in advance.

Questions inevitably arose about which types of property were subject to taxation. Typically, capital loaned out at interest or invested in business ventures was considered fully taxable. Land and buildings, investments that were not always revenue-producing, had already been exempted from full taxation in the medieval period.[7] With the increasing incidence of credit transactions, disputes and disagreements arose among scholars as to the tax status of businesses conducted with other people's money or in partnership with people from other communities.[8] Various interest groups with constantly changing memberships debated how to tax such businesses. When we consider the undefined nature of capital based on credit, it is no wonder that the assessors, and perhaps even the capitalists themselves, found it difficult to assess the property for tax purposes.[9]

In addition to this property-based tax (*skhumim*), there were also consumption taxes imposed upon meat, salt, wine, and other products. Moreover, it was accepted that certain outlays, such as support of the poor, maintaining the synagogue, and so forth, should be covered out of donations or fines paid by those who broke any of the bylaws (*takanot*). A third method of covering certain expenditures was to divide the amount among those of means on a per capita basis rather than in accordance with assessed wealth. According to the original halakhic sources, this procedure was to be followed concerning expenditures for the physical defense of the community in times of danger, something that affected rich and poor equally.[10]

Apparently the available legal precedents and principles were insufficient to allow the distribution of the tax burden among the various groups and classes without dispute and contention. Concepts drawn from Jewish tradition and local practice could provide only a framework within which the communal leadership functioned, influenced always by the relative strengths of the various interest groups and social forces. Halakhists did occasionally decide specific points of dispute by referring to traditional principles, but they generally found it difficult to apply "Torah law" (*din tora*), even in the broader sense of the term, to these matters.[11] Hence, rather than issuing binding rulings, they would suggest a compromise or hand the case over to the communal leaders.[12] Thus the real decision was the product of the various pressure groups and was executed through the coercive powers vested in the communal leaders.

The Kehila as a Financial Institution. On the whole, the *kehila* required only limited powers of enforcement because, in most aspects of life, its function was limited to supervising and overseeing (rather than initiating and implementing). In the economic sphere, however, the power of the *kehila* became more critical, at least in those regions where the *kehila* acted as a financial institution in its own right. This happened in particular in seventeenth- and eighteenth-century Poland and Lithuania, where the *kehila* held the exclusive right to distill liquor, collect taxes and duties on behalf of the non-Jewish authorities, etc. It is clear that the *kehila* leadership, lacking a staff of professional administrators, could not undertake to direct these enterprises itself. In effect, the *kehila* merely held the right to sublet its concessions, and it profited from acting as middleman between the authorities and the Jewish sub-concessionaire. In this way the *kehila*, because of its many obligations, became something of a financial institution in its own right, lending and borrowing, profiting and losing in such financial transactions.[13]

The *kehila*'s expanded financial role also led to new institutional pressures and distortions. So long as the *kehila* remained a merely supervisory body, its concern with economic activity was merely tangential. The *kehila* might, for example, call upon a tax farmer to submit his tariffs to the approval of the communal leaders or forbid an individual to borrow money from non-Jews without communal license. But such rulings were intended essentially to prevent the community as a whole from being harmed either directly or indirectly. The tax farmer might rouse hatred by charging more than was his due; the borrower might tarnish the community's reputation by defaulting on his debts.[14] Of course, intrigue and favoritism could lead to abuses, even in matters that were merely supervisory, but these were recognized as distortions of justice and deviations from the type of behavior incumbent upon the communal leaders. But once the community became a financial entity in its own right, it was almost inevitable that conflicts of interest would arise. Once the heads of the community were obligated by the government to assume, and then to sublet, certain tax farms, to borrow and to lend, they became involved in ongoing activities that, even when performed honestly, could lead to individuals' benefiting at the expense of the public. The leadership's power to decide and enforce now easily became a tool for economic exploitation for the leaders' own benefit.

The Power of the Community and the Rights of the Individual. The control of the *kehila* leadership over the life of the individual was extensive but by no means absolute. If an individual saw himself as harmed by a decision adopted by the community or its representatives, he always had the right to appeal to a halakhic authority. Even if the halakhist held a communal appointment, he was required to act impartially and could not appear to favor the community over the individual. Of course, there were psychological pressures on any rabbi to decide for the communal government of which he was a part and against the individual. But even ignoring this, we may well ask whether the judicial theories under which he operated favored one side or the other. In theory, the Halakha did not grant preference to the community over the individual. Halakha derived its rules governing communal life from the laws of partnership, as if the community were nothing but a group of individuals associated for some specified and limited purpose.[15] This legal approach did, at times, serve to protect the rights of the individual against oppression by the majority.[16] But the same logic could also be used to prevent an individual from withdrawing from a "partnership" whose obligations he had de facto accepted up to that point.[17] In fact, the halakhic authorities were not consistent in following up this notion of partnership. In many cases, they supported the majority against the individual; most prominently they ruled that the demands of the *kahal* were assumed to be justified until proven otherwise. Thus, the individual was required to pay any sums demanded of him, and only afterward could he sue the community for redress.[18] In theory, the concept of a partnership between equals would not have allowed such a policy.

The preference given to the power of the majority over the rights of the individual was already implicit in the medieval Jewish tradition, and exegetes found support for it in the Talmudic sources.[19] Because, in our period, *parnasim* were elected rather than assuming power on their own, yet another basis was available through which to legitimize communal power: the notion of representation. The leaders were conceived of as loyal agents of the community, even when they did things that went against the individual's desires.[20] The halakhists consistently gave preference to the community over the individual and, as we have seen, opposed the leaders only if they demanded arbitrary legislative powers and ignored basic concepts of propriety and justice.[21]

Lay Courts. The role of the halakhic authorities was supervisory: Rather than planning and executing policy, their task was to prevent anything that might destroy the structure of tradition. This was true also in the sphere of jurisprudence. Not all legal questions were brought before a halakhic court. To a not insignificant degree, the lay leaders of the community also served as judges, especially in matters akin to criminal cases, such as quarrels, insults, brawls, and beatings.[22] Even if the *parnasim* asked the city rabbi to join them when they sat in judgment, they did so only to strengthen their own authority.[23] They remained merely a disciplinary body, deciding both procedural and sentencing issues according to precedent and the rulings of the *takanot* rather than according to halakhic principles.

The same was true in civil cases. Judges were selected from among the members of the community in the same fashion as all other appointments. This judgeship was not merely an honorary appointment but rather a license to provide a certain service. The litigants would pay a certain fee to the judges in accordance with the size and importance of the legal matter in question.[24] These appointed judges were, of course, not always scholars. Hence, it was also true that they did not always judge their cases according to pure halakhic principles. Not only did they not base their decision on Talmudic sources; they did not even rely on halakhic sources in the broader sense. They decided according to their own best judgment, presumably using precedents drawn from their limited local experience.[25] Nevertheless, the Halakha did not, *eo ipso*, deny the legitimacy of such procedures. Litigants had always been allowed to bring their case before laymen on the condition that both parties freely accepted the judges. On the other hand, the community had the right to force its members to obey its decisions in civil matters. Judges appointed by the *kehila* were thus considered equivalent to judges whom the individuals had chosen for themselves, and they were therefore not required to decide cases in accordance with Talmudic law.[26]

Judges' Fees. There was similarly no reason to object to these judges for taking fees for their services—no more than there was for objecting to halakhic judges, who had long been charging fees. Social necessity had long ago overwhelmed the principle of *imitatio Dei* in this regard ("just as I judge for free, so also shall you"). Taking a fee from litigants (according to the size and importance of the case, and in such a manner that both sides would bear the costs equally) was a further step on the road to rationalization. The Talmud had already moved in this direction when it allowed the payment to judges of *skhar-betila de-minkara* [a fee in compensation for an appreciable loss]—i.e., recompense for the money that the judge had lost by not engaging in his own profession during the time of the trial.[27] The idea of paying judges a fixed salary from communal coffers had already been raised in theoretical terms as a method of freeing judges from economic dependence on any of the litigants who came before them.[28] But in reality this proposal was never acted upon—just as it was never instituted with regard to communal functionaries, as we have seen—except in the case of rabbis of the very largest communities, who received part of their salary as *skhar batala*, or fee for time lost that might otherwise have been used in the pursuit of profit.

As may well be imagined, though they accepted the lay court, the halakhists never were completely happy with the institution and they justified it only on the grounds that it was at least better than turning to *arka'ot shel goyim*—gentile courts—in places where there were no sages capable of serving as judges.[29] While this reasoning was appropriate to conditions in Poland, Lithuania, and even many places in the German lands through the second half of the sixteenth century, the large-scale derogation of civil matters to lay judgment did diminish the authority of the scholarly halakhic tradition. Hence, during the seventeenth and eighteenth centuries, when Torah study flourished, Talmudic scholars multiplied, and each community had its own *av bet din*, or communal rabbi, the demand arose to have civil cases judged by the Halakha and its interpreters once again. We therefore hear fierce criticism of lay courts by rabbis and scholars.[30] In many areas, these efforts met with a certain success, either because a rabbinic court was established alongside that of the laymen, or because a rabbi or scholar was appointed to the lay court. But lay courts were never eliminated altogether, and the struggle between scholars and lay judges continued. Even during the second half of the eighteenth century Rabbi Ezekiel Landau was still complaining in Prague that only minor cases were handed over to scholars to judge, while the important cases were adjudicated before lay courts.[31]

Apparently, lay courts were preferred because they provided more rapid decisions and implementation. The communal bylaws often fixed a maximum period over which trials might drag on.[32] On the other hand, a "rabbinic" trial could drag on because of the very specific rules concerning evidence and proof, as well as because of appeals to rabbinic authorities in other centers—something that was quite common in the Middle Ages and that had not disappeared from communal life in our period. Both of these types of courts shared one advantage at least in handling cases between members of the same community: It was possible to force someone to appear in court and to obey the court's decision. The community's enforcement apparatus (which did have some power) was available to the litigants in order to force the recalcitrant to obey.

The Prohibition against Recourse to Non-Jewish Courts. The jurisdiction of Jewish courts was limited by the charters issued to the Jews by the government. Certain types of legal matters, such as the transfer of real estate, were usually subject to the non-

Jewish authorities.[33] In some matters, individuals were allowed to choose between Jewish and non-Jewish courts—and the community waged an ongoing struggle to dissuade the individual from exercising this right. The act of turning to a gentile court was considered a religious crime, and the term *arka'ot* (gentile court) gained a negative emotional content, to be equated almost with a non-Jewish house of worship.[34] Though there was no place where Jews did not resort to gentile courts for some matters, the community and its representatives insisted on their right to determine in which cases this would be permitted.[35]

Obviously the extent to which the community could control the individual in matters of litigation was a function of the power and authority of the specific *kehila*. In Poland, for example, resort to gentile courts was relatively rare, while in the small towns and newer communities of Germany it was much more common.[36] And the community always reserved this option as a last resort—as, for instance, in dealing with powerful individuals against whom it was otherwise helpless. In such cases, an explicit license would be issued for those who sought to bring suit in gentile courts against such powerful people.[37] Once this precedent was set, however, it was often difficult to prevent litigants from continuing to use gentile courts on the grounds that their opponent would not appear before a rabbinic court or would not obey its sentence. This happened especially in inter-communal cases.[38]

Capital Offenses. In order to protect the community from lawless individuals, confirmed criminals, and government informers, who all endangered the existence of the community and the life and property of individuals, Polish Jewry reinstituted the law of *moser* (informer) as it had existed in Spain. Though there may have been cases of death sentences issued by Jewish authorities in medieval Ashkenaz, almost no trace of these has survived in the halakhic literature. But sociopolitical conditions similar to those that had applied in Spain now led the sages of Poland to turn to the Sephardic sources in which the practical aspects of such matters had been discussed.[39] And indeed, the death sentence as well as corporal punishment was decreed by communal leaders in secret, and sometimes even with the acquiescence of the authorities.[40] Now, recognized rabbinical figures ruled that a *moser* could be subjected to corporal punishment, maimed, or even executed. We have clear evidence of such sentences being carried out with the approval of the great rabbis,[41] although there was also a certain recoil from this and an attempt to arrange for gentile courts to carry out the despicable deed.[42] In any case, a formalized judicial procedure for capital cases never developed anywhere. It may also be noted here that by their very nature, the laws of *moser* were applied not by a regular court but by a sort of "underground" court in which the accused was judged in absentia and without the wealth of fine safeguards that the theoretical judicial tradition of the Halakha had developed.[43] This type of case proves that the existence of the Jewish community depended upon severe internal discipline and radical dissociation from the outside world.

Excommunication. It is thus clear that the *kehila* did not hesitate to resort to coercion in order to maintain its authority. In sociological terms, the community's "power of enforcement" was not limited to the usual disciplinary measures at the disposal of the courts: confiscation, fines, corporal punishment, imprisonment and whipping, and, in exceptional cases, death.[44] Alongside these were two other means of coercion—*ḥerem* (plural: *ḥaramot*; excommunication) and the handing over of Jews to the secular authorities—both of which reflect the nature of Jewish communal existence as a traditional-religious minority within non-Jewish society.

In a formal halakhic sense, the *ḥerem* implied removing the individual from the community—that is, preventing his participation in the mutual relationships of community members in both the real and symbolic spheres of life. In the mishnaic period, the *nidui*, as it was then called, served as a means of internal discipline among the various groups of sages. In later years it served as a means of enforcing the opinions of either the rabbis or the lay leadership (depending on who was then dominant) on the public at large.[45] Preventing an individual from participating in communal life was one of the outstanding disciplinary measures of the *kehila* in the sixteenth through eighteenth centuries. The extent of the ban depended upon the seriousness of the offense. On occasion the punishment amounted to no more than the denial of some privilege in the political or religious sphere, such as a temporary disqualification from holding public office, leading religious services, being called to the Torah, or being counted in the quorum for prayer.[46] The formal declaration of the *ḥerem* included all of these and added that social contact with the individual and his family was forbidden: His son was not to be circumcised, the marriage ceremony was not to be performed for his children, nor were they to be given a Jewish burial.[47] The threat it posed to one's physical existence was not the only intimidating aspect of the *ḥerem*; it also meant that the individual would not be able to perform his religious obligations, of primary importance to anyone raised as a religious Jew. Moreover, since the

Jew's primary social contacts were restricted to his own society, the *ḥerem* was tantamount to cutting him off from all social contact. The excommunicated individual felt himself losing his place in both this world and the next. This explains the tremendous emotional impact of the very term "*ḥerem*," an impact that was intensified by the ceremony that accompanied its declaration: opening of the Ark, blowing of the shofar, and the lighting of black candles.

The efficacy and force of the *ḥerem* derived primarily from the society's traditional, religious nature. In some cases a *ḥerem* could be enforced through physical means; for instance, a Jew under *ḥerem* who entered the synagogue could be physically ejected.[48] But this was not the case when a *ḥerem* was declared against those who engaged in some undesirable economic or social practice in private—as, for example, coin clipping or slandering an adversary. Here, the efficacy of the decree came from the magical powers associated with the *ḥerem*. We should not forget that this society believed in the magical power of words per se, and of holy words in particular, and the declaration of a specific formula could therefore lead to radical sociological results.[49]

The term *ḥerem* came to be associated with other ancient prohibitions. The *ḥezkat yishuv* (the right of residents to keep out potential competitors) was also called *ḥerem ha-yishuv*, and the term *ḥerem* was also applied to an entire series of prohibitions in the spheres of sexual and social relations.[50] The term was also applied to new prohibitions imposed by the communal and supra-communal institutions, as for instance, the *ḥerem* against farming taxes or duties at certain times in Poland, the *ḥerem* against buying a rabbinical post, etc.[51] It is clear, however, that in cases where the *ḥerem* came into conflict with powerful personal interests, it could not serve as an absolute barrier to maleficence. There were constant complaints about people who ignored and transgressed the *ḥaramot*. Because of this there were some who objected to the use of the device in the first place, arguing that the sin thereby committed by those who did not observe the rules outweighed any practical benefit.[52] But this itself demonstrates the magical and religious power of the *ḥerem*. We may assume that those who transgressed the *ḥerem* did not deny its power and did not mock it in principle; rather, they found some way to justify their actions by arguing that the *ḥerem* did not apply to their specific deed.[53]

The *ḥerem* once again exemplifies what we said above—namely, that even in places where leadership rested in the hands of laymen rather than religious functionaries, the basic institutions of government depended upon concepts whose force derived from the religious sphere. Who had the right to excommunicate remained a bone of contention between lay and rabbinic leaders. But even in those areas where the power was in lay hands, the actual issuing of the decree, and, of course, the supervision over its enforcement, remained in the hands of those expert in religious matters—i.e., the halakhists.[54] It was they who decided whether a *ḥerem* applied to a given act or object, thus determining the scope of the essentially irrational *ḥerem* through the rational modalities of thought at their disposal.[55]

Handing Jews over to the Gentile Authorities. The surrender of Jewish criminals to the gentile authorities is a reflection of the fact that Jewish society was independent only to the extent that surrounding society would allow. Since individual Jews functioned, especially economically, in the non-Jewish world, they were also subject to its laws and rules of behavior. Anyone who violated those laws was subject to the gentile authorities and could not flee back into Jewish society. In such a case the Jews had no basis on which to appeal. On the other hand, a Jew might fall into the hands of the government not because he had broken the law but simply because of an arbitrary decision by the ruler or because of a false accusation brought against him. Under these circumstances, Jewish society felt itself obligated to do everything it could to save the Jew.[56] This fact created a very strong tie between the Jew and his community, for if Jewish society ceased to protect him, he was defenseless and virtually on his own. And indeed, the public warnings about proper behavior toward gentiles sometimes threatened not to defend the transgressor.[57] Such a warning was apparently more frightening than various threats of punishment at the hands of Jewish courts. As for the more severe cases, not only did Jewish society reserve the right not to defend the individual before the authorities; it actually handed over the criminal, even in cases where this would certainly result in the death sentence.[58] This was a radical and final disciplinary measure that involved the same ethical problem implicit in the use of force by any state: the paradox that in the last resort the individual is necessarily prevented from using force only by the public use of force. Jewish society, as we know, forbade resort to gentile authorities and gentile courts, and defended Jews against the arbitrariness of those institutions. But Jewish society succeeded in this only by allowing itself to use these forbidden means when absolutely necessary. The same doubts and hesitations that we find in general society concerning the implementation of the death sentence were expressed also by Jewish judges who were asked to decide whether or not to hand over an individual to the gentile authorities. They confronted the same ethical polarity. The issue was to decide not between what was permissible and what was obligatory, but rather between what was forbidden and what was obligatory.[59] In any case, authoritative halakhists recognized the legitimacy of surrendering an individual to the gentile government when necessary and in fact even ruled on occasion that this be done. This was the ultimate threat by which the *kehila* could try to control the actions of its members vis-à-vis the outside world, actions that might lead to serious consequences for the entire community.

11

The Composition of the Kehila

The *kehila* was normally composed of the permanent residents in a given locale, and one of its prerogatives was the right to decide who might or might not settle there. Each *kehila* sought to gain recognition of this power from the local authorities on whom it depended for its political and judicial autonomy. From the point of view of Jewish law, this prerogative was based upon a medieval tradition that, though originally not universally accepted, had by this time come to be seen as authoritative.[1] Whether or not the individual was granted *ḥezkat ha-yishuv* or, more briefly, the *ḥazaka* (as the right of settlement was usually called) depended on two factors: the terms of the community's original charter (*kiyum*), which usually limited the number of settlers, and economic conditions generally, which determined whether the Jews saw an increase in the Jewish population as a threatening or a promising economic development. (In our period, in most places the former was the case.) Of course, much depended on the individual involved: rich people who could help support the *kehila*'s activities were welcomed, while poor people might be encouraged or even forced to give up their *ḥazaka* and leave.[2] It was customary to give preferential treatment to exceptional scholars, who were not considered bound by the laws of *ḥezkat ha-yishuv* and might settle anywhere.[3]

Terms for Joining or Leaving a Community. Often new settlers would be granted temporary residence rights. Such a person was termed a *nokhri*, or stranger, so long as he had not officially been granted a *ḥezkat yishuv* by the *kehila*.[4] On a political level, he could neither vote nor stand for communal office; in "civil" terms, he did not enjoy full freedom to trade and was not given the same religious honors, such as being called to the reading of the Torah or reciting the *kadish* on the anniversary of the death of a close relative (*yahrzeit*).[5] On the other hand, the *nokhri* was not obliged to share in the costs of communal membership, except insofar as he came to some personal arrangement with the *kehila* leaders.[6] A *nokhri* became a full member through the formal and official addition of his name to the list of householders.[7] From then on, the new member would share in all the financial burdens and would usually also contribute a one-time "advance" to the communal coffers.[8] Of course, especially during the formative period of a *kehila* it no doubt often happened that a *nokhri* would gain membership without undergoing any formal procedures.

The *ḥezkat yishuv* was a personal right, retained only so long as the individual kept up his residence in the locality. There were cases in which an individual maintained his *ḥazaka* even after moving away by continuing to pay a share of the expenses of the *kehila* at a rate fixed by custom or determined ad hoc. In the absence of such a prior arrangement, however, one's *ḥazaka* ended a year or more (depending on the local custom) after leaving a place.[9] Since *ḥezkat ha-yishuv* involved obligations as well as privileges, individuals were sometimes eager to have this period shortened so as to hasten their freedom from financial responsibility. It was decided, however, that anyone leaving a community was obliged to continue to participate in the expenses of that community for a certain period of time, usually a year or two. Sometimes the right to leave was made conditional on the deposit of a security adequate to insure that the individual would honor his responsibilities even while living elsewhere. In other cases we find the individual ending his obligation by making a one-time, fixed payment.[10] It was legally impossible to stop someone from leaving a *kehila*, but we in fact know of cases in which members of a community forced an individual to take an oath that he would not abandon them.[11] This would tend to happen especially in smaller communities where everyone depended on the continued residence of a few wealthy individuals—and sometimes just one.

Family Members' Rights of Residence. Barring local *takanot* to the contrary, one's *ḥezkat yishuv* also included members of the household, including even domestic servants. Still, there had to be some limits on who might legitimately be included in the "household." As we shall see, in this period the nuclear family was often joined by secondary relations, and the *kehila* was forced to protect itself against people using their family connections to settle illegally. There was, however, never any doubt that relatives of the first degree were included in *ḥezkat ha-yishuv*. Sons and daughters, stepchildren from either parent, and grandparents—in other words, all those whom one was halakhically obliged to support—had the right to join the household of the *kehila* member, even if they had not been born in the locale or lived there before.

On the other hand, these individuals could only participate in the personal right of domicile of the householder; they did not automatically gain this right for themselves. Usually, one could transfer *ḥezkat ha-yishuv* only to children, male or female, and even this was not absolute and unconditional. As a general principle, the children of *kehila* members could acquire the *ḥazaka*, even if they had previously lived elsewhere, so long as they requested it within a given time period—customarily two or three years after their marriage. Unless specifically stated otherwise, the *ḥazaka* also included the right to establish a family in the area.[12] Sometimes, even a *kehila* member was not automatically allowed to marry off all his children locally unless he could provide an adequate dowry for each. This was another method by which the community tried to limit the number of members who were unable to carry their full share of the financial burden.[13] In areas without such a limitation, children had the automatic right to request the right of residence, and the usual preconditions for acceptance were either waived or considerably lightened for them. But even here, their automatic right to request did not guarantee them membership, and if they did not exercise their right to request membership within a certain period of time, it lapsed too.

Appointments and Offices Are Temporary. Let us turn now to the methods by which offices were transferred and personnel changed within the communal leadership. Even these purely functional details of government cannot be ignored. The methods of changing leaders, as, indeed, the very fact that offices did change hands, were important determinants of the social character and function of *kehila* government.

A primary characteristic of *kehila* institutions was the fact that no office was held for life, much less could it be passed from father to son. This was as true for elected leaders as it was for paid functionaries. The rabbi and *shtadlan* served for fixed periods of time, and even if these appointments could be renewed or extended, whether or not to do so remained the decision of those who had made the original appointment. A *shamash*, scribe, or other minor functionary might, it is true, be appointed without time limit, but these were after all subordinate positions ultimately dependent upon those with real authority. They could always be fired for poor performance or for disobedience toward their superiors.[14] Conversely, the elected officials, who could not effectively be disciplined during their term of office, served for only limited periods.

The sociological intent of these arrangements is clear: Change of personnel prevented individuals from monopolizing offices and turning them into permanent sources of income or bases of power. Limiting the term of office prevented individuals from abusing their positions. This was especially important since there was no other effective, institutional mechanism through which to control the leaders' performance. The *takanot* emphasized and stressed that the annual (or, in the case of the supra-communal institutions, the bi- or triannual) elections must take place on time.[15] It was not a question, merely, of others eagerly awaiting the opportunity to displace the current officeholders. Even in places where the pool of potential officeholders was actually quite small, the community stressed the importance of changing personnel because this forced officeholders to consider public opinion and symbolized the fact that authority derived ultimately from the community at large.[16]

Criteria for Officeholding. The criteria for holding office varied. There were no predetermined rules regarding who might be appointed as a paid functionary; these appointments were left up to the officials. The rabbi had to have been ordained by his teacher, a recognized Torah authority, or one of the provincial rabbis,[17] but beyond that, the decision was based upon the candidate proving in person that he was qualified to serve as the head of a *yeshiva*, a judge, and a spiritual leader. In many places it was also stipulated that the candidate for a rabbinical post could not be related to members of the community,[18] but this requirement was not universal.[19] The increasing insistence on this point was a reflection of the emerging role of the rabbi as the primary judge and arbitrator of disputes. Since family ties provided the major focus around which group loyalty was formed, it was logical therefore that the rabbi could not be related to any of the groups that strove for power in the community.

Age and Officeholding. The primary qualification for public office at the local and supra-communal level as well as for the rabbinate was age, usually calculated in terms of the number of years since the candidate's marriage.[20] This method of calculation reflects the tendency to marry early. The minimum age rose with the importance of the office, and special *takanot* were issued to raise the minimum age of rabbis and of those who held office in the supra-communal organizations. Even where we do not have such explicit *takanot* it is almost certain that public office was not open to anyone who had not attained a certain chronological maturity. The traditional nature of the society demanded that public positions be given only to those who had already absorbed the tradition and had demonstrated it before the younger generation. Moreover, in some places election to higher office was made conditional upon prior service at some lower level.[21] This guaranteed that the candidate would gradually gain experience in handling public affairs, and to a certain extent the system provided opportunities for observing and selecting the best candidate.

Taxpayers as Officeholders. While age and experience requirements did not present absolute barriers to an individual's rise, there were two others—one based on property and one based on learning—that had much more far-reaching social implications. Anyone who enjoyed local residential rights was considered a member of the community. But the *ḥazaka* did not automatically qualify its holder to vote or stand for public office. For this, one had to be a taxpayer: that is, one had to be a property owner whose assets were regularly assessed and who shared in the communal expenses in proportion to the extent of those assets.[22] Even taxpayers could not all stand for every office. In some places the taxpayers were divided into categories—usually three—and each level had its own specific and defined rights. The major offices, such as that of *parnas*, were open only to members of the highest category.[23] No one in our period questioned this link between political privilege and the size of one's contribution to the communal burden, even if there were inevitably struggles between those of more modest means and those with greater means over the strength of this link.[24] The only factor that somewhat mitigated this "plutocratic" tendency was the custom of accepting a certain level of education as a partial substitute for property. As we shall see, scholars of this era acquired titles of *ḥaver* and *morenu*, which were treated as partial equivalents of the property qualifications required for appointment.[25] As is obvious, this custom had far-reaching sociological implications, which we shall discuss when we turn to the question of stratification in this society.

Nowhere did the electorate at large vote directly for candidates of its choice. Rather, appointments were decided upon by a limited group of from five to seven *mevorerim* (selectors), who decided upon the suitable candidate by majority vote. These *mevorerim* were selected, in turn, either by a yet larger group of selectors or by the drawing of names at random from among all those with the right to stand for election. In those places where taxpayers were divided into categories, the upper classes were given preference in that a larger number of their members were included in the pool from which *mevorerim* were chosen.[26]

The electoral system was semirationalized in the sense that election was determined by two principles: chance (in determining the makeup of the nominating body) and evaluation of personal merit (in the direct election of officials). The element of chance implied that in selecting the *mevorerim* matters were left in the hands of heaven. But the selectors themselves relied on personal judgment in selecting the most suitable candidates. The selectors were usually required to take an oath that they would carry out their task honestly (*le-shem shamayim*) and impartially.[27] On a certain level, this method was merely a compromise between radical democracy and oligarchy, or, as traditional sources had it, between "minyan" and "binyan"—that is, between giving a relatively large number some role in the election process and limiting office to that smaller group who were generally regarded as suitable. Be that as it may, the system performed the necessary social function of giving the members of the community the feeling that it was they who determined who would lead them. Despite the relatively weak connection between the voters and the results of the election, the system was able to maintain this sense of participation, and even though the pool of qualified candidates for office might be quite small, the public set great store by the elections. There was an ongoing struggle in most communities to enlarge the franchise, and suspense over the outcome of elections always ran high. Even though officeholders were elected time and again from among the same limited circle, competition within that group kept up public interest.

The *kehila* had always to take precautions lest leadership become the monopoly of a small group. Given the close ties in Jewish society even between relatively distant relations, it was important not to let relatives hold multiple offices for an extended period of time. Hence the *kehilot* took special care that members of a single family not be chosen for offices that had dealings with each other. Indeed, the *takanot* of the *kehilot* and other public institutions all included rules that aimed at distancing members of the same family from each other, and struggles between various factions often centered on the interpretation and application of these very rules.[28] Another factor that could lead to overconcentration of power was the involvement of the secular authorities. Opposition to accepting appointments to Jewish communal office from the secular authorities can also be understood as an expression of the fear that a *parnas* appointed in this manner would not step down from office after his term was finished. Finally, the political independence of the community was also threatened if the official gained his position through absolute economic dominance, as in a case where the majority of the community depended economically on a wealthy member. These dangers, particularly problematic when economic power was linked to political influence at court, severely limited the political independence of the communities, especially toward the end of our period, as we shall soon see.

12

Inter-communal Relations

Our picture of Jewish communal organization has so far focused on the *kehila*—the organizational and administrative unit of the Jewish community in a single city. We shall now complete the picture by treating aspects and forms of communal organization that do not exactly fit within this narrow rubric.

Yishuvim—Smaller Settlements. First, we should note that *kehilot* often included residents of small neighboring settlements (*bnei yishuv*) as members. Both the individuals involved and the *kehila* had an interest in encouraging such membership. For the isolated individual or the group of Jews too small to maintain communal institutions of its own, membership in the larger *kehila* provided vital services: aid in cases of conflict with non-Jewish society,[1] and religious necessities such as occasional public prayer, religious education for children, religiously supervised marriage and divorce, kosher foods, and, perhaps most basically, final burial in a Jewish cemetery. Physical distance meant that such individuals could not be active partners in the *kehila*'s institutions, nor could they enjoy all the benefits to which they were entitled, but they did receive the most vital services, even if with some difficulties.

For their part, the community and its agents were also eager to bring such nonresidents into the *kehila*. For one thing, as members they were obligated to share in the common burden, and their participation thus helped to ensure the existence of the *kehila*'s institutions. Communal functionaries such as the rabbi, the preacher, and the head of the *yeshiva*, who derived their livelihood either from set fees for services rendered or from donations given them on specific occasions, also saw the addition of new members to the community in a positive light, since it inevitably meant a broadening of their base of material support.[2] But even leaving personal interests aside, leaders who identified with their communities naturally sought such expansion as a sign of communal greatness and glory.

Once the population of an outlying settlement grew to the point that it could sustain independent institutions of its own, conflict could arise. The leadership of the established community would argue for retention of the status quo, while the *yishuv* Jews would argue that their needs and rights were being ignored because they lived so far from the communal institutions. Such disputes often reached the rabbinical courts, as did disputes between established *kehilot* about which held jurisdiction over settlements lying between them.[3] In the absence of any clear legal basis for deciding such disputes, the issue remained essentially political, and the function of the rabbinic court was more to encourage compromise and appease the parties involved than to issue a binding decision, unless the court was associated with a supra-communal organization that the litigants were both required to obey.

The Provincial Kehila. Another form of communal organization was found where all the Jews of the outlying settlements in a province (*medina*) belonged to a single, provincial *kehila*. This form of organization was found in the principalities of Germany where Jews settled primarily in villages and small towns and where there was no large, central community. By their very nature, such organizations could deal primarily with the administrative side of Jewish life: allocating financial obligations, raising taxes, and maintaining a provincial rabbi in the largest of the Jewish settlements. This rabbi would serve as a judge, arrange marriages and divorces, and supervise the ritual slaughterers. But in anything related to the daily life of the communities, such as the maintenance of institutions for education and prayer, the provincial *kehila* could provide only limited and irregular services.[4] On the other hand, the very limited nature of these institutions bears witness to the almost absolute nature of the Jews' need for ties to communal organization. Even when such institutions did not provide all of the individual's needs, they were still considered worthwhile for the minimum they did provide. The government's desire to keep its Jewish subjects within a single rubric and to levy taxes from them in some centralized fashion further encouraged the creation and maintaining of these organizations. But even this governmental attitude indicates that despite their dispersal, the Jews continued to form a unitary body whose members could not be linked except to each other.[5]

Inter-communal Cooperation. Having described the different forms of communal organization, let us turn now to the problem of the relations between them. Every *kehila*, whether associated with a specific city or a province, was an autonomous organizational unit with no obligatory relation whatsoever to any other. The *kehila* had authority over its members even when the latter were outside its territory,[6] and over strangers so long as they were within its territory. On the other hand, the *kehila*'s decisions were in no way binding for members of other *kehilot*, much less for their institutions.[7] But these clear-cut lines of jurisdiction among communities existed only from the point of view of legal theory. Individuals did not lead lives completely contained within the framework of the *kehila*; in the spheres of economic life, family life, and education, members of one *kehila* inevitably depended on individuals from other *kehilot*.[8] Even the communal organizations themselves had to help each other with regard to issues where joint action was preferable to action on the part of a single community. When the Jewish community faced danger because of pressure or abuse on the part of the government or because of accusations and pogroms on the part of the masses, the situation was not usually limited to the territory of a single community. In such cases cooperation on the part of many organizations was a vital necessity. Indeed, representatives of different communities customarily consulted with each other and called ad hoc conferences even in regions where no permanent, regular, inter-communal organization had been institutionalized.[9] *Kehilot* were likewise called upon to assist one another in the event of natural disasters—most frequently a fire[10]—and to share in the costs of ransoming prisoners.[11] Such reciprocity was of a spontaneous, rather than a formally institutionalized, nature: mutual aid was requested and extended on the basis of a common sense of national unity, and an awareness of a common destiny that linked all the scattered sections of the people. Extending aid to another community was seen as legally obligatory only when it might be reasonably supposed that the danger facing that community was likely to strike directly at others as well. This legal requirement, articulated by R. Joseph Colon in the second half of the fifteenth century,[12] was the first break in the principle of the total legal autonomy of each *kehila*.

Reciprocal relations were also maintained between communities both near and far for purposes of internal defense against religious deviators. The outstanding example of this was the war against the Sabbatean sect in the period after Sabbetai Ẓvi's apostasy (1666). The battle was carried on mainly by communal leaders, both rabbinic and lay. They collected testimony, issued proclamations, pronounced the ban, and otherwise punished transgressors whom they could apprehend.[13] But their proclamations were not addressed only to the members of a single *kehila*. Rather, they addressed Jewish public opinion in general and assumed that where the principles of Judaism were concerned, there was no geographical limit to the authority of the individual community. This same feeling of unity resounded in the eighteenth century in the proclamations of the opponents of Hasidism, for the most part also *kehila* leaders.[14] One of the signs of the isolation of the rabbinate in the Haskala period is the fact that they carried on their struggle against the *maskilim* largely on their own, without support from the *parnasim*. And at the same time, both the *maskilim* and the Hasidim, as leaders of new popular movements, relied upon independent individuals rather than recognized public institutions, as we shall see.[15]

Inter-communal Disputes. This sense of a national unity transcending the local *kehila* was also apparent when a controversy broke out among the leaders of a community, and particularly when rabbinical judges disagreed over a legal ruling. Such controversies tended to arise in towns where there was no clear hierarchy obligating one rabbi to accept the opinions of another. Once a controversy did break out, however, it generally spread beyond the limits of the *kehila*; almost invariably one or both parties would take their case to halakhic authorities elsewhere.[16] By the very nature of these controversies, there was little chance of obtaining a uniform opinion from all the scholars consulted, for the issue generally turned on questions not clearly decided in the halakhic sources. A binding decision could have been handed down only by an institution or individual with undisputed authority, and there was neither a rabbinic institution that transcended its local base nor a single halakhic scholar who was recognized as the supreme authority of his generation—except in a metaphoric sense. On the contrary, our period—the sixteenth through eighteenth centuries—is marked both by a multiplicity of organizations and by a wealth of rabbinic scholars who functioned side by side without any one succeeding in imposing his authority on the others. This explains the large number of controversies stemming from differences in rulings on religious law. The contemporary system of establishing the law was both complicated and dependent upon a high degree of acuity, and it often prevented any absolutely clear decision. Occasionally, of course, clashes of personalities and ideological leanings further complicated the theoretical dispute, and virtually precluded any possibility of compromise.[17] Essentially, however, the widespread phenomenon of legal controversy should be seen as a manifestation of a structural paradox: Jewish social units were tied to one another by a common system of law and justice but lacked a binding organizational format through which to express this unity.

The Ḥerem of Rabenu Tam. In the absence of any institution authorized to decide disputed cases, the demand that court rulings not be questioned once they were promulgated could obviously rely on little more than moral suasion. This is clear from the fate of the *ḥerem* of *Rabenu* Jacob Tam (twelfth century), which threatened excommunication to anyone challenging the legality of a bill of divorce already issued.[18] The explicit intent of this edict was to guarantee inappellable validity to a court action once it was complete. And yet, people's fear of the *ḥerem* and their great reverence for the sage who had first proclaimed it did not prevent endless appeals and controversies about the legality of bills of divorce even after they were delivered. Such disputes arose even within single *kehilot* wherever there was no central court,[19] and were still more common when more than one community was involved. For one thing, the courts of different *kehilot* were, in a sense, competitors—either for prestige or for simple financial gain, since the issuing of divorces was always an important source of income for local rabbis.[20] But, even assuming that the rabbis were completely innocent of selfish motives and of any desire to outdo their colleagues in halakhic learning, controversies were still liable to arise on religious grounds. The prohibition against appealing the already-implemented decision of a court was counterbalanced, after all, by the obligation to prevent people from falling into sin. Were one to accept an invalid *get* (bill of divorce) and thereby permit what was actually forbidden, the woman might improperly remarry and thereby bring illegitimate children into the world.[21] Here we arrive at the heart of the matter.

The Legal Relations between Different Communities. The right (and duty) of a rabbinic judge in one city to contest the ruling of a colleague elsewhere was based upon two assumptions. The first had to do with the legal nature of the Halakha, which, as received religious law, was subject to clarification but not to change. The task of the rabbi was therefore to discover the law that applied to the pending case. Were he to err in this, his ruling would be null and void, regardless of his formal authority or his position as rabbi of the community. Hence, and this is the second assumption, if a colleague felt that a judge really had erred, it was the former's duty to protest and thus prevent a miscarriage of justice and its repercussions.

The mutual responsibility for maintaining the Torah was not limited by geography. There was only a gradation of responsibility: Those nearest the scene of action and those living within the same country had the primary obligation to rectify the error if they were in a position to do so.[22] Indeed, the prevalent view was that the court closest in proximity had the primary duty to protest, but that it was thereafter the duty of anyone else to do so. On the basis of this assumption, as is well known, protagonists in halakhic controversies sometimes succeeded in drawing scholars of distant lands into the argument. In any case, until the dissolution of the traditional structure toward the end of the eighteenth century, the scholars of one land, much less one city, never argued that their counterparts in another land or city had no right to intervene.[23] National unity was maintained in this period and never challenged, at least with regard to matters of faith and religion.

The absolute autonomy of the community was restricted to those matters that might be classified as *inyanei mamon*—that is, the political, economic, and legal rights that were the subject matter of most *takanot*. And in fact, we can see an expression of this autonomy in the preferences granted to the local residents over "outsiders" (*nokhrim*) who either passed through, or actually lived in, a given place.[24] It never would have entered anyone's mind to demand equal economic rights for a Jew who just happened to be staying in a particular city. But this autonomy did not mean that the *kehila* could deal arbitrarily with members of other *kehilot*. The same legal tradition that empowered the *kehila* to issue regulations for the benefit of local residents also established the minimal rights of outsiders and required that they be protected.[25]

None of the fundamental elements that were added to the Jewish legal tradition during the Middle Ages ever sought to undermine the universal orientation of the original Talmudic law, which had encompassed all Jews, or at least all those living within a single state. Moreover, the historical situation of the sixteenth through eighteenth centuries, particularly in Poland but elsewhere as well, once again approximated the social structure of Talmudic times. Once again we find dense Jewish settlements, relatively differentiated in occupational terms, maintaining close social and economic ties with each other, and, to a large extent, basing their income on that fact. It is sufficient to note the increasing mobility of basic groups in this society: there were tradesmen who traveled to fairs, young men who wandered from one *yeshiva* to another, itinerant preachers, and, of course, beggars, who were considered a veritable plague.[26] The sense of unity among the different parts of the nation, which had not been eliminated even in the Middle Ages, was now strengthened by economic and social realities. In the legal realm, this sense of unity found expression in the multiplicity of claims and counter-claims between members of different *kehilot*. Which court had jurisdiction over such cases—that of the plaintiff's city or that of the defendant's? Did the litigants have the right to take the case to a neutral court, and, if so, what should the nature of such a court be? None of these questions were adequately thrashed out or decided even in theory in the legal tradition of the period.[27] And the absence of any enforcement mechanism with authority over the two cities involved in a given case made it even more difficult to achieve satisfaction from a lawsuit. For this reason, already in the Middle Ages communities resorted to the questionable measure of sequestering the property of the defendant—deposits or loans that were in the hands of others—in order to compel him to stand trial in the plaintiff's city or in the place where the property was located.[28]

The Aspiration toward Supra-communal Institutions. In a period such as ours of interlocking economic ties, when capitalists based their livelihood upon such arrangements as the transfer of merchandise from place to place and the acceptance of commercial paper drawn against an anonymous market, such legal uncertainty was an intolerable impediment. It is no wonder, therefore, that people looked to supra-*kehila* bodies, which were in a position to guarantee the stability of legal arrangements between parties who had constant economic dealings with one another. The gentile government and its courts of law provided another venue in which members of distant communities might air their petitions. But this solution contravened an unquestioned national-religious inhibition, and it was therefore essential that the deciding body be found within Jewish society.

It was the Talmudic legal tradition itself that supplied the concepts necessary for a solution in the notions of the *bet din gadol* (high court) and *bet vaad* (house of assembly), to which, under certain conditions, individuals who refused to accept the decision of their local courts might appeal. In Palestine and Babylonia there had existed national organizations that lent real enforcement powers to these institutions. During the medieval period, a period marked by organizational fragmentation, these legal terms were used to justify the activities of judges with spontaneous, as opposed to institutionalized, authority. This might occur when the two litigants (or, in exceptional periods, as in the days of R. Meir of Rothenburg, the entire people) accepted the authority of a certain individual.[29] In our period of increased inter-communal contact, no single scholar could have satisfied the need for an ultimate arbitrator—even if an individual of unquestioned authority could have been found. The system of assigning authority in an ad hoc fashion did not, by definition, provide a permanent solution; it worked only if both parties in a given instance agreed. But an economy based upon credit depended upon guarantees that agreements would be carried out, and could not accept such a system at all. It sought, therefore, to create permanent institutions of justice with authority over broader areas, and, indeed, did so in all regions where the secular government did not specifically prevent this development. In 1603 in Germany, for example, a congress at Frankfurt tried to lay the groundwork for such a legal institution but was frustrated by the government.[30] This case demonstrates that in areas where such supra-communal institutions *were* established, we should not assume that the motivating force derived from the government, even if the latter used these institutions for its own needs and sometimes even helped to create them. Moreover, even if the government had sought to create them, it could not have done so without the basis of Jewish legal concepts and the Jewish public consciousness. The government could only support or block such a development. The source of the supra-communal institutions lay in the need for organizational unity perceived by a Jewish society that, on the one hand, avoided resorting to state institutions and, on the other, was maintaining ever-increasing contacts among its own component parts.

13

Supra-Kehila Organizations

It is not our intent in the present study to describe the development of any particular supra-communal organization, just as it was not our intent to describe the growth of any particular *kehila*. The supra-communal organizations flourished in the different countries of central Europe—in the German Empire and in Poland-Lithuania—from the mid-sixteenth until the second half of the eighteenth century. Each organization, called a *medina* (literally: state), underwent a development of its own, and is worthy of independent historical treatment. (Indeed, this remains a major desideratum of Jewish history.) But beyond any individual variations, we find characteristic features that were common to all these organizations and arose from the similarity in the factors that gave them birth: prevailing conditions, functional patterns, institutional structures, and operational systems. In our study of social history, we are therefore justified in trying to abstract the essential nature of the *medina* and to trace the universal aspects of its development.[1]

By way of summary, let us list the principal facts that call for analysis. Supra-*kehila* organizations existed and functioned from the second half of the sixteenth centuries to the first half of the eighteenth in Poland, Lithuania, Moravia, and western Hungary. The sphere of jurisdiction of such an organization was called its *galil* (district) or *medina* (state), and these names were also applied to the organization itself, as, for instance, in composite terms such as *vaad ha-galil* (district committee) and *maẓav ha-medina* (condition of the state). Organizational structure differed from place to place. In Poland and Moravia, the communities of the *galil* chose representatives who then acted on behalf of the entire *medina*.[2] In Lithuania, on the other hand, in matters relating to the district as a whole, all the *kehilot* were subject to the leadership of the principal *kehila*, even though they had no role in forming its executive institutions. In practice, the leadership of the principal *kehila* and that of the district were identical. Whatever the method of electing the organization's lay leaders, the unity of the member *kehilot* found both actual and symbolic expression in the person of the *rav ha-medina* (the rabbi of the supra-*kehila*) or the *av bet din* (the chief rabbi of the principal *kehila*), to whom all the *kehilot*, including the principal one, were, at least theoretically, subject.[3]

The *galil* represented the first level of supra-communal organization. Where a number of such districts existed within a single country, the districts themselves united into yet a broader organizational unit. The *medina* of Moravia encompassed three districts, that of Lithuania between three and five, and the Polish lands from four to ten, the increasing number of districts reflecting growing population as well as the maturing of new centers. In all cases, the executive institutions of these organizations were chosen by representatives of the component bodies.[4]

The Role of the State. The creation and functioning of the *galil* and *medina* were conditioned by the same factors that affected the basic unit of internal Jewish self-government, the *kehila*. None could have existed but for the grace of the ruling authorities. The European state of the sixteenth through eighteenth centuries was based upon a system of "estates," each one of which existed as a political and social unit unto itself, and was occasionally even represented as such vis-à-vis the central government. Thus, recognition of the supra-*kehila* did not involve any special concession. On the contrary, it corresponded to the degree of rationalization of government characteristic of the period, by which the respective estates were held responsible for the conduct of their internal affairs and were obliged only to contribute their share to the maintenance of the state. For the Jews, this latter meant tax payments in cash—payments that were made not by individuals but by the community as a collective. The state agreed to the existence of the central, supra-*kehila* organization and granted it some of the political power normally accorded to the local *kehilot* because it found it more convenient to deal with a larger organization and especially to have the collection of the Jews' taxes centralized in this manner.

It should be noted that for purposes of the kind of social history in which we are engaged, it is irrelevant whether these organizations were created by the state as a means of controlling the Jews or resulted from an internal Jewish initiative.[5] Whoever the initiator, the supra-communal organization could not have existed without the welcoming context of the corporate state on the one hand, or the frequent contacts and deep sense of interconnectedness that linked the various Jewish communities on the other.

Negotiations between the government and the supra-communal

organization did not end once that organization had been created. Determining reciprocal rights and obligations was an unending process that required constant attention. Representatives of the organizations and of the government negotiated constantly over the level of taxation, over special levies, and over whether the community was responsible for the actions of its members and constituent subgroups. The representatives would also protest any abrogation of Jews' confirmed rights, arbitrary actions by government officials, and encroachments by the authorities on their organizational autonomy.

Lay and Rabbinic Leadership. Let us turn now to a description of the internal structure of these organizations. On a formal level, the structure of the *medina* appeared quite similar to that of the *kehila*. Both were headed by *parnasim* elected by the members—in the *kehila*, by local householders, and in the *medina*, by representatives of the communities or districts. Election procedures were also similar. In Lithuania and Poland, those who elected the *kehila* leaders also directly chose their representatives both at the district level and to the Council of the Four Lands; these representatives collectively formed the leadership of the supra-communal organization. In Moravia, on the other hand, it was the representatives of the *kehilot* who in turn elected some of their number to serve as *parnasim* and lead the *medina*.[6] Appointments to the supra-*kehila*, like those to the *kehila*, were honorary posts with no financial recompense. Accordingly, the extent of one's contributions to *kehila* taxes was an important factor in determining eligibility. Officeholders were, on principle, not entitled to derive material benefit from their post, though they were reimbursed for their expenses from organizational funds.[7]

In addition to its lay leadership, each supra-communal organization was headed by a rabbi, who exercised religious-halakhic authority. This was either a specially appointed, regional *rav ha-medina* or the *av bet din* (chief rabbi) of the principal community in the region. In the Council of the Four Lands and the Lithuanian *medina*, both composite organizations, rabbinic leadership was vested in a committee of rabbis each of whom enjoyed equal authority.

The division of power between the lay and rabbinic leadership was likewise very similar to that which obtained at the *kehila* level. The lay heads of the *medina* decided on all measures of communal policy and "foreign" relations. It was they who distributed the tax burden and special levies, again through assessment committees, as in the *kehilot*.[8] The *takanot* adopted at committee meetings were sometimes written by experts specially appointed to the task, but they were nevertheless issued in the name of the *parnasim* and the heads of the *medina*. The same was true for regulations dealing with ritual questions such as prohibited foods, Sabbath observance, the prohibition of usury, and the confiscation of usurious profits. Such *takanot* could have been formulated only by outstanding scholars and, as a rule, they should be attributed to the rabbi or rabbis of the supra-*kehila*. But even these were proclaimed in the name of the lay leaders of the supra-*kehila*, who, like the lay leaders of the *kehila*, recognized their obligation to uphold religious law.[9] Indeed, there was no clear-cut demarcation between the lay and rabbinical spheres of authority: the *parnasim* assisted in ensuring the dominance of religion in public life, and they were assisted in turn by the rabbis, the preeminent representatives of religion, in enforcing the *takanot* in other spheres. As in the *kehila*, there were sometimes differences of approach between lay and rabbinic figures at the *medina* level, sometimes even leading to outright protests by the rabbis against the actions of the *parnasim*.[10] But the mutual interdependence of the two authorities, combined with the fact that the officeholders in both groups belonged to the same social class, were sufficient to reconcile such conflicts. In their public proclamations, the lay and rabbinic leaders appeared as virtually a single entity. The rabbis did not hesitate to sign regulations pertaining to economic or political matters; indeed, it was assumed that they approved of the lay leaders' decisions unless they actively objected. It is not mere happenstance that even though the *parnasim* did not necessarily solicit the active assistance of the rabbis, they couched their proclamations in religious terminology and used a mechanism deriving from the religious sphere—the decree of excommunication—as a method of enforcement.[11]

To the extent that they served as judges and issued halakhic judgments in the broad sense that we discussed in chapter 10, the rabbis enjoyed independent status within the structure of the *medina*—as in that of the *kehila*. That they would be able to rise above particularist interests, including those of the *kehilot* in which they functioned as rabbis throughout the year, was ensured by their close ties to, and dependence upon, the source texts of halakhic justice.[12] Theirs was the court of last resort in all inter-*kehila* and inter-regional disputes. The very existence of a central court of this sort epitomized the unification of the *kehilot* into one overall body.

The Absence of an Executive Apparatus. Despite the structural similarity between the *kehila* and the supra-*kehila*, however, there were great differences in their operative methods and mechanisms.

Note, for instance, the very limited size of the supra-*kehila*'s bureaucracy in comparison with the breadth of issues for which, in principle, it was responsible. This is a good indication of the difference between the two organizations. The supra-*kehila* maintained a permanent staff only to keep up its contacts with the external authorities, to collect taxes, and to keep the books. The judicial function, which, as we shall see, was of fundamental importance in the life of the *medinot*, was exercised only periodically—whenever there was a fair or congress. Only in Moravia are there indications of one degree or another of continuous judicial activity by the heads of the *medina* even while they stayed in their hometowns, and with and without rabbinic participation.[13] To perform its functions, the *medina* employed, first of all, the *shtadlan*, who acted as deputy of the *parnasim* in dealings with the authorities. In addition there were the *ne'eman* (trustee), the *sofer* (scribe), and the *shamash* (attendant). The first two worked as bookkeepers and clerks, and issued the documents of the council. To the extent that the activities of the council were seasonal, even the scribes and the attendants were employed only during congressional sessions and fairs.[14]

The size of this staff was trivial in comparison with the scope and nature of the decisions issued by the councils. It is therefore not surprising to find that many of the *medina*'s decisions were to be carried out not by its own institutions but by those of the *kehilot*. It should be borne in mind that for most of the year, for all practical purposes the *medina* did not exist and its leaders were dispersed to their respective communities. True, they continued to bear the title of *rosh medina* (head of state), *rosh galil* (head of district), or *manhig vaad arba araẓot* (leader of the Council of the Four Lands), and they (or their replacements) would have to report on the implementation of the committee's decisions at the next session, but this report would turn principally on what had, or had not, been done by the *kehilot* rather than by the leaders of the *medina* themselves. With regard to most of their decisions, the task of the supra-*kehila* leaders involved control and supervision rather than direct implementation.[15] Execution was left to the *kehila* leaders and the paid officials at their disposal. The *medina* leaders would merely encourage *kehila* leaders and, if necessary, report the latter's refusal to obey.

In the final analysis, we thus conclude that the supra-*kehila* organization was completely different from the *kehila*. Whereas the *kehila* was a ruling body with powers of enforcement, the supra-*kehila* was merely a federation of autonomous entities joined around recognized common interests. It is true that the members of the federation theoretically restricted their own freedom of action, but they never made that restriction permanent and obligatory by handing over the means to execute government decisions to the central organization.

Another indication of the sociological distinctness of the *kehila* and the supra-*kehila* lies in the means of enforcement exercised by each. The *kehila,* as we have already seen, used practically all means of punishment—from monetary fines to curtailment of free movement to corporal punishment. The supra-*kehila* also proclaimed such sanctions against those who violated its rulings, but its announcements of fines, threats of dismissal from office, and the like always required enforcement by the local *kehila.* It could almost be stated that the supra-*kehila* had no practical power at all, were it not for the significant level of obedience that a recognized and respected institution backed by exalted religious authority could elicit, especially in our period.

One of the proclamations regularly resorted to by the supra-*kehila* was the decree of *ḥerem.* Admittedly, most such decrees were directed not at specific individuals but rather at transgressors in general, and as such (as we have already noted in chapter 10) served more as a means of intimidation and deterrence than as actual punishment.[16] But the leaders of the *medina* did proclaim the ban against specific violators, either individuals or entire communities, when necessary. And the *ḥerem,* unlike other means of enforcement, was well suited to the supra-*kehila*'s organizational structure, for it did not require any action on the part of the issuing authority or its agents. It was the public at large that was requested to have no contact with the excommunicated person and even to cause him direct harm. In social terms, the implication of the ban was to withdraw the protection of institutions of government and justice from the individual. This type of sanction was typical of a weak governmental organization that had not the means to execute punishments on its own. Even the largest supra-*kehila* organization of the period, the Council of the Four Lands, had no means of imposing its authority directly on a recalcitrant community—unless it was willing to invoke the assistance of the secular government. But just the threat that the council might not defend a community against arbitrary actions by the authorities amounted, ipso facto, to an effective means of enforcement. It was even more effective to remove a community's legal protection vis-à-vis other Jews and, for example, to release the community's debtors from paying their debts, or to permit seizure of members' goods while in transit.[17] No *kehila* could withstand such measures for an extended period of time.

The *medina*'s powers of enforcement thus depended, in fact, upon the entire community's identifying with its purpose and decisions. The minimal preconditions necessary for creating a central government with the power to enforce its decisions were totally lacking. Hence, we should understand the existence of these councils and *medinot* and their activity (especially in those spheres in which they were not supported by the secular authorities) as an expression of the recognition that such activity was ultimately of benefit to the entire community. In some areas, this recognition developed into a sort of "*medina* consciousness," with an ideology that demanded of individuals that they promote the existence and unity of the *medina*. By the very nature of things, such an ideology derived its terminology and drive from the traditional religio-national sources. Emotive terms such as *tovat ha-klal* (the common good) and *ẓorkhei ẓibur* (communal need) came up often in the decrees of the central councils; in extreme cases—as with regard to the activities of the Council of the Four Lands—contemporaries even used the sanctified terms *bet din gadol* (great court) and *sanhedrin gdola* (grand Sanhedrin).[18] The primary bearers of this ideology were presumably members of the upper leadership class, who derived prestige and status, and often material benefit, from their activities on behalf of the *medina*. But at least indirectly, these concepts also penetrated the general public awareness, and thus allowed the central leadership to maintain control far in excess of what was warranted by its real power of enforcement.

The Authority of the Medina and Its Advantages. What matters could be better promoted by the *medina* than by the *kehila*? In the last chapter we discussed the entire complex of problems that arose from the fact that the Jews constituted a single society—both economically and socially—but were dispersed over wide areas. An institutional solution to these problems was sorely needed. The *medina* represented an attempt to arrive at a partial solution, at least with regard to the *kehilot* located within the territory of a single kingdom.

In the first place, the ability of the Jewish community to withstand external threats was strengthened by the existence of the national organization. A threat or a false accusation (*bilbul*) directed at an individual or a local community was ordinarily referred to the central organization, the heads of the *medina*, and its *shtadlanim*, or intercessors. For many reasons, the arguments of such *medina* representatives carried greater weight than those of local functionaries. Moreover, the *medina* implied, ipso facto, the required participation of all its members in any such rescue activity. Members of a *medina* could have no doubts as to whether they were obligated to participate. The abstract legal principle of mutual aid, the development of which we discussed in the previous chapter, here received stable institutional expression.[19] The issue was not just one of quantity; the accumulation of power in the hands of the supra-*kehila* made a qualitative difference as well. The *medina* could afford representatives with far higher qualifications than could the *kehilot*. The *medina* could even refer cases of accusations directly to higher gentile authorities with relative ease—an accepted strategy of Jewish self-defense. The Council of the Four Lands, for example, sent an emissary to the pope requesting a statement against blood libels.[20]

Because they were supra-communal organizations, the *medinot* enjoyed a distinct advantage in the legal sphere. The problem of deciding controversies among members of different *kehilot* or among different *kehila* organizations was resolved by the establishment of a central court to which both sides were subject. The central court of the *galil* or the *medina* held jurisdiction over all Jews living within its territory.[21] The actual power of this court depended on whether it had sufficient means of compulsion to force the parties to attend court and abide by its decision. But be that as it may, the legal anarchy of the preceding period, under which anyone with a claim against someone outside of his *kehila* did not know where to turn, was eliminated by the establishment of the supra-*kehila* organizations. There were now judicial frameworks with binding authority over extended areas, which could provide the sense of security that made possible frequent and close financial contacts among Jews of the region.

The creation of the central organizations also had some impact on the local judicial system. Henceforth, the individual no longer saw himself as completely under the local *kehila* court, even if the *takanot* always took care to ensure that the central organization did not infringe upon the jurisdiction of the *kehila* over local residents. There were various restrictions on appeals to the central authority: In Moravia such appeals were limited to suits over a certain sum, and all court costs were to be borne by the individual who had first appealed to the non-local court; in Lithuania, appeals to the council court were allowed only with the permission of the two principal *kehilot* or an affirmation from the local *av bet din* (chief rabbi) that he had refused to confirm the ruling of the *parnasim*.[22] Such restrictions were designed to dissuade people from resorting to appeals lightly. But in serious cases, and especially in cases of disputes between individuals and their *kehila*, the door was open for the individual to fight for his rights and to prove the justness of his cause. In at least one region, in Moravia, there was actually a special appeals court before which one could appeal a ruling of a *kehila* court, even if it had already been promulgated.[23] But everywhere the *medina* broke down the closed judicial framework of the *kehila*. References to a *bet din gadol* are thus not merely a rhetorical device; the *medina* courts were a real authority and they fulfilled the function of a supreme judicial body in those areas of society over which they had been assigned power.[24]

There are several other areas, aside from the appellate-judicial, in which the supra-*kehila* was superior to the local community even though it actually depended upon that community to enforce its rulings. Certain types of decisions, for example, were effective only if they were issued centrally, thus serving as a guide for all the *kehilot* concerned. A ruling that a particular tractate of the Talmud be taught during a given period in all the *yeshivot* of Poland and Moravia served as a means of aiding the publishing houses in finding a wide market for a volume fresh from the press, but it also amounted to technical aid in the central supply of educational materials, as well as an educational policy that facilitated students transferring from one *yeshiva* to another.[25] It is unlikely that there was significant opposition to such obviously beneficial rules, but the rules could nevertheless never have been issued except by a supra-communal organization.

Other decisions dealt with distributing financial burdens among different bodies: for example, whether settlements that had no *yeshiva* should be charged with the maintenance of *yeshiva* students during vacation periods, or whether communities were obliged to accept students from other *kehilot* or orphans from other *medinot*.[26] Even though the implementation of the ruling fell to the same bodies who were financially affected by it, the authority of the issuing institution was probably sufficient to ensure obedience. Without such a decision, matters of this sort would have been left to chance—to the detriment of the students and orphans.

In other cases where implementation was the task of the local bodies, the decision of the central organization served to protect the public against a too-powerful individual. Prohibitions on farming the customs tax in Poland or calls for supervision of tariff levies in Moravia were rulings implemented by others, but we may assume from the fact that the councils took the trouble to issue them that these rulings had some impact.[27] They strengthened the position of the community vis-à-vis powerful individuals, and provided at least partial protection against arbitrary acts on the part of the latter.

One of the most important functions of the central leadership was simply to bolster the authority of the *kehila* leaders in matters that the latter could presumably have accomplished entirely on their own initiative. It was *kehila* functionaries who carried out the decision of the Moravian *medina* to allow collection of a *MaMRaME* (promissory note) even if it lacked the legally required endorsement of signatures.[28] The execution of this decision required the use of force and occasionally even cruelty, going as far as the quick sequestration of the defendant's home and property. This and similar rules governing bankruptcy, which we have already discussed, were issued with the intention of ensuring confidence among businessmen. But even though these stringencies were recognized as important public necessities, their actual execution was likely to be difficult, particularly in small communities whose members were all linked by blood and friendship. The decision of the central organization presumably served to dispel doubts and to bolster the law.

Similarly, we find rulings explicitly designed to combat individuals' feelings of compassion in cases where the public good required severity. Paupers roaming from place to place were a virtual plague for the Jews of Europe, as for the rest of European society. In an attempt to restrict the poor to their own locales, the Lithuanian council called on *kehila* leaders not to assist wandering beggars and not to allow them to stop even temporarily. It is clear from their wording that the authors of this decision saw Jewish compassion as the main factor inhibiting the implementation of their decisions.[29]

Clearly, we are witnessing a broad sociological phenomenon: Within the framework of a many-faceted society there was an increasing tendency to institute administrative and judicial measures without regard to their effect upon the individual. The small society of the medieval *kehila* was not capable of developing abstract principles of this sort, but neither had it required them. Problems of this kind were resolved on an ad hoc basis. But once the isolated *kehila* became part of a society with wide-ranging reciprocal relationships, the leadership was forced to develop an overall, abstract system. From this point on, problems were considered as they affected the existence and welfare of the society as a whole. The fate and suffering of the individual seem to have become irrelevant to those who formulated and executed the laws. This was both the strength and the price of the supra-communal form of organization.

14

The Family

Let us now go from a description of the framework that society imposes upon the individual—that is, the *kehila* and the supra-*kehila*—to the institution of the family, into which the individual is placed at birth by nature. This transition from the coercive institutions of government to the family, the institution that provides the individual's needs, is somewhat arbitrary. But our treatment of the family at this point at least has the advantage of presenting the opposite end of the spectrum of human social existence. From the formal and organizational, we move to the intimate and personal. All other religious and educational institutions existed between these two poles of coercion on the one hand and primary care on the other.[1]

Structure and Composition of the Family. The Jewish family in our period was, in sociological terms, of the small type. It was composed of the married nucleus—that is, husband, wife, mutual offspring, and any children from earlier marriages living with them. Family members shared a single housing unit. Assets upon which the family drew for its sustenance were the legal property of the husband, whether the family was extraordinarily wealthy or had only the barest amounts necessary for daily survival. The wife had certain rights to use this property: She took care of regular household expenses and certain religious and ethical expenditures, such as the giving of charity in acceptable and customary amounts. To the extent that it was customary for the wife to participate in her husband's business, she was his full equal in daily economic activities. On occasion, part of the burden of supporting the family, or the entire burden, was borne by the wife, while the husband devoted his time to the study of Torah.[2] Children were considered dependent on their parents, and especially on their fathers; they were without economic, legal, or political independence.[3]

The nuclear family was not infrequently joined in its living arrangements by secondary relations: for instance, the husband's or wife's parents. The rights of parents to be supported in old age by their children was guaranteed by both custom and law.[4] Other relatives, and sometimes even unrelated orphans, might also be supported, out of traditional Jewish charity and loving-kindness. Sons- and daughters-in-law living with the family during the first few years of marriage occupied a somewhat intermediate stage: They were primary relations but their participation in the family was determined by a contract that promised support for the young couple for a predetermined number of years.[5] A completely contractual relationship with no familial element governed the status of yet other members of the household—namely, the male and female domestics, the cook, and the wet nurse, and even the teacher (*melamed*), who often served as a household tutor in the wealthy homes of the day.[6]

This family, monogamous and patriarchal, would appear to be typical of urban, burgher society as it had developed in European culture. True, there are certain features unique to the Jewish family and to underlying Jewish attitudes toward family life. But it is not our purpose here to compare and contrast familial structures; we shall content ourselves with trying to understand the Jewish family per se—its structure, its functions, and the atmosphere that pervaded it. If one may be so bold, we are trying to grasp the spirit that gave the Jewish family life.

Creation of the Family: Betrothal and Marriage. The first point to notice about any familial structure is the mechanism by which it is created. In our period, the Jewish family was created by an agreement between those considered the couple's logical representatives—the parents or, if they were no longer among the living, the couple's relatives or publicly appointed guardians. It is true that the formal bond of matrimony (*ishut*), the bond that could be severed only by a bill of divorce, was established only through the direct action of the couple themselves—by the man's act of betrothal and the woman's voluntary acceptance. This bond took effect under the marriage canopy (*ḥupa*) when the marriage ceremony was actually performed. (This differed from the usual practice in the Middle Ages, when it was customary to have the betrothal precede the marriage ceremony by several months, or even years.[7]) Still, betrothal was always preceded by the writing of *tna'im* (conditions)—a contract in which the parties committed themselves to the marriage and specified other terms, such as the amount of the dowry, the time of the wedding ceremony, and the couple's place of residence. As a rule, the couple had no voice whatsoever in formulating these terms. Only in a second marriage, where the participants were already domestically independent, or in rare cases where marriage was delayed until the participants had reached social and economic independence, were these *tna'im* determined by the couple themselves.[8] And even in these cases, formal signing was delegated, as a matter of convention, to the parents or other representatives.

As noted, the signing of the *tna'im* did not create a matrimonial bond, nor did their cancellation require a bill of divorce. But for all practical purposes, the *tna'im* contained guarantees of sufficient substance that the couple's future might now be seen as entirely settled, no less than if an actual betrothal had taken place. First, each agreed to pay a heavy forfeit—usually half the dowry—for violating the contract. Second, and more important, the agreement included a *ḥerem*, a decree of excommunication, on anyone who broke the agreement and abused the good name of the other family. This ban was understood to be a "ban of the *kehilot*"—i.e., a decree dating back to the ancient Sages. In Germany it was sometimes allowed that the ban would be lifted upon payment of a fine, but in Poland the *tna'im* explicitly stated that the *ḥerem* would apply even after the fine was paid. The seriousness of the relationship forged by the *tna'im* was supported by public opinion, which frowned upon any abrogation. The *tna'im* were written at a public ceremony in the presence not only of family members but also of communal officials such as a rabbi or preacher, a scribe, and witnesses.[9] Since the match had not been based on "irrational" considerations of a personal and intimate nature, any abrogation necessarily implied that there was something wrong with the marriage partner or his or her family. Hence, anyone who broke the agreement without first receiving permission from an appropriate rabbinic court would not only have to suffer the consequences by paying a forfeit, but would also be held in contempt, and their chances of again making a suitable match would be diminished.

The Role of Parents in Arranging a Match. The enormous degree of control that parents exerted over the match reflects the fact that the engaged parties themselves were expected to be young, lacking in experience, and unable to know their own minds. And indeed, marriage at as early an age as possible was typical of the era. This tendency stemmed, first, from the parents' desire to settle their children's future while they, the parents, were still alive. But beyond any personal and material concerns, we have here a reflection of the traditional religious and ethical norms regarding sexual activity. All sexual contact and erotic satisfaction was forbidden outside of monogamous marriage. The ideal of sexual purity applied equally to both men and women. In fact, sinful thoughts were considered worse in a man than in a woman, for they might lead him to nocturnal emissions or masturbation, sins for which there was almost no atonement except through difficult and bitter self-mortification. This concept of sexual ethics was drawn from the Talmudic literature. Contemporary *musar* (ethical) works elaborated and popularized it, adding also the particularly strict views of sexuality that they drew from the *Zohar* and other kabbalistic texts.[10] On the other hand, that very same literature, from the Talmud and Midrash right down to the contemporary *musar* books, was keenly aware of the intensity of sexual temptation. Talmudic Judaism was far removed from the optimism of Catholic sexual ethics, which believed in the power of the individual to overcome his desires. Nor did it share the liberal tendency to gloss over the problem and minimize its importance. Jewish halakhic and *musar* literature stress in unambiguous terms that he who is without a wife has almost no hope of withstanding the temptations of the flesh. A Jew who had grown up with this view was left with no choice but to arrange as early a marriage as possible for himself and his sons. At most he might delay marriage for a few years in order to study in a *yeshiva* on the grounds that "his soul longed for Torah." But even for Torah scholars, the ideal was to marry first and to study Torah afterward "in purity."[11]

Age of Marriage. There were thus many incentives for early marriage, and anyone who could, fulfilled this ideal. Sixteen was considered the proper age for a girl, and eighteen at the latest for a boy. Parents were never censured—indeed, they were praised—for arranging a match for daughters of thirteen or fourteen and sons of fifteen or sixteen, and even for marrying off their children at such young ages.[12]

The Function of Dowries. But it would be an error to suppose that all members of society were married so young. The age of marriage was delayed for some, although not by the sort of subjective factors operative in societies where marriage depends on a personal attachment between the parties. The great majority of matches were arranged through the agency of others, and every eligible person was the target of marriage proposals, especially from professional marriage brokers (*shadkhanim*) operating on the local, inter-communal, and even international level.[13] We may assume that anyone who had the necessary qualifications for marriage was able to meet suitable candidates of the opposite sex. But fulfilling these "necessary qualifications" was sometimes much more difficult than we might imagine, and marriage might consequently be delayed. The establishment of a family was considered the foundation of a new economic survival-unit. True, the new couple would commonly live with one of the sets of parents for two years or more, but this was never intended as a permanent arrangement. This period was considered an extension of the boy's education. He would either continue his Talmudic study at home or in the local *beit midrash*, or else he would be given his first lessons in commerce or some other common trade of the day. Once the fixed time of support was passed, the new couple would leave the parents' home and begin establishing their own household.[14] In order to make this economic independence possible, one or both families offered a dowry to the couple. If the families did not have the wherewithal to provide a dowry, they would resort to other sources: relatives, altruistic patrons, charitable associations that were sometimes specifically designated for this purpose, or even the coffers of the community and supra-communal institutions.[15] The willingness of many individuals and public bodies to aid in the marrying off of poor girls is proof of the religious value that was attached to getting young people married as early as possible. But it is also an expression of the universal assumption that marriage required economic means that could serve as the basis for establishing a home, and in general would also be the first tool for independent economic activity. The prime prerequisite, therefore, for marriage was the existence of a suitable dowry. The larger the dowry offered, the greater the chances of obtaining a suitable match.

Other Factors for Marriageability. The dowry was not, of course, the only value to be considered in deciding on a match. The new couple would have to obtain a residence permit in a community. If one of them was heir to such a right, and if that right could extend to the other partner in the match, this might be a first-rate marriage opportunity. It happened on more than one occasion that a marriage was delayed by the communities, which, wishing to limit the number of competitors in a given area, forbade marriages for a specified period of time, limited their number, or made licenses to marry dependent upon the property of the candidates.[16] In other places it was necessary to buy the residence permit from the local non-Jewish authorities, and the obligation of one of the parents to purchase this license was made a precondition of the match from the start.[17] Sometimes the couple was promised a salaried communal position by the bride's parents.

During the period when rabbinic positions were sold in Poland, this was apparently sometimes a condition for a marriage, although it was scarcely ever explicitly stated in the formal *tna'im*.[18] Marriage into a family with social and economic contacts was considered valuable even without any explicit promise of immediate profit. Similarly, a certain value was ascribed (albeit a relatively limited one, as we shall see in chapter 19) to lineage (*yiḥus*)—that is, to descent from Torah scholars or famous men of the past. On the other hand, a familial blemish—sexual licentiousness or apostasy occurring among the proposed spouse's relatives—was a negative value that had to be balanced out by other, positive assets.[19] And finally, there were also personal marriage values: the young man's scholarship or the young woman's efficiency (if one was dealing with a girl who had already had some experience running a household or helping in a first husband's business). Beauty and good appearance were also considered, although they were not as important as they would be in a society that based its marital system on free choice.[20]

It was thus possible to estimate how well and how soon a person would marry from the degree to which he or she possessed the socially approved marriage qualifications. Members of the wealthy, scholarly ruling classes would likely marry into families of their own class, usually at an early age, in accordance with the contemporary ideal. The high degree of mobility that characterized this class allowed marriages to be arranged between prospective brides and grooms from quite distant places, sometimes even from different countries, the only limit being the social and cultural frontiers of the Ashkenazic Jewish world. Members of the lower classes were more limited, in both the quality of match to which they could aspire, and the age at which they could expect to marry. Similarly, the geographic area from within which a match would be proposed to them was also more limited. Their marriages were essentially local affairs and occurred at a later age.

Of course, the personal qualities of the candidates also affected their marriageability. A widow or widower, a status quite common in those days of early mortality, would perforce be content with a mate from a lower class than the one to which he or she could normally aspire, particularly if the widowed person was left with a number of children. This was even truer in the case of a person with a physical deformity or in whose family there had been some sort of scandal, even through no fault of his own.[21] Conversely, anyone possessed of learning, physical beauty, or outstanding economic skills could use these to marry into a higher class. Such people, however, tended to delay their marriage until their skills or attributes reached full maturity—the talented student until he had attracted the attention of senior scholars and the entrepreneur until his business ventures had borne fruit.[22] In fact, only members of the highest classes who possessed both learning and wealth could afford the luxury of marrying off their children at a very young age with no thought to better opportunities in the future. Their very class guaranteed them a suitable match. Members of the lower classes, on the other hand, had to carefully balance their present prospects against future possibilities before making a decision.

Even the weight attached to the religious ideal of early marriage varied with the individual and depended on that person's degree of loyalty to religious values. *Musar* works reflect this tension when they warn against delaying marriage in the hope of obtaining a better, wealthier match later on. The middle classes were particularly subject to this dilemma. The destitute lower classes, on the other hand, were largely subject to forces over which they had no control: the charity of others, finding a domestic position that did not interfere with maintaining a family, securing a permit to live in a particular place, and so forth. In such cases the religious ideal of early marriage operated more through its influence on communal institutions that facilitated marriages than through any direct impact on the personal aspirations of the individuals.

The Suppression of Erotic Considerations. The outstanding characteristic of this society's approach to marriage was the extreme rationalism with which it calculated the chances of that "proper match" to which each aspired in his own way. Such criteria as personal compatibility, not to speak of romantic attachments, were not considered at all. This does not mean that young people did not meet, at least in the course of everyday life, and fall in love. In many places there were even opportunities for contacts that possessed a degree of erotic tension, such as dances and excursions on the occasion of celebrations or holidays. But even so, erotic attraction was not allowed to determine one's choice of a mate, even if a person had been "caught in the web of desire." Love was certainly never considered a necessary prerequisite for a match. Even if, by chance, personal attraction had determined the choice of a mate, a matchmaker (*shadḥan*) would still be used for appearance' sake, and the negotiations and the writing of the *tna'im* would certainly be handed over to the parents or their substitutes.[23] Every effort was made to give the impression that the match had been arranged in the usual manner. Finally, it was virtually axiomatic that the young couple would forgo their love match if their parents objected. They would not have found it easy to go against their parents' wishes in any case. The *responsa* literature frequently discusses cases of "secret marriage," in which a youth was betrothed to a girl in the presence of witnesses but without prior matrimonial negotiations. The rabbis usually annulled such marriages on formal grounds—the witnesses had been unfit, the girl had not given proper consent, etc.—or insisted that a bill of divorce be issued. No halakhic scholar ever suggested that the couple's marriage be recognized and accepted. Marriage without prior formal negotiations was already in Talmudic times seen as somehow morally blemished. In our period public opinion condemned such marriages as an attempt by socially irresponsible individuals to usurp the parents' legitimate right to decide their children's fate. Moreover, such surprise marriages were condemned because they broke down the barriers between the classes insofar as they provided a mechanism by which a member of a lower class could trick his way into a match beyond his station.[24]

This final consideration will help us to understand one of the reasons for the opposition to marriages based on free choice. This society, as we shall see, was based on rigid class divisions but it lacked adequate means to differentiate between the social status of the various classes. From a purely halakhic point of view, "every family was assumed to be fit,"[25] and was therefore allowed to intermarry with any other. On rare occasions such inter-class marriages actually occurred. But precisely its theoretical openness meant that the society could not allow the choice of a spouse to be determined by chance encounters. It was in the nature of life in isolated communities that members of different classes would occasionally meet. Members of the same class, on the other hand, who on the basis of objective criteria could be considered suitable marriage partners, were often geographically dispersed and would meet only if the matter was deliberately arranged beforehand.

Of course, the rejection of love matches stemmed from more than class considerations; it was also intimately bound up in the society's understanding of love and sexuality. Although, as we have noted, the power of the sexual urge was clearly recognized and openly acknowledged, there was never any deliberate cultivation of the erotic life in which the individual might find release from tension or even room for self-expression. Sexuality—indeed, any form of eroticism—belonged exclusively within the strict confines of married life. And even in that context, sexual activity was limited by the religious laws relating to the menstrual period (*nida*), which added approximately one week of ritually enforced abstinence to the monthly period during which physiology ruled out sexual intercourse. It is true that sexual activity within marriage was not totally subjugated to the formal religious purpose of fulfilling the commandment to "be fruitful and multiply." Intercourse between man and wife was allowed even when conception could not possibly result, as, for instance, if the wife was already pregnant or was sterile.[26] The moralists all found ways to resolve the apparent contradiction between this lenient approach and their strict censures against "spilling one's seed in vain."[27] The very strictness of their rules against any sexual contact or thoughts outside of marriage is what forced them to allow satisfaction at least within the permitted framework of marriage. It is interesting to note in this connection that the halakhic and *musar* texts seem to consider the woman's needs even more than the man's. Thus, any tendency to encourage asceticism on the part of the husband and to limit his sexual activity to the minimum was counterbalanced by the husband's halakhic obligations toward his wife. And their mutual relation included an erotic component. The wife was commanded to try to attract her husband's attention to the point of exhausting his sexual appetites, while the man was commanded to approach his wife out of genuine affection and tenderness. He was at least required to take her feelings into consideration and not to see her as merely a means through which to satiate his lust or to fulfill a commandment.[28] Kabbalistic works, such as that of R. Isaiah Horowitz, even taught that there was a spiritual dimension to the erotic life within marriage by popularizing the notion that the sexual joining symbolized parallel processes in the divine sphere.[29] And it was certainly accepted that the degree of mutual sexual satisfaction achieved was a valid criterion by which to judge the success of a marriage.

It was always understood that some marriages worked and some didn't. It was not, however, assumed that attachment or love before marriage would in any way guarantee the eventual success of a marriage. Success was guaranteed, people felt, by objective conditions, such as the sort of homes in which the couple were raised. To the extent that personal attributes such as physical beauty were taken into consideration, even these were not left up to the personal eye of the beholder but rather were given over to experts who had both experience and authority. Hence the marriage of two young people who had met each other only shortly before their wedding was not considered a denial of the young people's rights. True, this sort of arrangement was generally limited to the wealthy, scholarly classes, who brought their spouses from afar; among the lower classes it was often the custom to bring the engaged couple together in an intentionally erotic context.[30] But even in the latter case, this occurred only *after* the match had been arranged, and it is doubtful whether this erotic tension was meant as a test of mutual compatibility. In any case, even when there had been no opportunity to get to know one another in advance of the wedding, the young couple did not see their rights as having been violated. As in everything else, once all rational efforts had been expended to achieve the goal, after others had done everything in their power to choose the best possible mate, one could only hope for luck and pray to Him in Whose hands man's fate was always entrusted.[31]

Restraints on Divorce. Nor would one generally break up a marriage except in cases of clear and absolute failure: total sexual dysfunction; adultery (especially on the part of the wife); barrenness; or radical incompatibility (as displayed in constant, open quarreling), etc. People had not been raised ideologically to expect happiness, and the absence of romantic satisfaction in a marriage would not lead to divorce.[32] There were, moreover, tremendous hardships involved in divorce. The husband had to consider the economic cost. The *ktuba* was still in force in this period—that is, the legal document that spelled out the couple's mutual obligations and whose main purpose, according to the Talmud, was "that it not appear easy in his eyes to divorce her." The amount of the *ktuba* was proportional to the amount of the dowry[33]—and that money had usually been invested in such a way that its withdrawal would have destroyed the family business. Women, on the other hand, knew that divorce would leave them with a much reduced status. A divorcée's chances of remarrying were slim, especially if she had been the cause of the divorce, whether because she had produced no children, or because she was suspected of adultery, or because she was obviously argumentative. Independence was in no way an advantage to a woman in this society. Only a widow with children to raise could be seen as, in effect, substituting for her husband and could thus maintain the economic and social status of the family—as occurred in the case of Glückel of Hameln. But it was doubtful that a young divorcée could find a viable economic role for herself; there was certainly no independent social role for her. Of necessity she was forced, therefore, to seek refuge in the house of others by returning to her parents or relatives, or, for the lower classes, by taking a job as a household domestic.

For these reasons divorce was generally rejected as a quick solution to family tension. In many cases, halakhic authorities were asked to find a way for a marriage to continue even though, according to the letter of the law, the husband was obligated to divorce his wife, as, for instance, when she had not given birth within ten years of marriage.[34] The secondary economic and social functions of marriage were so important in this society that they were often sufficient to sustain a match that was no longer fulfilling its primary erotic and biological function.

Sexual Deviance. Despite the tremendous pressure to marry, however, there were obviously some who remained single. There was no positive social value attached to remaining single; even someone who had lost more than one mate to divorce or death would try to marry yet again. Still, the same factors that often delayed marriage could also prevent it altogether.[35] Hence, the problem of sexuality, and, even more so, of eroticism, was not completely resolved. The possibility remained of the type of sexual activities that the society labeled as deviant to a greater or lesser degree. It is difficult to determine the extent of such activity, but its occurrence is not open to doubt. The *takanot* of the major communities establish policy toward deviance, and the *responsa* literature deals with real cases in every generation and in each locale. The source of such deviance was, as noted, enforced bachelorhood: young men and women who had not yet found their mate, male and female domestics whose situation precluded marriage, widows and widowers who were left without families, *agunot* (grass widows) who had given up on their missing husbands, bachelor teachers who had left their homes in search of a living, wandering merchants and traveling charity collectors. Because of their life-styles, all of these were suspected of licentious behavior,[36] and they were a constant source of temptation to such behavior for others. For that matter, marriage itself provided no immunity from the "evil desire." As the Talmud puts it realistically: "There is no guardian against unchastity" (*Ktubot*, fol. 13b).

Hence even this society had to fight against licentiousness. But at least we can say that everyone in the society, even the promiscuous, shared in the battle against perversion—their own, and that of others. Deviance did not derive from an ideology of licentiousness; it was universally considered a blemish and a sin even by the deviants. Hence we find frequent requests in the *responsa* literature for methods to atone for sexual sins, sins varying from the "spilling of seed in vain" to adultery with a married woman. The term *baal tshuva* (penitent) was restricted almost exclusively to sinners in a sexual sense. Only accidental homicide and apostasy (by choice or enforced) were treated with the same severity. This society had inherited a rich legacy, an entire code of rules regarding penitence for each and every sin from the thirteenth-century German Pietists (*Ḥasidei Ashkenaz*). The severity of punishment and personal degradation connected with repentance went far beyond what we would consider reasonable or humanly bearable today.[37] The fact that the deviants themselves requested these punishments in order to atone for their sin—and there are cases in which rabbis assigned more stringent punishments only in order to appease the petitioner—indicates that even if sexual purity was not absolute, it remained the ideal, both limiting deviation and restoring equilibrium should such deviance occur.

15

The Extended Family

The family inevitably fulfilled an entire range of secondary social functions, which can be understood in detail only after we have analyzed the various religious and educational institutions of the society. For now it is enough to note that the family served as the base for a significant portion of all social activity, and provided the setting for a number of religious ceremonies. It was the primary and "natural" tool by which each new generation was socialized.

Relations Based on Familial Bonds. Beyond the nuclear family, a formally defined and recognized social institution, there lay a less formal set of relationships based on both blood and marriage, which linked uncles and cousins, in-laws and in-laws of in-laws, into what was accepted as an extended family. If this extended family was not institutionalized and if it did not bind its members as formally as it would have in societies based upon the tribe, neither was it totally ignored. The extended family seems to be a universal human phenomenon rooted in the individual's need for social relations of graded intimacy. The primary intimacy of the nuclear family is transferred through connecting links—my father is your brother, his wife is your mother, and so forth—to family members with whom the individual does not live on a day-to-day basis. The extended family may thus be seen as an anthropological phenomenon that varies with sociological circumstances. And the analysis of our society will not be complete if we ignore the ties of kinship that applied within it.

Legal Definition of Kinship. Traditional Jewish society understood kinship inclusively, both as to whom it encompassed and as to the obligations that relatives had to each other. The Halakha defined kinship in the context of deciding which relatives were forbidden to marry or were disqualified to serve as witnesses. Marriage was prohibited only within the inner circle of relatives: a brother and sister, an aunt and nephew (but not an uncle and niece).[1] Even great-uncles and cousins (whether male or female) were disqualified from bearing witness and from serving as judges in cases involving each other, with no distinction made between ties of blood and those of marriage: men were disqualified even if they were related only through their wives.[2] This definition served also as a basis for disqualifying relatives from serving together on the governing bodies of the *kehila* and supra-communal organizations. In legal and constitutional cases, the intention was to maintain a distance between relatives and a fixed legal definition of kinship was required. On the other hand, when the intent was to obligate the individual through feelings of family solidarity, no such limiting definition was applied. The Talmud had understood Isaiah's admonition (58:7) "not to ignore your own kin" as an expression of the obligation to help one's relatives when possible. In our society, it was considered as applying to all relatives, whatever the degree of kinship.[3]

The Obligation to Support Relatives. Aid to one's relatives meant first of all financial support in the event of economic failure or true poverty. That relatives had priority over other poor people was already accepted in the ancient Halakha.[4] But in our period it was further accepted that kinship obligated one actually to give more than one would normally have been ready to give to others of the needy.[5] The obligation of financial support was especially emphasized with respect to marrying off daughters of relatives, during the lifetime of their fathers and all the more so after their death. The raising of a poor orphaned relative and the arranging of his or her marriage was considered an especially meritorious religious deed, which charitable persons took pride in fulfilling.[6]

Contemporaries accepted the call to support their relatives—each individual in accordance with his generosity—as a recognized social norm. Family honor and status was, at most, a secondary consideration, for as we shall see, no family, including the wealthiest, could hope to maintain even an approximately uniform socioeconomic status for all of its members. The fundamental precondition for this—namely, property of permanent value, such as real estate—was totally absent. The nature of Jewish business and the conditions under which it was carried out led to constant ascents and descents on the social ladder. Even the richest families kept their poor relations in mind; they could perhaps save them from destitution but they could not provide them with a firmly based socioeconomic position.[7]

Familial Ties Provide Economic and Political Benefits. The social norm requiring aid to the extended family derived ultimately from the real function that kinship ties served in this society. As we have already seen, Jewish society profited economically from its unity despite geographic dispersion—in other words, from the fact that Jews could use their shared language and culture to maintain contacts with other Jews living in distant lands. Kinship ties among even distantly related individuals provided further such advantage when it came to competition among the Jews themselves. And there were noneconomic advantages as well. Familial ties were also useful when common political issues arose, whether they involved intercessions with the non-Jewish authorities or negotiations with one of the internal Jewish organizations. Such contacts in other places were useful in many circumstances. The Talmud student traveling from center to center in pursuit of his studies, the rabbi who accepted an appointment in a new *kehila*, and even someone seeking a match in a distant city all required local support, if only to provide them with information and the like.[8] The society's need for inter-urban contacts far exceeded the means available through existing institutions. Only the "natural" ties of kinship could answer this need.

Within the *kehilot*, too, factions in the struggle for power, economic advantage, or social status often formed around patterns of kinship. Here too, the reason was, in the first place, negative; that is, there were no ideological or class bases strong enough to serve as poles around which such factions could crystallize. The contests were usually between economic, social, and ideological equals who struggled over which of them would acquire that power, status, honor, and prestige that the society could offer its members. Under such conditions, it was natural that factions would form according to primary kinship ties, and we find in the history of contemporary *kehilot* that entire families struggled with each other, sometimes remorselessly.[9]

We are now in a position to refine our definition of the social conditions that fostered Jewish familial solidarity in this period. We have before us a society whose economic, political, and social activities had reached a high enough level of differentiation and diversification that belonging to secondary associations offered real advantages. These conditions led, as we shall see, to the rise of confraternities, which fulfilled the need for secondary association on a local level. But even before that, these conditions strengthened the existing "natural" tendency to association through the family.

Governmental and Judicial Functions Transcend Family Ties. The obligation for members of the family to aid each other was accepted as an unquestioned principle. The individual obeyed this principle, whether or not it was to his own benefit. But inevitably the realities of social life dictated that loyalty to one's family would also lead to some degree of conflict with other principles. Family obligations existed alongside, and functioned within the framework of, larger public institutions. These institutions, whether legal, administrative, or economic, were, by their very nature, established on a basis that transcended the family, and they therefore had to serve members of different families and operate irrespective of family connections.

The need to separate public institutions and family ties was evident in the case of the judiciary. The Jewish court was a public institution that had been consciously and as a matter of principle withdrawn from the familial context that bound members of the society. Talmudic law transcends the family and does not recognize any rights of the individual derived from a family relationship between the judge and the judged. In this regard, Jewish society of our period was based on a clear tradition that came into being under conditions similar to its own. For already in the mishnaic and Talmudic periods (although, in certain respects, not the biblical period), justice was based on this public concept, which went beyond membership in a family or clan. In fact, as the Halakha developed, it tended to react to expanded notions of the family by becoming even more strict about not allowing people related by blood or marriage to judge each other.[10] In any case, there was absolutely no ambiguity about the radical separation of legal process and family ties. Anyone who transgressed the instructions of the law concerning the makeup of the court or who judged a case according to family considerations was, in his own eyes and in those of others, deviating from the principles of Halakha and ethics and behaving improperly.

The situation was somewhat different with regard to administrative institutions. In principle, the *kehila* and the supra-*kehila* organizations were also perceived as standing above family ties. Hence we find *takanot* forbidding relatives from serving together in these institutions, on the *kehila* administrative body of *parnasim* and *tovim*, or on the committees of the various provincial and national councils. This was especially stressed with regard to the assessment boards that assigned the individual's tax burden. In fixing the degree of family relationship permitted, the *takanot* relied upon the accepted tradition with regard to judicial institutions.[11] But it is clear that there was no fixed and clear tradition concerning this matter. Hence differing customs grew up and disputes arose concerning the degree of relatedness that was to be permitted in secondary public institutions. Were relatives to be forbidden to serve only on the administrative body of *parnasim* and *tovim*, or were they also to be forbidden on wider communal bodies, such as the board of electors—that is, the committee that was set up to choose the *parnasim* and *tovim*?[12] A similar question arose concerning the rabbi and his congregants. In many places the selection of the rabbi was made conditional on the fact that he not come from the community or have any relatives there.[13] It is possible that in this the communities were trying to ensure that the rabbi would be able to serve as the head of a court in any dispute that arose among their members. But it seems also that the general position of the rabbi as bearer of supreme authority within the community led people to seek for this position a man who stood above the conflicts that, as we have seen, periodically arose along family lines. However, even this rule concerning the rabbi was not universally or systematically enforced. Not all *kehilot* insisted on it, and even where it was enforced, it often applied only at the start of a term of office. If the rabbi subsequently married into a local family, he did not thereby lose his post.[14] And the same was presumably also true with regard to the holders of administrative offices; if members of two different families married, they did not therefore lose their positions. It was never possible to establish a completely clear-cut rule against relatives serving together on administrative boards because such administrative institutions, unlike judicial ones, were not defined by strong halakhic traditions. Even where such a principle was accepted in theory, there was no sufficient guarantee that it would actually be carried out in practice. People certainly were not as careful about preventing relatives from serving together in administrative institutions as they were with regard to judicial ones.

The lack of a straightforward principle concerning separation of family and communal interests can be seen in other areas as well. As we know, the *kehila* guaranteed its members equal opportunities for making a living, while strangers and nonresidents were given only minimal rights. Merchants from outside the community were allowed to trade only to the degree that this did not harm the livelihood of locals. Theoretically this restriction should have applied to all foreigners, whether or not they were related to members of the community. On the other hand, the livelihood of many was based specifically on family ties that created the economic contacts necessary in trading between different localities. If the community were to forbid, for example, receiving goods on commission from foreigners on the grounds that any sale would profit the nonresident, did this ban apply also to a brother or father who lived elsewhere? The trans-familial principle upon which the community was based suggested forbidding such an arrangement. But the deep family ties, rooted in group consciousness and reflecting real economic needs, militated against consistency in this matter. In some places the *kehilot* tended to enforce the trans-family principle and forbade giving any advantage to nonmembers; elsewhere, the tension between the two principles led to a compromise even in theory. Compromises were certainly worked out in practice everywhere.[15]

Thus, neither the *kehila* nor the other supra-familial institutions completely abrogated the principle of family ties; indeed, there were cases in which they used it in order to transfer their own responsibilities onto the shoulders of the family. This is clear with regard to the support of those who had failed in business and the poor. The supra-familial institutions felt obligated to care for these people, but required that the individual first try to get help from wealthy members of his own family. If one of the pauper's relatives was capable of supporting him, the community no longer felt obligated to help him.[16] Thus, the very *kehila* that sought to base itself on the principle of transcending the family used the family when it was to its own benefit, while the individual was required to support his own poor relatives and the poor of his city as well.

Just as contemporary economic activity had a unifying effect on the extended family, it also had a disruptive and isolating impact. For the most part, Jewish economic activity in this period was based on money, or at least on goods that could be evaluated in terms of money. Because of this, each nuclear family unit stood on its own independent economic base. Once they had received their dowry, sons and daughters ceased to be economically part of the family except insofar as they entered into a formal partnership in the family business. (In this case, of course, the relationship was fundamentally no different from that which applied between any other business partners.) After the settlement of the dowry, the only economic ties existing on the basis of family relationship were those of inheritance and those of support in times of need. On whatever level such support was extended—whether it amounted to outright charity or special help to a relative in business—this family relationship did not eliminate in any way the distinctions drawn between the individual families, each of which stood economically on its own. And the more economic activity moved in the direction of anonymous credit transactions, the more calculations of profit and loss became impersonal. The promissory note (*MaMRaMe*) that was passed from hand to hand would eventually be collected by someone other than the person to whom the borrower was first obligated. Once the note entered the market, the lender could no longer forgive the debt even if he wanted to do so. To an ever-increasing extent, the individual confronted not people he knew but rather a large market that encompassed also all of his relatives and friends. And since each nuclear family formed an independent economic unit, the primary feeling of economic responsibility was felt toward this unit. A far-reaching concession to others could destroy the equilibrium of this independent economy. The Talmudic adage "Your life takes precedence over that of your fellow" (*Bava Meẓi'a*, fol. 62a) was interpreted in this period as applying to family members as well.[17]

In summary, in the economic context the family played a positive role as link and intermediary and in providing aid. But the primary fact of economic life was the independence of the nuclear family, and the individual and his household were left to their own luck and skills. Despite the well-known closeness of the Jewish family, we are dealing with a society in which the responsibility of individuals to each other, and even to those family members who did not live within the same household, was quite limited. The true fighting unit in the struggle for survival was the nuclear family, and in times of need it could rely only on more or less weak support from members of the extended family.

16

Confraternities and Social Life

In traditional Jewish society the life of the individual was inevitably defined by two institutions: the family and the *kehila*. Born into the former, he was forced to accept the dominance of the latter because of its powers of enforcement and control. But there was also room outside these two spheres for forms of social activity in which not all members of either the family or the *kehila* participated. These ranged from friendships between individuals to the formation of groups dedicated to specific economic, political, religious, or social purposes. Such social activity could be merely temporary in nature, but sometimes the grouping recurred often enough to became a permanent, defined association separate from the family and the *kehila*. In such cases we may speak of a secondary group within the *kehila*. If the association was formally organized, with defined goals and rules of procedure, and especially if there were criteria of eligibility for membership, a formal division of tasks, and rules about relations among members, then we may speak of a confraternity (*ḥavura*). The confraternity differs from the *kehila* in its restrictedness: only those who wished to do so would join, and not everyone was accepted for membership.

There was presumably some room for free social activity and temporary social association in all communities, however small. But formally organized confraternities are a product of population increase and social differentiation, as occurred among Ashkenazic-Polish Jewry during the sixteenth through eighteenth centuries. In the smaller communities, even spontaneous group activities seem to have remained within the institutions of the *kehila*. This was true, for example, of Torah study among adults.[1] On the other hand, in communities numbering in the hundreds of thousands, the overall organization of the *kehila* was, in the first place, too large to serve as a framework for social-religious activity by its members. Second, with the increase in the number of people in the community, the likelihood also arose that individuals would find others who shared their own interests and level of ability and that they would join together in activities that set them apart from the rest of the community.

Synagogues as a Divisive Factor. The first split in a community might well derive from necessity rather than conscious choice. As population grew, the local synagogue would simply no longer be able to hold all the worshipers. More recent immigrants and those who had newly reached adulthood would be forced, against their will, to find a new place in which to pray. In places where people of different ethnic origin and customs settled, the liturgy in the new synagogue might differ from that in the old. But even if exactly the same liturgy was used, and no new essential religious split or variation was expressed, a social split was created de facto. First, a different social status was attached to each synagogue, based on seniority or other factors.[2] Moreover, the frequent daily contact among members of a given synagogue was likely to create a social division vis-à-vis members of the other synagogues. The significance of this distancing becomes clear if we remember the sociological importance of religious ceremony for the participants. As we shall see in chapter 17, the daily religious ceremonial could provide a framework for group identity. Undoubtedly, different customs developed ex post facto in the different synagogues. Even if these were merely minor variations with no halakhic importance—differing tunes, the addition of specific chapters of Psalms, a change in the time of prayers (such as waiting after the afternoon prayer in order to say the evening prayer on time or reciting the *shma* at dawn *ke-vatikin*) and the like—they would foster a sense of uniqueness among the members of each synagogue and create divisions even within the intimate sphere of religion. Of course, there was even more of a tendency to social differentiation wherever truly new approaches to the essence of prayer took hold and different patterns of behavior and new customs arose—in the East as a result of the spread of Kabbala and the rise of Hasidism, and in the West with the beginnings of Reform. But individuals and small groups had even earlier sought to create separate *minyanim* (small prayer circles) for themselves, and the communal leadership had been powerless to stop the process.[3] The religious variation implicit in the rise of Hasidism and Reform only completed the weakening of the *kehila* framework already underway.

The Burial Society (Ḥevra Kadisha) and Its Functions. The organization of the prayer service and the development of the synagogue provide one of the main themes in the history of the social differentiation of Jewish communal life; the social element is hidden behind the ostensibly religious facade. This was also true for most of the formal associations that organized around specific objectives. The association's right to exist derived from its identification with one of the accepted social values: the study of Torah, charity, or the performing of various types of *gmilut ḥesed* (acts of loving-kindness). The value of providing proper burial for the dead, referred to as *ḥesed shel emet* (literally: an act of true loving-kindness) was the first to take on separate, institutionalized form.[4] The members of this association, eventually called the *ḥevra kadisha* (holy society), took it upon themselves to care for the dead and sometimes also to provide bedside care for the sick and dying. Even though there is already evidence for such confraternities in the Talmud and the writings of the medieval jurists (*rishonim*), the confraternities of our period were more than continuations of past institutions. The small Ashkenazic community of the Middle Ages had not required such a division of tasks within society. The existence of the confraternities is the product of life in large communities such as Prague and Frankfurt, in which the very size of the population prevented the members of the community from relating to the concerns of the individual. Once they were established in the big communities, these confraternities spread also to the smaller communities, which might not have otherwise needed them.

The *ḥevra kadisha* answered two sets of needs: those of its members and those of the community at large. On the one hand, the society guaranteed its members that in their own hour of need they would all be taken care of in accordance with the full ritual traditionally prescribed for death and burial. On the other hand, the existence of the society allowed for the transfer of at least the essential core of the obligation to provide *ḥesed shel emet*—that is, to bury one's fellow Jew in a Jewish cemetery—from the community to the confraternity. But even when all of the *kehila*'s responsibilities relating to burial were transferred to the confraternity, the latter did not therefore become a part of the *kehila* administration. Members retained certain special rights: They were buried in a desirable location, the funerary ritual was conducted with special care for them, and so forth. Therefore the *ḥevra kadisha* remained a closed society, and membership in it depended, at least in theory, upon possession of appropriate personal qualities. The members of the society saw themselves, and were seen, as a sort of ethical social elite.

Other Religious Confraternities. The other associations also justified themselves on the grounds of one or another of the religious ideals accepted by society. There were associations for study that sponsored Torah classes at various levels of expertise, charitable societies that were concerned with the needs of the poor in general or with the particular needs of a specific group, such as dowering brides of good but poor families or providing heating fuel to scholars.[5] There were also *talmud tora* societies, which cared for the education of the poor or of all the youth of the *kehila*. All of these were tasks that in essence belonged to the general *kehila* organization, and in the absence of special confraternities they were carried out to one degree or another by the *kehila*.

Artisans' Associations. An apparent exception to what we have said here would appear to be provided by the artisans' associations found in Moravia, Bohemia, and Poland-Lithuania beginning in the seventeenth century. These confraternities were devoted to maintaining the economic status of their members by the typical methods of the time: protecting the interests of Jewish artisans vis-à-vis their Christian competitors, systematizing relationships among the Jewish artisans themselves, controlling competition among them and keeping out anyone not recognized as a craftsman, supervising production quality, and ensuring propriety in relations with the customer.[6] In this sense, membership in these associations was not voluntary. All practitioners of that craft were required to belong.

But this is the exception that proves the rule. Contemporaries saw no justification for any association that did not engage in realizing one of the religious and ethical values of the society. Thus these associations also defined themselves and functioned as promoters of social values —offering public prayers, maintaining a rabbi or teacher, helping those of their fellows who had fallen on hard times, and generally coming to each other's aid in life, and sometimes even in death. The economic motivation that led to the initial formation of these associations on a craft basis was insufficient to justify their existence. Only dedication to the practical religious obligations typical of the other confraternities lent public approval to the artisanal associations. We have here more than merely ex post facto rationalization: The founders and members saw it as legitimate to refer to these artisanal associations as "holy" confraternities, just as was done with regard to the other associations. Economic interests and religio-ethical values were intertwined from the start. The latter not only justified the existence of the associations; they also aided in maintaining the groups by providing the identity symbols and by creating the atmosphere of mutual interrelations without which the association would probably not have been able to survive, for all its clear economic purpose.[7]

Incidental Activities of the Confraternities. The confraternities always functioned in more than one area. Even if its ostensible purpose was promotion of one of the sacred traditional values, each confraternity came incidentally to fulfill other functions as well. The members of burial and charitable societies also established fixed times for study together, while a study group often served to provide mutual aid to its members. There were also confraternities, such as the society for providing firewood or the one for distributing free *ẓiẓit* (ritual fringes), whose declared purpose was no more than a sort of pro forma justification to create an organization whose major activities were along such "incidental" lines, such as organizing study groups or maintaining a synagogue.[8] The confraternities also engaged, whether sporadically or on certain fixed occasions, in totally secular activities. Every confraternity sponsored celebrations and banquets for its members—as when a new Torah scroll was installed in the synagogue, the group study of a Talmudic tractate was completed, or the "society dinner" was held to commemorate some event in the history of the association or an important date in Jewish tradition. Thus the dinners and celebrations were accepted as legitimate because they could be associated with the general air of sanctity that justified all of the confraternities' activities, and in this way they were spared the ethical suspicions that applied to all social entertainment that had no link to a religious-ethical purpose.

Legitimizing Social Recreation. The need to impose a religio-ethical context on essentially "neutral" social activity is typical of this society. Social activity per se—that is, gathering together for the sake of simply enjoying being in a group—was considered religiously and ethically dangerous. If the grouping included men and women, the danger was an erotic one. As we already noted in chapter 14, the regnant sexual ethic required males to remove any thought of sin from their heart and to distance themselves from anything that was likely to stimulate the senses erotically. Social diversions involving both sexes were therefore considered an intentional incitement to sinful thoughts.[9] There was even some ethical suspicion concerning social gatherings of members of the same sex. These were considered temptations to the sins of gossiping, maligning, and quarreling.

The Religious Obligation to Study Torah versus "Wasting" Time. On another level, social gatherings were also rejected as a waste of time. Ideally, a man was to use his time only for Torah study. Any time, however brief, that remained after the performance of the obligatory commandments, earning one's livelihood, and taking care of the other necessities of life was to be devoted to the study of the Torah. In practice this ideal was actually achieved only by a few special individuals who devoted their time totally to the Torah. But the theoretical obligation remained an unquestioned part of the social consciousness and was promoted even by the popularized halakhic and ethical works aimed at the masses. This widely accepted ideal further discouraged any activity that was merely social entertainment. Any social diversion, even a friendly meal or the invitation of a friend to one's house without an ostensible religious justification, was considered a waste of time and a distraction from study—aside from the other concerns it raised.[10]

Of course, there was a great difference between the demands of principle and the realities of life—more so here than in most other areas of religion and ethics. The ideal of total devotion to study was, first of all, innately difficult to fulfill. But even beyond that, there was a tremendous difference in ability between those who espoused the ideal and those expected to fulfill it. While Torah scholars were capable of devoting their time exclusively to independent study, individuals with little Torah education had to be content with following a lesson taught by someone else. They could "fix times for Torah study" in their homes or within the framework of public institutions, but this still left time—a little or a lot, depending on circumstances and social class—that had to be spent in some way.

Social diversion was not totally absent from the community; rather, it was limited, restricted, and, to some extent, frowned upon. Walks on the Sabbath and holidays, dances on vacation days, and games such as cards and chess were to be found almost everywhere. Community *takanot* limited such diversions to specific days and events; for instance, a woman recuperating from childbirth was allowed to play cards with her female neighbors.[11] But social entertainments and other neutral forms of association were never totally eliminated. Nor was there really a clear and decisive desire to do so.

Religious Meals. In the end, the need to socialize could not be satisfied by means that involved circumventing recognized prohibitions. Those who aspired to live up to the high ethical demands of the religious ideology and Halakha could never be satisfied with such artificial rationalizations. For such people, and thus for the entire society, the solution lay along a different path: the intertwining of social diversion into the network of institutions whose religio-ethical function camouflaged their secular aspects. The family and the confraternities provided the framework for all social activity. Actually, even these institutions were not entitled to sponsor social events per se, but in-their capacity as the accepted social framework for religious ceremonies, they provided opportunities for legitimate socializing as well. People tended to take advantage of this license and to expand it as far as possible. A family occasion such as a wedding, for example, expanded into many parties. A long series of festive meals came both before and after the main wedding meal. Similarly a circumcision was anticipated by a party the evening before as well as by the *zakhar* party on the preceding Sabbath eve. In some places, there was yet another meal, on the third day after the circumcision. There were also those who held a party upon naming a baby daughter and in honor of the new mother's first leaving her house and coming to the synagogue. The ceremony for redeeming a firstborn son was everywhere a reason for inviting in friends. A meal in honor of a Bar Mitzva was, in this period, a fixed custom, to celebrate the first time a young man was called to the reading of the Torah. There were those who added to it a party on the Sabbath when a boy, at an earlier age, was first honored with the recitation of the reading from the prophets in the synagogue. The building of a new house justified a house-warming party.[12] The halakhists tried, in their way, to fix which of these parties were to be considered *se'udot miẓva* (religiously obligatory meals) which the Talmud permitted, and in which even scholars were allowed to participate. They tended to expand the category and to include within it even meals that the Talmud and early codifiers had not mentioned or had not considered *se'udot miẓva*.[13] In the popular consciousness, all such meals ceased being "optional"—that is, mere opportunities for socialization—even if the halakhists did not find any basis to authorize them as *se'udot miẓva*. The leaders of the *kehilot* and other organizations aspired to limit such socializing. Their motives were both economic and social: They sought to limit the waste of money on the consumption of luxuries and to limit social competition among individuals and between social classes.[14] But the *takanot* of communities and other organizations never tried to forbid such parties outright; they sought only to limit their size and to ensure that the guests were closely related to the family.

These *takanot* assumed an ascetic character only during periods of great public mourning, as, for example, after the pogroms of 1648–49, when the Lithuanian Council made the usual restrictions much more severe and forbade, inter alia, the playing of musical instruments "even for the entertainment of the bride and groom . . . except at the wedding ceremony itself and at the ceremony of veiling the bride [*bedeken*]."[15] But this prohibition was limited right from the start to a three-year period, and the basic concept that the institution of the family legitimized social diversions was not abrogated.

The same was true with regard to the confraternities. The learned societies held parties upon completing a Talmudic tractate, and these meals were considered *se'udot mizva*, that is to say, religiously obligatory.[16] But the annual banquets of the other confraternities, especially those of the burial societies, could not rely on the traditional sources for legitimation. There is some evidence that the custom of banqueting, as, indeed, some of the ceremonial detail involved in these banquets, was taken over from local Christian confraternities.[17] But the participants were normally unaware of the historical origins of these rituals. The meal was lent a Jewish, and indeed a sacred, character by the fact that it was preceded by a day of fasting and by linking it to a date of some significance in the Jewish calendar—the seventh of *Adar*, the day of Moses' death, or the like. And of course, everywhere the meal was capped by a scholarly discourse on the Torah, an edificatory address, and the singing of Psalms and hymns. There were even attempts to draw upon the Jewish tradition in order to lend a metaphorical meaning to the rituals practiced.[18] The participants felt that the meal was divested of any day-to-day, secular associations. At the same time, it served as a time of fellowship for the members, and distinguished between them and the rest of the *kehila* who did not belong to the society. With less ritual, but with an approach very close to that of the burial societies, the members of the other confraternities celebrated their particular holidays. The overall function of these parties was to satisfy the need to socialize under the aegis of accepted values and institutions.

The Middle Classes and the Confraternities. To complete our sociological analysis of the confraternities we must now ask in what way they contributed to the maintenance of the society as a whole, to preserving its structure and values. We must seek the answer to this question in the fact that the emergence and growth of the confraternities was linked to the growth and expansion of the *kehila*. A *kehila* of hundreds, and sometimes thousands, of members could not transmit the feeling of direct belonging that the individual needed. Moreover, the positions of leadership in the central *kehila* institutions were quite limited in number; most members of the society had no opportunity for public activity. These two factors encouraged individuals to establish or join confraternities.

The confraternities were established and functioned under the control of the central leadership, and in some instances a part of the association's leadership was appointed directly by the *kehila*.[19] At least, the elections among the members of the confraternity were held in the same fashion as in the institutions of the *kehila* itself.[20] It seems that the founders of the confraternities, and those who were active in them, were members of the middle classes who were capable of public activities but who could not hope for a role in the central leadership of the community. The "middle-class" nature of the confraternities is clear when we note that their spiritual leaders were always preachers (*magidim* and *darshanim*) rather than halakhic scholars of the first order. The same was true with regard to the lay members: The most experienced and wealthiest Jews were normally drawn to the central administration, while the middle ranks had to be satisfied with leadership of the confraternities.

The Confraternities as Instruments of Social Control. Even though there was sometimes tension and even real struggles between the confraternities and the central *kehila* administration, on the whole the *kehila* profited from the existence of these societies. The fact that a large number of people were thus provided with opportunities for communal activity prevented excessive competition for positions within the primary leadership. On the other hand, young people and those of the middle class found a way to test their mettle in communal activity on a lower level, prior to assuming responsibility for leadership of the entire congregation.[21] The societies also served as social loci for mutual control, something that was difficult for the larger *kehila* to provide. While membership in a closed confraternity lent prestige, it also demanded that the individual live up to the values that the society espoused. Sometimes this responsibility was explicitly stated in the society's *takanot*. The members of the confraternity might be threatened with fines if they did not appear for prayers or classes.[22] The leadership of the confraternity reserved the right to expel any member who was found not to live up to its particular values and to those of society as a whole.[23] But the control was exercised primarily not through formal mechanisms but through the creation of a framework by which members of the societies could identify with the values represented by their group. And guaranteeing loyalty to the particular values of the confraternity meant also guaranteeing loyalty to the values of society as a whole.

17

Religious Institutions

In our description of Jewish society, we have repeatedly come across religious concepts and institutions affecting all aspects of life: relations with the gentiles, economic activities, communal administration, organization of the family and society, and, as we shall see in the next chapter, education. Everywhere, religious values set the goals and encouraged or forbade given actions. Indeed, the traditionalism that we have labeled as the defining characteristic of this society was religious in content, and religion provided the justification for preserving all aspects of that tradition. Even halakhically trivial details such as one's style of dress or one's language were granted at least a secondary religious basis, if they were not brought fully under halakhic *imprimatur.*[1]

But the all-pervasiveness of religion should not be understood to mean that there was no specifically religious sphere or that there were no specifically religious institutions. Even in this so-to-speak completely religious society there were areas in which religion was the ultimate purpose of an institution and not merely a background factor in its governance. Both the synagogue and the rabbinate were explicitly aimed at satisfying religious needs—the former as a place for public worship and religious ceremonial, and the latter as the judicial and regulatory authority deriving its legitimacy from religious law. While it may be true that in practice the synagogue also served as a social gathering spot and the rabbinate as an adjunct of the communal government, these functions were secondary and ex post facto.

Let us look first at the rabbinate and the way in which it fulfilled the religious functions for which it was primarily designed. We use the term "rabbinate" here in a somewhat different sense than we did when discussing the *kehila*. Then, we were speaking of an office granted formal recognition within the *kehila* structure. The local rabbi was given the authority to regulate and decide any matter that could be defined as religious. As a result of holding this authority, the rabbi became a sort of representative symbol of the *kehila* vis-à-vis both Jews and gentiles. Thus, the rabbi's authority derived from the *kehila*, just as the *kehila* was strengthened by the religious legitimacy of the rabbi even in economic and financial spheres, where religion played a regulatory role at best.

But the rabbinate existed in Jewish society independent of the *kehila* organization. As a religion of positive precepts (or, at least, as one including positive precepts), Judaism required an authorized body to rule on questions that were likely to arise and that the layman was incapable of deciding. A Jewish education and participation in the life of the community usually gave the average Jew sufficient knowledge of the tradition to conduct his daily life. But circumstances changed and the unusual or unexpected arose on an almost daily basis. Questions about the dietary laws, worship, or the prohibition of work on the Sabbath and festivals were always likely to arise. No one could know what was expected in every situation solely on the basis of common practice, especially if the issue was one over which even the more erudite halakhists disagreed. Questions occasionally arose for which even the learned did not have a ready answer. Such cases called for a decision by qualified persons who not only were thoroughly versed in tradition, but also regarded themselves as authorized to interpret it and to apply accepted rules to new circumstances.

Those who, in fact, fulfilled this rabbinical role were the scholars and recognized halakhic authorities, whether or not they held official *kehila* appointments. In this sense, the existence of the rabbinate did not derive from, nor was it dependent upon, the *kehila* organization. It stemmed, rather, from the essential nature of Judaism. We can be more specific. The rabbinate emerged out of both aspects of the tradition: the tradition as it was expressed in social institutions (the family, the synagogue, etc.), and the literary tradition, which could be mastered only through purposeful study and inquiry. The Jew could "act as his own rabbi" only to the extent that he had acquired traditional knowledge and mastered its decision process. He had to "acquire a rabbi" to the extent that he had to ask others to decide religious-halakhic questions for him. It was irrelevant whether the rabbi in question held a formal position or was simply serving as a scholar and teacher. Indeed, during our period, the right to decide what was permitted and what forbidden in halakhic terms was never restricted to holders of rabbinic office.

Though there were certain prerequisites, of which we shall speak below, the title *morenu* (our teacher) was conferred on anyone who had attained a certain level of halakhic scholarship, and it authorized the recipient to hand down halakhic decisions whether or not he held rabbinic office at the time. It was not even absolutely essential that he hold the title *morenu*. If no one with this title was available, anyone who was versed, or felt that he was versed, in the relevant sources might lay down the law. Only in such very weighty halakhic issues as divorce and *ḥaliẓa* (levirate marriage) was it regarded as essential that the authority be ordained, or even that he hold an official rabbinical post.[2]

In any case, the function of deciding the Halakha was in fact concentrated in the hands of those who were ordained and held office, even if not necessarily the office of *kehila* rabbi. Judges, heads of *yeshivot* (who were not always rabbis), preachers, and even teachers were all assumed to be competent to issue rulings, each in accordance with his level. To whom an individual directed his question was a function of the faith he had in the ability of a given figure to decide the matter. Whether the authority would answer the question himself or redirect it to a higher authority depended in turn on his own conscience and his view of his own abilities. There was a sort of unofficial hierarchy of scholars qualified to rule on Jewish law even though its ranks were not clearly defined or marked. "Spontaneous" public opinion in the *kehila*, in the supra-*kehila*, or even within the Jewish world at large determined the place of each jurist in this hierarchy of halakhic authority. Obviously, opinion was not always unanimous in evaluating different rabbinic figures. As a result, the spontaneous hierarchy could not guarantee authoritative rulings, much less could it institutionalize judicial review of "lower" courts by "higher" ones (though rulings were sometimes set aside if they were questioned by a higher recognized authority).[3]

The existence of casuistic literature and summary codes such as the *Shulḥan Arukh* would appear to have simplified the task of issuing religious rulings, but in fact did not render the rabbinate superfluous. Mastery of this literature required halakhic training, and though halakhic learning was widespread in this period, authoritative knowledge remained the property of a small minority. In fact, the increased number of teachers and scholars implied not only that more individuals could rule on issues clearly decided in the halakhic literature but also that there would be more questions deriving from their study and from an education directed at detailed observance of the commandments. Such questions would never have occurred to the average Jew, who lived according to a tradition learned through daily practice. No one could ever be so expert in the tradition that he would by definition never have to ask the opinion of others. Unlike those of a Catholic priest, a rabbi's rulings were not issued ex officio on the basis of institutional authority. It was the rabbi's knowledge of the Halakha and his ability to deduce a new ruling from existing precedent that lent authority to his decisions. If the rabbi was unable to make up his mind definitely, he was not competent to judge. A sense of modesty and reluctance to decide for fear of making an incorrect decision sometimes kept even leading rabbinic authorities from handing down judgments on their own. Many *responsa* penned by leading authorities conclude with the proviso that their conclusions should be considered valid only if other authorities concurred.

Intellectual certainty and a sense of religious and ethical responsibility were what determined the limits of a rabbi's authority. Only the mystics (or, better, those who had undergone a mystical experience) saw their intellectual certainty as strengthened by transcendental inspiration. For them, the stock phrase "Thus did they instruct me from heaven" became a concrete expression of their state of consciousness.[4] But this transcendental source was never seen as providing more than psychological support for the individual's judicial abilities or an explanation for the rapidity with which a decision had been reached. Transcendent certainty remained irrelevant when it came to determining the halakhic basis of a ruling, and certainly in fixing the institutional authority of the jurist. The influence of the mystical experience was perceptible only between the lines, or on rare occasions from external evidence. In its public and communally recognized role, the rabbinate functioned as interpreter of, and advisor on, Jewish law. Its authority derived directly from that law. A rabbi's official and personal charismatic status were only psychological supports for his intrinsic authority. In terms of the norm that governed the rabbinate and determined its standards, that institution derived its status and effectiveness only from administration of the law and loyalty to it.

In addition to interpreting religious law, the rabbinate, in the broader sense that we have been using in this chapter, was charged with the task of public exhortation to the observance of the law. Unlike the issuing of halakhic rulings, which the rabbi did only when specifically asked, this urging and exhortation were spontaneous functions that the rabbi initiated on his own. The formal justification for such activity lay in the commandment "Thou shalt surely reprove thy neighbor" (Leviticus 19:17). In other words, Jewish mutual responsibility with regard to religious precepts was not limited in any way, either by geography or by class. In theory, nothing prevented anyone from rebuking his fellow man for misconduct; to the contrary, everyone had a clear obligation to do so. In practice, however, Judaism differed from other religious denominations in never developing "lay preachers" who would emerge from within the community and publicly point out the sins of co-religionists.[5] The reason for this lies, again, in the nature of Judaism—a religion of practical deeds and of casuistic ethics. Ignorance was regarded as at least as great an obstacle to the fulfillment of religious obligations as perverseness of heart. And while the enthusiasm of a lay preacher might be even more effective than the sermon of a scholar in correcting perverseness of heart, only a person qualified to lay down the law could cure ignorance. Aptness at administering reproof was not enough.

Indeed, the task of preaching had always been reserved for members of the scholarly class. The aim of their sermon was as much to teach as it was to admonish and inspire. Instruction in the sermon ranged from practical rulings on specific questions of religious law to truly abstract halakhic disquisitions. Talmudic casuistry, or *pilpul*, was then in its final and most radical stage of development. Even non-halakhic sermons included a sprinkling of biblical, midrashic, and Talmudic citations. This was true even in the popular sermons delivered to the general public by professional or amateur preachers. Since the sermon had to impart knowledge, the position of preacher was reserved for the knowledgeable expert who had been trained in a *beit midrash* (house of study) or *yeshiva*.

The role of preacher and the task of regularly admonishing the community on moral matters fell, at least in theory, to the *av bet din* (official *kehila* rabbi), who in this period represented the authority of the Torah in the life of the community. He was expected to deliver a sermon on at least two Sabbaths a year—on *Shabat ha-Gadol* (the Great Sabbath), immediately preceding Passover, and on *Shabat Tshuva* (the Sabbath of Penitence), between the New Year and the Day of Atonement.[6] The *Shabat ha-Gadol* sermon exemplified the instructional function of the rabbinate. The communal rabbi instructed his congregants in those special laws relevant to the upcoming holiday, and admonishments entered only as asides. On *Shabat Tshuva*, on the other hand, the need of the hour was to rouse the people to repent and the sermon was devoted to ethical exhortation and chastisement. Both of these major sermons were linked, in content and timing, to the ancient tradition. But depending on the size of the community, the individual rabbi's talents, and local custom, there might also be sermons on the festivals or on other special local and national occasions.[7]

In fact, the institution of preaching expanded to such an extent in our period that the local rabbi was no longer able to handle the role on his own. In the larger *kehilot*, official preachers were appointed whose principal function was to deliver sermons at fixed times and on special occasions.[8] Throughout this period there were also itinerant preachers, who held no regular position but wandered from place to place. They were paid for their sermons out of *kehila* and private funds.[9] Since the sermon did not involve binding halakhic rulings, the right to preach was not made dependent on the title *morenu*—that is, in effect, on rabbinic ordination. There never was ordination for preachers (as there was, for example, for ritual slaughterers). Some preachers were, of course, scholarly men, and in the larger *kehilot*, the position was often filled by individuals who were destined to become the halakhic leaders of their time. But in principle, specific requirements of training or knowledge were never spelled out for preachers. The preacher had only to prove that he could speak intelligently and well.[10] A measure of public control was required to prevent the possibly unbalanced, immoral, or heretical from appearing before the public. This was especially necessary after the rise of Sabbateanism and Hasidism, deviant movements whose spokesmen often used preaching as a method of publicizing their views. But the need for control was felt even earlier, particularly with respect to itinerant preachers, who lacked any fixed institutional tie.[11] Still, such control was not exercised formally. A written recommendation from some authority, or an interview with the local rabbi or lay leadership, was enough to open the doors of the synagogue to the preacher, unless there was a regulation that limited the right to preach to a rabbinic incumbent or the like.[12]

The existence of the institution of preaching, as we have said, should be understood in terms of its fundamental religious purpose: to fill the need for public exhortation. The preacher exploited the religious atmosphere of the synagogue and the inspiration of the Sabbath or festival service in order to remind the people of the system of values to which society adhered. The preacher used the yardstick of fundamental values to evaluate the behavior of his audience, or else he acted as the voice of public opinion in criticizing the community's institutions and leaders. The congregation and its leaders here allowed themselves to be reproached and did not respond, but we need not assume therefore that they actually put the preacher's words into practice. Though preaching was an institution of public criticism and control, it was not revolutionary even in the sense of seeking extremist consistency in the realization of accepted ideals.[13] There were some preachers whose presentations were marked not just by emotionalism but by an ecstatic tone that gave the audience a sense of exaltation and of having undergone a deep religious experience. These preachers sometimes succeeded in persuading their listeners to lead changed lives, confess their sins, and adopt self-imposed castigations to atone for their sins.[14] But as a rule, preaching played no revolutionary or reformatory role. It acted rather as an emotional safety valve, something in the nature of a public catharsis intended more to preserve the customary way of life than to inspire real change.

Aside from these fundamental religious and moral functions, the preacher incidentally answered other needs as well. His listeners gained intellectual pleasure from his exegetical insights. If on the practical level the preacher merely reminded his audience of things they had forgotten, on the academic level he was expected to come up with new ideas as introductions to his ultimate moral message.[15] It was the promise of some surprise that kept the attention of the congregation over a long period. The pilpulistic or casuistic approach, which had then established itself in the field of halakhic learning, also affected the style of preaching. On the one hand, the method made it easier to come up with new insights, often no more than the "discovery" of some imagined meaning in a verse or rabbinic saying, or an association between quite-distant concepts or verses. On the other hand, the widespread familiarity with the pilpulistic method of study trained the audience to follow the complicated argument on which the sermon was based.

At the height of the development of homiletics in the seventeenth and eighteenth centuries, outstanding preachers achieved amazing artistry in the construction of their sermons. An opening theme would serve as a central thread joining all sections of the talk. Sometimes that theme would disappear as the preacher went off on quite tangential matters, but suddenly it would reappear and give the audience a satisfying sense of coherence. Finally, the preacher would conclude by returning to his point of departure and offering a solution to the original problem that he had deliberately left open.[16] The listeners who had followed these mental gymnastics derived aesthetic pleasure from the tension and its release. Moralists questioned the legitimacy of this method of preaching, arguing that it used the words of the Holy Writ for amusement and made an entertainer of the preacher, whose real task was the moral guidance of his congregation.[17] As we shall see, these same arguments were used in slightly different terms against *pilpul* in Halakha. Entertainment in sermons was suspected of not being conducive to correct action; entertainment in study was suspected of diverting the student from discovery of the truth. In both spheres, we see religious values forced to do battle on their own territory with secular temptation.[18]

Next to the rabbinate, the second classic religious institution was the synagogue, the institution dedicated to public prayer. No Jewish community was without one. Here, too, in attempting to understand the functions and structure of the institution, we must concentrate first on extracting the significance of its basic function—public worship. This function was clearly a religious one. Prayer may be emptied of content if faith is undermined and the attachment to transcendental values weakened. But so long as prayer exists, it is nourished by the human need to approach God, to petition for one's needs, to confess sins, to seek communion with, or bond to, God (that is, to achieve *dvekut*, in the various senses in which that term was used), or even simply to leave the mundane sphere and enter the realm of the sacred.

The goals of private and public prayer varied even within traditional Jewish society in accordance with the religious convictions that lay behind it. But differing views concerning the nature and function of prayer did not prevent worshipers from participating in a common service. Only the devoted mystics gave public expression through the prayer service to their special views by changing the words of the liturgy or the way in which it was pronounced and by establishing their own places of worship.[19] In general, however, fixed traditional patterns for prayers reigned supreme.

These patterns had been handed down since the mishnaic period and even earlier, with a few minor elements added in the Middle Ages and through local usage. A Jew who moved from one place to another might encounter different melodies, variant readings, and unfamiliar customs in the new congregation, but these did not affect the basic, overall structure of the service. Within the territorial confines of a single center, such as the German-Polish one that we are discussing, distinctions were nothing more than slight variants that would not have prevented the newcomer from immediately, or quite soon, feeling comfortable in the new prayer setting.

Traditional Jewish prayer is public prayer, not only in its content, but even more so in the manner in which the ritual is performed. Halakha does require the individual to pray thrice daily, even when he is on his own, and such private prayer is considered complete fulfillment of one's obligation even when it would have been equally possible to attend a public service.[20] But in our period—in contrast to the mishnaic era itself—private prayer was seen as a last resort. The desirable and usual form of worship in those communities large enough to maintain a regular *minyan* (a quorum of ten males aged thirteen and over) was public prayer in the synagogue, the *beit midrash* (house of study), or a private home in which one or two rooms had been set aside and equipped for the purpose by the installation of an Ark with a Torah scroll. Such improvised synagogues were the rule in towns with small

Jewish populations, and they were later resorted to also in the large cities, when the decomposition of the communal framework began. But during the apogee of the traditional *kehila*, small and medium-sized *kehilot* had a single synagogue proper, while large *kehilot* would have a number of parallel synagogues as well. Even these auxiliary synagogues, however, preserved their public character and were subject to all local customs and to the authority of the community.[21] Somewhat more detached was the *beit midrash* of the *rosh yeshiva*, where the rabbi prayed together with his students whenever he was not obligated to appear at the *kehila* service.[22] Only the kabbalists of the Lurianic stream established truly secluded *batei midrash* or *kloyzim*, attended only by adherents of their specific liturgical tradition.

That public prayer was preferable to private was stressed even in Talmudic tradition. The first ten men to arrive at the synagogue were deemed especially meritorious, for they had ensured that public worship would be possible on that particular occasion. The superiority of public prayer even received tangible expression by the addition of the *kadish* and *kdusha* prayers, which could not be recited unless there were at least ten men present. Because of their quasi-mystical content and exclusively public character, these selections were accorded particular attention by the commentators and were considered especially important by the worshipers. Anyone who did not attend public prayer forfeited the reward that religious belief accorded such participation, and was in fact deprived of a religious experience.[23] But one way or another, the obligation to join the congregation in prayer as often as possible was based on the Jewish conception of the nature of prayer as it was traditionally practiced: Prayer was not simply composed of private entreaties. In certain passages where the cantor acted as a substitute for the congregation or as its leader, he would recite the prayer and the congregation would simply respond "amen." In other passages, the cantor would read the opening or closing lines, and the congregation would follow his tempo. Through his emotional exaltation and his awareness of his own role, the cantor became the representative of the community before God. His role was to project this sense of exaltation by rendering the liturgical melodies that were fixed by custom but that still left room for varied emphases in accordance with his own ability and taste.[24]

But alongside—or, better, at the very heart of—the shared public ritual of the prayer service there also lay fundamental elements of private prayer. This was not merely a case of the individual spontaneously pouring out his heart in the middle of the service. Rather, the individual was to concentrate carefully on the literal meaning of the liturgy or dwell upon secondary interpretations of the prayers that he had gleaned from the commentaries on the prayer book. The apex of such individual prayer was reached in the *shma* and the silent, individual recitation of the *amida*. At this point, the public context of prayer served only a preparatory function. The individual's readiness and ability to concentrate on the meanings of the words and on their associated implications were enhanced by the earlier shared parts of the service and by the awareness that he stood within a congregation. The danger that one would cease to pay attention to a well-known, even too-familiar, liturgy was recognized, and worshipers were repeatedly warned to train themselves to concentrate on the meaning of the prayers and to bear in mind the special concepts (*kavanot*) embedded in them.[25] Reciting one's prayers in a group in the synagogue was always considered one of the best mechanisms to ensure this. Paradoxically, therefore, the emphasis on personal prayer became a major motivation for encouraging individuals not to absent themselves from public prayer and not to be satisfied with praying in private.

The individual's desire to perform his duty in the best possible fashion was not the only factor behind public prayer. The congregation, as an organic unit, regarded itself as responsible for the maintenance of public worship. The right that the Talmud granted members of a congregation to force each other to erect a synagogue was later extended, with some qualification, to the right to force each other to maintain a quorum in the synagogue for daily prayers. Of course, this was even more the case with regard to prayer services on the Sabbath, Festivals, and the High Holy Days. Public prayer was equated with the *tamid*, the daily offering in the Temple, and failing to hold public prayer was therefore tantamount to abrogating that daily offering.[26] A community that had not been able to maintain this shared obligation saw itself as guilty not only because, as individuals, they had failed to fulfill a precept, but also because, as a community, they had lost something that in a sense legitimized their existence. The *ḥerem*—the decree of excommunication—derived its power from the individual's sense of obligation to participate in public prayer. The first stage of *ḥerem* was to deprive the offender of the right to participate in the service. Conversely, the importance of public prayer lent power to victims of injustice, who could interrupt the service and thus compel the congregation to attend to their grievance.[27] In the case of *ḥerem*, the individual felt himself excluded from the ranks of those privileged to take part in the cardinal obligation of public prayer; in the case of interrupted prayer, the entire congregation was prevented from performing this duty and saw itself as discredited and, so to speak, condemned before God.

As we mentioned before, the importance of praying with the congregation varied with the importance for the individual and the community of the specific day on the Jewish calendar. Even Mondays and Thursdays, though weekdays, were marked by extra prayers and by the reading of the Torah, which could not be duplicated in private prayer. Through their emotionally charged ceremonials, Sabbaths, Festivals, and of course the Days of Awe became occasions when the individual was almost totally identified with the community, even though the specific obligations that these days entailed—hearing the shofar on the New Year and fasting on the Day of Atonement, for example—did not require one to gather with the congregation.[28]

Public prayer had a social, as well as a religious, aspect. Social circumstances determined the extent to which this religious ideal could be realized, while the ideal itself also helped to shape social realities. For example, we need only recall that the daily obligation to participate in public prayer, morning and evening, implied that Jews live in compact neighborhoods, that they engage in types of work that did not require their continuous presence, and that the general conditions of production and existence did not yet demand that every moment be exploited in order to gain economic success. Synagogue attendance was facilitated where the workplace—a store or workshop—was located on the same premises as the home. When the menfolk were away—and it was only the men whose attendance was required in the synagogue—the women could substitute for them. At least it was not necessary actually to close the store at prayer times. Under such conditions, one could very well formulate a halakhic demand that the entire congregation assemble for public prayer twice a day and expect it to be implemented. The concentration of homes in one area also made it possible to announce the hour of prayer, and the beadle knocking on doors to summon worshipers was a characteristic feature of life in the Jewish quarter in this period.[29] Similarly, synagogue attendance was also easily subjected to mutual control, and the admonitions of the rabbis and preachers were supplemented by the informal criticism of the congregation itself. In the small *kehilot,* this control was exercised by the *kehila* leaders themselves, while in the large *kehilot,* it was accomplished through the *ḥavurot* (confraternities), which obligated their members to attend services and even maintained a certain measure of control in this regard.[30]

Even so, the ideal of the entire community attending synagogue twice daily was never realized completely. Certain occupations took some individuals away from the Jewish quarter, particularly at the hour of afternoon prayer during the short winter days. Servants, paid employees, and artisans were tied to their work at prayer times. The moralists and authors of *takanot* tended to make fewer demands of such people, insisting only that they attend synagogue on Mondays and Thursdays, when the Torah was read, or at least on Sabbaths and festivals.[31] The greater the significance of the day, the less need there was to encourage and demand synagogue attendance. There is ample evidence of preaching and moralizing regarding the importance of participation in public prayer on weekdays. But there is no trace of such sermonizing with regard to Sabbaths and festivals. Attendance was assured by the stronger drawing power of the synagogue on those days, and because the factors that stood in the way of the would-be worshiper during the rest of the week were now absent.

And just as social circumstances determined the extent of participation in public prayer, the emphasis on public prayer shaped social realities. The synagogue was given multiple secondary functions as part of the communal administration: It was there that warnings were issued, decrees of excommunication pronounced, and oaths taken, and it was exclusion from the synagogue that constituted the punishment of the disobedient. The synagogue itself required organization and management. These functions were entrusted to *gaba'im* (wardens), who discharged them in person or through beadles. The *gaba'im* were appointed in the same way as other communal leaders and sometimes the post of synagogue *gabai* served as the stepping stone to advancement because of the experience in leadership it afforded. And the synagogue also fulfilled less obvious social functions. As a regular meeting place for members of the community, it provided an opportunity for purely secular conversations and even for business negotiations.

Admittedly, religious law forbade discussion in the synagogue of any matter that did not concern the prayers themselves.[32] But precisely because of the frequency of meetings in the synagogue, this rule was no longer observed in our period. Indeed, the leaders themselves took advantage of the community gathering for their own purposes, and the rank and file followed their example. It is unlikely that they had any qualms about discussing business in the synagogue at those times when absolute silence was not required by the liturgy. But the principal social use of a visit to the synagogue was simply as a setting for light conversation, which arose in the course of the constant contacts among the worshipers. Even the formal Halakha distinguished between various parts of the service and required absolute silence only during the central prayers and major ceremonies. As for the rest, the prohibition of talking in the synagogue remained somewhat vague and ill-defined.[33] Strict and thoroughgoing moralists sometimes attempted to prohibit all secular talk within the confines of the synagogue. But the frequency of contacts between members of an all-inclusive congregation militated against acceptance of this stringency.[34] This demand could be realized only in the synagogues of groups of ascetics, which arose spontaneously within the community.

In addition to fulfilling its central task in the life of the community, the synagogue also provided a method of marking off the social strata within the community and of fixing the distinctions between various levels. Seating arrangements provided an opportunity for expressing these distinctions. Proximity to the Ark, the reader's desk, the rabbi's seat, or the platform from which the Torah was read all reflected one's relative importance. In addition, a seat in the row nearest the eastern wall (*mizraḥ*) had a value of its own. This was because those who sat there at times faced the congregation. Seats were purchased outright by the members of the congregation and they sometimes passed from father to son. It may well be that the seating arrangements did not always reflect the actual state of stratification, since it was quite common for social status to change from one generation to the next. The sons of good families held on to their honored seats even if others had meanwhile eclipsed them in terms of property or status. If a family were totally impoverished, however, they were usually stripped even of their synagogue seats.[35]

The synagogue offered the well-to-do various methods of displaying their wealth. Rich families could donate Torah scrolls, curtains for the Ark, and ritual objects. In a manner typical of the period, such gifts did not become an undifferentiated part of the public property: The donor's name was inscribed on his gift, and he and the members of his family were honored every time their gift was used at the appropriate time. More than once, a quarrel would break out over the question of whose gift should be used on a particular occasion.[36]

Another guide to a person's social rank lay in which *aliya* (being called to "ascend" to read a portion of the Law) he was given. Here, too, there were gradations, depending on the importance of the day and other considerations. *Aliyot* were purchased, the buyer either taking the honor for himself or bestowing it on someone else. They also served as an opportunity to announce contributions to charitable causes and, at the same time, as a means of publicizing one's financial capacities. Nevertheless, the honor of an *aliya* did not depend solely on financial considerations. The *kehila* and supra-*kehila* regulations reserved certain *aliyot* for those who represented other communal values: The local rabbi, the district rabbi, other scholars, and local or regional community leaders were also guaranteed an *aliya* in accordance with their status. The minuteness with which the rules were set forth in the regulations of both *kehilot* and supra-*kehilot*[37] is evidence of the sensitivity of people with regard to fixing a person's place on the social scale. The synagogue ritual afforded the principal opportunity for public demonstration of this status.

The assembly of the community on Festivals and Holy Days offered other opportunities to exhibit one's wealth not specifically linked to the service itself—through the clothes and jewelry one wore. Men could adorn themselves with silver *atarot*, or collars on their prayer shawls; women found the best opportunity for displaying their wealth and position in the luxurious items they wore to the synagogue. Sumptuary laws regulating the use of luxuries sometimes specifically exempted synagogue attendance, or were at least more lenient in its regard. Traditionally, the honor of the Sabbath and Festivals required one to be well dressed, and this could serve as a pretext for displaying social status.[38] Even if the intention of the individual was simply to observe the precept of glorifying the Sabbath or Festival, the fact remains that each person's appearance in public, dressed in keeping with his purse, served as a means of social classification.

The phenomena described above are secondary social functions that became attached to the religious institution, not always in accordance with its original aims and at times even in explicit opposition to them. Be that as it may, the chief social function of the synagogue was not in these incidental demonstrations. The synagogue served to maintain the society precisely where, and to the extent that, it avoided all involvement in social goals. The congregation that assembled for prayer united insofar as it succeeded in forgetting itself and communed, in accordance with its religious consciousness, with its God.

We have already observed that the more the religious ceremony was charged with sentiment and focused on the worshiper's experience, the more the individual was tied to the congregation in his worship. At the climax of Jewish public devotions, on the New Year and the Day of Atonement, when the likelihood was greatest that the individual would turn his thoughts away from his own interests and social ambitions, he was likely to be absorbed almost completely in his society and community. This experience of fusion, albeit temporary, must have left a lasting impression. The internal cohesiveness of the Jewish community was undoubtedly nourished by the depth of the ever-recurring religious experience of the ritual. Durkheim's judgment on the unity of religion and society is substantiated here, although not in the sense that religion loses its independence and becomes a mere function of society. Only where religion lives on its own independent resources—man facing God—is it unconsciously and paradoxically also transformed into a primary social preservative.

18

Educational Institutions

Until now, we have treated traditional Jewish society as static and unchanging. In that way, we were able to establish a ''base reading'' as a starting point for our investigation. But the picture would remain incomplete were we not now to add a description of the transformations and development that the society characteristically underwent over time. Change is inevitable even in traditional societies not enamored of change per se. Generations come and go, the aged must retire and the young must be incorporated into the social fabric. Every society must both consider, and actively prepare for, its future.

The fact that Jewish society was a traditional one—that is, that it based itself on knowledge and values drawn from the past—does not mean that it ignored the future. Rather, the Jews' strong attachment to the past meant that the *present* became less important; the *future*, on the other hand, became a time when, it was hoped, the values of the past would be restored. Future generations—and sometimes the one immediately to come—became bearers of this hope for the renewal of society. It was vital to involve the next generation in the effort to reform the future—paradoxically, through maintaining the tradition. As in every other idealistic society forced to compromise with reality, the hope for fully realizing the ideal was transferred to the coming generation. While it matured, the new generation was temporarily exempt from the struggles of life and did not have to resort to the compromises that reality imposed on the active members of society. It was logical that educational institutions became the chief representatives of society's values vis-à-vis the rising generation. In traditional Jewish society, informed by the ideal of fulfilling the religious heritage in its totality, educational institutions served to promote the traditional values and to transmit them to the new generation.

Family and Synagogue. The education and ''socialization'' of the new generation—that is, the introduction of the young into the framework of social life—was not carried out only by those institutions specifically designated for the purpose. The other institutions of society shared in this function, each within its own sphere. Though created originally to cater to the needs of the existing society, they were also charged with the auxiliary task of serving the requirements of the rising generation.

The foremost of these secondary institutions of education was, of course, the family, which, at least in one sense, was defined as a mechanism for providing for the needs of the next generation. But the family's educational role derived from more than biology. The traditional Jewish family served as a primary educational institution because of the role ascribed to it by society at large, because of the cultural values which it was assigned, and because of its internal structure. It was in the framework of family life that the child absorbed the atmosphere typical of traditional society as a whole. The structure of the family paralleled that of society. The father headed the family by virtue of the traditional values he represented. The mother was close to him in status, though not in authority. The children and the other members of the family each occupied a position in accordance with their age and ability.[1] The child who grew up in such a family was trained to think in hierarchical terms and was accustomed to a discipline in which the young obeyed their elders.

The family became a bearer of religious values because it was the locus for certain religious ceremonies, especially at meal times: daily, to the extent that the family dined together and recited the blessing before, and the grace after, meals; and then of course on Sabbath eve and at the Passover Seder.[2] The child's psychological attachment to his family gave an emotional dimension to the religious experience of participating in the ritual; both religious and family ties were strengthened and values were transmitted to the new generation.

The family similarly served, almost unconsciously, as an instrument of education as it fulfilled its various social functions. Through it, children participated in the principal framework for adult social activity, accompanying their parents on visits and receiving guests in their homes. Presumably it was in these early-childhood experiences that the foundations of broad family solidarity were laid. The child could observe the close relations and intimacy that existed between members of the extended family. Finally, to the many ways in which the family provided a "teaching environment" for children, we can add the expressly pedagogical tasks incumbent at least initially on its adult members: The child would learn good manners and moral behavior as well as the elementary customs of religion and tradition—prayers, benedictions, and the like—from the older members of the family, either through formal lessons or by simple and repeated imitation.[3]

The services at the synagogue occupied second place among the auxiliary educational institutions. From their earliest years, children attended the synagogue with their parents or, as we shall see, under the supervision of their teacher. The service was conducted by adults, and until they were almost thirteen, children played no active part. Still, they joined the congregation in reciting the prayers and in responding "amen." Through daily exposure, they learned the customs connected with the service, the text of the prayers, and the accompanying melodies.[4] Through direct participation in the prayer services on Sabbaths and holidays, the child acquired that total spiritual attachment to the religious community that gave life to the mythos through immediate contact with the divine. Similarly, it was in the synagogue that he acquired a portion of his knowledge of the ritual aspect of the tradition and absorbed, by listening to sermons and debates, at least part of what was formally taught in the educational institutions.

In this broader sense, all the *kehila* institutions must be regarded as mechanisms for educating the new generation. Under the cramped conditions of existence, with the activities of the public institutions as intertwined with one another as they were, it was obviously impossible to keep the children from seeing and hearing everything that took place in the community. The life of the community was carried on as in a public arena, before the eyes of young and old, and children absorbed whatever they were intellectually capable of absorbing. Thus, even though one could actively participate in communal government only from a relatively advanced age, and even though there were almost no special institutions in which younger people could gain political training,[5] effective leadership of the *kehilot* and other organizations was assured from generation to generation. Presumably, young people gained an understanding of the problems of government and leadership through observation of the actions of the leaders, and they gained experience by gradually taking on tasks of greater and greater responsibility once they had attained the age then deemed appropriate for public activity. Of course, sons and sons-in-law of the leading families had an advantage in this respect through their personal contact with those who already held office.

Practical Education. The child was prepared for making a living in a similar fashion. Here, too, there was no formal training of any sort. At the very most, we might argue that learning to write Yiddish or Hebrew and mastering the basics of arithmetic, either in the *ḥeder* or elsewhere, were tangentially preparatory for earning one's living. The children of the rich also had the opportunity to study the local vernacular or the language—often Latin—used by the government, under private tutors.[6] A knowledge of these languages made it easier to deal with the authorities, and a person with such knowledge had a better chance of winning the post of *shtadlan* and of exploiting his direct contacts with government representatives.

The knowledge required for running a business was acquired through practical experience. A good opportunity for this was offered by the first years of marriage, when the couple lived with one or another set of parents. The commercial methods in vogue among both Jews and non-Jews in this period made such a method of training feasible. The merchant's expertise was of a practical sort and did not involve systematic conceptualization or require prior theoretical training. The economic and financial considerations involved in successful business operations were nothing more than practical rules that anyone with a business sense could learn from an experienced guide. The same was true of the manual trades. The apprentice learned his trade by helping his master, observing him, and imitating him.[7] The training for other vocations—rabbis, preachers, teachers, and sextons of all types—was even less formalized. It is true that, with the exception of the sextons, these latter relied on knowledge they had acquired in a formal fashion, as we shall see below. But how to apply that knowledge in practice—in halakhic rulings, sermons, and classroom teaching—was learned by personal experience. At most, a rabbi might serve for a period as "clerk" to a well-known halakhic authority, and a teacher might assist someone more experienced than he. But as with the apprentice craftsman, this is training through service and observation. In this period, it was not customary to train anyone formally for any social role.

The Ḥeder and the Financing of Elementary Education. We must now define the methods and content of the *ḥeder* and the *yeshiva*—the society's two formal educational institutions. These sought to teach only that knowledge that constituted the essential value system of the society. Their principal function was to transmit Jewish tradition at various levels of difficulty and abstraction. The *ḥeder* supplemented the knowledge of tradition that the child absorbed directly from the society (via the family, the synagogue, the street, etc.) with the basic knowledge stored in the people's religious literature. In keeping with its broad-ranging communal function, the *ḥeder* was entrenched throughout the length and breadth of traditional Jewish society. Even the isolated Jew living in a remote village tried to keep a tutor for his children or to send them to a nearby town where they might be familiarized with the fundamentals of Judaism.[8] Nor did poverty usually stop parents from providing at least an elementary education for their children. By religious law, it was the father's duty to educate his children at his own expense. The extremely wealthy sometimes employed a private tutor for their children; the tutor lived with the family and served as both teacher and mentor to the children, with whom he stayed all day long.[9] But on the whole, education was carried on in an institution that, while not directly created by the community, was subject to public supervision. Though the primary obligation to educate the child fell to the father, education was regarded as more than a private duty. By Jewish law, hiring a teacher was one of the duties that members of a community could force each other to support. In this period matters rarely got to that point. For the most part there was an ample supply of teachers offering their services. The *kehila* thus did not bear the expense of instruction, and usually did not even have to organize the educational system. Its task was limited to supervising the teachers and providing for the education of those children whose parents could not afford to pay. In the smaller *kehilot*, these functions were entrusted directly to the *kehila* leaders. But in *kehilot* large enough to allow for differentiation in the allocation of duties, special trustees, known as *gaba'ei talmud tora*, were appointed for this task. In other *kehilot*, there were special associations, known as *ḥevrot talmud tora*, whose officers were responsible for supervising the teachers and, especially, for ensuring the education of the poor. Fulfilling this function required considerable financial resources. Accordingly, certain sources of income were specially allocated to the *talmud tora* fund. Part of the general contributions made in the synagogue were set aside for this purpose. The *talmud tora* trustees were also permitted to solicit donations on certain occasions. In some localities, a tax was levied on the members of the *kehila* to cover the education of needy children. Special teachers were employed, and occasionally, special premises were set aside for this purpose. Elsewhere the poor were given direct aid to help them pay for private lessons. In yet other places, private teachers hired for the children of the well-to-do were required to teach a poor child free of charge or at a reduced fee. Except in the smallest *kehilot*, where there were not enough families to support a private tutor, it was not common for the community itself to hire a single teacher for all the children.[10]

Public Supervision of the Ḥeder. Education was therefore a "public" responsibility not in an organizational or financial sense, but only insofar as the community supervised and controlled it. But the community's supervisory role did not include the selection of qualified teachers through prior examination. Since there was no formal licensing system for teachers akin to the *smikha* for rabbis or *kabala* for ritual slaughterers, nothing could prevent any local resident from hiring himself out as a teacher through a private arrangement with a parent. Only nonresidents, who would anyway have been watched by the community, were required to obtain official permission to practice their profession. And even in such cases, supervision was more a matter of deciding whether or not to let such newcomers live in the town than of any real judging of their professional abilities as educators. Only if such foreign teachers became a serious threat to the livelihood of locals were they asked to demonstrate their pedagogical abilities, something that could justify employing them even though they came from the outside and did not hold the *ḥezkat yishuv*. Sometimes such proof of ability was also demanded of locals, as in cases where it was decided that only those who had been granted the title "*ḥaver*" from the local rabbi might serve as teachers. Even so, such a title attested only to the individual's personal learning and to the fact that he had followed the accepted path of formal education by spending a number of years in a *yeshiva*.[11] Thus, such control as did exist applied, at the very most, only to the teacher's knowledge, while his pedagogical ability could be proven only in the course of actual teaching. The success of a teacher was measured by his pupils' level of achievement. It was customary for the pupils to be examined periodically by public officials: the rabbi or someone acting for him, the *gaba'ei talmud tora*, or someone else specifically appointed for the purpose.[12]

Supervision was aimed primarily at ensuring the conditions necessary for successful teaching. The teacher was not allowed to take on more students than it was considered possible to teach, he might not reduce the number of instructional hours, and he was not to engage the children in non-educational tasks.[13] Supervisors also looked into fee schedules, the times of payment, the method of collection, and the prevention of unfair competition when the supply of teachers was greater than the demand.[14] Supervisors also ensured that parents did not put their children to work or place them as domestics at an age when it was customary to have them at school. The minimum working age varied from place to place, but it generally ranged between thirteen and fifteen.[15]

Thus, elementary education in the *ḥeder* was entrusted, in essence, to teachers distinguished by neither knowledge nor formal training for their job. Even though society placed a high value on teaching, the *melamdim* who actually performed this task were given neither status nor prestige. They were trapped in a job that demanded all their time, paid little, offered no chance for advancement, and left them totally dependent on the goodwill of others.

The Curriculum. It was a religious duty to educate one's child, and the community cajoled and pressured its members to fulfill this obligation. Consequently, almost everyone in the society had a traditional education, and what was absorbed during those first stages of *ḥeder* education became the basis of the national and religious consciousness of the entire community. The earliest years were devoted to Bible study—at first in translation into the local vernacular, and then with the commentary of R. Solomon ben Isaac (RaSHI).[16] The special status of the Jews as a chosen people, the essential and mythic distinction between Jews and the other nations, an understanding of the fate of the Jewish people in exile, and a belief in the people's ultimate redemption—all of this penetrated the child's consciousness through the popular homiletic illumination of RaSHI's commentary, itself originally written with a didactic purpose in mind during a period of great religious tension and awareness in the Middle Ages.[17] Children thus acquired the fundamentals of their faith through study of the classic texts, particularly the Pentateuch with RaSHI's commentary. While the teachers might also review and emphasize these fundamental principles, there was never any attempt at teaching them systematically. The lack of systematization and comprehensiveness in pedagogical goals was a typical feature of this educational system. Even in teaching the Pentateuch, rather than following the biblical story consecutively, the teacher would begin the section to be read that week in the synagogue, even if he had not finished the portion of the week before.[18]

There was a close tie between the school and the synagogue dating back to the very beginnings of Jewish schooling in antiquity, a link that was strengthened by the need to prepare the students for participation in the main prayer service and Torah reading on the Sabbath. This link took precedence over any desire to establish a pedagogically logical course of study based on the nature of the material itself. Even the practical requirements of the halakha were taught only as time would permit and as the need to know them arose in the life of the congregation. Aside from laws needed on a daily basis by the children (blessings, the laws of phylacteries just before the boy reached the age of Bar Mitzva, etc.), the laws of the holidays were studied only as the specific holiday approached.[19]

By any rational criterion, this method of teaching must be considered unsatisfactory, and the system had its critics—notably R. Judah Loew (MaHaRaL) of Prague. Despite the considerable public attention paid to education, there were those who never learned to read, much less to write or even to sign their own name. Even those who did absorb what the *ḥeder* had to offer were left with only fragmentary knowledge.[20] Still, from the point of view of social function, this education achieved what was required of it. Anyone who attended a *ḥeder*, even if only for a few years, would have absorbed the rudiments of the tradition and could help to preserve it. Even if he did not know its details, he knew what it required of him. His knowledge and religious attachment were sufficient for him to join the congregation in prayer and follow its major customs.

Critics of the *ḥeder* attributed its academic shortcomings in part to the fact that teachers failed to adjust the curriculum to the pupil's age and mental capacity. Familiarity with the Bible and training in Mishna were seen not as accomplishments in themselves but only as preparatory to the ultimate educational goal: creating a *talmid ḥakham* who had extensive knowledge of the Talmud and halakhic codes. Obviously only a small minority of students could hope to attain this ideal—those with the ability and the desire to devote many years to their studies at a *yeshiva*, traditional society's highest educational institution. Nevertheless, the *ḥeder*, an institution apparently designed to serve the general public, was also made subservient to the ambitions of the minority. Pupils were introduced to Talmud before they had acquired a fundamental knowledge of the Bible or even of the Pentateuch. The *melamed* was evaluated primarily with respect to his achievements in the area of Talmud. Clever teachers, whose livelihood depended after all on making a good impression on parents, perfected techniques, such as rote memorization, that led to remarkable accomplishments, which were illusory and even harmful in the opinion of some of the best of their critics.[21] Ultimately, however, the *ḥeder* was simply a reflection of the system of values upon which all of Jewish society was built. Even if only a minority could actually engage in it, study of the Talmud was a primary value for the entire society. The educational goals for the people as a whole, knowledge of the fundamentals of Judaism and the fulfillment of its precepts, were considered as no more than by-products of an educational system directed at developing Talmudic scholars.

The *ḥeder* was only a first, preparatory stage in the journey toward this ultimate goal. The educational setting for the training of Talmudic scholars was the *yeshiva*. This institution depended, first of all, on the presence of a rabbi who was himself a *talmid ḥakham* capable of teaching Talmud and the halakhic codes. He had not only to know the material; he had to be able to generate new insights into the sources on his own. Of course, the level of one's knowledge and originality cannot be defined in exact terms. What was expected would vary from place to place. There was no formal license for the head (*rosh*) of a *yeshiva* (as there was for a rabbi), nor was there any institutionalized supervision of the *yeshiva* (as there was of the *ḥeder*). An individual's suitability to head a *yeshiva* might be raised formally during the appointment process of a new communal rabbi (in those areas where he served also as *rosh yeshiva*), but ultimately, suitability was decided by whether or not he was accepted by the broader society of the learned and whether or not he could attract students. As students would come and go, moving from one *yeshiva* to another, the reputation of specific scholars would spread and a consensus emerge about their relative merits. Though of course it was always possible to influence and direct public opinion in an "illegitimate" manner, it is reasonable to assume that this sort of free public criticism usually managed to keep the level of study as high as possible.

Supra-communal Aspects of the Yeshiva. This brings us to one of the most outstanding characteristics of the *yeshiva*. Unlike the *ḥeder*, a local institution that did not serve people from outside the town except in cases where such children were sent to live with local families, the *yeshiva* was an institution that provided education to individuals from a number of different communities, sometimes quite far apart.[22] This is partly a function of the age of the pupils. The *melamed* taught students up to twelve or thirteen years of age; after that point, students would usually enter a *yeshiva*. These teenagers were both capable of living outside the family setting and eager to do so—to leave their family and spend their adolescence among people of their own age in the circle of a specific *rosh yeshiva*. It was not only a matter of wanting to study with a teacher on a level higher than what might be available locally. Even youths from large communities who had fine teachers at hand would nevertheless leave home and travel elsewhere. By cutting himself off from his family and associating completely with his educational institution, the young man was able to devote his adolescence totally to the development of the life of the spirit. He was freed from any worries about making a living and uninvolved in the daily activities of the society. He took no part in its economy, politics, or even volunteer activities. In return, he was assured that if he had the requisite intellectual ability and moral character, he would eventually become one of the spiritual leaders of that community. Society was sufficiently differentiated to allocate leadership to a defined class, that of *talmidei ḥakhamim*, or talmudic scholars. Hence the development and transmission of spiritual values had to occur in institutions cut off from other aspects of life. In such institutions, which brought together pupils from around the region, we see clearly articulated the internal cultural unity of each area within the Diaspora. In this sense, the wanderings of the *yeshiva* students clearly defined the cultural-geographic extent of each center.

It was the out-of-town students who lent the *yeshiva* its particular character. The nucleus of the *yeshiva* would be formed by those pupils who depended for their right of residence, their local ties, and even their daily bread on the rabbi.[23] Once that nucleus had formed, local elements might join: pupils just beginning their studies, young men living with their in-laws, and other householders and scholars who came to hear the lectures at the *yeshiva*.[24] But even though locals often formed a significant part, and sometimes even the majority, of the student body, they remained on the periphery of the institution—the reverse of the situation with all other communal institutions, which were always dominated by the local Jews. The "foreign" students formed the heart of the *yeshiva* because only they fulfilled the criteria of total dedication to learning and absolute and perfect dependence on the rabbi, the representative of the value system that they had gathered to absorb.

Hence, another prerequisite for the existence of the *yeshiva* was a method of providing for the needs of the out-of-town students. Because the general community placed a high value on Torah study, it solved this problem through both communal and supra-communal institutions. A rabbi who intended to maintain a *yeshiva* would generally make it a condition of his contract that the community agree to support a fixed number of students.[25] Direct responsibility for the support of the youths lay with the community's appointees, who were sometimes given a special title: *gaba'ei ha-kupa* (wardens of the fund). Just as in the case of the *ḥeder*, funds for the *yeshiva* would be raised through semi-voluntary levies on the householders. Sometimes individuals would spontaneously make donations to the *yeshiva* or establish endowments on its behalf. But the wardens also had the power to require householders to participate directly in maintaining the *yeshiva* by opening their homes to the students and providing them with room and board on weekdays and, even more so, on the Sabbath and holidays.[26] For their part, the supra-communal institutions would constantly encourage the local communities to fulfill their obligation in supporting *yeshivot*, and they would sometimes lend support to, or at least define standards for, those aspects of the *yeshiva* that were beyond the authority of the local community. They were involved, for example, in dividing up the students such that their number in any one *yeshiva* did not exceed the financial capacity of the local community to support them. The supra-communal institutions likewise sought partial support for the *yeshivot* from those communities themselves too small to maintain one on their own. Such smaller communities were required to raise money at fixed times for the *yeshivot*, and in fact they would actually support the students directly, since during "intersessions"—a not-insignificant period of time—the students would take up residence in these settlements. Here, too, the supra-communal institutions tried to systematize matters by dividing up the levies fairly and by assuring the educational needs of the migrant students.[27]

The elite of the Jewish intellectual world was trained in our period in the *yeshivot*. There was a large stratum of *yod'ei sefer*—that is, of individuals educated in the *ḥeder* who were familiar with the customs of Judaism and could understand the basic texts (the Pentateuch, the Mishna, and aggadic anthologies such as the *Ein Yaakov*) or at least follow a rabbinic talk about them. This group formed the middle stage between the Talmudic scholar (*talmid ḥakham*) and the ignoramus (*am ha-areẓ*). But it was the *yeshiva* that provided the highest degree of intellectual training available for the Talmudic scholar in our period. The *yeshiva* students' training was at such an advanced level of complexity and acuity that anyone who had not spent a number of years in intensive study in a *yeshiva* would not be able to follow a lecture by, or even the conversation of, these *talmidei ḥakhamim*.

Pilpul and Ḥilukim. This situation resulted from developments in the manner in which halakha was studied. Especially after the publication of the *Shulḥan Arukh*, halakhic study had separated into two streams: those who were interested in elucidating the practical implications of the law, and those whose goal was purely speculative study. Practical halakhic decisions were arrived at, for the most part, through reliance on earlier authorities. The study of primary sources was merely an opportunity for exegesis and development of the halakhic mentality for its own sake. This separation of study of the primary sources from any practical halakhic concerns encouraged the tendency to over-intellectualize and to indulge in logical games without defined purpose. In its most radical form, such developments, from the sixteenth century on, led to the development of the well-known system of "*ḥilukim*." Practitioners of this style of argument raised admittedly hypothetical problems in the Talmudic text and in the commentaries and resolved them on the basis of logical assumptions of admittedly doubtful value. Their method of study, which neither led to the discovery of truth nor guided Jews in practice, was justified with the pedagogic theory that preoccupation with such *ḥilukim* sharpened the mind and prepared the students for future study of a more desirable sort.[28]

In fact, students spent only a part of their time in such study. There were two *zmanim* (terms) lasting three and one-half months each: in the summer from the first of *Iyar* to the fifteenth of *Av* (approximately late April to late July), and in the winter from the first of *Ḥeshvan* to the fifteenth of *Shvat* (approximately early October to late January). These were subdivided further. During the first half of each term, in the summer through Pentecost and in the winter through Hanukkah, studies were conducted in the pilpulistic fashion, which culminated in the presentation of the *ḥiluk* by the rabbi or someone else whom he decided to honor. During the second half of the term, the students would devote themselves to the *poskim*—halakhic codes—both early and late.[29] Here the need to determine how the final decision was derived from the sources and to see how to apply the law inevitably limited the students' tendency to unrestrained casuistry. But even here, the manner of understanding the early codes was also quite complex, such that only a number of years of study in a *yeshiva* could provide one with the ability to participate actively.

The Titles of Ḥaver and Morenu. One way or another, ongoing and continuous preoccupation with one's studies became the prerequisite for being considered a *talmid ḥakham*. Teachers in the *ḥeder* could not prepare their pupils for this. Even in the *yeshiva*, students were divided in two groups: *baḥurim*, or "young men," who studied Talmud on their own, and *naarim*, or "lads," who still needed help from others. In return for the financial support that they received from the director of the *yeshiva*, the *baḥurim* were obligated to teach the *naarim*—that is, to help them prepare for the rabbi's lecture.[30] The basic study of the text, and presumably also a review of the rabbi's insights, was conducted in small groups of a "teacher" and two or three students. These groups met in their separate rooms for most of the day and came into the *beit midrash* (study hall) only to hear the rabbi's lecture.[31]

Even continuous study in a *yeshiva* at the rank of *baḥur* did not necessarily make one a *talmid ḥakham*. At approximately eighteen, the student would usually leave the *yeshiva* to marry. If he continued to study, on his own or at a local *yeshiva*, for at least another two years after his marriage, he would be given the basic title of *ḥaver*, possibly by the local authority rather than by his own teacher. Further years of study were needed before one was given the title of *morenu*, which authorized one to decide halakhic questions. The number of years of study required for each of these titles was fixed in the *takanot* of the communities and supra-communal institutions. That the community and supra-communal organizations supervised the allocation of such titles was no mere coincidence; after all, these titles brought with them a special status and privilege within the community with regard to taxation, officeholding, etc. This is why, even though training for these titles went on completely within the framework of the *yeshiva*, the titles themselves were granted by communally appointed rabbis, sometimes under the direct supervision of the communal and supra-communal leaders.[32]

The Rosh Yeshiva as the Embodiment of Values. The *yeshiva* of the fifteenth through eighteenth centuries was distinguished not only by its approach to study but also by its characteristic linking of the functions of public teacher and intellectual—of rabbi and *rosh yeshiva*. As in all periods of its history, the *yeshiva* was devoted to educating the masses of the Jewish people; the great scholars had always seen it as their special duty to teach publicly and to cultivate large student followings. But it was not enough just to teach the views of earlier scholars. Psychologically the scholar obviously benefited from having an audience to whom he could describe the results of his own studies and thinking as well. This linking together of the functions of intellectual creativity and public teaching marked the *rosh yeshiva* as superior to the *melamed* or *ḥeder* teacher. Since knowledge of the Torah was not presented in instrumental terms, the rabbi also was more than a transmitter of mere information. Vis-à-vis his students, he became the very embodiment of those ideals that he presented to them in intellectual terms. Personal attachment to the rabbi was further encouraged by the fact that the students who formed the *yeshiva*'s nucleus were young people with no other local institutional ties. These conditions allowed for the emergence of a uniquely intensive educational setting.

The Limits of the Yeshiva. Still, it is unlikely that this potential was realized often in our period. The merging of the functions of communal rabbi (*av bet din*) and *rosh yeshiva* decreased, rather than increased, the likelihood of this. Caring for the *yeshiva* was, after all, only one of the many tasks of the rabbi. True, the rabbi would see in the *yeshiva* a kind of "escape" from his public duties and struggles. Here he was in his own element, and he exerted virtually total control. From here as well derived the prestige that he carried with him into all other spheres of his activity.[33] His scholarly accomplishments were measured by the number of students he had and the closeness of their ties to him. The attitude of the community toward its rabbi, often complex and tense, was balanced by the special prestige deriving from his role in the *yeshiva*. The honor accorded him as *rosh yeshiva* and teacher, roles that were universally respected, strengthened the rabbi's hand also as bearer of the moral authority of the entire community. Nevertheless, it is also true that the educational function was therefore carried out by someone whose major function lay in another sphere. The limiting of the school year to seven months was not so much an accommodation to students' needs as it was an acknowledgment of the limits of the rabbi's time and of the supporting community's resources.[34] The long inter-session and the wandering of the students from *yeshiva* to *yeshiva* weakened the contacts between the rabbi and his pupils and prevented the total identification of pupils with specific teachers.[35] By the end of the seventeenth century we find the supra-communal institutions and moral preachers warning *rashei yeshiva* not to turn the *yeshivot* into sources of private income by taking tuition from the students.[36] This is a clear indication that the educational functioning of the *yeshivot* was being limited.

Despite the decisive role of out-of-towners in establishing the *yeshiva*, the institution was an integral part of the local community that supported it, and there is no indication that the *yeshiva* of this period felt itself religiously superior to the rest of that community. Later, when the unifying power of the *kehila* was in decline, the *yeshiva* took upon itself the responsibility for maintaining and developing the tradition. In our period, however, the *kehila* was still responsible for this function, and the *yeshiva* was essentially one of its institutions.

19

Stratification and Mobility

Up to this point we have described traditional Jewish society as a single functional unit, within which each institution had its own vital role to play. In this "functional" approach, no attempt was made at ranking the social roles of institutions and individuals, since each was necessary for the complete picture of the society. Admittedly, this egalitarian approach to social function was sometimes resorted to by members of the society itself, especially when they sought to appease those who played low-status roles in the community. Society was compared to a living organism, as in the ancient Roman parable, and people were told how important *each* task was and how mutually dependent the various classes were.[1] In fact, however, all such reasoning implicitly recognized that distinctions did exist between the various social functions; the very need to justify and appease indicates how sensitive members of society were to the status of their social role, and despite the efforts at appeasement, there was a constant struggle to attain those roles that were considered of elevated status and importance. Unless, therefore, we are willing to treat this society in merely static terms, with no interest in its internal dynamics, we must now turn our attention to the hierarchy, or hierarchies, of function within it, and trace the paths along which roles and status were transferred among individuals and groups. In other words, we must explore the extent and direction of mobility within the society.

Stratification. Social stratification, as well as constant fluctuations in hierarchical position, did exist within traditional Jewish society. True, the Jews formed only one division within society as a whole, thus limiting the opportunity for stratification. Nor could occupation provide a basis for stratification since there was no wide-ranging occupational differentiation among Jews. Only artisans tended to form a kind of circumscribed vocational group whose status almost at the bottom of the social ladder was determined by the nature of their occupations. But even this collective body never became anything like a closed, hereditary caste. Whether or not one was allowed to join the vocational association and thus to practice a craft depended upon the extent to which the other members feared increased competition. On the other hand, there were never any rules that prevented the individual from leaving a given craft for another vocation if he was capable of doing so. No ideology ever appeared to justify the separation of the artisan group; earning one's living through the crafts was never seen as anything more than an unfortunate necessity and no one was prevented from bettering himself.[2]

Political Power and Social Stratification. Nor could political power serve as a basis for fixing the social hierarchy permanently, either due to the Jews' relationship with the non-Jewish authorities or through the performance by Jews of political tasks assigned to them. The Jew's dependence on the authorities had a decisive impact on his status within his own society. If he gained his residence privileges directly from the authorities (rather than through the community) and, even more so, if he performed some economic or administrative function for the government, his status rose also within Jewish society. In some places, the authorities doled out privileges to the Jews according to a sliding scale: Some received a permanent residence privilege, which might be inherited by their heirs, while others were granted residence only for themselves, or for a limited period of time. Yet others were merely tolerated or were dependent on the residential rights of fellow Jews, thus becoming, at least *de jure*, the retainers of the Jews who enjoyed protection, even though they sometimes used their supposed dependence as camouflage for engaging in business on their own.[3] Still, their lack of any personal residence privilege also impaired the status of these Jews even within Jewish society.

The Jew could acquire influence and even real power in non-Jewish society, but he could never convert this influence and power into a social position within that society because of the deep divisions, both communal and cultural, between the Jewish and gentile worlds. The individual's power could be expressed in social terms only internally, vis-à-vis Jewish society. There was no objection on principle to the use of this external source of power to buttress one's position internally; "closeness to the authorities" (*kirva la-malkhut*) could, after all, be seen positively as a form of informal representation of the interests of the Jewish community and of Jewish individuals to the government.[4] If one fulfilled this function as the ideal demanded, one gained legitimate honor and prestige within Jewish society. Only if one sought to use one's personal relationship with the authorities to break the bonds of Jewish society—as, for instance, by trying to obtain communal office through the government—was such power seen as illegitimate, and *kirva la-malkhut* equated with abuse and treason, or *mesira* (literally: informing).[5] In such a case, external political power lost its social legitimacy; even if society did not succeed in routing the "abuser" or "informer," the esteem ordinarily due him would be converted on social and ethical grounds into contempt and disgust.

Considerations of the possible misuse of power aside, political influence could serve as an openly recognized, legitimate base for stratification, and in those areas where individual Jews enjoyed differing rights, one can speak of classes almost tantamount to estates within Jewish society. These externally derived distinctions were more than *de facto*; they were openly recognized by the authorities as legally binding, and it was this sort of legal basis that lent an absolute and permanent character to divisions between estates, as opposed to the more transient divisions of class. In this sense, social differences in Jewish society were given bases no different from those operative in the surrounding society.[6]

Status Could Not Become Class. But another fact must be noted that weakens this comparison: The privileges that a Jew might acquire from the authorities never became permanent and hereditary, as did those of the indigenous nobles. Even the highest ranks attained by a Jew remained "acquired" positions that the authorities granted to anyone able to pay the price. Only in exceptional cases were privileges granted to Jews because of some personal service they had given the government, as in the case of certain Court Jews. But from the point of view of Jewish society, even these were "acquired" positions that in principle had no value status and were therefore never marked by external trappings, a justificatory ideology, or an aura of ancestral privilege and status. Whereas the high status of communal leaders and scholars was transferred in part to the coming generation, political prestige, including *kirva la-malkhut*, remained a purely personal matter. Elevated political position remained, in fact, nothing more than a convenient base of operation for other activities; it never achieved intrinsic value in its own right.

Similar conclusions can be derived from examining the internal government of the Jewish community and its leaders. As we saw in our analysis of the *kehila* and supra-*kehila* institutions, officeholders enjoyed material advantages and were distinguished from the masses through badges of honor that symbolized the importance of their task. There is no doubt that people were willing to fulfill these functions in part because they sought the elevated status and honor associated with them. Communal office thus provided a basis for the stratification upon which the social hierarchy was constructed. It is equally clear that climbing this hierarchical ladder was not an option available to all. The exclusion of the poor was given an explicit institutional expression in regulations that limited the electorate to taxpayers and scholars. At times the various communal and supra-communal offices were monopolized by a limited circle, and the process of appointing new officers was no more than a mechanism to regulate the reshuffling of positions among a limited circle of candidates.[7]

But none of this implies that officeholders constituted a ruling class that excluded all outsiders. Rotation, even if only among a small minority of *kehila* members, did prevent any vested claim to permanent office. Moreover, a relatively large group participated in political activity through voting or working to influence public opinion in favor of one candidate or another. Hereditary appointment, the classic method by which a minority deprives the majority of a chance at officeholding, was never a real possibility. The fundamental fact remains that the twin conditions for joining the electorate—property and learning—could be acquired by anyone. An individual who was excluded from officeholding by these prerequisites did not therefore regard himself and his descendants as permanently barred from the positions of leadership. He might himself one day accumulate the necessary financial means; no miracle was required for a man entirely without means to rise to the top of the ladder under the dynamic economic conditions of the time.[8] And the family could acquire learning either directly, if the sons were academically gifted, or indirectly through money, if the daughters were married off to outstanding scholars.

Transience of Economic Power. We have argued that the circle of those enjoying political privilege never became closed because the acquisition of capital in this society was never totally class defined. Just as with regard to those who held political office within the *kehila* and those who relied on political power from outside, so also in the economic sphere, those who had power and privilege were never able to insulate themselves behind exclusive class barriers. This was a result of the political conditions that determined the framework of Jewish society's existence. The Jews' inability and even unwillingness to acquire real estate meant that even the highest economic achievements would continue to be linked to liquid capital. This fact reduced the assurances that capital could be transferred from one generation to another. Political insecurity—i.e., the possibility of unrestricted levies and even of outright expropriation by the authorities—was not the only source of danger for Jewish capital. The very fact that the Jew's capital was liquid put its stability over a period of generations into question. Sudden impoverishment as a result of unsuccessful business ventures was a common occurrence. Conversely, the swift accumulation of wealth through good luck and business acumen was not unusual.[9] Yet another result of this situation was even more important from the point of view of class differentiation: Even the greatest Jewish capitalist could not give his economic achievements qualitative expression by investing his commercial profits in real estate. During this period, many non-Jews did exactly this, not only gaining stability and security for their property but also giving a different qualitative expression to their economic power and thus giving themselves a social status quite different from those who held only liquid capital. Since this path was blocked for Jews, even the tremendous differences in personal wealth that existed within Jewish society in this period remained merely quantitative.

Lineage and Learning as Bases for Stratification. The third principle (alongside political power and economic wealth) that commonly serves as a basis for stratification in human societies, lineage, was similarly almost entirely lacking in the religious-sacral sphere of Jewish society. Judaism did distinguish, it is true, between the sacredness of Priests, Levites, and Israelites. This distinction was based in theory on the respective real roles these groups had played in the Temple service, and it had once given them definite and tangible privileges and obligations in daily life. Moreover, maintaining this distinction in the post-Temple period was undoubtedly linked to the messianic hope for the rebuilding of the Temple and everything which that implied. But in fact, this sacral distinction made little practical difference except for a few restrictions on whom a Priest might marry (he could not, for example, marry a divorcée), his exclusive privilege to fulfill certain ceremonial religious functions (the priestly blessing and the redemption of the firstborn), and his precedence when it came to the allocation of public honors such as being called up to the reading of the Torah.[10] But all of these rights and obligations affected each Priest as an individual and never brought all Priests together into a social group; in the post-Temple period, one cannot treat the Priests or Levites as a social grouping in any real sense of the phrase.

Once the real basis for the sacral distinction between Priests, Levites, and Israelites had disappeared, no similar basis for stratification emerged. We do find, it is true, a certain claim to hereditary privilege among descendants of outstanding religious personalities—pietists, kabbalists, or Torah scholars—to whom spiritual or magical powers were sometimes attributed. The claim could easily be put forward that these charismatic qualities were hereditary, and the way was thus open for establishing a new basis for sacral-lineal stratification.[11] But, at least until the rise of Hasidism, this possibility was never actualized as a new basis for stratification even over a few generations. The essential condition for this was lacking: an attachment of the dynasty to some kind of temple, or at least to some stable center of worship. The conditions of existence in the Diaspora—geographical dispersion, political insecurity, and the absence of a strong bond to one's place of residence—undermined the value of lineage as a stabilizing factor that could be passed on to future generations.

Existing conditions were far more favorable to the scholarly type, the *talmid ḥakham*, whose religious authority rested upon the acquisition of knowledge that was portable and independent of time and place. The scholars had inherited the role of the Priests ever since the destruction of the Temple, and they held it until the period of Hasidism and the Haskala. Scholars were in a position to guarantee their sons a superior "head start" in life by giving them an outstanding scholarly education and providing an atmosphere of learning from youth. But even they could not bequeath their learning to their sons or block the rise of the sons of the uneducated. In theory, at least, positions of religious leadership remained accessible to the entire community. In practice, no one was disqualified absolutely on an ascriptive basis, though there were various types of obstacles to be overcome. Those ritual or ceremonial functions that Judaism retained after the destruction of the Temple, such as kosher slaughtering and serving as cantor or reader of the Torah, were likewise dependent on knowledge that, in principle, was accessible to all.[12]

Concentration of Stratification Factors. Thus, from all points of view—occupational, political, economic, and religious—traditional Jewish society appears to be an open society, or at least not one in which certain positions were reserved on principle to specific individuals or groups. But saying that Jewish society was open does not, of course, imply that everyone had an equal chance of achieving each and every position. No matter which yardstick we use, there were great gaps between those at the top and those at the bottom of this society: wealth and poverty, learning and ignorance, political power and powerlessness, distinction of pedigree and complete absence of family prestige—all coexisted in extreme form. Admittedly, there were no symbolic barriers to keep individuals from aspiring to any status;

indeed, in the field of scholarship the individual was actually commanded to strive to reach the top. Even so, we must be extremely cautious in assessing the extent of mobility within the society. Restrictions, absent in theory, existed in practice. Sources of power tended to become concentrated in the hands of the same individuals. Political office went hand in hand with wealth: without wealth one could not attain political office and political power likely led to increased wealth. The other two bases for status—scholarship and family connections—tended also to be linked with these. The sons of the rich could afford to continue their studies until they attained the high level of scholarship necessary to become rabbis. And once they reached that stage, their wealth, their family connections, and sometimes even their influence at court helped them to find appointments as *kehila* rabbis and thus express their learning in an institutionalized fashion.[13] Someone who was financially independent could also more easily obtain a position as *rosh yeshiva*, even when this was not linked to appointment as rabbi of a community. This was even more true if the individual or his family could help support the needy students as well.[14] Sometimes this linkage of scholarship and wealth occurred in the reverse direction: Rabbis here and there managed to accumulate capital from their incomes, and heads of *yeshiva* were sometimes showered with so many gifts from their admirers that they became wealthy.[15]

Scholarship and wealth might also be linked in an indirect fashion. If an unlettered person married into a family of scholars, he could bask in the reflection of their glory. Generous financial support to scholars earned one the reputation of "cherishing the Torah," and tradition equated the merit of such a man with that earned by the scholar himself.[16] The *kẓinim*—the Court Jews of Germany in the seventeenth and eighteenth centuries—resorted to this approach extensively. They established foundations to support houses of study (*kloyzim*) and their students.[17] They also gained honor from the reflected glory of Torah study by assisting scholars in publishing their books. Hardly a book was printed in Germany during this period whose title page did not mention the name of a *kaẓin* whose support had made its publication possible.

Concentration of the various sources of power in the same hands serves as an indication of the steep structural stratification maintained at all times in this society. Each person's position in the social hierarchy was known not through visible signs of class, but through the verdict of public opinion, which set a value on the position of each individual. In this, the public opinion was based on well-known and available facts. Everyone knew the extent of a person's influence with the authorities and, of course, about any position held in the *kehila*, the supra-*kehila*, or one of the local associations. The official titles given to scholars, as well as the public discussions among them, gave authoritative indications of their respective merits. Even pedigree and family ties could not be hidden in a society in which, at least at the upper levels, everyone knew everyone else. Finally, the community could estimate the individual's economic position quite closely, even if precise information was not always available. Assessment of taxes was public, charitable contributions were announced in public, and even the amount of dowries given one's children was publicized, thus providing people with the means to identify each member's place in the hierarchy.[18]

Competition for Status. One sees in all this an excessive sensitivity to class, which, incidentally, characterized contemporary non-Jewish society as well. This sensitivity expressed itself in the demand, expressed in moral terms, that each person be given the respect due him according to the sum of his positions on the various scales of stratification.[19] Calculation of this sum was not, of course, merely mechanical. Even if one's position on each scale was known clearly, there was no objective, certain standard by which to evaluate the various scales, one against the other. It was relatively easy to rank two scholars, two leaders, or two rich men, but it was much harder to find criteria according to which all of these might be ranked on a single scale. This problem of ranking the different criteria for status is found in all societies, but it was intensified among Jews because of the absence of secondary social structures that could provide a framework for those who possessed each type of status. Because of the restricted sphere of Jewish life—physically, occupationally, and socially—such structures could develop only in the most rudimentary form. A man's wealth or political influence could likely be disregarded in the house of study during a discussion of Halakha, where knowledge of Halakha alone determined one's status. But unlike learning, the other bases of status—wealth, official position, and lineage—did not each have a separate milieu in which they could be expressed. Those possessed of any of these marks of status were constantly competing against each other, especially in the synagogue, the common meeting point of the entire community and the place that provided an opportunity for public demonstrations of social differentiation. A good illustration of this is provided by the question of precedence among those to be called up to the reading of the Torah, something that caused no little friction in communal life. Similarly, at the sessions of the supra-communal councils where representatives of various public bodies came together, there were constant problems in determining precedence in being called to the Torah, in giving sermons, and even in seating. Those who prepared communal bylaws made considerable efforts to arrive at acceptable rules for such occasions.[20] But, of course, *takanot* could only lay down general rules; they could not provide a clear-cut solution for each and every eventuality.[21] Friction over status continued in the synagogue and at the general councils.[22] There are grounds for assuming that the multiplicity of synagogues, especially in the eighteenth century in the larger communities, must be attributed in part to the desire, especially of the very wealthy, to avoid this social friction by building private synagogues of their own.[23]

Social Mobility. If the absence of mechanisms through which to express each of the various forms of elite status tended to increase the friction between members of the elites, it also facilitated social mobility overall. Marked pluses in one area could compensate for minuses in others and make possible an astonishingly rapid social rise. We see this expressed clearly in the custom of waiving for scholars the usual restrictions governing the right to vote or to stand for communal and supra-communal office. Scholarship, in this instance, served as a substitute for such things as wealth and residence rights.[24] This same compensatory system also applied in arranging marriages. A person's prospects in making a match were determined by his status on the various scales of stratification. Money or scholarship could compensate for lack of pedigree, and vice versa.[25] In this way, paths of upward mobility were created. Not all paths upward were equally fast. Wealth could raise a person's status to astonishing heights within his own lifetime. Scholarship and lineage, on the other hand, could be consolidated only in the course of a number of generations—with a son or son-in-law at the earliest. Even so, when compared with truly class-defined societies, even this was easy. As soon as even one generation of a family excelled in wealth, in public leadership, or in learning, the succeeding one benefited not only from improved opportunities, but also from the reflected genealogical glory. The rise of a nuclear family indirectly affected the status of its entire extended family; not only could they provide direct assistance of the sort that we have already discussed, but they also shed an unquantifiable distinction on everyone.

On the other hand, no family was able—or, for that matter, even tried—to shut itself behind a class barrier. Because those attributes that determined status were of a "personal"—or, to use the sociological terminology, achieved, non-ascriptive—nature, families could not guarantee a substantial share in them to all their members. Learned men could hardly make scholars of all their relatives. Even the wealthy could do no more than support and help their poor relatives; they could not guarantee them riches or even a comfortable living. The "distinguished family" of Jewish society was not the same as its counterpart in aristocratic society, all of whose members shared the social standing deriving from its status. When we say that a family had status (*yiḥus*)—whether of wealth or learning—we mean only that there were some wealthy or learned people in the family. But alongside the scholars and the wealthy men there were always relatives lacking these qualities who merely hung on, with more or less success, to the family's more fortunate members. Hence, just as there was no uniform level of status among the members of "distinguished families," there could be no complete segregation from undistinguished families. Some exceptional individuals possessed of a specific attribute—such as intellectually gifted persons or the newly rich—could always penetrate into even the best families. Even children of distinguished families might have to resign themselves to marrying persons without special *yiḥus* or pedigree. For example, it often happened that a widower with a number of small children could not aspire to a wealthy or pedigreed girl, but had to settle for a capable, hardworking wife from an ordinary family.

Thus, the picture of social stratification that emerges is one of a society steeply stratified and with tremendous gaps between its peaks and valleys. What made up for this gap, even between those most differentiated from each other in the structure—was the fact that there was no insuperable barrier between them. He who aimed to reach the peak had a long, steep road to climb, but if he had the strength, the ability, and the will, nothing would prevent him from achieving his desire.

PART III

THE BEGINNINGS OF BREAKDOWN

20

The Impact of Historical Events

So far we have described traditional society as a stable entity and have disregarded any changes and variations in it. Our analysis of stratification and mobility highlighted only the way in which individuals or groups would gain or lose relative social position, rather than changes in the underlying structure or functioning of society. Every society must undergo at least generational transfer of functions from fathers to sons; this cannot be taken to imply a structural change in that society.

Social and Spiritual Change. But even our traditional society did undergo significant change over the period with which we are dealing. Aside from the transfer of positions from one generation to another and the social ascent or descent of individuals, we have already noted variations in the functioning of institutions that can be properly labeled as structural and functional change. For instance, we noted a change in the status of the rabbinate at the start of our period, and the strengthening of the artisan class during its latter half.[1] In the sphere of culture and ideas, the most obvious relevant phenomena are the spread of *pilpul* (casuistry) as a style of study in the *yeshivot* at the start of our era[2] and the penetration of kabbalistic ideas into the ethical and homiletical literature during its latter half. The spread of Kabbala, which we shall explore further, is proof of the tremendous influence that an internal religious development could have on the structure of society as a whole. In short, it is not illegitimate to speak of ''development'' even in this ostensibly stable society. Despite the ideology of traditionalism, which saw the present as no more than an attempt —always unsuccessful—to maintain the ideals of the past, each generation in fact added a new story to the structure of tradition. These additions reflect both the generations' creative spirit[3] and their reactions to the events of their specific time.

Reactions to 1648–49. Of course, the traditional nature of this society did severely limit the extent of possible change. Even the most serious events were likely to evoke reactions only within the framework of traditional modes of thought and action. This is shown, for example, by the impact of the massacres of 1648–49. The slaughter of tens of thousands, the flight of many more before the sword, the destruction of communities, and the deprival of entire regions of their means of existence—all of these traumatized the Jews, undermined their sense of security, and forced them as a community and as individuals to reevaluate their status. But the Jews' reaction remained within the traditional patterns of thought and practice. True, the extent of the rescue effort and the number of people involved in it were larger than before. True, Jews from all over Europe and even the Ottoman Empire took part in the rescue activities. And true also, the *kehilot* broke with past patterns and ignored their own bylaws aimed at preventing outsiders from entering the community and seeking their livelihood there.[4] But the effort itself remained extemporaneous and ad hoc. There is no record of any plan of action to prevent a recurrence of the disaster. The Jews were not unaware of the real causes behind the events, but drew no practical political or social conclusion from their historical experience. In fact, realistic explanations were overshadowed by the traditional providential explanation and the assumption that the ultimate lesson to be derived from any evaluation of the catastrophe was a religious and moral one. The composition of penitential prayers (*seliḥot*), the proclamation of a day of fasting, the imposition of more severe restrictions on dress and banqueting, and repetitions of the standard warnings about observing the commandments—these constituted the sum total of the reaction in the area of social values.[5] The reaction was not qualitatively different from that of any other generation to the events of its time during the period of traditionalism.

No matter how much this generation added to the traditional superstructure, no matter how deep its reaction to the events of its day, its essential attitude toward tradition did not change. A real break with tradition occurs only when events are accompanied by a total reevaluation of tradition itself, and when tradition, rather than serving to justify events, becomes the point of departure for reservation and criticism. Seen in this way, Jewish society can be said to have preserved its traditional character until the second half of the eighteenth century.

The Sabbatean Movement. Admittedly, one momentous event did occur in our period that briefly broke down Jewish society's conscious traditionalism: the appearance of Sabbetai Ẓvi (1666). Ẓvi presented himself as the Messiah and claimed that it was his prerogative as such to abrogate accepted norms and to open a new chapter in the history of lawgiving in Israel. At the time, most Jews accepted his authority. Though Ẓvi did not, during his brief career, manage to whittle down many traditional practices, his abrogation of sacrosanct holidays and his institution of new ones indicate the extremes toward which he was headed.[6]

In fact, however, Sabbetai Ẓvi's actions do not represent a break in the tradition. His appearance constitutes a natural awakening of forces always latent in traditional society; he was the actualization of a preexisting longing for redemption. Traditional messianism had already included the notion that the authority of tradition would be abrogated at the "end of days." Such annulment by the Messiah would represent the fulfillment of tradition rather than its repudiation and essential abandonment. The faithful expected not a gradual social change but a complete new order of things—in both the material and spiritual sense—and at the time of the Messiah's revelation in the person of Sabbetai Ẓvi the Jews were prepared for this crisis, for the expected single, catastrophic change.[7] With the collapse of the movement after Ẓvi's conversion to Islam, the tension of the messianic moment relaxed and society as a whole returned to its state of relative stability—though bearing with it the memory of its reaction to a shattering event and an inner concern lest it be repeated. But the authority of tradition per se, and even of the messianic idea itself, was not weakened, and the hope for redemption remained an unquestioned article of faith for coming generations.

It is true that a small minority of Jews were not able to return to the status quo ante. They continued to believe in the messianic pretensions of Sabbetai Ẓvi even after his conversion. For them, Sabbetai Ẓvi's messiahship remained real despite the fact that the messianic objectives had not been achieved. They believed that the messianic period had begun with the revelation of Sabbetai Ẓvi, and this inevitably led them to certain conclusions regarding the authority of tradition. We know that even these Jews were divided over how far to take these conclusions.[8] Some maintained all laws and customs except those, like the fast of the Ninth of *Av* and *tikun ḥaẓot* (the recitation of the night prayers for the restoration of Israel), that directly expressed the belief that Jews were still fully in exile. The removal of these symbols was sufficient, in the view of the moderate Sabbateans, to demonstrate their belief that the period of redemption had begun. None of the other elements of tradition was discredited, and the traditional mindset itself remained in force.

On the other hand, some Sabbateans drew the logical conclusion that the beginning of redemption implied the total abrogation of tradition and of its entire system of values. As far as they were concerned, the way had been cleared for a new, truly revolutionary, historical development. In practice, the members of this sect did not really follow up on their belief. They did not seek to change the structure of society, or even work toward the realignment of social classes and the elevation of their own status. Nor, with the exception of Jacob Frank (1726–1791), did the sect try to publicize its views. Frank attempted to maintain his community as a separate denomination, neither Jewish nor Christian, but in the end found it necessary to convert to Christianity and to take his followers with him. Frank's failure was proof of the impossibility at this juncture of maintaining a social unit midway between Jewish and Christian societies.[9]

The external norms of traditional Jewish society imposed themselves even on the radical Sabbateans. Their teachings denied traditional society's underlying values and allowed all forms of behavior when the members were among themselves, but these same teachings continued to enjoin members to conform to traditional social norms in public. The Sabbateans believed that the public revelation of their doctrine and its acceptance by all of Jewish society would occur only after some future messianic act of catastrophic proportions. In practical terms, therefore, even the radical Sabbateans agreed that, at least for the time being, the institutions of Jewish society would not, and should not, be changed. The Sabbateans were social revolutionaries only in their hearts, and when they were among themselves. If even those who denied the society's values to themselves were unable to rebuild that society on any new basis, it is clear that the objective conditions that would have allowed such a new organization did not yet exist.

Thus, for social historians, the Sabbatean movement poses only a question of secondary importance. We may ask whether there was any link between social class and response to the movement. To put the question in another way, was membership in the movement a function of chance and individual psychology, or was there, perhaps, some connection between Sabbateanism and a given social stratum? If the former, Sabbateanism should be evenly distributed over all social strata with access to the new teaching; if the latter, membership should be concentrated in a specific stratum. From what we know about those who belonged to the crypto-Sabbateans, it appears that social class did have a significant effect. Though members of all the various strata were to be found among the Sabbateans—from *parnasim* in Germany to the simplest Jews in the towns of Podolia—the movement had special appeal for what can be termed the "secondary intelligentsia" of Jewish society: preachers, *SHaDaRim* (emissaries of charitable institutions), and scholars living on communal charity but without any official role. There is no doubt that this group was tremendously overrepresented among the Sabbateans.[10] The phenomenon requires little explanation. A movement such as Sabbateanism, which could not publicize its views, could also not have open symbols of identification. The masses would join such a movement only in locales where a charismatic leader appeared, as happened in the case of Frank. But the rest of the Sabbatean "prophets" were itinerants, driven from place to place, who could do no more than leave behind their teachings, which attracted, in the first place, those individuals already immersed in the world of kabbalistic thought from which the concepts derived.

Of course, one should also recall the sense of frustration that typified this "lower class" of scholar, frustration that could itself motivate individuals to deviate from what was official and accepted. Moreover, maintaining such a dual life—that is, conforming to society's life-style while denying its moral values—was easier for someone who had no direct responsibility for the leadership of that society. A rabbi, called upon to decide halakhic cases for others, or a *parnas*, required to compel the people to fulfill the commandments, would have been placed in much greater psychological distress by denying the real value of these commandments than would a contemplative student, an emissary from the Holy Land moving from community to community, or a preacher, whether itinerant or locally established. It is these latter types who are found most frequently among the Sabbateans; the rabbis and leaders of the large communities were, for the most part, among the opponents and suppressors of the movement.

Sabbateanism and the Events of 1648–49. Historians have sought to explain the appearance of Sabbetai Ẓvi in 1666 as a result of specific historical events that immediately preceded it. There is no firm basis for such an argument, and our characterization of the movement as the actualization of messianic belief is intended to imply that the timing of its emergence was a matter of mere historical chance. The movement could have appeared much earlier, or not have appeared at all. There is only a remote connection between the messianic movement and the massacres of Polish Jewry in 1648 and 1649.[11] Despite clear references to these pogroms in Sabbetai Ẓvi's words, his original inspiration cannot be attributed directly to events that he knew about only from hearsay. And the public reaction to his appearance among the Jews in the countries affected by the pogroms was little different from that of Jews living in relative peace and quiet, such as in Holland, Italy, and Turkey itself.[12] No specific event led to Sabbateanism; rather, it was the consciousness of exile itself that again and again gave rise to such movements. If Sabbateanism exceeded all preceding movements in its scope and impact, this was the result of a number of historical circumstances, of which proximity to the events of 1648–49 was only one. The extended scope of the movement was, as I indicated in chapter 1, the result of the increased national unity that Jews had achieved in this period through more intensive reciprocal contacts between different regions. Improved means of communication, increased mobility of the Jewish elite, the rise of Palestine as a real center connecting the Diaspora—all of these developments heightened the ability of the dispersed communities to respond in a sort of national chain reaction to what would otherwise have remained a limited, local phenomenon.[13]

Sabbateanism and Lurianic Kabbala. The encompassing national scope of the messianic eagerness contributed both to enlarging the movement's range during its heyday, and to deepening the disappointment that followed its failure. Indeed, one of the major arguments for the truth of Sabbateanism—that the Holy One, blessed be He, would not mislead His entire people—derived its weight from the national scope of the events.[14] But it was not the depth of Sabbateanism's impact per se that explains why, unlike almost every other messianic movement, this one was not totally forgotten after it was proven false. The survival of Sabbateanism derives from the religious stream with which many connected it from the start—that is, the Kabbala of Safed. If, for the masses, the news of the redeemer simply represented the realization of popular messianism, for the movement's central leaders and wide circles of kabbalists, the revelation of the Messiah at that time signified the culmination of a process that their system of Kabbala had predicted from the start. According to Lurianic Kabbala, from the time of Rabbi Isaac Luria (1534–1572) the world had entered a final stage of *tikun* (repair), which required only a slight final effort in order to achieve its goal: the advent of the messianic era. Lurianic Kabbala had become very widely accepted approximately a generation before Sabbetai Ẓvi, and in the circles of its adepts there was a heightened expectation of the Messiah's appearance. This anticipation was the direct cause for Nathan of Gaza's naming Sabbetai Ẓvi the Messiah. The widespread, public character of this feeling of anticipation constituted at least a secondary factor in intensifying the reaction to the movement within communities that included Lurianic devotees.[15]

The link between the messiahship of Sabbetai Ẓvi and this widespread current of kabbalistic thought is also the reason for the persistence of the movement even after its failure. The confusion that prevailed after the Messiah's conversion demanded some form of response, but this could take various forms. The majority reacted by completely effacing the episode from their memory. But another reaction was also possible: the rejection of the messianic doctrine itself, or even the total renunciation of Judaism and the adoption of the gentiles' faith. These were possibilities that had concerned the opponents of Sabbateanism from the very start.[16] If these fears were not realized to any appreciable extent, and if those who could not forget the impact of the events reacted by creating a secret, antinomian sect, this was because the kabbalistic system of thought provided them with a mechanism to do so. The kabbalistic system presented redemption as a process occurring in stages and left room for an ambiguous stage that was no longer *galut* (exile) but not yet redemption. This blurring of the distinction between the period of *galut* and that of redemption inevitably raised questions as to the applicability of Jewish tradition in the intermediate era. Tradition claimed authority only until the coming of the messiah, but not afterward. During this intermediate period, then, tradition lost some of its authority. And for those interested in *tikun ha-olam* ("repairing" the world), it was now only a short step from perfect piety and detailed observance of the commandments to viewing everything once prohibited by religion as a sacred duty appropriate to an era in which exile and reform were themselves no longer distinct. For the Sabbateans, it was the advent of Sabbetai Ẓvi as redeemer that had marked the transition into the new period. But it would not be too bold to suggest that even had Sabbetai Ẓvi not appeared on the stage of history, there was a significant possibility that an antinomian deviationist sect would have arisen through the internal religious development of the Kabbala and its adherents. Be that as it may, to the extent that Sabbetai Ẓvi's appearance can be seen as an "inevitable" historical development of the time, its inevitability derived from the spread of the kabbalistic thought associated with Safed in the previous generation.

Now, taken by itself, the development of the Kabbala is an immanent, religious process whose unfolding cannot be understood in terms of one-time events (that is, historically) or as dependent on given social conditions and circumstances (that is, sociologically). Still, it is certainly not true that the overall tendency of the Kabbala bore no relation to historical reality: the Kabbala's doctrines constitute an expression of the nation's consciousness of its being in *galut* (exile) and the loss of any rational approach to the determination of its own fate. As we already saw in chapter 3, Jewish society in this period typically segregated itself, to the point of losing all contact, including a polemical one, with the outside world. This introversion prepared the way for acceptance of a doctrine that based the future of the nation (and indirectly, that of the world, as well) on an internal Jewish religious process and that saw advancement of the world's perfection through careful observance of the religious precepts together with the kabbalistic devotions associated with them. This disregard of what was happening in the outside world, and even of what the world was doing to the Jews, reached its height in the kabbalistic ethical and homiletic writings through which, from the beginning of the seventeenth century on, the essentials of kabbalistic thought were popularized among the Jewish masses. Not only was there no longer any trace of disputation with the beliefs of the other nations; there was even considerable indifference about representing the Jews and Judaism to the outside at all. The process of development that would effect the perfection and redemption of the world became an internal matter between Israel and its God.[17] Even though the Sabbateans deviated, to a greater or lesser extent, from accepted Jewish norms in the areas of dogma and ethics, they represented no more than an extreme expression of the historical consciousness shared by the entire people.

Kabbala and the Practical Commandments. The major impact of the Kabbala on the national plane is to be seen not in the Sabbatean deviation, but in a general shift in religious values—a shift that, beginning in the latter part of the seventeenth century, went hand in hand with the social changes then becoming manifest. The shift was reflected in the new significance attached to performance of the practical commandments. While halakhic and ethical literature of the time saw observance of the commandments as, first and foremost, obedience to the will of the lawgiver, the kabbalist viewed such observance as a sort of mechanism for setting the machinery of the upper spheres in motion. Each tiny particular of each commandment was linked, in this scheme, to a specific point in the divine system, and anyone who performed that commandment was thereby directing the operation of that system. This in turn determined not only the fate and reward of the individual, but also the advancement or retarding of the perfection of the world as a whole.[18]

The interpretation was not simply a matter of abstract theological thought. It also influenced religious life in practice. First, it brought with it a new appreciation for *dikduk ba-miẓvot*—careful observance of all the minutiae of the laws and customs as they had been handed down and codified. The kabbalistic approach included a complete system of explanations for all the commandments. Each detail had a specific explanation, and its particular influence on the divine order was noted. What marks this system of explanations for the commandments as unique is that it did away almost entirely with the differences of degree between one precept and another, between law and custom, between a biblical ordinance and an extra restriction imposed for the especially pious by later legislators.[19]

Ritual Creativity of Kabbala. The flexibility of the kabbalistic system in creating a symbolic link between a religious act and the kabbalistic conceptual framework allowed for basing the entire ritual on kabbalistic ideas. Moreover, it even allowed for the introduction of new details. The kabbalistic circles in Safed as well as the kabbalistic popularizers—first and foremost Rabbi Isaiah Horowitz, author of *Shnei Luḥot ha-Brit*—all stand out for their productivity in the area of ritual. Though innovations were based formally on halakhic concepts, the true impetus to development undoubtedly came from the link with a system of thought in which every movement of the hand and every murmur of the lips assumed an almost metaphysical significance.[20] Nor was Kabbala's contribution to the ritual limited to a few practices and some new interpretations. It also added an entirely new dimension—the *kavanot* (singular: *kavana;* intention, concentration, or conscious devotion). The concept of *kavana* derives from the Talmud, and requires that in performing a commandment the individual be conscious of a religious purpose to the action. The *poskim* (halakhic legists) agreed that such *kavana* was mandatory, but they allowed for certain exceptions and distinguished between various precepts as to whether *kavana* was required.[21] The kabbalists charged the concept of *kavana* with a specific mystic content that varied with the symbolic significance that their system attributed to the precept concerned. Performance of the commandment had to be accompanied by conscious attention to the symbolic significance of all the minutiae involved. The kabbalists were much more rigorous than the halakhists in insisting on these *kavanot.* For them, performance of a commandment without *kavana* virtually lost its religious significance.[22]

Kabbalists: A Religious Elite. On a practical level, this development implied that complete observance of the commandments was limited to a handful of persons. The masses, and even those with a basic grounding in religious law, lacked not only the knowledge but also the time and the power of concentration required for the observance of the daily ritual with such exactness and mystic purpose. The popularization of the Kabbala thus did not achieve its aim of making all

Jews into adherents of this occult mode of religious practice. In fact, the result was the exact opposite of what had been intended. The scholarly elite and the masses were already split in their abstract conceptualizations of Judaism. Now this split was extended to the practical sphere of observance.[23]

Moreover, the split now existed within the ranks of the elite itself. Henceforth, traditional Jewish society contained not one elite but two—one that had mastered halakhic knowledge and one, kabbalistic *kavana* and doctrine. Although these two elites occasionally overlapped in theory, they in fact came close to being rivals. Kabbala competed with straightforward Torah study as a field of endeavor and speculation. Of course, a knowledge of religious law remained a basic prerequisite for study of Kabbala. Educational institutions such as *yeshivot* and *batei midrash* were never called upon to teach Kabbala instead of, or even alongside, Talmud. But the study of the Kabbala did compete with the study of the Talmud as a final goal and supreme value. The individual who attained a sufficiently advanced level of knowledge of Halakha was enjoined, in the kabbalistic view, to devote his time to the esoteric teachings that alone could impart to him true knowledge of God's Torah.[24]

This approach was not new in itself. Already the *Zohar*, and in particular the section of it entitled *Raaya Meheimna*, had elevated the status of scholars occupied with the esoteric above that of those who dealt only with the exoteric law. But so long as the Kabbala itself was limited to closed circles, this distinction would remain nothing more than the self-appraisal of those few who dealt in the occult teachings. Once the kabbalistic teachings had been popularized by way of ethical and homiletic works, however, this view of the kabbalist as superior spread too. The main point is that once the kabbalistic elite had become an identifiable social phenomenon, this theoretical evaluation had a clear-cut point of reference in the real world. People began to reevaluate the traditional *talmid ḥakham* (scholar). The social utility of the regular *talmid ḥakham* was obvious: He served as a religious authority, community leader, head of a *yeshiva*, and the like. The kabbalist, on the other hand, had only to occupy himself in his own private studies, or at most to study with a few of his contemporaries. Much of the prestige attached to a *talmid ḥakham* who devoted himself to Torah study without hope of personal gain was now ascribed not to those individuals who employed their learning in the areas of communal leadership, halakhic rulings, and the teaching of the Torah, but to those engaged in studying the kabbalistic teachings and carrying out the commandments in accordance with them, in a fashion open only to initiates. As a reward for his non-utilitarian occupation, the kabbalistic *talmid ḥakham* was considered worthy of the same public support given to those who filled practical positions involving mastery of the Torah, such as judges in the religious courts, rabbis, and preachers.

In our period we hear calls for the establishment of houses of study devoted to *tora li-shmah*—a phrase that now might mean not disinterested personal dedication but study specifically of the esoteric doctrines. And indeed, there is evidence for the actual establishment of such institutions and for support of this sort of secluded scholar.[25] Thus reclusive pietists were able to gain public support in exactly the same fashion that other scholars had done until that time. But the ideological explanation for this support had characteristically changed. The kabbalists differed from the traditional *talmidei ḥakhamim*, whether rabbis, judges, teachers, or preachers, who had been paid for performing functions necessary to religious life. The link between the service rendered and the salary paid had been an eminently rational one.

True, there had been scholars before who had devoted their lives to study, had fulfilled no communal office, and had nevertheless received support. These scholars were supported on the grounds that they realized, as few others could, the supreme ideal of Torah study. Their support was rationalized ideologically by the argument that their heavenly reward for study would be shared with the individuals who had supported them and thus made the study possible.[26] The support given to the kabbalistic pietists could draw on this precedent and use the same rationale by identifying study of the Kabbala and fulfillment of the commandments in accordance with its teachings with non-mystical Torah study. But now there was a new thrust to the argument, derived from kabbalistic concepts. Support of the *talmid ḥakham* was no longer simply a religious obligation that earned one a reward. It was now a mechanism for cleaving to the *shkhina*, the divine presence, something of which the ignorant man (*am ha-areẓ*) was unworthy, but which the scholar achieved through his study and thought.[27] It is clear that what is meant here is the kabbalistic scholar, to whom the notion of "cleaving" (*dvekut*) applied in a mystical fashion. The notion of a reward to be divided between the patron and his client did not apply to him. The goal of his studying was *dvekut*, and even the ignorant man achieved this through his support of the kabbalist. But the sponsor's *dvekut* would remain indirect, with the *talmid ḥakham* both a link and a barrier in the connection. There are Talmudic antecedents for this concept of superior individuals mediating in the service of the Creator, but the idea appeared as a new one within the traditional social framework of our period, and bore within itself far-reaching dialectical possibilities.

We have traced the influence that Kabbala exerted in the social sphere—influence that, as we shall see, was bolstered by other changes in the social sphere itself. If the new religious elite of kabbalists clipped the wings of the talmudic scholars, it should also be noted that this was preceded or paralleled by an independent decline in the latter's status. The rise of one religious elite—the kabbalists—was facilitated by the undermining of the status of another—the scholars. It is true that the new elite did not literally supplant the old. Moreover, its relationship with the community—that of a chosen group that required separation and seclusion—differed from that of the old. The scholarly elite saw itself as set off from the masses by the attainment of a high degree of knowledge, and it was this knowledge that gave them the authority to teach and guide the masses in practical matters. But the kabbalist elite saw itself as divided from the masses by a wide chasm even in the practical sphere. The only relationship possible between them and the masses was one of *shliḥut* (agency or proxy). The few were transformed into exacting performers of the precepts on behalf of the many. It is certain that the extreme demands of the kabbalists made it impossible for them to serve as models for the masses. The chasm gaping between them revealed itself wherever the kabbalists became homilists and ethical preachers and then tried to apply unsuitable criteria to the masses. To an extent exaggerated even for ethical literature, preachers of the day portrayed their contemporaries as a sinful generation with no redeeming qualities. There is no doubt that the problems of the times, the havoc of war, and governmental persecution on the one hand, and the seizure of internal offices by the powerful with a concomitant weakening of communal institutions on the other, led to failures and abuses by the communal leadership. But if we examine the lists of faults that the preachers found in their audience, it is clear that their horrifying descriptions were also the product of a set of radical demands that even a generation of angels could not have fulfilled. Things that had long been allowed by custom and by accepted legal practice were now labeled as unforgivable sins.[28] This was simply a case of the moral and religious system of a group divorced from public life becoming the standard by which the entire community was judged. This social divide between those who cultivated the religion and their unsophisticated followers constituted one of the signs of the crisis into which traditional society entered at this stage of its development.

21

Historic Turning Points

All of the events and changes that we described in the previous chapter can be seen as mere variations within the framework of traditional society. But two movements arose in the second half of the eighteenth century, Hasidism in eastern Europe and Haskala in the West, that were perceived from the start not as mere variations on past themes but as major turning points in the history of Jewish society. What do we mean by a "turning point," and how may we distinguish between a mere variation upon the norm and a truly fundamental change?

Variety in Traditional Society. Inevitably, there are variations even within a traditional society. In fact, the society that we have been describing—Ashkenazic Jewry of the sixteenth through eighteenth centuries—was itself only one among many variations on traditional Jewish society. This society had achieved its full character at the very latest by the start of the Diaspora period and subsequently underwent merely minor changes in the many lands where Jews settled. The basic characteristics of this society were shared by all Jewish communities. Jews everywhere had similar attitudes toward gentiles and parallel values concerning all areas of human endeavor, from making a living to sexuality. Their basic institutions—the family, the house of study, the synagogue, the rabbinate—fulfilled similar functions everywhere. Heinrich Heine's witty remark that traditional Judaism was a sort of "portable homeland" is not without a measure of truth.[1] These fundamentals served the Jews over and over as a basis upon which to rebuild their society wherever they settled.[2]

Of course, a comparative study of the many manifestations of traditional Jewish society in various lands would undoubtedly reveal differences in detail regarding each of the aspects that we have considered. Indeed, even our treatment glossed over many distinctions between German, Moravian-Bohemian, and Lithuanian-Polish Jewries of the sixteenth through eighteenth centuries.[3] Nevertheless, as we said, Ashkenazic Jewry of this period should be understood as one concrete example of what happened to the Jews at all times and in every place of their dispersion, and to the extent that we have succeeded in describing the features common to its component communities, we have also presented a model of traditional Jewish society in the larger sense.

Haskala and Hasidism Are Unique. But at the end of our period we find this particular example of traditional Jewish society undergoing a radically new process. We are no longer speaking merely of exile and migration, of an uprooting and subsequent replanting of the same society. Now we see this society undergoing much more radical changes. In places that witnessed the Haskala movement and civil emancipation—France (Alsace), Germany, Bohemia, and Moravia in the second half of the eighteenth century, and Hungary a generation or two later—the fundamental structure of traditional society was actually destroyed. In Poland, the rise of the Hasidic movement likewise significantly distorted that structure.

That the Haskala movement caused fundamental changes in traditional society is generally accepted by historians and requires almost no proof. Obviously, Haskala affected the basic religious values upon which traditional society had been constructed. The movement's tendency toward secularization demonstrates its radical nature clearly. But it is not as obvious that Hasidism represented such a fundamental change. After all, the movement did not present itself as opposed to tradition, and it generally maintained accepted religious forms while apparently limiting the changes that it advocated to the realm of religious ideas and sentiments. Nevertheless, those who have studied Hasidism from a historical or sociological perspective have had no doubt that it too represents a fundamental change in traditional society. If Hasidism did not destroy the accepted religious forms, it certainly shifted their spiritual basis, and if it did not destroy the accepted social framework, it certainly introduced new principles of integration into it. Both movements, Haskala and Hasidism, established new values alongside those of tradition, and thus denied tradition's claim to exclusive authority. In each case we must ask what led to this new pattern, which was no longer merely a variation on the accepted but an unprecedented historic change.

Haskala as Derived from External Factors. Historians have found it relatively easy to explain the Haskala movement by seeing it as the product of yet another phenomenon, whose existence they accept as a given and therefore not in need of explanation. Since the Haskala movement parallels the rationalist movement and the rise of the general

European Enlightenment, the Jewish historian can conveniently make the Haskala a product of the broader movement.[4] The Haskala movement, even though the changes it wrought were obvious and radical, does not force the Jewish historian to take a stand concerning the very nature of social change. This is not true, however, with regard to Hasidism.

Hasidism as Derived from Kabbala and Sabbateanism. Hasidism cannot be explained as merely the reflection of developments in the outside world. Such parallels to it as exist among contemporary non-Jews cannot be seen as more than stimulants to change.[5] There is no evidence of any dependence on external factors in the development of Hasidism, nor, much less, in the consciousness of its leaders and members. On the contrary, one of the most marked characteristics of the movement was its exclusive Jewishness: It operated exclusively within Jewish society and drew its symbols exclusively from internal Jewish tradition. The rise of Hasidism must therefore be understood as a change within Jewish society, and any explanation must relate to what occurred within that society itself.

Two sorts of "events" have been cited as explanations for the rise of Hasidism. On a religious-social plane, historians have pointed to Sabbateanism and the rise of kabbalistic pietism as possible factors. And indeed, important elements of these two movements were absorbed by Hasidism, and the rise of Hasidism cannot be understood without reference to these movements. On the other hand, such an argument from chronology to causality is satisfactory only in part. Hasidism is so radically innovative, even vis-à-vis Sabbateanism and kabbalistic pietism, that any attempt to explain it as the outcome of these two is virtually tantamount to intellectual evasion. Such an explanation derives from the tendency of some historians who content themselves with trying to establish the continuity of stages of development, as if such continuity were sufficient proof that a later stage was a natural outcome of an earlier.

Weakening of the Social Structure. The second type of "event" that might serve as an explanation for the appearance of Hasidism lies in the realm of political, economic, and social change. We argued above that Hasidism was a disruptive factor vis-à-vis traditional society, but others have claimed the exact opposite: that in fact Hasidism was a product of an earlier breakdown of traditional society.[6] These historians can point to a number of important facts. The history of Polish Jewry in the first half of the eighteenth century was one of bitter economic struggle. Economic decline was evident at the institutional-communal level, in the growing numbers of impoverished Jews, and in the inability of institutions to pay off their financial debts. The relation between the Jews and the authorities was becoming increasingly strained. Official demands and pressure were the primary reason for the impoverishment of the *kehilot*. Most crucial, the political conflict within the kingdom of Poland itself led to the decentralization of political authority on the one hand, and to unsuccessful attempts at reorganization on the other. These processes led to a weakening of the supra-communal organizations and the subordination of Jewish communities to powerful local factors. The dismantling of the Council of the Four Lands in 1765 merely marks the final end of a long, sad process of decline in the Jewish institutions of government.

Crisis of Religious Institutions. The decline in the real power of these institutions was accompanied by an erosion in the moral authority of their leadership. It was now a daily occurrence to hear of the leadership taking advantage of its position for its own benefit. People acquired and held positions of leadership against the popular will. Leaders now arose and maintained their status as a result of their centralized economic power or with the help of the non-Jewish authorities with whom they were close.

The crisis also affected rabbinic and educational institutions. The institutions of Torah learning were in a state of decline from the end of the seventeenth century; because of the troubled times, communities wearied of supporting these *yeshivot*, or at least no longer supported them in the generous fashion of earlier times. We begin now to find what appears to be an unprecedented development in the history of the *yeshivot*: The teachers (*rashei yeshiva*) began taking tuition fees from the students who came to study with them.[7] As we explained in chapter 9, the prestige of the *av bet din* (chief rabbi) in the *kehila* stemmed from the fact that he fulfilled the function of a *rosh yeshiva* (head of an academy). Once he abandoned that function, whether or not it was his fault, and certainly once he used that position for profit, the *av bet din* lost one of his primary sources of authority. The purchase of rabbinic offices had long been a problem for the communities, but with the disintegration of the institutions of central government and the consequent subordination of the communities to the local nobility, the post of rabbi was often bought from the local lord. Not only was this morally offensive in its own right; it also opened the door for unqualified candidates to acquire this office. And indeed, from this period on we hear complaints not only about the purchase of rabbinical office per se, but also about the giving of this function to unworthy individuals, and even to youths who had not studied enough. The supra-communal organizations were forced to lower their standards regarding the qualifications for the rabbinate. In 1719–20 candidates were required to have studied for twelve years after their marriage, whereas in 1760–61, the authors of a new *takana* were content so long as the rabbi was over the age of twenty.[8]

And if the position of rabbi was no longer a guarantee of impressive scholarship, this was even more true with regard to the title *morenu*. From the end of the seventeenth century the requirements for receiving this title, as well as the title *ḥaver*, were lessened to the point that they became mere honorifics granted with almost no relation to the level of expertise and dedication in the study of the Torah.[9] The eighteenth century has been described as a period of increasing barriers between scholars and the unlearned, and this pattern has been used to explain the supposed rebellion of the common man embodied in the Hasidic movement. But this is simply not the case; instead of a widening gap, we have a distortion of the social scale, which made it difficult for people to perceive their own place and to accept the justice of existing hierarchical distinctions.

Understanding Causality. Thus we have historical and social conditions tantamount to what sociologically would be termed anomie, in which many individuals no longer had a sufficient attachment to existing institutions to be willing to undertake those activities upon which the existence of the institutions depended. Under such conditions there were increased chances of new social attachments forming among uprooted individuals. The slow rise of the kabbalistic elite is an early sign of this social process, and it parallels to a significant extent the decline of the *yeshivot* and the rabbinate. It was these same conditions that formed the background to the new social affiliation of Hasidism, which was far more radical than the rise of the kabbalistic elite. Historians were therefore correct when they refused to accept changes within the purely religious realm as a sufficient explanation for the rise of Hasidism and turned instead to the political-social spheres.

But admitting the connection between social conditions and the rise of this religious movement is not enough. We must also investigate the nature of this link. It is certainly not true that the new social conditions necessitated the rise of Hasidism and hence the consequent "distortion" of the structure of traditional society. To disabuse ourselves of this notion it is sufficient to recall that traditional Jewish society underwent greater crises—in the form of migrations and expulsions—than those that affected eighteenth-century Polish Jewry, and nevertheless managed to rebuild itself very much along the ideal lines expressed in the traditional value system. Moreover, events themselves disprove the idea of some necessary connection between social upheaval and the rise of Hasidism. In fact, traditional society was weakened over a broad geographic area—at least throughout Poland and Lithuania—while Hasidism arose initially only in limited regions of Poland (Podolia and Volhynia), conquered other regions in whole or in part only later, and eventually withdrew totally from Lithuania, after a long and drawn-out battle. Moreover, traditional Jewish society, based on the study of Torah as the supreme value, found renewed expression in Lithuania and in the western provinces of Hungary. Hence, any purely sociological approach that tries to link the emergence of Hasidism only to social factors would have to distinguish at least three different environments: one that was capable of giving birth to the movement, one that prepared the ground for its absorption, and one that absolutely prevented its spread. But there is no basis for distinguishing between social conditions in the various parts of the world we have been describing.

Hence we are forced, in summary, to say that the rise of the new movement was indeed made possible by certain social conditions, and it grew and prospered as a continuation of earlier religious changes and processes, but in its content and values, its makeup, and its historic development, Hasidism was something new. Everything that preceded it should be seen as not more than a constituent element of, or a stimulant to, the movement. The Hasidic movement itself was a new "historic creation," whose essential characteristics had not existed previously.

Charismatic Religion and Its Disruptive Power. The Hasidic movement can be understood best through comparison with similar historic phenomena, notably outbursts of charismatic religiosity whose force and authority stem from the consciousness of direct contact with the divine sphere. The values and characteristics of Hasidism are not, therefore, merely an addition to, and a variation upon, traditional values. Rather, they are, at least in part, a displacement and substitution for these traditional values. It is reasonable to theorize that were it not for the social convulsion that preceded it, Hasidism could not have arisen or spread. That convulsion, which implied a measure of abandonment of accepted values, did not necessitate or guarantee the creation of new values. Still, once the reaction to the situation had expressed itself in the form of a new movement, it created a real historical turning point.

Hasidism was made possible by the neglect of old values, but it in turn led to the renunciation of those values, something that went far beyond mere neglect. Neglect affects only the concrete manifestation of a society; it may be only temporary, and the traditional society can eventually reassert itself in its old form. Renunciation, on the other hand, actually injures the ideal image of the society to which its members constantly aspire. New values have replaced the old. And in such cases, the disappearance of the old values becomes permanent. The renunciation blocks the way to the reacceptance of traditional values.

Hasidism and Haskala exemplify the two methods of renunciation by which traditional society could be affected: one that was based on charismatic religious factors and one that resulted from rationalist critique. In the coming chapters we shall describe the realization of these two dangers, which descended upon traditional Jewish society and shook its foundations.

22

The Transition to Hasidism

From the 1730s and 1740s, Jewish society in Podolia and Volhynia saw the emergence of individuals and groups whose religious conduct was neither identical to, nor identified with, that which we have been describing until now. This new religious type was characterized by ecstatic behavior and the casting off of all emotional restraints during the prayer service. And such ecstatic outbursts were not limited to times of prayer. Rather, they affected the entire social experience of the devotee. He felt released from the mundane sphere even while dealing with his fellow man and even while imbibing strong drink, whether alone or with a group. It is clear that in the minds of those who experienced it, this ecstatic experience created a system of values that now challenged the accepted values of society.

The first scholar to cite and interpret the relevant sources was Gershom Scholem, and according to his analysis, these groups were composed of both traditionalist Jews and those who believed in the messiahship of Sabbetai Ẓvi.[1] Moreover, it seems that the impetus for the enthusiast movement derived from the Sabbateans, whose sectarian experience was also characterized by intense emotion and a relaxation of restraint. But the ties between Hasidism and Sabbateanism soon weakened. For the Hasidim, the shared experience of ecstatic religiosity became a source of independent religious authority, and even though they absorbed many Sabbatean elements into their customs, they severed all conscious relations with Sabbateanism, and distanced themselves from its sectarianism. With regard to observance of the practical commandments, the Hasidim did not follow the Sabbateans into antinomianism. Like the unsophisticated Jewish masses, these ecstatics accepted the traditional way of life as a given; indeed, in a fashion typical of such religious movements, traditional rites and customs now provided a method and occasion for attaining this intensified spiritual exaltation. What had changed was their overall understanding of the rituals of traditional observance. The essence of Judaism was no longer considered to lie in the minutiae of observance, much less in the theoretical knowledge of such details to be derived from the study of

Halakha. It was the accompanying religious experience that determined the value of performance of the precepts. It is thus no wonder that in the first accounts of their appearance, we hear of the Hasidic groups' contempt for the study of Torah, and hence of their lack of respect for those who devoted themselves exclusively to this study.[2]

The Movement's Leaders and the Baal Shem Tov. We can get an idea of some of the outstanding individuals within these early Hasidic groups from what has been preserved in the tradition. Some of them—for example, Rabbis Naḥman Kosover, Naḥman of Horodenka, and Leib Pistiner—were not only ecstatics in practice but also thinkers capable of expressing their views, at least by way of oral aphorisms.[3] In sociological terms, these figures were members of the secondary intelligentsia of Jewish society: preachers, exhorters, and *baalei shem* (that is, practitioners of folk magic). Each became the focal point of the movement in his own region, and there was a tacit struggle and a degree of tension between them over positions of leadership within the movement as a whole.[4] Rabbi Israel *Baal Shem Tov* (the BESHT) emerged victorious from this struggle, and it was owing to his intensely sensitive personality that the movement was channeled into a clearly defined course.

The BESHT was a fervid mystic who at times of successful religious exaltation achieved a feeling of direct contact with the divine realm, almost completely freeing himself from the real world.[5] Once he had become the central focus of the movement, he, his experiences, and his teachings became models for others. While he was still alive—and even more so after his death in 1760—he became the orientation point and the source of authority for all those who joined the movement.

The Movement's Spread. It is not the purpose of this work to trace the spread of the movement, especially once it split into various subgroups.[6] The principal stages of its development are well known.[7] Until the 1760s the movement remained within the provinces of Podolia and Volhynia. From that point on it spread westward, giving rise to offshoots throughout Podolia and Lithuania. In some areas, it won over a substantial portion of the Jewish population, or, at any rate, left a clear imprint on the life of the community. In the seventies and eighties, a backlash led to confrontation and a public struggle. In Poland, Hasidism emerged the victor, and in some communities and provinces, it became the dominant way of life and the basis for communal organization. In Lithuania, on the other hand, Hasidism was forced to retreat, and the Hasidim remained merely a tolerated social minority. Either way, the social implications of the movement were apparent from the start; it was clear that Hasidism was distinct from other trends within traditional society.

Hasidism, Kabbalistic Pietism, and Sabbateanism. Hasidism differed from Sabbateanism in that it both rejected the messiahship of Sabbetai Ẓvi and restrained the antinomian tendencies of the earlier movement. Hence, from the dogmatic and normative points of view, Hasidism represented a return to the traditional mainstream of Judaism. In this Hasidism was reacting to the Sabbatean failure: It not only rejected Sabbetai Ẓvi as the messiah but also suppressed active messianism itself—i.e., the tense anticipation of redemption and all religio-magical activity on its behalf. From this point of view, Hasidism differed not only from Sabbateanism but from kabbalist pietism as well. In the Hasidic approach, the practical commandments lost their magical-redemptive function. Religious ceremonies, prayer, and the observance of laws and customs were no longer aimed at activating the upper spheres through the ritual act per se. The aim was the personal religious exaltation of the individual, who was now commanded to strive for direct contact, whether mystical or contemplative, with the divine sphere. Prayer and fulfillment of the commandments became means toward, or at least an intentional framework for, this end. *Dvekut* ("cleaving," i.e., subjective communion with God) was the religious goal to which the rituals of religion and tradition were totally devoted. The link between observing the commandments and their subjective goal—the spiritual state of communion with God—is clearly to be seen in Hasidism's attitude toward the details of ritual observance, an attitude diametrically opposed to that of kabbalistic pietism. The new Hasidism broke away from the latter's absolute ritualistic attitude toward these details. Observance of the commandments was now assigned a new task. Instead of fulfilling an objective, metaphysical function (the hastening of redemption), the commandments were to serve as preparation and guide for subjective religious experience. The connection between means and end was clearly accepted: A commandment that led to the experience of *dvekut* had achieved its purpose; one that did not, had failed.[8] And experience was likely to show that success and failure were not dependent on the strict observance of small details.

In contradistinction to Sabbateanism and kabbalist pietism, the new Hasidism may be styled a "movement" in the full sociological sense of the word. Movement spokesmen—at first the BESHT and later his outstanding disciples—demanded and were accorded the right of leadership. This privilege was based on personal charisma, which derived in turn from the immediate religious strength of their personalities. These religious leaders gathered around themselves a group of loyal followers who looked to them for guidance, were prepared to follow their advice, and were ready to be swept up in the vortex of collective religious ecstasy.

The Ẓadik and the Masses. If we look at the historical link between kabbalistic pietism and Hasidism, we find a clearly dialectical development. Kabbalistic pietism had been unable to win over a broad following because of its stringent religious demand that the commandments be observed in an exacting fashion, with constant attention to their metaphysical implications. In theory the new Hasidism should have been even more restricted in its audience, since its inherent hallmark—ecstasy—could be achieved only by an extremely limited group of "religious virtuosos." In contrast to what is usually claimed, Hasidism actually widened the gap between the leader, the *Ẓadik*, and the masses. This was in line with Hasidism's basic theory: Since the masses were incapable of achieving contact with the divine, their performance of the positive precepts, simply a means to that end, was devoid of any ultimate religious value. In practice, however, the very principles that widened the gap between the *Ẓadik* and the mass of ordinary Jews also provided a method of bridging that gap. Ecstatic Hasidism was significantly different from earlier kabbalistic pietism. The latter could be acquired only by the individual himself actively imitating the behavior of a model. On the other hand, Hasidic ecstasy could be transmitted to onlookers who joined the community. Something of the *Ẓadik*'s ecstasy could adhere to those who joined the Hasidic group; even if they proved incapable of personally attaining the level of religious ecstasy on their own, they achieved something akin to it through their *rebbe.*[9]

Hasidic theory followed in the footsteps of its religious and social experience. Though Hasidism denied the leaderless masses any religious legitimacy, it restored their religious raison d'être once they had joined the *Ẓadik*. The concepts of kabbalist pietism were now given social expression in a new doctrine: The masses, by associating with scholars, could participate indirectly in the latter's immediate communion with God. The Hasidic community provided an institutionalized framework for direct contact between the leader and his followers, and the communion with God inherent in the *Ẓadik*'s enthusiasm was transmitted to his followers and strengthened by their group experience.

This doctrine of the dependence of the Hasid's religious communion on that of the *Ẓadik* also served as a convenient justification for the financial assistance that the *Ẓadik* received from his followers. There was nothing new in such assistance per se. Itinerant and local preachers, as well as scholars and kabbalistic pietists who devoted all their time to study, had long traditionally received all or part of their livelihood from personal benefactors. What changed now was the size of the sums involved. The *Ẓadik* had no practical source of livelihood, and he relied entirely on the contributions of his followers for his own support and that of his family. As early as the second generation, and perhaps even during the lifetime of the BESHT, an entourage began to take shape around the *rebbe*. The *Ẓadik* required attendants and emissaries. Guests came and went, sometimes spending Sabbaths and holidays at his home, and the *Ẓadik* had to provide for them. Even if the *Ẓadik* also held a local rabbinical post, his salary could not have come close to covering his expenses. The Hasidic community thus quite naturally became the financial support of the *Ẓadik* and his household. Upon visiting the *Ẓadik*, each Hasid left an appropriate gift.

This giving was fundamentally different from the traditional support given to scholars. The latter was always seen as charity. The traditional view that such donations were obligatory notwithstanding, they always implied a status differential between the giver and the receiver. True, gifts to a famous scholar, *rosh yeshiva*, or the like had about them the aura of acts of tribute that honored the donor no less than the recipient. But even in such cases, the relationship was at best one of reciprocity between two equal partners. One who supported a scholar received, in the accepted view, a part of the latter's reward for studying Torah. But with donations to a *rebbe*, the relationship between donor and recipient was inverted. Since the religious legitimacy of the Hasid depended upon his attachment (*dvekut*) to the *Ẓadik*, the economic patron became, in effect, the religious dependent. Here, giving no longer came under the heading of charity but served as a symbol of the Hasid's attachment to the *Ẓadik*.[10] This change in the nature of giving illustrates the tremendous social elevation of the status of the preachers and *magidim*, whom the new religious movement raised to the high level of *Ẓadik*.

It is thus clear that we are dealing with a twofold revolution, religious and social, in which both aspects were interconnected and interdependent. The shift in emphasis from the actual performance of the precept to the attainment of ecstasy through that performance constitutes the primary religious change. Had this idea been systematically pursued to its ultimate implications, this change could have totally subverted Judaism: after all, if the state of ecstasy was the main goal, then performance of the commandments was not the only mechanism that led to its achievement. Even the Hasidic leaders, including the BESHT himself, admitted that traditionally secular activities could become the means for achieving the sought-after exaltation.[11] Thus, when representatives of traditional Judaism pointed out that Hasidism was potentially heretical, their complaints were not totally without grounds. The fact that Hasidism never actually took its philosophy to such extremes is to be explained by reference to the specific character of the movement's leaders as well as to objective sociological factors that limited the extent of change. Given the real circumstances of Jewish communal life in eastern Europe and the fact that the demarcation lines between Jewish society and its environment were still quite firmly in place, it remained vital to preserve the identifying characteristics of traditional Jewish society. The fate of Jacob Frank and his followers in the generation following the death of the BESHT served as a clear warning. They tried to establish themselves as an independent sect, neither Jewish nor Christian, but though they inwardly retained a degree of mental reservation and an idiosyncratic ideology, they were forced ultimately to convert to Catholicism. Practice of the commandments was the single most representative feature of Judaism to Jews and non-Jews alike; ceasing to observe them would have placed Hasidism beyond the Jewish pale and would have raised, in the minds of both Jews and Christians, the same question that led to the crisis of the Frankist movement: "Whose side are you on?"

There was, therefore, no real correspondence between the radical internal experiential and philosophical revolution of Hasidism and the quite limited change that this engendered in the Hasid's actual religious practice. Change consisted more of a shift in emphasis and tone. Pre-Hasidic preachers, for example, treated purely speculative matters in their sermons and went off on convoluted pieces of casuistry and homily, but at the end or sometimes even in the middle of their talks, they would always return to the basic task for which they had come before the congregation: exhorting and warning about observance of the commandments between man and God and between man and man. In the sermons of the early Hasidic leaders, this type of exhortation about the detailed observance of the commandments is not to be found. They were concerned with the quality of religious worship, and, moreover, their concern was primarily with the worship of the chosen few, the *Ẓadikim* capable of *dvekut,* rather than of the community as a whole. Still, even they assumed that everyone, including the masses, would maintain the traditional way of life, which included observance of the commandments, even if without the niceties that the mystical pietists found so important.

Changes in Religious Practice. Only minor changes occurred as a result of the activities and teachings of the Hasidic leaders, and as a direct result of the new religiosity. An example of such a change is provided by Hasidic laxity about the time of prayers.[12] Whereas the halakhic tradition regarded prayer primarily as an obligation tied to the cycle of hours and days, Hasidism saw it as an opportunity for achieving communion with God. Inevitably, it was difficult for the Hasid to be always prepared for this experience at a prescribed time. But here again, there was no outright abrogation of the Halakha. Rather than altogether dismissing the notion of fixed times for prayer, the Hasidim accepted the legitimacy of an ex post facto delay until one felt ready for the ultimate sort of prayer. In the same way, with regard to revising the text of the prayer service, the Hasidim did no more than switch from the usual Ashkenazic liturgy to that of Rabbi Isaac Luria, which had already been adopted by the kabbalist pietists.[13]

But from the point of view of their social consequences, it was not the size of the changes that mattered. Small as they were, they sufficed to mark Hasidism as a separate social entity, to indicate the group's withdrawal from external society and to symbolize its independent identity. The fact that these changes pertained specifically to the order of prayers made them all the more powerful means of expressing this, since the liturgy was an area in which the unity of the community was classically given expression.[14] And there were other changes, at least at the start, which were similarly intended to separate the Hasidim from the rest of the Jewish community. The most far-reaching of these was the change in the custom of ritual slaughter. The Hasidic slaughterers were careful to use only particularly well-honed knives—a stringency that served to camouflage their real object, which was to avoid eating together with non-Hasidim.[15]

The Hasidim's open use of identification symbols as bonding mechanisms in the crystallization of their group was quite different from what pertained among the Sabbateans. The chief exponents of both movements were members of the secondary intelligentsia: preachers, scholars supported by others, ritual slaughterers, and teachers. But because of the Sabbateans' need for secrecy, membership in their movement could not lead to any change in the individual's social status. On the other hand, joining the Hasidim meant detaching oneself from the Jewish community and linking up with a Hasidic associative group.

Furthermore, the movement's central figures acquired their status as leaders on the basis of new criteria that were diametrically opposed to those by which traditional Jewish society had picked its leaders up to then. Halakhic erudition was no longer an essential qualification for leadership. Of course, Hasidism never denied the value of Torah study; it could not, since it had not rejected the halakhic basis of Judaism.[16] And, of course, it was advantageous for a Hasidic leader to add great scholarship to the list of his other qualities. This explains why Hasidic legend attributed this quality even to the BESHT, who did not possess it. Nevertheless, it is clear that halakhic erudition was not one of the basic marks of the Hasidic leader. The primary and ultimate prerequisite for leadership was an individual's ability to achieve communion with God and ecstatic contact with the divine sphere. This was a personal talent that could not be acquired through rational study; indeed, it could even be impeded by such study.[17]

Spontaneity rather than institutionalized and rationalized formality marked the Hasidic movement from the start. The *Ẓadik* emerged, or "was revealed," through the spontaneous *dvekut* of a small group of Hasidim to him, rather than through a rational method, such as that used to select a *kehila* rabbi. One joined the movement, at least in the early years, as one joined all movements based on an affective relationship—through a personal and voluntary act. And of course, some who came in contact with Hasidism became disappointed in the *rebbe* or the community and rejected both; this is what happened, for example, with Solomon Maimon.[18] But those who remained gave virtually unlimited faith and confidence to the movement because of their immediate relationship to the *Ẓadik*.

The Hasidic Community. It was also this spontaneous relationship of each individual to the *Ẓadik* that fashioned the Hasidim into a community. Even if they visited their *Ẓadik* only once a year, meeting him or even being near him that one time was sufficient to sustain the Hasidim for the entire year.[19] While away from the *Ẓadik*'s physical presence, the Hasidim would recount his teachings and relate details of his biography in order to maintain the sense of contact. This allowed the Hasidic community to exist even though its membership was widely dispersed. But communal cohesion was only a side benefit; the dispersed community was never organized in any fashion. Everything derived from the spontaneous relationship that each individual felt toward the head of the community. No intermediary came between the Hasid and his *rebbe*. There was no such thing as the *Ẓadik* of a single city in the fashion of a local *kehila* rabbi. So long as a particular *kehila* was not yet completely taken over by Hasidim—in other words, during the transitional period that interests us—the Hasidic community and the *kehila* might overlap to an extent. But the members of the Hasidic community, scattered over wide areas, were not organized in any fashion. Their membership was spontaneous, just as were their contributions toward the financial support of the *Ẓadik* and his community.

Conflict with the Bearers of Tradition. The twofold revolution—religious and social—inherent in the rise of Hasidism necessarily meant a clash with the representatives of traditional society. It is not our task here to follow the course of that controversy, which had already begun to emerge during the lifetime of the BESHT and which raged violently over the two generations following his death. We shall mention only the social basis of the struggle between the two camps. As already noted, Hasidism was rightly recognized by its opponents as a movement possessing charismatic religious authority and as a source of possible deviation from historical-institutional Judaism. The traditional bearers of authority—the rabbis, *yeshiva* heads, and lay community leaders—were threatened and antagonized by the fact that Hasidic leaders derived from the secondary intelligentsia and that the Hasidim held themselves apart from the *kehila*.

The weakening of *kehila* leadership and the geographic dispersal of Jewish settlements in the provinces of Podolia and Volhynia apparently helped Hasidism to gain its first foothold in those regions. The abolition of the Council of the Four Lands, which took place around the time of the BESHT's death (1765), removed the primary organizational instrument that might have checked the movement's spread. The struggle against Hasidism would now fall to communal officials—rabbis and *parnasim*—and individuals such as R. Elijah, the "Gaon" of Vilna, who considered themselves responsible for the fate and leadership of Judaism. Although this struggle was no less fierce than that waged against Sabbateanism, it did not result in an outright communal split. This is owing to the surprising moderation of Hasidism. Since the movement did not overturn the halakhic basis of Judaism or even abrogate the value of Torah study, Jews were never required to decide once and for all between the two camps. In the end, the struggle resulted in two coexisting sets of institutions—the rabbi and the *Ẓadik*, the study of the Torah and the study of Hasidic teachings. In other words, there evolved a sphere of activity neither entirely intellectual nor yet completely emotional, with preference given to the value of the *Ẓadik* and the study of Hasidism over the rabbi and the ordinary study of the Torah. We know that even among the early Hasidim there were some outstanding halakhic scholars. But it is also clear that even they ceased to regard this ability as an attribute of primary importance.[20]

For the most part, something like a division of labor emerged between the rabbi and the *Ẓadik;* the former was a sort of religious technician, an expert, as it were, in the halakhic rulings needed for formal leadership, while the latter was a teacher in the broadest sense of the word. Although the authority of the rabbi in his own designated field was apparently preserved, in fact his status had contracted and his influence had declined. A role reversal had occurred. In the traditional period, it was the halakhic scholar who represented the ultimate goal of religion—the observance of the precepts as prescribed—while the preacher, the teacher of *agada* and ethics, was his assistant. Now the situation was reversed. The goal was to achieve a certain standard of Hasidic piety, a standard embodied by the *Ẓadik,* who helped his followers achieve it. The halakhist rabbi had dropped to the rank of a mere aide.

The appearance of the new leadership was paralleled by the formation of the new community of Hasidim. This community existed, as we have seen, over widely separated areas. At least at the start, the movement was elitist rather than popular, and membership was an individual and voluntary process. Once the Hasidic community had emerged, however, its existence split the *kehila,* since a part of the latter now owed loyalty to a separate body. The weakening of the *kehila* organization in the period that preceded the rise of Hasidism presumably facilitated the movement's taking root. But once rooted, the movement also exerted a great deal of influence in the opposite direction. The penetration of Hasidism tended to weaken the power of the *kehila* to govern. This was the first time in the history of the *kehila* that a divisive principle had appeared that might itself serve as a basis for political cohesion in an internal power struggle. The victory of Hasidism over the length and breadth of Poland also meant the conquest of the *kehila* organizations by the Hasidim.

Weakening of the Family. The same was true with regard to the family. The individual joined the Hasidim after undergoing something resembling a conversion, that is, an unexplainable change of heart. By its very nature this was a personal experience that was not shared simultaneously by all members of the family.[21] Someone attracted to Hasidism might see himself as superior to the rest of the family. If other family members were sworn opponents of the "sect," this conversion was likely to lead to total estrangement. But even the family that embraced Hasidism as a body became different from the ordinary traditional family. Owing to the Hasid's visits to his *Ẓadik*, especially on Sabbaths and festivals, the chief basis of family cohesion—the celebration of the holidays together—disappeared or was weakened. Moreover, membership in the emotionally charged Hasidic community and the strong attachment of the Hasid to his *rebbe* to some extent replaced or weakened his feeling of belonging to the family. In extreme cases, even grief over the death of a family member took second place to that felt for the loss of the *Ẓadik*.[22]

Impact on the Jewish Mentality. The spiritual revolution in Hasidism penetrated into the depths of erotic life. The diligence with which religious devotion was practiced diminished erotic tension. Although Hasidism did not trigger a celibate movement, it displayed a clearly discernible tendency to deprecate erotic life, as well as to lower the status of women.[23] The Hasidic congregation was a man's world; unlike the family, it had no place for women. Nor was a parallel women's community organized, as in the *ḥavurot* or associations of the traditional *kehila*. The community of Hasidim grew, if not on the ruins of the traditional institutions of society, at least at their expense.

A religious revolution like that of Hasidism changes more than social institutions. It also influences the mental outlook of its adherents. In this sphere, too, it is more important to fix our attention on the psychological results of the initial religious revolution than to seek the reason for the emergence of Hasidism in prior psychological data. There is no doubt that Hasidism transformed the Jewish worldview, or at least influenced it enormously. The rationalistic approach to daily life gave way to passive expectation of some miraculous occurrence. To resort to rational means, such as medical science, was to invite suspicion of lack of trust in God; in one stream of Hasidism—that of the Bratslaver—this led to an outright prohibition on consulting a physician.[24] The same was true in other areas of life. The rational use of time—that is, its division and fullest exploitation for practical purposes and for the realization of religious values—was fundamentally restricted by the positive value that Hasidism attached to waiting for an opportune moment to achieve *dvekut*, a moment that might come and go and then return without the individual having much control over the matter. It is no exaggeration to call this the sanctification of idleness, an idleness made possible by social conditions and sanctified by the religious movement. The deep split that was felt in the post-Hasidic period between Hasidic Jews and those of the non-Hasidic areas such as Lithuania was the result of the religious revolution implicit in Hasidism.

23

The Emergence of the Neutral Society

So far we have emphasized the breadth of the transformation that Hasidism caused in traditional Jewish society. But this transformation affected only the internal structure of the society—its mode of organization, its sources of authority, and its criteria for stratification. Nothing changed in the society's relation to the outside world. The isolating barriers remained, and Jewish society's feeling of uniqueness vis-à-vis its surroundings may even have grown stronger and deeper. It is clear, therefore, that the changes brought on by Hasidism cannot be defined as disintegration in the true sense of the word. What happened was a change in the mechanisms that governed the life of society rather than a true disintegration, which would have implied the breakdown of the institutions of society and the dispersal of its membership.

Signs of Social Disintegration. Under normal circumstances a society does not totally disintegrate. Usually, institutions break up only to allow for the birth of new ones. Though contemporaries perceive their world as disintegrating, this is largely a subjective reaction to the transitional stage during which the old institutions have lost their authority and the new ones have not yet become established or formed a positive, binding relationship with the individual members of the society. But Jewish society really did face the possibility of true disintegration, since it depended for its existence on an intentional withdrawal from the surrounding society, a withdrawal buttressed by ritual barriers. Should the barriers crumble and the withdrawal end, a total breakdown of social institutions could occur, one that would not be followed by the emergence of substitutes. The individuals in Jewish society would then be absorbed by the surrounding society and would have their needs fully met through its institutions.

Jewish society, as the reader is aware, never went to that extreme, even where it was apparently given the opportunity to do so. But a tendency toward disintegration and self-liquidation did occasionally appear; a prime example of this is provided by the Haskala and emancipatory movement. This movement arose in the West contemporaneously with the rise of Hasidism in the East. The very fact that, within a society that had until then formed a unified continuum, there now simultaneously emerged two movements with quite opposite goals and ambitions is one of the signs of the breakdown of this society into its component parts.

A New Social Type—the Maskil. This watershed is marked by the emergence of a new social type, the *maskil,* who added such things as a command of the languages of the gentile environment, general erudition, and an interest in what was happening in the non-Jewish world to his knowledge of the Torah. This type began to multiply from the 1760s and soon constituted a defined subgroup within Jewish society, demanding for itself not only permission to exist but also the right to provide overall leadership and guidance. Programmatic statements presented new ideals of life-style, communal organization and leadership, scholarship, and education. And once the maskilic program came to dominate, even those who continued to adhere to the traditional values in which they had been reared began to feel a sense of crisis. Awareness of crisis imposed itself on contemporaries as a result of the changes in the objective facts that had hitherto determined the framework of Jewish life. Where the abandonment of the accepted and the traditional was carried to extremes, the consciousness of crisis became a conviction that ultimately Jewish society would disappear totally. This in turn justified, and perhaps even obligated, the individual to seek refuge outside the framework of the disintegrating society.[1]

The development of this sense of dissolution can be treated as an internal process within Jewish society, but its causes were rooted in processes operating simultaneously in both Jewish society and its surrounding environment. We must therefore broaden the scope of our analysis in order to include also those factors that brought about the change in relations between the two societies.

Estates Undermined. As our earlier discussions have consistently shown, the political and social boundaries of Jewish society were determined by the institutions of the surrounding society. On a formal level, it was the governing institutions of the state that fixed the sphere of Jewish existence. So long as the state was structured along corporate lines, the Jewish community could be allocated status akin to that of other estates. The Jews functioned very much like an estate even though the nature of their community differed from that of others and their rights of residence depended on negotiated charters or the goodwill of the rulers. But during our period, the structure of society had undergone significant change as a result of complex factors that need not be detailed here. For our purposes it is sufficient to summarize the results of these changes briefly: The absolute ruler—emperor, king, or prince—sought to concentrate power in his own hands with the aid of a bureaucratic apparatus. Under this new form of government, all the estates were gradually shorn of their autonomy, and the absolute ruler converted the members of the different estates into citizens. For the time being, the organizational framework of the estates was not destroyed, much less were the differentiated privileges enjoyed by members of the various estates abolished. But the affairs of each estate were transferred to the central authority of the ruler, and it was his orders that determined the functions, duties, and privileges of the members of each estate. Though the ruler would still take the traditional place of the estate into consideration, the right of the members of the respective estates to decide their own fate was now revoked. The central government was at least in theory required to direct the activities of all the classes so that they complemented one another for the good of the state, and the state itself was now held to be the political unit of supreme value and responsibility.

These changes in the structure of the state also affected the Jews. In the area of economics and occupations, the impact was less than might appear. There was some expansion of occupational opportunity, for instance, when a not-insignificant number of Jews took advantage of the permission granted from the seventeenth century on to study medicine in German universities.[2] But even in the absolutist state, most Jews continued to earn their livelihood by investing their own or other's capital. Only the *type* of investment changed to keep pace with economic developments.

Economic organization was also tied to the new form of government. A number of factors encouraged the linking of political and economic activity at this stage in the development of the modern state: Political leadership was concentrated in the hands of the ruler and his advisers; a national army and bureaucratic structure were created; the tax and customs network was expanded as part of a search for new financial resources; and new types of economic endeavor were sponsored by the rulers. These factors combined to make the government not only the center of political activity, but also the focus of economic and financial activity. Moreover, the development of a brilliant court life as a symbolic demonstration of the absolute ruler's authority made the courts of the princes and kings into unprecedented centers of intensive consumption.

Court Jews. These centers of power and conspicuous consumption became the spheres of activity of the Jewish type unique to this period, the Court Jew, who was to be found in the service of almost every single one of these absolute rulers.[3] The Court Jew fulfilled functions in the areas of financing and money raising; he farmed various state revenues (such as the minting of coins and collection of customs duties); he supplied the court and the army; he gave advice and at times even served as a political go-between.[4] The activities of these Court Jews sometimes became quite extensive, paralleling the growing needs of the absolute rulers, to the point that their wealth and influence placed them far above the rest of their community. Because of the means at their disposal, the Court Jews were able to develop a life-style that differentiated them from other Jews. But for reasons that we have discussed already, wealth did not bring with it a sense of a separate status. The Court Jews did not leave their community; rather, they became the permanent leaders and representatives of the *kehila*, and the patrons and sponsors of individual Jews, providing them with a livelihood and sometimes even with their very right of residence.[5] Under such circumstances, the *kehila* lost much of its "democratic" character. Elections, if they were held at all, were merely pro forma.[6] Still, the social, religious, and educational institutions, the family and the confraternities, the rabbinate and the preachers, all continued to function in the traditional manner. The Court Jews, or "*kẓinim*" (nobles), simply became their supporters and protectors.

State Involvement in Jewish Internal Affairs. So long as the absolute state affected only individual Jews, the institutional functioning of Jewish society was not restricted. But from the first quarter of the eighteenth century at the very latest, the absolute state interfered directly in the affairs of the Jewish "estate," as in the life of all others, and the internal autonomy of the *kehila* and *medina* was seriously breached. For the authorities it was no longer sufficient that the Jews paid their taxes, obeyed the local laws, and fulfilled the other preconditions for local residence rights. The ruler and the state administration were now interested in the internal financial and organizational management of the *kehilot* and *medinot*, and wanted to direct and control them.[7] Functions such as the collection of promissory notes and the liquidation of bankruptcy holdings, previously the prerogative of *kehila* institutions, were now transferred to the government bureaucracy. In this way, the *kehila*'s means of control over its members were weakened and its enforcement mechanisms restricted. The imposition of the ban (*ḥerem*) was either completely forbidden or made dependent on the special approval of the authorities. If the *kehila* leadership did exert compulsion on a member, that individual could easily turn to the authorities and induce them to review the action of the internal Jewish court.[8] Though the absolute state did not abolish the traditional *kehila* institutions, it was happy to take advantage of any opportunity to interfere with their activities.

Curtailing Jewish autonomy was easier than restricting the rights of the other estates. The latter could point to a history of rights, but Jewish autonomy had never been more than a voluntary grant by the ruler, to be extended or revoked at will. In the past the Jewish community had used all the means at its disposal to combat the occasional intervention of the state on behalf of one party or another in internal Jewish disputes, but now we find no attempts to oppose the more far-reaching intervention of the absolute state that affected the very basis of Jewish autonomy.[9] At most, some of the Jewish elders raised objections to a specific decision or tried to deflect it through their influence and status. In some cases, new *kehilot* were established from the start on the limited basis that the absolute state was prepared to allow. But even where the limitations were applied ex post facto, they were introduced only gradually, and there is no evidence that the members of the *kehilot* regarded the changes as decisive turning points in their lives. Moreover, from a historical perspective, it is doubtful whether these changes were of decisive social significance.

Ongoing Social Isolation. The restriction of the *kehila*'s sphere of activity loosened the bond between the individual and his community. But this loosening was neither preceded nor immediately followed by the individual's joining another society. The social-religious barrier between Jewish and non-Jewish society still stood. Admittedly, the Court Jews did meet with members of non-Jewish society, and not necessarily in a purely business context. Kings and princes occasionally accepted invitations from Jewish courtiers, attending the weddings of their children or even staying over in their homes. But such meetings with distinguished Christians or the appearance of such people at Jewish celebrations was more an act of condescension than the sign of a reciprocal relation between equals. For the Jew, too, such meetings represented a signal honor that demonstrated his achievements to the members of the Jewish and non-Jewish societies. But these meetings, which remained isolated occurrences in the Jew's life, did not represent any shift in his social position.[10] At the most, a personal tie might form between the Court Jew and his master, whom he served loyally and devotedly.[11] Social life and, even more, cultural and religious life remained bound to the inner Jewish circle. Even individuals who gained power and influence through their economic achievements in the non-Jewish world directed their social aspirations toward the internal life of the Jewish community. It was here that they sought positions of leadership, status, and prestige. The non-Jewish world, although it had lost something of its hostile and threatening character, remained alien and could be entered only through conversion. If the frequent and varied contact of the Court Jews in this period increased the number of converts to Christianity, particularly among the children and grandchildren of those who had achieved greatness, this did not affect the existence of traditional society, which was capable of preserving its principles and its special character despite these defections.[12]

Jews Gain Citizenship. A decisive turning point in the history of Jewish society occurred only when its individual members transferred their social aspirations from the context of their own community to that of the surrounding non-Jewish milieu. This happened when they began to regard the non-Jewish society not only as a framework for economic activity but also as a source of social gratification. Up to this time, if such a change in social goals had taken place, it led the individual to a transfer from Jewish to non-Jewish society. That the outward-directed Jew now did not have to convert to Christianity was a function of the fact that a new social class had emerged in non-Jewish society, a class that no longer saw religious differences as a decisive factor. This class gradually emerged under the wings of the absolute state through the coalescing of a new group, the independent middle class, itself the consequence of economic activity in the free market that the absolute state tolerated and sometimes even encouraged. The absolute state aimed at stripping the existing estates of their political power, but unintentionally it also encouraged the weakening of their social framework. More and more, individuals were unable to find satisfaction within the framework of the accepted estates—merchants and artisans in their guilds and confraternities, and the nobility in their estate-bound occupations and social life. These unsatisfied individuals found support in free economic activity based on the rational calculation of market prospects. The emergence of the free market correlates directly with the number of individuals who defected from their estates. The two phenomena were conditioned by numerous and complicated political and technical factors whose full description is beyond the scope of this study.

This historical process affected Jewish society only in its later stages, when the fluctuations in the economic-social area were no longer isolated phenomena. Economic and social independence had by then become a primary experience for an entire class that now sought expression and justification for itself in doctrines and demands derived from various theoretical sources. "Natural law" supported the claim that every person possessed the right to unlimited independence. Rationalist philosophy authorized man to govern his own actions on the basis of his reason alone and to sweep away the restraints imposed by cultural and religious tradition. Utilitarian ethics identified the good with the useful and gave moral sanction to the individual's efforts to achieve his own practical ends. All the principles of rationalism and the *Aufklärung* were mobilized in order to paint a picture of a new world that differed from that which actually existed. In this image of the future, class and religious differences disappeared, and all that remained was the direct bond between one enlightened man and another. It is no wonder, therefore, that the Jew was also included in this rationalist dream of human society—not as a member of a specific religion or nation, but simply as a human being without any special qualification.

The Rationalist Vision of the Future. The rationalist vision of the future began to take shape in the middle of the eighteenth century, and from the last third of that century it specifically included the Jews.[13] The vision could not yet affect the social status of Jews in the real world: the Enlightenment in both France and Germany would often become engrossed in principles that it was powerless to implement. But in the meantime, these principles could find expression in peripheral phenomena. Here and there, they served the adherents of the ideology as a basis for a new type of grouping within society. In the older corporate structure, there had been a group of intellectuals attached to each estate: Writers and lawyers served at the courts of kings; priests and teachers provided for the needs of the commonalty; and Talmudic scholars did the same for the corresponding niche in Jewish society. Now the intelligentsia coalesced into a separate stratum that presumed to be above and beyond all estates. This stratum defined itself as a "spiritual elite," and the precondition for membership was a dedication to the fostering of spiritual values.[14] Though this elite was a by-product of the emergence of the middle class, the two groups were not identical, and not all members of the intelligentsia were drawn from that class. Once the new ideas were formulated and articulated, they attracted further adherents by virtue of their internal consistency, by satisfying the demands of justice, and by guaranteeing a better world. Soon the Enlightenment ideals would intrigue some of the very people—nobles, priests, and even princes and kings—who until then had been in control of the older divisions of corporate society.

A Spiritual Elite. This new development began to influence Jewish society when Jewish enlightened *maskilim* came to identify socially with their gentile intellectual counterparts. This was not the same as the earlier phenomenon of individual Jews, fully ensconced within the world of tradition, who admired and respected gentile intellectuals and differentiated between them and the masses of non-Jews whom they disparaged.[15] This had been a purely intellectual identification that yielded no concrete social results. A true social transformation could occur only where enlightenment came to serve as a basis for social grouping. This occurred from the middle of the eighteenth century, particularly in the German states, when "intellectual" changed from an attribute of individuals to a membership criterion for a well-defined social group. Links were forged between individual intellectuals in various ways—by reading the same books and periodicals, by holding informal or organized meetings, and, finally, by creating social circles designed solely to foster the values of the Enlightenment within a single social framework.[16]

From our point of view, this social form had special significance. In consequence of the new sociological nature of the grouping, it paved the way for yet a further innovation: even Jews could be accepted into it as equals. An association formed around the values of the Enlightenment could not restrict membership to the adherents of a single religion. Transcending religious distinctions lay at the heart of the rationalists' creed, and excluding Jews from their group would have struck at the very heart of their principles.[17]

But however implicit the admission of Jews was in the rationalists' ideology, from the point of view of the Jews themselves, such admittance was profoundly revolutionary. What was new, of course, was not the actual encounter between Jews and non-Jews, but its sociological basis. Hitherto, meetings between members of the two groups had been exclusively utilitarian and directed at some ulterior purpose. The meetings of these societies, on the other hand, were valued in their own right. They were intended to give the participants a feeling of belonging to a primary, intimate group. It is probable that those who joined the new social group did so because they had cut themselves off from their class and felt relatively isolated. Be that as it may, they found their chief satisfaction in the meetings themselves, and if they assigned other purposes—such as the fostering of learning or mutual assistance—to their societies, these were only secondary aims. The principal function and justification for these meetings was in the pleasure of the contact with kindred souls that they afforded. This was the surprising fact as far as Jewish society was concerned—that some of its members were, in some aspects of their existence, transplanted to a common socio-cultural milieu with non-Jews.

The social manifestation outlined here served as the background and precondition for the development of the personality of Moses Mendelssohn and many others of lesser ability and character. Mendelssohn fell in with a group of rationalist intellectuals in Berlin, and there he remained until his entire spiritual being and all his social activity were defined and conditioned by a dual allegiance—to his religious community, and thus to traditional Jewish society, on the one hand, and to the rationalist circles, and consequently to the neutral European society, on the other.[18]

Mendelssohn in Two Worlds. It amazed contemporaries to see Mendelssohn living simultaneously in two worlds that for most people were still separate and linked only by utilitarian concerns. Hence, there were repeated attempts to convince Mendelssohn of the necessity of choosing between the Jewish and the Christian worlds. The best known of such attempts is Johann Casper Lavater's public challenge to Mendelssohn to admit or refute the truth of Christianity.[19] But in fact, such appeals missed the point, for the essence of the rationalists' social achievement lay precisely in their creation of a neutral common ground above religious differences. The human and universal had been transformed into an intrinsic value, which served as a unifying principle for all who accepted it. The demand that one decide in favor of either Christianity or Judaism lost its urgency and acuteness. From this point on, there was a third sphere—the neutral, humane one—to which members of both religions could belong. Intellectually, this sphere had arisen on the basis of the universal values of the Enlightenment; socially, it had been built within the framework of the rationalists' neutral associations. There is clear historical evidence to prove that in the German lands this third sphere gained in strength particularly in the decade from 1770 to 1780.[20]

The Ideology of Those Who Converted. Belonging to the third sphere did not uproot the intellectual from his original social world. In most cases, the new framework encompassed only a part of the individual's life. In various contexts of life, Christians remained

Christians and Jews, Jews. Mendelssohn and other *maskilim* like him preserved their attachment to the life and principles of their original culture, and divided themselves between the two worlds. But such duality was not easy to maintain. For many Jews, the neutral contact with non-Jewish society led to a complete separation from Judaism. The supposedly neutral intellectual circles sometimes served Jewish *maskilim* as a way station in the transition to Christianity. The famous salons of Jewish women were particularly intensive loci of this process of alienation in the generation after Mendelssohn's death. The salons of both Rachel Varnhagen and Henrietta Herz in Berlin and of Fanny (Feigele) Arnstein and Zipporah Eskeles in Vienna were ostensibly neutral meeting grounds where Jews and non-Jews could spend time in one another's company, with their differences of origin forgotten. However, since the unifying feature of the salons was social amusement for its own sake, they established a style of behavior that clashed with the traditional way of life to a far greater degree than did that of the intellectual, rationalist circles in which Mendelssohn and the others had participated. In fact, the salons transferred the life-style of court to the Jews and were revealed to be an assimilatory social framework in which non-Jewish culture was dominant. Participation in salon life generally led Jews to join the non-Jewish society outright, to the point even of adopting its religion and its church.[21]

If the new converts required ideological backing for their decision, they could find it in the idea of a common positive core to all religions, a notion that denied any importance to the specifics of the historical religions. The theory of the positive nucleus common to all religions discredited completely the claims to uniqueness of each religion. A person who accepted this theory could believe that in changing his religion he was simply altering the external trappings, which were unimportant in any case. On the basis of this theory, one public figure, David Friedländer, thought it possible for the entire Jewish community to be absorbed into Christianity without having to renounce what really constituted its fundamental beliefs. For those individuals who were enticed by social inducements to accept the prevailing religion, this theory no doubt served to soothe their conscience and remove their psychological inhibitions.[22]

To no small extent, therefore, the creation of a neutral zone between Jewish and non-Jewish societies led to the absorption of sectors of Jewish society into the Christian world. But if this had been the only result of the process, it would not have constituted a turning point in the life of Jewish society as a whole. Even greater numbers of Jews had deserted traditional society in other periods without destroying that society.[23]

The Elite of Jewish Maskilim. Paradoxically, it was not those who abandoned Jewish society outright who mark this period as a watershed in Jewish history, but those among the *maskilim* who opted to remain *within* the fold. Abandonment of Jewish society was, after all, only one possible reaction to neutralization. Mendelssohn himself, it may be recalled, did not take this course. But neither was he capable of maintaining a dualistic partition of his life into a Jewish and a neutral sphere. From the time of his debate with Lavater in 1770 and in the light of increasing indications of impending changes in the system of the corporate state in general and of the status of the Jews in particular, Mendelssohn was drawn further and further from his passive stance. Out of a sense of responsibility for the fate of Jewish society, he agreed to undertake tasks that more or less defined the future course for all those *maskilim* whose identification with the values of the neutral society set them apart from traditional society but whose attachment to the values and the culture of their original milieu did not allow them to divorce themselves completely from it.

The lives of many Jews of that generation bear witness to a struggle over whether to preserve the link with one's Jewish origin or to convert. Precisely because the decision was ultimately up to the individual, it was influenced by a multitude of psychological and social factors; the outcome could obviously not always favor conversion. First, there were *maskilim* whose attachment to Judaism was so deep that the idea of conversion never entered their minds, even as a theoretical possibility. Moreover, not all *maskilim* had equal prospects of being absorbed into Christian society. Wealthy Jews had an advantage in this regard, and their children all the more so, since, in addition to their wealth, they had an education and a life-style that paralleled those of their Christian contemporaries. But *maskilim* in reduced circumstances, and particularly those who still bore evidence of their origins in their appearance and accent, had difficulty in finding their way not only into the salons, but also into the neutral associations. Despite the principle that called for the removal of the barriers between Jewish and non-Jewish societies, these *maskilim* associated only with one another.[24] This intermediate class, halfway between Jewish and Christian society, was sure to continue to exist.

Thus we have a stratum of *maskilim* defined by identification with its society of origin, but feeling strong reservations about that society's traditional system of values. If the members of this group did not actually join the neutral associations, they did identify with them. In sociological terms, the neutral associations had become the reference group for the *maskilim*. It was from the neutral associations and their doctrines that these *maskilim* derived their criteria for appraising Jewish society itself. Certainly, the status quo could no longer be justified by an appeal to tradition. The *maskilim* now held up the institutions of traditional society to the test of reason, intellect, and nature—terms that, for them, were practically interchangeable.

Most important of all, the *maskilim* pictured the future of Jewish society in accordance with the model and the values of the neutral society. In their aspiration to shape the future of their society, they assumed the right to serve as mentors to the entire community. If diehard traditionalists regarded the *maskilim* as heretics and deviationists, in their own eyes the latter were pioneers and heralds of the future. From the 1780s onward, the *maskilim* emerged as a group with a clear-cut social-ideological character, which laid claim, much like any other social elite, to the leadership of society as a whole. The rise of this new elite alongside the traditional society constituted the decisive event in the Jewish social history of this period.

24

The Haskala's Vision of the Future

From its inception, the Jewish Haskala movement, like the Enlightenment in general society, envisaged a future quite different from contemporary reality. At first the future was imagined simply as the converse of what already existed, but gradually the vision took on an intellectually defined shape of its own and began not only to critique the faults of the present but also to hold up an independent ideal reality. Henceforward, the Haskala was no longer based merely on dissatisfaction with what was; rather, its appeal and moral authority derived from its logical consistency and the fundamental justness of its demands. The ideal became the standard by which reality was to be evaluated and judged, and thus a decisive factor in the active advancement of the historical process. For our purposes, we need not follow the development of the Haskala over its entire history. We shall limit ourselves, as with Hasidism, to describing the emergence of the new vision of the future. Even so, to understand this vision is also to grasp the overall direction of the breakdown of traditional society as a whole, since the Haskala presumed to criticize every principle and institution of contemporary reality and thus effectively influenced the shape of the future. Let us therefore try to imagine the traditional institutions as they must have seemed to the critical eye of the *maskilim*.

Desire for Vocational Diversification. Both Jewish *maskilim* and their non-Jewish counterparts found the economic structure of Jewish society to be distorted and illogical,[1] and with good reason. So long as the Jews were perceived as one of several corporate classes within society, each with a specific task to perform, the one-sided occupational structure of Jewish society could be justified to some extent. But once people came to perceive of society as composed of individuals who were free to move from one social status to another, the fact that Jews were linked to a restricted number of professions became something of an anomaly. But evaluations of the phenomenon were not uniform. Hostile critics censured the Jews for their attachment to commerce and finance and their shunning of the crafts, physical labor, and the liberal professions. All of the opprobrium that was normally the lot of merchants, moneylenders, and financiers in general was applied with special force to the Jews. It is one of the indications of the close dependence of Jewish *maskilim* on their non-Jewish counterparts that the former identified with this criticism. True, the *maskilim* tended to soften the implicit moral censure by arguing that the one-sidedness of Jewish economic activity was the result of restrictive legislation imposed on the Jews by the state.[2] Mendelssohn even justified commerce on economic grounds, by ascribing productive value to the transfer of goods from one area to another.[3] But Mendelssohn also saw the need to expand the fields of Jewish endeavor in the future, and to stress especially the free and intellectual professions.[4] The *maskilim* came close to believing that if only the state would allow it, the Jewish economy would diversify totally into the crafts, farming, and even the military.[5] Everyone agreed that Jewish economic specialization could not survive in the fully mobile society that the Enlightenment envisaged. But the Jewish *maskilim* saw economic diversification as more than possible, and even desirable; for the *maskilim*, economic diversification was an obligatory ethical demand.

Criticism of Jewish Institutions. The *maskilim* similarly criticized traditional Jewish institutions of self-government. Mendelssohn, the major spokesman of this view, was quite extreme in this. Even though he had seen the extensive public activity of these institutions, he could not be objective about them and labeled any claim to enforcement powers by Jewish organizations as an ill-conceived imitation of the Christian Church. And working from this assumption, Mendelssohn concluded that in the future, Jewish organizations would exist only as voluntary unions of individuals based on a common faith and liturgy. The function of the Jewish community, as of any other religious organization, would be to serve as a framework for the advancement of that which was the essential purpose of religion—namely, the fostering of a proper set of attitudes that would lead in turn to proper actions. The state, on the other hand, was permitted and obligated to enforce obedience, but it did not have the right to inquire into the intentions that lay behind the act.[6] Mendelssohn even found it difficult to compromise with tradition and agree that there was still a role for Jewish courts within the community; this he granted only so long as the Jews involved in a suit voluntarily accepted the jurisdiction of Jewish law in advance.[7] Compulsory powers, to the extent that these were required by human society, could be exercised only by the state. Religion and the state differed in essence, and were therefore necessarily distinguished in their modes of behavior. Only if they were separated could religion and state complement each other. Needless to say, this view was far removed from the reality of 1783, the year in which it was formulated by Mendelssohn in his book *Jerusalem*. Here again, we see the *maskil* speaking in terms of broad principles and demands. Through his great moral fervor, Mendelssohn portrayed what was an accommodation to reality as a vision for the future and a realization of absolute values.

The *maskilim* also adopted new forms of social association among themselves. Those who had reservations concerning the values and institutions of traditional society could hardly find social satisfaction in the traditional social groups that were then available. As we saw in the last chapter, even the neutral associations did not absorb all of the Jewish *maskilim*. To the extent that the *maskilim* sought to fulfill the function of a guiding elite and point the way for the rest of the Jewish people, the neutral associations could not serve their purpose. Only within the framework of special Jewish associations could they foster specifically Jewish expressions of enlightened values, and only through presenting themselves as a cohesive social group could they hope to influence a Jewish public that was still aloof from, or even actively opposed to, the Haskala.

These circumstances provide the background for the rise of maskilic societies from the 1780s on: for example, the Königsberg *Ḥevrat Dorshei Sfat Ever* (Society of Seekers of the Hebrew Tongue), established in 1784, which changed its name two years later to *Die Gesellschaft zur Beförderung des Guten und Edlen* (The Society for the Fostering of the Good and Noble), and the Berlin *Gesellschaft der Freunde* (Society of Friends), established in 1792. The Königsberg society undertook to publish a Hebrew monthly magazine, *Ha-Me'asef* (The Gatherer), in order to popularize Enlightenment values among the Jews, and the Berlin society was formed in order to force the local Jewish burial society to wait several days after a member's death for burial—a demand that became a rallying cry for the modernists in their war with the traditionalists, since it represented being guided by logic and scientific fact as opposed to blind obedience to tradition and the past.[8] These societies thus fulfilled functions that were at the very heart of the maskilic program. But they incidentally also offered mutual aid, support to those in need, care for the sick, preparation of the dead for burial, and the like.[9] They further provided their members with recreational opportunities.

The apparent parallels between these associations and the traditional "holy societies" are only superficial. First of all, the values to which the societies were dedicated had changed: they were directed no longer at fulfilling religious precepts but rather at spreading Enlightenment and achieving rationalist goals. Second, social recreation no longer had to justify itself in terms of religious precepts. It was now seen as legitimate in its own right—an expression of sociability, which, for the Enlightenment, was one of man's innate values.[10] Hence, it should come as no surprise that in maskilic circles, there were attempts at canceling or limiting some of the customary *se'udot shel mizva* (religiously prescribed banquets), such as the *zakhar* on the Friday evening after the birth of a male child, and the festive meal immediately following a circumcision. The official reason given for this stance was hygienic—to protect the health of the new mother. But we may also see here an expression of the fact that the *maskilim* no longer needed religious sanction to satisfy their social needs.[11] Without consciously intending to do so, the *maskilim* undermined religious values and weakened traditional institutions.

New Educational Goals. It was in the field of education that the conflict between tradition and innovation became open war. A new educational philosophy had appeared within non-Jewish society advocating uniform education for all children, regardless of their religion. This ideology was articulated in both theory and practice in the Philanthropic schools, such as that of Bazedow in Dessau, where children of different religious groups were educated together. The pupils were allowed, and given the opportunity, to participate in the rituals of their respective faiths, but the fact that members of different faiths were being educated together meant, *eo ipso*, that within the all-day institutions themselves there could be no fostering of attachment to their ancestral religions. The educators saw in this not a lamentable compromise, but an integral part of their original plan, for the Philanthropists really sought to shunt positive religions off to the sidelines and replace them with natural religion, whose deistic principles and ethical message they taught to all their students. The Philanthropist schools were the educational expression of the neutral society. Once the Jewish *maskilim* had accepted the ideal of the neutral society, they found it difficult to qualify their approval even when the issue had moved from meetings between members of various faiths on a basis of mutual tolerance to the more radical notion of creating a new generation on a totally neutral ground.[12] Of course, there was no chance that this sort of common education would totally displace traditional Jewish schooling. It was clear to everyone that those who were educated in the neutral atmosphere of the joint institutions would end up without a strong attachment to Judaism. Hence, these institutions could serve only those parents who themselves were almost totally alienated from Jewish society. The schools never really appealed to those *maskilim* who remained tied to Jewish society and wished only to change its value system from within.

One such *maskil*, deeply involved in the world of traditional values, did bring forward a systematic plan whose subjective goal was creative rather than destructive. This was Naphtali Herz (Hartwig) Wessely, whose proposal was contained in his propagandistic pamphlet "Words of Peace and Truth," written, as is well known, in reaction to the publication of the *Toleranzpatent* of Joseph II in the Austrian Empire. The emperor's edict served as an appropriate occasion for advancing the educational program that had already taken shape within maskilic circles. The author clearly identified with the values of the neutral society. The basis of education was to be *torat ha-adam* (literally: the Torah or teachings of man)—that is, the educational values shared by all men. *Torat ha-elohim* (the Torah or teachings of God), by contrast, encompassed the Jewish religious tradition, and for Wessely it became merely a special supplement for the education of the Jew. The value of this supplement depended, moreover, upon prior mastery of the universal principles.[13] Wessely's identification with the neutral society is clear in the strong emphasis he placed on subjects then considered basic for a general education: the local language, geography, history, etc. Moreover, even within the framework of Jewish studies, preference was given to subjects that could be seen as representing values shared with the outside society—biblical studies, Hebrew language and grammar—as opposed to Talmud, which was seen as distancing the Jew from his fellow man.[14] The real impact of this educational program lay in the fact that it granted autonomous importance to subjects and intellectual endeavors that until then had been seen as, at best, no more than intermediary and propaedeutic. Indeed, Wessely did not support his proposal primarily with practical arguments; rather, he argued for it on the grounds that it led to the achievement of perfection and salvation for the individual Jew. In presenting his educational blueprint, Wessely used the same moral fervor to which Mendelssohn had resorted for his political platform.

The representatives of the old system of values understood the true implications of the new educational program better than did its proponents themselves, and Wessely's book spurred the conservatives to warn publicly against the danger threatening the foundations of the entire society.[15] Wessely himself tended to play down the implications of his words.[16] But as events would prove, his proposal represented not merely the ideas of an individual but a fundamental shift of consciousness within the entire community. Slowly institutions were created dedicated to educational programs similar to that of Wessely. They received strong public support and thus provided a serious alternative to the traditional schools, which gradually disappeared in the generation following Mendelssohn. Here political factors also came into play: The government also desired to have Jews educated along lines similar to those used for the population as a whole. But in this the authorities were clearly relying on Jewish public opinion, and only a few powerless diehards from the past voiced any objections.[17] Once the traditional educational institutions had disappeared, the basic tool that traditional society had used to guarantee its survival was gone.

Romantic Love as the Basis for Family Life. This period is also marked by changes in the Jewish family, but the nature and direction of these changes were radically different from those that we have seen so far. In the economic, political, and educational spheres, behavioral norms were now fixed by rational criteria rather than through reference to accepted tradition. But with regard to marriage, the intent now was to abandon rationalistic decision-making, and to make the erotic experience the foundation upon which the family was built. What was new was not, of course, the erotic experience per se; rather, innovation lay in the elevation of this experience to the status of a determinative norm as a prerequisite for the social acceptability of a marriage. Whereas in traditional society, anyone who fell in love before marriage had to camouflage this fact behind an ethical-rationalist justification, it was now the other way around: Even marriages that were arranged along rational lines were now given the appearance of resulting from personal attachment.

Mendelssohn serves as a prime example of this change in Jewish society. He tried to portray his engagement as a private and personal affair, though he certainly had not undergone a tempestuously amorous experience, something that would have been quite alien to him. It seems that he met his spouse through mutual friends, but afterward he customarily described their meeting as spontaneous. He refused to commit himself to give his bride the traditionally prescribed gifts, and further broke with the social norm by corresponding with his fiancée. In these seemingly trivial matters, Mendelssohn was trying to emphasize that everything connected with the marriage had been his own personal decision. In this he broke with the accepted norms and rejected them on principle.[18] Moreover, Mendelssohn was only giving expression to a widely held tendency: virtually overnight, arranged marriages ceased to be socially acceptable. It was not that they disappeared. Rather, they were forced to adapt to the new social ideal. The marriage broker had to perform his duty discreetly. The dowry was now haggled over behind closed doors. The engaged couple presented themselves as lovers who had met accidentally. In some circumstances, the erotic desire was actually given free rein. Mendelssohn's daughter, Dorothea, left her husband and children because she felt she should not repress her erotic feelings. In her the romantic ideal was expressed so radically that the institution of the family was totally destroyed. For most Jews, the effect of the ideal was less intense, but it nevertheless reinforced the new norm of marriage based on free choice by the partners.[19]

It was not coincidental that the idealization of romantic love in both Jewish and non-Jewish society occurred simultaneously with the breakdown of the barriers between these two worlds. There was a common historical root for both phenomena. The weakening of those frameworks that had bound social units together left the individual on his own. Thus isolated, the individual was mentally prepared to form his social associations along new lines. Moreover, that same isolation forced him to find an experiential basis for intimacy in the realm of friendship and love. But whatever the cause, rational ideals and erotic experience both emerged as norms at a time of class dissolution and the liberation of the individual from class boundaries. These developments were two sides of the same coin.[20]

Attitudes toward the Practical Commandments. For the bearers of the new spirit, no institution of Jewish society retained its traditional authority completely—not even the religious institutions that gave voice to Jewish national identity. "Natural religion"—that is, principles of faith that suited the rationalist approach of the *maskilim*—became the standard by which all positive religions, Judaism included, were to be evaluated. The practical conclusions actually drawn by Jewish *maskilim* and gentile *philosophes* concerning specific positive religions ranged over a very broad spectrum. Some dissociated themselves completely, while others were able to harmonize their views with the theoretical teachings of religion and continued to fulfill the practical obligations of their faith. Moses Mendelssohn saw Judaism as identical with natural religion, and saw the practical commandments as training the Jew in the purest forms of natural religion's precepts.[21] But already Mendelssohn's contemporaries pointed out that his rationalization of the commandments abrogated their absolute authority. For if the principles of Judaism were identical with the principles of natural religion, they were already widespread among gentile thinkers, and observance of the commandments no longer had any real purpose even for the Jewish *maskil*.[22] Such reasoning might well lead to abandonment of practice even by those who followed Mendelssohn. And in fact, even *maskilim* who did not cut off all ties to Judaism no longer believed in the absolute authority of the commandments. On the contrary, it was precisely such *maskilim* who were left perplexed and troubled regarding the form of the new Judaism once it had, in their view, lost its traditional, absolute nature.[23] For them, the Halakha had ceased to serve as the final arbiter of that which was permitted or desirable. True, they continued to use the Halakha as a proof-text when it suited their needs in debates over details, but halakhic literature had now become no more than a storehouse of weapons for those who knew how to use them. No longer would one follow the rabbi's ruling automatically. Thus, the decline of the rabbi's authority meant, at the same time, the end of a cardinal principle of traditional Judaism.[24]

The New Image of the Synagogue. It appeared that the institution to suffer least in the transition from traditional society to new social forms was the synagogue. Anyone willing to grant Jewry a raison d'être tied this to its unique religious service. But in traditional society, as we have seen, the synagogue functioned in diverse secondary administrative and social roles. Once the *kehila* itself lost its governmental functions, and social life was expressed in various independent settings, the synagogue was restricted to fulfilling its primary function: namely, the assembly of the faithful for common prayer. No one questioned the obligatory nature of public prayer, but its frequency declined and the attitude toward it changed.

And even in this area, tradition ceased to serve as an absolute authority in determining that which was desirable or permissible. The content and language of prayer, the layout of the synagogue, and the style of the ceremony were now evaluated according to standards drawn from contemporary taste and consciousness. As we shall see, even Mendelssohn noted a contradiction between the content of the prayers—the desire to return to Zion—and the conscious aspirations of his contemporaries. Because of his formal conservatism, Mendelssohn did not allow himself to suggest a change in the liturgy, but those who came after him had no such compunctions, and in the confrontation between the tradition and what they found acceptable, the decision went against tradition.[25]

The same was true with regard to matters of beauty and aesthetics. The structure of the synagogue, the style of the prayers, and even the tunes and melodies used in the reading of the Law suddenly struck the *maskilim* as strange, offensive, and lacking in good taste.[26] Clearly, their identification with an external group planted a certain reservation in the hearts of the *maskilim* about their own cultural tradition, even in spheres that were not a matter of rational decision.

Eliminating the National Basis. For traditional Jewry, religion had always included a national element. There was a consciousness of belonging to a people, a sense of participation in the common past and future, and a feeling of solidarity with contemporary co-religionists. The breakdown of traditional society now divided the religious and the national consciousness. Because of the unique nature of Jewish society as a minority within a larger society, this differentiation between the religious and the national had quite different implications than it had for non-Jews. Radicals among the gentiles, even if they broke with the Church and other religious institutions, were not thereby cut off from their national culture. Their national cultures had also been connected to, and encapsulated within, a medieval religious heritage, even if not quite to the extent that was true for the Jews. But the weakening of the medieval religious institutions did not destroy this national link. On the contrary, it prepared the ground for a new crystallization of society around modern nationalism. This could occur where the primary elements of nationality—language and land—were real and immediate facts. But Jewish nationality was, as we saw in our analysis of traditional society, built primarily on mental substitutes for such real data: on a secondary use of a nonspoken language, on a memory of, and hope for, a land in which they did not dwell, and on bonds of religious and historic consciousness that flowed through the literary and institutional channels of tradition. Any Jew who did not remain within the Jewish fold, and, even more so, any Jew who rejected the Jewish faith and religion, found it easy also to free himself from the symbols of nationalism. Breaking off ties with one's origins was for the Jews more fundamental and rapid than for philosophes from other social groups. The latter, even if their links to their origins were weakened, did not exchange their own society for a neutral one that, in fact, was nothing more than a temporary social grouping on the one hand, and a utopian vision of the future on the other. Jewish *maskilim* sometimes had no choice but to live in an illusory world in which they eventually found it difficult to survive.[27]

Even those who otherwise remained completely loyal to Judaism sought to free themselves from the symbols of nationalism. Thus Mendelssohn and Wessely sought to eliminate Yiddish as a language of communication among Jews.[28] Even in this period, when European nationalism had not yet attained its full dynamic power, civil integration into the surrounding society meant that Jews were obliged to abandon their hope for a national future in the land of their origin. In his typical compromise fashion, Mendelssohn left the prayers for the return to Zion in the liturgy, but he declared that such prayers had no real meaning for the worshipers.[29] Here, too, we see the abandonment of the nationalist position.

Weakening of National Unity. Once the national symbols lost their power, the feeling of unity that until then had linked Jews in all lands also disappeared. The first sign of this was the desire to assimilate linguistically. Once Yiddish had been declared unacceptable as the language of internal Jewish communication, a wedge was driven between western Jewries and the Jews of Poland, whose exclusive vernacular was Yiddish. Educational reformers in particular blamed the cultural backwardness of western Jewry on the fact that the schoolmasters were all from the East.[30] The desire to acculturate led logically to opposition to the language that until then had provided a basis for the unity of traditional Ashkenazic society. The possibility for personnel exchanges between East and West gradually disappeared. Western Jewry henceforth longed for cultural autonomy from eastern European Jewry.

The Reaction of Conservatives. The process of breakdown that we have been describing was, from the start, pioneered by a minority that claimed the right to define and lead society. But the activities of this minority created a feeling of crisis in the entire people, a sense that the foundations of society were crumbling. At the same time, even the world of the traditionalists underwent a change: Once the guardians of society, the traditionalists had now become a class on the defensive. Until the 1770s, no one—not even an acute observer like R. Jacob Emden—realized the nature of the changes about to occur in Jewish life. Only from the seventies and eighties, when pressures for change were expressed in slogans, philosophies, and demands, did the conservatives understand that they were at a turning point. They resorted to the traditional weapons for suppressing deviance and apostasy: denunciation, public punishment, and excommunication. At first they didn't realize that they were facing a completely new type of opponent. No longer did their opponent accept their definition of him as a sinner and deviant; now he justified his actions in accordance with his own, independent value system. That is why the war carried on by the *parnasim* and rabbis sometimes seemed grotesque. They didn't realize that their weapons were covered with rust. Though at first they were no more than a tiny minority, the *maskilim* had the upper hand. At this decisive juncture, the god of history was on their side.

Afterword: *Tradition and Crisis* and the Study of Early Modern Jewish History*

BERNARD DOV COOPERMAN

Jacob Katz's *Tradition and Crisis* marked an important milestone in the study of pre-modern Jewish societies. On the one hand, the book summarized generations of earlier research into the local history, institutional development, and modernization of Ashkenazic Jewry. On the other hand, it also marked the path for future researchers into all pre-modern Jewries, Ashkenazic and otherwise, and defined important positions in the debate about Jewish modernization generally. By demonstrating the coherence and deliberateness of social policy in the autonomous Jewish communities of pre-emancipation Europe, Katz legitimized a more rigorous use of rabbinic literature as a primary source for social history. By insisting on a formal analytic structure, by adopting a declaredly sociological methodology, and by defining his subject according to new chronological and geographical parameters, Katz challenged many standard assumptions of older Jewish historiography and provided crucial building blocks for later innovations in the study of the Jewish past.

Indeed, so much of *Tradition and Crisis* has become axiomatic in the writing of Jewish history that it is surprising to discover that the book received quite harsh reviews when it first appeared. Two leading Israeli historians, Haim Hillel Ben-Sasson and Shmuel Ettinger, devoted long and critical essays to the book in major scholarly journals of the day.[1] This treatment was quite unusual within the intimate circles of Jewish historical scholarship of the time. The length and forcefulness of the critiques reveal clearly how innovative Katz's work was in the late 1950s, and how many basic assumptions it challenged. Some of the reasons for this will become clear as we explore the basic themes of Katz's approach.

* This afterword aims at assessing the impact of Professor Katz's overall approach to the study of Ashkenazic Jewry in the four decades since *Tradition and Crisis* first appeared. In keeping with the audience for this translation, I have restricted references almost completely to works available in English.—BDC

Periodization: Between Medieval and Modern Let us begin with Katz's decision to focus on the sixteenth through eighteenth centuries. Historians of European Jewry had conventionally divided the past into medieval and modern, with no intermediate stage leading from one period to the other. For Jews, the "Middle Ages" had simply gone on and on until suddenly ruptured by some radical process or event, whether Sabbatean messianism, spiritual westernization, political emancipation, or the start of mass *aliya* (immigration to Israel). Thus, while historians may have differed as to the cause and date of the shift to modernity, they were unanimous in emphasizing its revolutionary and absolute nature. By comparison, the many earlier centuries of Jewish life in Europe seemed to blend together into an undifferentiated "age of tradition." In Jewish historiography, then, there had been no intermediate pattern worthy of separate analysis, no "early modern period" with independent defining characteristics of its own and no clear pattern of development leading from medieval through Renaissance to our own age. At best one could point to the "proto-modern," suggesting only that isolated Jewish societies had displayed aspects of the modern prematurely, and without lasting impact.[2] At worst, historians like Heinrich Graetz simply dismissed the period as merely a final dénouement of medieval greatness, as marked only by population shifts and kabbalistic fantasies.[3]

Though Katz did not break terminologically with the conventional periodization, his approach and emphases marked a significant shift from earlier historians' indifference. While he continued to call the sixteenth through eighteenth centuries simply "the end of the Middle Ages,"[4] he gave them a new importance in the working out of Jewish national history. For Katz these centuries were "particularly eventful." They were marked by demographic expansion, literary productivity, and spiritual enthusiasm (chapter 1). In the period's population growth and communal flowering, in its flood of ethical works and halakhic manuals, Katz found evidence of a living social organism, one characterized by creativity rather than stasis and by vitality rather than decay. The period became more than the last link in a long, continuous chain of tradition stretching back to Talmudic times. It was also the start of a new chain leading forward to change and crisis.

Archival Research In part, Katz's interest in the early modern period is the Jewish parallel to increased awareness of this period among historians of Europe generally after World War II. Specialized scholarly associations, new journals, and important monographic studies have stressed the uniqueness and importance of these centuries. Not entirely unlike Katz, these historians have tended to focus on broad social process rather than on individual events, on the popular as opposed to the elite. But this analogy should not be taken too far. Katz did not undertake the sort of massive archival investigation that lies at the heart of the new historiography, nor was he interested in the material aspects of culture on which much recent research has concentrated. Katz's theoretical constructions were drawn largely from Max Weber rather than from the anthropologically and psychologically informed views of more recent scholars.

Still, as Theodore Rabb has already noted, the historical investigation of these centuries has certain special features that tend to lead the historian—whatever his or her specialty—in similar directions:

> In no other field of European history is there so comfortable a balance between paucity and abundance of documentation. With the growth of bureaucracies . . . in the sixteenth century, archives become sufficiently rich (at last) to answer most of the major questions asked by modern historians. As the paperwork and its survival rate multiply, however, there comes a point . . . when the volume of materials starts to cause severe problems of digestion. It may well be, therefore, that only in the early modern period could the type of research done by the [French] *Annales* school have seemed so comprehensive, with such revolutionary consequences for an *entire* subject.[5]

For Jewish as for general European history, the late sixteenth century provides a sudden mushrooming of documentary evidence for social institutions and daily life. From the 1890s, and more intensively in the period between the two World Wars, Jewish scholars began collecting, analyzing, and publishing these documents, largely in studies devoted to local history and institutions. One of the reasons for the powerful and long-lasting impact of *Tradition and Crisis* was that the book was the first to effectively synthesize and organize this wealth of information according to the broad sociologically defined categories, institutions, and structures of daily life. (The present translation includes the scholarly footnotes precisely in order to provide the English reader with access both to Katz's erudition and to the chain of scholarship upon which he drew for his generalizations.)

For some years after World War II the archival and documentary wells relevant to early-modern Ashkenazic Jewry appeared to have dried up and were assumed to have disappeared forever. In fact, however, much survived the carnage, and the last two decades have witnessed renewed and innovative research in these areas. Israeli institutes have mounted a determined effort to locate and catalogue the many documents referring to Jews in German, Polish, and now Russian state archives.[6] Extensive microfilming, cataloguing, and analysis of German materials has been fostered both in Germany and in Israel, and has been published by a number of programs, especially the various branches of the Leo Baeck Institute in London, New York, Berlin, and Jerusalem. More recently, Polish Jewry—the population reservoir of the Jewish people in the early modern period—has similarly become the subject of intensive archival research. Specialized journals, international symposia, and institutes for Polish-Jewish studies in Jerusalem and Oxford all give evidence of this increased interest.[7] Rich treasure troves of material about Jewish legal status and daily life have been discovered in the surviving archives of the great magnate families in whose towns and villages most eighteenth-century Jews lived.

The new research has already begun to yield important results. Systematic collection of the many Jews' charters has demonstrated that these were informed by consistent patterns of legal theory, precedent, and practice. Bench marks have now been established by which we can evaluate changes in the Jews' status and compare their position at any given time with that of other minority trading groups such as the Italians, Scots, and Armenians in Poland.[8] Jewish economic activity had been largely ignored or disparaged in class terms by Polish historians. The new quantitative data have revealed an extensive and ramified Jewish economy, which was crucial to the development of the large latifundia and private towns of the era. The archival records also require that we modify the commonly accepted picture of rigidly separated Jewish and Christian worlds. In *Tradition and Crisis,* although Katz acknowledged that a Jewish community formed a "subgroup" of local, non-Jewish society, he emphasized those symbolic, social, and ideological structures that, in fact, kept the two worlds quite separate. He argued that in the early modern period these two societies were so radically separated (except on a utilitarian level) that even the polemical tension characteristic of the Middle Ages had largely evaporated into irrelevance. Katz's position has not been without its critics, and the issue can obviously be debated on many different levels. But at least with regard to the give and take of daily life revealed in the archival documents, it seems clear now that Jewish cultural isolation was not nearly as total as has been suggested. Similarly the older assumption that Jews were more or less passive victims of capricious and malevolent magnates has been replaced by a more nuanced assessment of the Jewish-magnate relationship that stresses mutual interdependence and a social dynamic based on the informed self-interest of both parties.[9]

When used in conjunction with traditional Jewish sources, the new archival findings provide a more balanced and more nuanced social history of early modern Ashkenazic Jewry. Even material from non-Jewish archives can tell us much about Jews' *internal* affairs. Based on his research into the archives of the Sieniawski–Czartoryski family, for example, M. J. Rosman has demonstrated that the eighteenth-century decline of the *kahal* came not because of pogroms, invasions, or traumatic impoverishment but rather through the cumulative effect of the magnates' continuous efforts to weaken what was, after all, a rival governmental system. Perhaps the most startling result of Rosman's study is new insight into the rise of Hasidism, which, he shows, "was neither born in poverty nor . . . as inimical to the Jewish establishment as has often been supposed." He ends his study by suggesting that both the traditional communal authorities and the magnates may have encouraged the charismatic *rebbe* as a potential ally in their ongoing struggle for control over Jewry.[10]

Internal versus External Factors in Jewish Historiography

Not many historians have been willing to follow Katz's lead and attempt synthetic treatments of the early modern period. For the years up to 1650, the student can now consult the relevant chapters (and the extensive bibliographic footnotes) of Salo W. Baron's monumental *Social and Religious History of the Jews*,[11] while Raphael Mahler, for all his somewhat outdated Marxist approach, provides useful insights into the development of Hasidism and Haskala—the two movements whose emergence signaled, for Katz, the end of the period.[12]

Recently, Jonathan I. Israel offered a new, comprehensive overview of *European Jewry in the Age of Mercantilism 1550–1750*.[13] Israel's approach and emphases are quite different from those of Katz, and a comparison of the two works helps us better to identify Katz's goals in *Tradition and Crisis*. Israel argues that the early modern period, what he called "the emancipation of the seventeenth century," was unique in witnessing extensive Jewish participation in, and influence over, European society *without* the concomitant breakdown of traditional Jewish society so characteristic of later years. In keeping with his thesis, Israel devotes extensive space to Levantine Jewry and the Sephardic settlements of western Europe, which Katz had intentionally omitted. Israel also emphasizes legal, economic, and intellectual developments in the surrounding society as causes of, and models for, Jewish behavior. On the other hand, Israel largely ignores the rich Hebrew, and especially halakhic and homiletic, material of this period, while Katz worked primarily from Jewish communal records, religious works of ethics and polemic, and, above all, Halakha. Thus, Israel's scope is at once broader and narrower than that of Katz. While Israel emphasizes Jews' contact with *outside* societies, Katz was more interested in *internal* patterns of tradition and change.

This distinction is essential. It reflects not only Katz's extensive training in the use of rabbinic materials but also his orientation as part of the then-emerging nationalist school of Jewish historiography. When he wrote *Tradition and Crisis*, Katz was living and working among the Jewish people in the newly independent State of Israel.[14] Like Ben-Zion Dinur, Gershom Scholem, and other Jewish nationalist historians, Katz could not share the once-accepted view that placed political emancipation, social integration, and cultural westernization at the teleological center of Jewish history. The Holocaust had put the lie to these pivotal dreams of nineteenth-century Jewry. The rise of the State of Israel had pointed to the true source of dynamism in Jewish modernity: a revived national identity and newly reorganized community life. This is why Katz devoted his energy to a study not of westernization but of internal Jewish social and communal organization. For him, the forces that had shaped Jewish history were imminent rather than external. The outward-turned Haskala, which had demanded an end to Jewish communal authority, was a sign not of progress but of crisis.

Social History, the Typical and the Deviant Katz's emphasis on internal dynamics and communal authority stems also from his methodological assumptions about the application of sociological categories to Jewish historiography. In a detailed article published in 1956, Katz outlined his understanding of "The Concept of Social History and Its Possible Use in Jewish Historical Research."[15] This article amounts to a statement of purpose for *Tradition and Crisis*. In it, Katz labeled the global Jewish histories written by Graetz, Baron, and others as artificially eclectic on both theoretical and substantive grounds. Because, at least in a political sense, "the Jewish nation in the Diaspora [had] ceased to exist as an historical unity with its own unifying content," a comprehensive history of the Jews could not be organized around political institutions. On the other hand, unifying criteria such as a shared religion and literature were not adequate to justify and inform a history that included the many secular and non-literary aspects of the national past.

In place of all these inadequate organizing principles, Katz offered the methods of social history, which derived, he said, from the sociology of Comte and Weber. The social historian sought to comprehend *all* of society by abstracting from the mass of details those features that were "typical," "conventional," and normative. It was the conventional, argued Katz, that provided the individual with a point of reference for his or her behavior in every aspect of life from the most public to the ostensibly most private. The heart of *Tradition and Crisis* is a path-breaking, systematic description of pre-modern Jewry expressed in such typological categories. Rather than treating each event as a separate topic, each *kehila* as a specific case, each individual as a particular example, Katz tried to determine what occurred "typically" within the society as a whole. He sought the *norms* and institutionalized conventions that guided Jews' lives. He sought what was customary, that "accepted pattern" that the "average member of society" followed if he or she did not wish to be labeled as deviant.

But how can the historian know what was "typical" in a past society? In his review of *Tradition and Crisis*, Shmuel Ettinger argued that Katz had set up an unachievable goal for the historian. Since the sophisticated sampling and polling tools of social science could not be applied to the past, it was simply impossible to know what the "average man" of past times had thought or done. Rather than establishing the typical, argued Ettinger, Katz had too hastily assumed that the *officially* normative—that is, the prescriptive materials preserved in halakhic works and communal records (*pinkasim*)—had in fact guided the lives of every man. Katz had relied too heavily on halakhic and ethical works without checking them adequately against the available *realia*.[16]

Ettinger, it has been argued, was here articulating the general rejection of social scientific methodology that would remain the rule rather than the exception for Israeli historians for decades to come. And it is certainly true that Jewish historians everywhere have tended toward the idiographic (individualizing) rather than the nomothetic (generalizing) approaches so popular among general historians in Europe and America.[17] But it would be a mistake to assume that Katz's work was without impact. For one thing, certain analytical concepts—such as the "[semi-]neutral society," which Katz coined, quickly entered the common vocabulary of all Jewish historians. And recently there have been more Jewish historians with a social science background who have quite naturally seen Katz's work as both a resource and a model for their own. A good example is provided by Shlomo Deshen, an anthropologist and ethnographer who deals with the Jews of North Africa. In his book on the *mellah* (urban Jewish quarter) of Morocco—a book that he dedicated to Katz—Deshen acknowledged the impact of *Tradition and Crisis* on his own approach:

> Katz raised new questions about the structure of Ashkenazic society, and he viewed it in terms suited also to the study of other Jewish societies. The effect has been to move the study of the social history of late medieval European Jewry away from parochialism and toward more general mainstream sociological issues.[18]

It should also be added that the contemporary field of social history is quite different from what it was when Katz was making his powerful case in the late 1950s. On one level, the pendulum has shifted away from abstraction and back to in-depth archival research and the hunt for quantifiable data. But with regard to conceptualization and theory there have been even greater changes. The categories of Max Weber, which informed *Tradition and Crisis,* have lost ground to other traditions of social theory—that of "historical anthropology" and "thick description," which traces its roots through Clifford Geertz and his colleagues ultimately back to Emile Durkheim, to that of structuralists such as Claude Lévi-Strauss and poststructuralists such as Jacques Derrida and Michel Foucault.[19]

For our purposes, what is perhaps most important about this shift is the new requirements for establishing what was "typical." The assumption of multiple "frames of interpretation" or "codes of signification" within given social situations has raised questions about the normative postulate that lies at the heart of Katz's work. Much recent work on popular culture and on groups previously ignored or even excluded by history—women and children, the native as opposed to the colonizer, the insane, the heretic, the witch, etc.—has implicitly challenged Katz's equation of elite norms with the behavior or even the aspirations of the average individual. Folklorists have vehemently declared the importance of studying "the totality of all those views and practices of religions that exist among the people apart from and alongside the strictly theological and liturgical forms of the official religion."[20] Recent years have also seen growing interest in the spiritual life of Jewish women. Studies have investigated both the content of woman's spirituality and the construction of gender in traditional Jewish society.[21]

How we can incorporate these new research agendas into Jewish social history is still somewhat unclear. The Jewish past has left us with very few sources through which to document non-elite culture and religiosity, and the danger of projecting present categories onto the past is correspondingly increased. There has not yet been a completely satisfactory definition, for example, of what a specifically woman's spiritual life might have been in the Jewish context, and anthropologists evaluating the impact of modernization on Jewish women's religiosity have been able only to imagine a traditional world which "empowered" women by sacralizing the separate, mostly domestic, spheres of their lives in some manner free of male (and literate) norms.[22] We can certainly assume, however, that any future social history of the Jews will have to address the issue of the "non-elite" to a greater extent than did Katz.

The same is true with regard to the deviant. One of the major strands of contemporary social and cultural history is the argument that society defines itself through a process of labeling the deviant. Rather than emphasizing, as Katz did, the way in which articulated norms provide the reference point for social behavior, many historians now look at the process in reverse: The acceptable is distinguished and limited by that which is excluded. This change goes to the heart of Katz's approach, not just on theoretical grounds but also because the process of modernization among Jews has been marked by an especially shattering internalization of alien values and a resultant legitimization of what had been deviant forms of behavior.

How did the deviant become normative among early modern Ashkenazic Jews? This question became the focus of considerable debate soon after the appearance of *Tradition and Crisis* when Azriel Shoḥet published a study analyzing the *Beginnings of the Haskalah Among German Jewry*.[23] Shoḥet sought to antedate the birth of the modern among German Jewry to the *first* half of the eighteenth century on the grounds that already by that time there was strong and increasing evidence of deviance from halakhic norms. In an oft-cited review, Barouh Mevorah questioned both Shoḥet's methodology and his conclusions. He argued first that by focusing exclusively on deviant behavior without the context of the normative and typical, Shoḥet had necessarily misrepresented the valence even of the deviant. Even Shoḥet had admitted, moreover, that the "deviant" of the early eighteenth century had not yet been informed by any new ideological construct. "It seems to me," wrote Mevorah, "that even those who treated the commandments and traditional social values lightly [in this earlier period] were aware of being deviant, knew they were giving in to [the demands of] reality or sought to justify their actions by invoking some other traditional value." Mevorah argued that a deviant act *that was acknowledged to be deviant* by the person who performed it could not be seen as a sign of incipient modernity. Only an act justified by a new ideological construct could be interpreted as such, for only such an act indicated that the old values had truly been replaced by the new.[24] Katz himself echoed this position in his later book, *Out of the Ghetto: The*

Social Background of Jewish Emancipation, 1770–1870, urging that "only insofar as it can be proved that some of the basic tenets of Judaism were called in question can there be talk of an indication of change."[25]

It may seem puzzling that a social historian should insist that true social change require ideological underpinnings. But in arguing thus, Katz was not merely giving in to the well known intellectualist bent of Jewish historiography. As we have seen, for Katz, social history was a method of discovering the ideals and norms that informed typical behavior. Hence, even if one (or several) members of society did not conform completely to the ideal, so long as that ideal was shared and acknowledged by all as the *desirable* mode of behavior, it had not lost its binding power. In traditional societies, people "assume that all the practical and theoretical knowledge that they require has been inherited by them from their forefathers, and that it is man's duty to act in accordance with ancient customs." Only when people have begun to question that fundamental premise and to aspire toward change as an ideal can we argue that the traditional society is in crisis.[26]

A different picture of the breakdown of traditional behavior patterns is presented by Todd Endelman in his stimulating study *The Jews of Georgian England*. In his portrayal of the Jewish middle class, and even more so in his detailed chapters on the peddlers, pickpockets, and pugilists representative of the Jewish poor, Endelman describes an indirect, uncertain, and, above all, non-ideological process of acculturation, which was not so much an identification with the articulate world view of gentile intellectuals as a gradual imitation of the behavior patterns of one's economic peers. Endelman acknowledges that his model cannot be applied directly to the central European heartland of Ashkenazic Jewry. He distinguishes carefully between the patterns in England and those that applied on the continent, and attributes the difference to the special circumstances of Anglo-Jewry: the dislocating experience of immigration and the absence of any long-established community that could impose the discipline of tradition. Katz, for his part, similarly acknowledged that *his* model did not apply to areas such as England, which lay outside the territorially contiguous zone he had defined as a unified society. Still, Endelman's model of acculturation is a powerful one and deserves consideration especially as research into court and police archives tells us more about the poor Jews who, even on the continent, often lay beyond the purview of the official Jewish community.[27]

Katz acknowledged, of course, that deviance need not be informed by a coherent ideology whether articulated or tacit. He also acknowledged that one set of norms can lose its binding power *before* it is replaced by another, and that behavioral deviance, if common enough, is in itself a sign of cultural crisis. Indeed, he described the latter part of our period as one of "anomie" (end of chapter 21), when "many individuals no longer had a sufficient attachment to existing institutions to be willing to undertake those activities upon which the existence of the institutions depended." The decline of the *yeshivot* and the rabbinate, on the one hand, and the parallel rise of a new kabbalistic elite claiming exclusive religious legitimacy, on the other hand, created an institutional crisis throughout Ashkenazic Jewry. This crisis—Katz calls it a social convulsion—did not in itself "necessitate or guarantee the creation of new values." But it allowed two types of challenge to tradition, one charismatic and one rationalist, to take hold and become the bases for new movements. Though Jewish society had weathered these types of challenge before, its weakened condition in the late eighteenth century allowed the formation of two movements—Hasidism in the east and Haskala in the west—which renounced the old values and replaced them with new ones of their own.

Katz's pairing of two movements—so bitterly opposed to one another—is certainly the most paradoxical argument in *Tradition and Crisis*, but it follows consistently from his emphasis on internal factors as the primary forces in Jewish historical development and from his understanding of social history. In the name of discovering what was truly conventional and typical, Jewish social history had to do more than lump together parallel social institutions from different lands and point to their shared talmudic inspiration.[28] Social history could only treat geographically contiguous "centers" within which the Jews had enough mutual contact to allow for shared normative standards. Katz was aware that his division of the Jewish world into centers ran counter to both traditional and contemporary nationalistic perceptions, and he stressed repeatedly that the Jews had remained a single nation through their shared past and sense of a common destiny. But for purposes of social history, he argued, each center had to be treated separately.

But if intimacy of the contact is what defined these centers, it also implied that any (internally generated) weakening of the shared norms would be felt throughout the center. While local, external conditions could lead to variety in the *response* to the crisis, the crisis itself would be universal. And so Katz argued logically that the apparently traditionalist Hasid and the apparently radical *maskil* (advocate of Enlightenment) were both reacting to the same social convulsion, and that there were elements of the "modern" in both their responses, even though each responded in accordance with local conditions.

Toward a History of Halakha One of the characteristic features of *Tradition and Crisis* was the book's use of halakhic and *musar* (ethical) literature as a guide to the social thought and typologies it sought. This was part and parcel of a number of basic principles in Katz's approach: his emphasis on internal factors in Jewish history, his equation of prescriptive norms deriving from the elite with that which was typical of the society as a whole, and so on. But Katz's approach also alerts us to important issues in the history of Jewish thought, issues that have been at the heart of Jewish scholarship for many years now.

First, there is the global problem of Halakha's relation to developments in the "real" world. As Isadore Twersky noted in his review of *Tradition and Crisis,* "there is here a sustained attempt at balancing . . . approaches to the history of Halakha—of recognizing the relevance of historical-sociological explanation while not eclipsing the immanent development [of] halakhic concepts."[29] Before the historian can be sure of the contemporary motivations for a given legal position, after all, he or she must be aware of the legal tradition itself, of the range of possibilities and "halakhic options" that stood open before the court in the first place. This brings us to a second, even more basic methodological question: How does one identify innovation within the stylized rhetoric of rabbinic discourse? How does the historian identify comprehensive theories veiled by the rabbis' preferred modes of commentary and case-specific legal opinion? This issue was one of the central foci in the debate between Ḥ. H. Ben-Sasson and Katz after the appearance of *Tradition and Crisis.*[30]

In the years since, Katz has authored a number of important case studies of changing halakhic attitudes on issues ranging from levirate marriage to rabbinic ordination, from the proper time for prayer to the practice of allowing gentiles to provide services for Jews on the Sabbath.[31] In all of these, his aim has been to go beyond the merely biographical and bibliographical and to contribute to the history of Halakha itself as a living system of thought. Most historians had been content, when dealing with rabbinic responsa, simply to note the final rulings and had therefore been unable to evaluate the halakhists' real positions and motives. In contrast, Katz stressed analysis of the juridical argumentation itself as the key to a ruling's historical significance. He also argued that modern halakhic research had erred in assuming that the Halakha was infinitely flexible and adaptable, that in any confrontation between Halakha and economic or social need, Halakha would simply forego its internal principles and find a way to sanction that which was desired. Katz argued that halakhic adaptability was limited both by the integrity of the halakhic system and by the Jews' "ritual instinct," which might bend on an "instrumental" question but never on a "personal" one. With regard to the "shabbes goy," for example, the people might tolerate a gentile performing actions that were technically forbidden to Jews on the Sabbath, but only so long as the Jew was not personally involved. Even this restricted "bending of the rules" was, of course, a breakdown in the absolute control of Halakha and halakhic authorities. Katz identified it as a characteristic feature of the early modern period, and attributed it not just to economic changes, "which fueled the drive for permissive rulings," but also to the institutional separation of communal leadership and halakhic authority necessitated by the large size of Jewish communities in Poland. Once halakhic authorities had become merely advisers to local, regional, and national lay organizations, the community came to trust its own "ritual instinct" and no longer felt obliged to seek official rulings about the details of observance.[32]

Katz's work on the history of Halakha has been paralleled by an enormous growth in the study of Halakha on two fronts. First, the contemporary revival and expansion of "traditional" Jewish scholarship in both America and Israel has provided a tremendous impetus to the publishing and republishing of primary source works, many of which were previously unavailable. Comprehensive anthologies, encyclopedias and indices have appeared which provide both the raw materials of scholarship and wonderful introductions and guides for beginner and experienced scholar alike. Technological improvements have allowed for the concentration of vast libraries of manuscript materials on microfilm in central depositories, and recently even computers and CD-Roms have been utilized to make this material both more available and more useful to scholars. On another level, we have also seen the expansion of *mishpat ivri*—that is, the exploration of the Halakha's internal development using the critical tools of modern legal historians. Here, too, journals and symposia, comprehensive guides, and systematic expositions of central issues give evidence of intellectual vigor.[33]

The cumulative impact of this halakhic research on our understanding of the dynamics of traditional Jewish society has been tremendous. Biographies of leading figures have become far more sophisticated and can give full attention to the conceptual halakhic issues that lay at the heart of their subjects' concerns.[34] On another level, our understanding of the theoretical underpinnings and practical functioning of the *kehila*—the traditional institution of Jewish self-government—has been considerably enhanced by both historians and political scientists.[35]

Israeli Supreme Court Justice Menaḥem Elon and others have outlined the manner in which medieval and early modern Jewries both legitimized and limited the authority of their *kehila*, how they allocated power and ensured the participation of the less wealthy in the election of communal officers, and how they used logical argument to supplement precedent and ensure the flexibility and viability of communal law.[36] In a number of innovative volumes, Daniel J. Elazar and Stuart A. Cohen have used the terminology of the political scientist, not always with complete success, to offer a more systematic approach to Jewish communal history and the theory of Jewish self-government.[37]

Dynamics of Jewish Spirituality *Tradition and Crisis* does not limit its analysis of Jewish religious literature to the purely halakhic. As we have noted, the book placed great emphasis on the popularization of Kabbala in the early modern period. The mystical redefinition and amplification of ritual observance and the emergence of a kabbalistic religious elite separate from the communal rabbinate are the primary internal factors that Katz cited for the institutional decline and "social convulsion" that marked the dissolution of traditional society (chapter 20). Similarly, Katz analyzes Hasidism as a charismatic religious movement valuing the personal, ecstatic exaltation of the believer as the ultimate religious goal (chapters 21 and 22). In this he was explicitly rejecting older explanations of the movement that linked it to external models or social (that is, class) tension. In its analyses of the dynamics of Jewish spirituality, *Tradition and Crisis* was an important contribution to a central effort of Jewish scholarship in the twentieth century.

In the years following the publication of *Tradition and Crisis*, Katz has continued to contribute to this effort in particular through explorations of the relationship between Halakha and Kabbala, their competing claims to authority within Judaism, and the manner in which each contributed to the formulation of Jewish society.[38] In his articles, Katz not only explicated and helped to define the ongoing problem of the relations between Halakha and its "explanatory counterpart," but he also provided detailed analyses of the manner in which Kabbala intruded itself into the practice of halakhic jurisprudence and decision making. His efforts, together with work by a number of prominent scholars whom he directly inspired, have gone a long way toward upgrading scholarly discussion of Jewish spirituality generally and of the early modern period in particular. It has taken us beyond the formalistic categories of philosophy and Kabbala, and the tendentious interpretive grid of rationalism *versus* obscurantism, to a much more complex discussion of competing trends within a universal search for the life of the spirit.[39]

Indeed, perhaps the only area of early modern Jewish spirituality in which Katz's views have not had a major impact is in the study of Hasidism. The chapters of *Tradition and Crisis* dealing with the Hasidic movement attracted considerable criticism from reviewers. Twersky did not find the view of Hasidism as socially disruptive and religiously revolutionary "persuasive." Ettinger noted that the movement's emphasis on *dvekut*, or ecstatic exaltation, was not new and that whatever socially revolutionary fervor motivated the early leaders, this soon evaporated as the movement served to unite rather than split the community. Both Ettinger and Ben-Sasson accused Katz of too easily accepting the caricature of Hasidic behavior promoted by the movement's early opponents. Since Katz himself has not returned to the topic in more than four decades, it would seem that any attempt to synthesize the enormous amount of scholarship about the movement, which has appeared during that period, would take us well beyond the scope of this afterword. Suffice it to say that both archival research and explorations of the movement's theology have tended to emphasize continuity over fracture and social coherence over polarizing split.[40]

Haskala and the Transition to Modernity But if *Tradition and Crisis* has had little impact on the study of Hasidism, the very opposite is true for the study of the Haskala, the other movement which, according to Katz, marked the end of the traditional period. Here, too, Katz's approach marked a considerable shift in emphasis. For one thing, Katz substantially broadened the parameters of the process through which Jews entered the outside society. Jewish acculturation was not just the result of gentile hostility overcome, of Christian barriers removed. Both in *Tradition and Crisis* (chapters 2–5, 23) and in *Exclusiveness and Tolerance*, a study of *Jewish-Gentile Relations in Medieval and Modern Times*, which appeared three years later, Katz had stressed that separation of the two societies had been integral to *both* their world views. Breaking down the walls involved a two-way process, with complex changes of attitude on both sides.[41] We have already noted the universal acceptance of the term "neutral" or "semi-neutral society"—Katz's description of the changed gentile world, which made Jewish aspirations to integration possible. Equally influential was Katz's emphasis on the parallel changes in Jewish attitude toward the outside world, what he called "the reeducation of Jewish society . . . [to] universalistic ethics."

Katz has also strongly influenced the way in which historians now treat the *maskilim*. Previously, emphasis had been placed on the careers of individuals, most notably, of course, Moses Mendelssohn, and on their knowledge of outside society. Katz, however, directed our attention to the social character of the Haskala. The secular enlightenment of individual Jews "began to influence Jewish society when . . . *maskilim* came to identify socially with their gentile intellectual counterparts," when Enlightenment came to require that Jews be accepted on an equal basis with gentiles. But this new social type "began to multiply from the 1760s and soon constituted a defined subgroup within Jewish society, demanding for itself not only permission to exist but also the right to provide overall leadership and guidance." The *maskilim* claimed to form a Jewish spiritual elite just as much as did the Hasidim. Katz showed us, in other words, that *maskilim* sought not to flee their community but to reform it.

Katz's presentation of modernization emphasized, therefore, the changes in Jewish/gentile perception of the other, on the one hand, and the changes in Jewish society's vision of itself, on the other hand. These themes have informed two important books and a host of articles that Katz wrote on nineteenth-century Jewish history and the background to legal emancipation. In his studies of Jewish participation in Freemasonry, Katz brilliantly used that order as a microcosm through which to locate and map the semi-neutral society, and to illuminate how and why Jews sought to be absorbed into it.[42] In *Out of the Ghetto*, his treatment of the great changes in West European Jewish identity over the century of emancipation, the same themes were developed, and the book reads very much as a continuation of the last chapters of *Tradition and Crisis*.

Over the last four decades Jewish scholars have devoted a great deal of attention to the Haskala, and it is well beyond the scope of this afterword even to attempt a summary of their achievements. But several themes stand out that are not unrelated to the approaches suggested by Katz. Biographical treatments have stressed continuity between traditional Jewish culture and the new ideology, especially when treating those associates of the Berlin circle who spread Haskala ideals to the east.[43] The Haskala's preoccupation with control of the community and its claim to leadership have been made clear by the carefully annotated translation and publication of Mendelssohn's *Jerusalem*, with its expressive subtitle: *On the Religious Power and Judaism*.[44] The social circles within which the Haskala operated and which it helped to create have been illuminated by innovative studies of those individuals who subscribed to Mendelssohn's translation and commentary on the Bible.[45] Both class- and gender-specific aspects of identification with the new movement have been explored.[46] But perhaps most important in the systematic treatments of nineteenth-century Jewries that have appeared in great numbers over the last decades, historians have focused not just on the achievements of individuals but on the transmutation of the group, not just on the new ideas imported from outside but on the continuity of traditional values and learning.[47] In a significant sense, Jacob Katz's *Tradition and Crisis* set the agenda for Jewish scholarship for decades to come.

Notes

Preface

[1] *Die Entstehung der Judenassimilation in Deutschland und deren Ideologie* (Frankfurt am Main: 1935), published in *Nach'lat Z'wi* 5–7 (1935–37) and reprinted in Jacob Katz, *Emancipation and Assimilation: Studies in Modern Jewish History* (Westmead, England: 1972), pp. 195–293. References are to the latter edition.

Part I. The Basis of Existence

Chapter 1. Definition of Our Subject

[1] For a more comprehensive discussion of the methodological problems involved in social history, see my article "The Concept of Social History and Its Possible Use in Jewish Historical Research," *Scripta Hierosolymitana* 3 (1955), pp. 292–312.

[2] The problem of the nature of Jewish unity during the Diaspora period is treated by many historians. See, e.g., Heinrich Graetz, "The Structure of Jewish History," in *The Structure of Jewish History and Other Essays*, ed. Ismar Schorsch (New York: Jewish Theological Seminary of America, 1975), pp. 63–124; Simon Dubnow, *Jewish History. An Essay in the Philosophy of History*, tr. Henrietta Szold (Philadelphia: Jewish Publication Society, 1903; reprinted in Koppel Pinson, ed., *Nationalism and History* [Philadelphia: Jewish Publication Society, 1958], pp. 253–324); Ben-Zion Dinaburg [Dinur], *Yisra'el ba-Gola* [The Jews in the Diaspora], part I, vol. I [=*Toldot Yisra'el*, V] (Tel-Aviv and Jerusalem: 1926), Introduction, pp. ix–xxxi [and in the corrected and expanded 2nd edition (Tel-Aviv: 1961), pp. v–lvi—*tr.*], available in an edited English version in Dinur's *Israel and the Diaspora* (Philadelphia: Jewish Publication Society, 1969), pp. 3–76; Yitzhak Baer, "The Unity of the History of the Jewish People and Problems in Its Organic Development" [in Hebrew], *[First] World Congress of Jewish Studies (5707 [1946–47])* (Jerusalem: 5712 [1951–52]), pp. 337–43; and see my "Concept of Social History," above, n. 1.

[3] Selma Stern, *The Court Jew* (Philadelphia: 1950), pp. 203–7.

[4] See chapter 20.

[5] Most of the material collected in Abraham Yaari's anthology, *Shluḥei Ereẓ Yisra'el* [Palestinian Emissaries] (Jerusalem: 5711 [1951–52]), derives from this period. See my review of that book, "Sociological Notes on a Historical Work" [in Hebrew], in *Beḥinot* 2 (Tamuz 5712 [June–July 1952]), pp. 69–73 [now reprinted in the author's *Le'umiyut Yehudit. Masot u-Meḥkarim* (Jewish Nationalism. Essays and Studies) (Jerusalem: 1983), pp. 252–60—*tr.*].

[6] See Gershom Scholem, *Sabbatai Ṣevi. The Mystical Messiah 1626–1676*, Bollingen Series, no. 93 (Princeton, N.J.: Princeton University Press, 1973), especially chapter 1, pp. 1–102. I explore Scholem's views further in chapter 20 of this volume.

[7] See my "Concept of Social History," above, n. 1.

[8] See Max Weber, *Wirtschaft und Gesellschaft, Grundriss der Sozialoekonomic* (Tübingen: 1947), pp. 142, 758–59.

[9] There are many examples of rational critique of the traditional bases of Jewish society, especially in Spain. See Yitzhak Baer, *A History of the Jews in Christian Spain* (Philadelphia: Jewish Publication Society, 1966), pp. 96–110, 289–305, as well as my Hebrew article "Religious Tolerance in the Halakhic and Philosophical System of R. Menahem ha-Meiri," *Zion* 18 (1953), pp. 15–30 [reproduced in slightly different form in Jacob Katz, *Exclusiveness and Tolerance: Studies in Jewish-Gentile Relations in Medieval and Modern Times* (Oxford: 1961), chapter 10: "Men of Enlightenment," pp. 114–28—*tr.*]. On the place of the mystical stream in Judaism and its relation to tradition, see Gershom Scholem, *Major Trends in Jewish Mysticism*, 3rd revised edition (New York: Schocken, 1954), pp. 7–10.

Chapter 2. Jewish Society and Its Environment

[1] See Arthur Ruppin, *Ha-Soẓiologiya shel ha-Yehudim* [The Sociology of the Jews] (Tel-Aviv: 1931), I, p. 62. B. Dinur, *Be-Mifne ha-Dorot* [English title: Historical Writings] (Jerusalem: 1955), p. 272, n. 1, believes that Ruppin's figures for the end of the eighteenth century must be revised upward. See also S. W. Baron, *The Jewish Community* (Philadelphia: 1942), III, pp. 106–8. The half-million Jews of eastern Europe prior to the pogroms of 1648–49 were the result of population growth during the previous two generations. At the end of the fifteenth century the number of Jews there was approximately 100,000.

[2] See Baron, *Jewish Community*, loc. cit.

[3] See Guido Kisch, "The Yellow Badge in History," *Historia Judaica* 4 (1942), pp. 95–144; Raphael Straus, "The 'Jewish Hat' as an Aspect of Social History," *Jewish Social Studies* 4 (1942), pp. 59–72; Raphael E. Aronstein, "The Jews' Hat" (in Hebrew), *Zion* 13–14 (1948–49), pp. 33–42.

[4] As is well known, Goethe intentionally learned the street argot of the Frankfurt Jews and even used it on occasion. See Johann Wolfgang von Goethe, *Aus meinem Leben. Dichtung und Warheit*, IV [ed. Siegfried Scheibe (Berlin: 1970), p. 107; English translation: *Poetry and Truth, From My Own Life*, tr. Minna Steele Smith (London: 1908), I, pp. 106, 129f.—*tr.*]

[5] The cultural-historical approach provides the most reasonable explanation for the origins of Yiddish. See M. Mieses, *Die Entstehungsursache der jüdischen Dialekte* (Vienna: 1915); S. Birnbaum, "Jiddisch," *Encyclopaedia Judaica* (1932), IX, pp. 112–18. The attitude of the *maskilim* toward Yiddish further proves the mutual dependence of linguistic and cultural-religious elements. See below, chapter 24.

[6] On the development of these policies, see Yitzhak F. Baer, *Galut* (Berlin: 1936), pp. 10ff. [English edition: *Galut* (New York: 1947), pp. 14ff.—*tr.*]; G. Kisch, *The Jews in Medieval Germany* (Chicago: 1949), pp. 129ff. The sociological ramifications of the situation are especially clear in James Parkes, *The Jew in the Medieval Community* (London: 1938), pp. 101–207.

[7] See Baer, *Galut*, pp. 11ff. [English edition, pp. 15ff.]. This view was accepted up until the emancipation period. In the view of R. Ezekiel Landau,

> it is clear that this tax is [in payment for the fact] that we live in their lands, and it amounts to a rent. . . . What, after all, is the difference between rent for the right to live in a house and rent for the right to live in a country? It is because of our payment of rent that they allow us to live among them.

Responsa Noda bi-Yhuda, first collection (Prague: 1775–76), *Ḥoshen Mishpat*, §22. In his sermons, Landau makes a similar statement:

> In fact the tax which we pay is just, for he is the lord of the land and it is proper and fit that all who take shelter under his wing should pay a tax, and the king who is filled with righteousness does not make the tax burden too heavy. What he levies he takes justly and righteously for his own sake, as the man who leases out an apartment in his house.

This view was uttered in response to the *Toleranzpatent* of Joseph II. Landau is consistent in seeing this decree as an act of kindness, and he warns his congregants "not to become boastful or engage in self-exaltation. It is proper that we act respectfully to the local people who possess the land, for we are but strangers here"; *Drushei ha-ẒLaḤ* (Warsaw: 1886, and many subsequent printings, including Jerusalem: 1965–66), fol. 53a. Conservatives retained this view even after Jewish citizenship status had changed. R. Moses Sofer may have been articulating a more extreme form of this theory when he rejected the idea that improved government treatment of the Jews meant that messianic prayers for redemption could be omitted from the liturgy. "We are," he wrote, "so-to-speak prisoners of war ever since the destruction [of the Temple], but out of His mercy . . . God granted us favor in the eyes of the kings and officials of the nations"; *Ele Divrei ha-Brit* (Altona: 1818–19; photographic reprint, Jerusalem: 1969–70), p. 6.

[8] For an example of negotiations over accepting Jewish settlement, see Selma Stern, *Der preussische Staat und die Juden* (Berlin: 1925; reprint, Tübingen: 1962), I, pp. 11–14; II, pp. 7–16. For plans to expel the Jews, see I. Halperin, "On the Danger of Expulsion of All Polish Jews during the Second Half of the Seventeenth Century," *Zion* 17 (1951–52), reprinted in Halperin, *Yehudim ve-Yahadut be-Mizraḥ Eyropa. Meḥkarim be-Toldoteyhem* [English title: *Eastern European Jewry. Historical Studies*] (Jerusalem: 1968), pp. 266–76. A summary of the arguments used in favor of allowing Jewish settlement is to be found in R. Simone (Simḥa) Luzzatto, *Discorso circa il stato de gl'Hebrei et in particolar dimoranti nell'inclita Città di Venetia* (Venice: 1638; reproduced with an introductory essay by R. Bachi, Bologna: 1976). The work, published in Hebrew as *Maamar al Yehudei Veneẓiya* (Jerusalem: 1950) [and analyzed and partially summarized in Benjamin C. I. Ravid, *Economics and Toleration in Seventeenth Century Venice* (Jerusalem, 1978), pp. 49–93—*tr.*], was formulated with respect to the specific situation of Jews in Italy, but the arguments are nevertheless typical of the type of argumentation used elsewhere in Europe as well.

[9] Moses Schorr, *Rechtsstellung und innere Verfassung der Juden in Polen; ein geschichtlicher Rundblick* (Berlin and Vienna: 1917), p. 8.

Chapter 3. Barriers against the Outside

[1] The blessing said before reading from the Torah uses the term "torat emet" (literally: true teaching) to express this idea. Maimonides, *Mishne Tora, Laws of Kings*, IV, 10, uses the term "dat ha-emet" (true religion), and the phrase "dat emet" is also found in the morning service for the Day of Atonement, in the prayer "enosh ma yizke." In the philosophical literature of the Middle Ages we find the terms "conventional" or "natural" religion sometimes used to describe Christianity or Islam. See my "Religious Tolerance in Menaḥem ha-Meiri" and *Exclusiveness and Tolerance*, chapter 10. But in the popular mind, the distinction between true and false religion was more widespread. See for example, for our period, the phrasing in R. Benjamin Wolf b. Mattathiah, *Tohorat ha-Kodesh*, first edition (Amsterdam: 1732–33), II, fol. 10b: One who learns from the gentiles or teaches them "is exchanging a true teaching for a false one."

[2] See my "Religious Tolerance in Menaḥem ha-Meiri" and *Exclusiveness and Tolerance*, chapter 10.

[3] See *Shulḥan Arukh, Yore De'a*, §148.12; Sabbetai b. Meir Kohen, *Siftei Kohen* [*SHaKH*], ad loc., §13; as well as *Shulḥan Arukh, Yore De'a*, §151.1, and *SHaKH*, ad loc., §7.

[4] R. Solomon ben Isaac [RaSHI], *Tshuvot RaSHI* [English title: Responsa

RaSHI], ed. Israel Elfenbein (New York: 1943), §58, pp. 55f. ("In our areas the gentiles do not offer wine in libation to idols and therefore people have begun to act leniently and allow profiting [from the wine, but not drinking it—*le-inyan heter hanaa*]"), and §327, p. 337; idem, supposed author, *Sefer ha-Ora*, ed. Solomon Buber (Lemberg: 1905; photographic reprint, Jerusalem: 1966–67), p. 148; R. Simḥa ben Samuel, *Maḥzor Vitri*, ed. S. Hurwitz (Nürnberg: 1923), p. 774, §115; *Tosafot, Avoda Zara*, fol. 58b, s.v. "Katav"; *Arbaa Turim, Yore De'a*, §123.

[5] According to R. Meir b. Gedaliah (MaHaRaM) of Lublin, from the time of Rabbi Moses Isserles the rabbis of Cracow had tried to stop the merchants of Rimanov from engaging in the wine trade. But the merchants argued that they drew the main part of their livelihood from this trade, and the rabbis had desisted. MaHaRaM himself tried once more to limit the license to situations in which the wine was offered in payment for debts, but it is clear from the responses of the Rimanov merchants that they treated this as, in effect, a license for all forms of trade. Nor was this a matter of a single town. As MaHaRaM testifies, there was a general proclamation made on "market day"—apparently in Cracow—forbidding all trade in gentile wine. *Responsa*, §50. This proclamation may be the *takana* hinted at in the *takanot* of Cracow of 1594–95 concerning gentile wine; Israel Halperin, ed., *Pinkas Vaad Arba Arazot. Likutei Takanot, Ktavim u-Reshumot* [The Register of the Council of the Four Lands. Collected By-Laws, Writings, and Notes (1580–1764)] (Jerusalem: 1945), p. 452. The MaHaRaM served as rabbi of Cracow between 5347 and 5355 (1586–95). Cf. Sabbetai Kohen, *Siftei Kohen* [*SHaKH*], *Yore De'a*, §124.71. In any case, the struggle arose as the supervisory powers of rabbis rose in general. Before this, it seems that people simply engaged in this trade with no hesitation at all. The struggle would continue in Cracow in the next generation as well. The halakhists excommunicated "anyone drinking, or trading in, gentile wine," but this was in vain as we see from the testimony of the town rabbi; R. Joel Sirkes, *Responsa Bayit Ḥadash ha-Ḥadashot* (Koretz: 1784–85; Jerusalem, 1958–59), §§29–30. For a similar situation in Moravia, see R. Menaḥem Mendel Krokhmal, *Responsa Ẓemaḥ Ẓedek* (Amsterdam: 1675), §§12, 74, 87, and 116. Here permission was somewhat restricted, but the householders certainly tended to extend the license. See also Israel Halperin, ed., *Takanot Medinat Mehrin* [By-Laws of the Province of Moravia] (Jerusalem: 1951), index, s.v. "yayin."

[6] At the end of the eighteenth century, R. Judah Loeb Margalioth gave explicit halakhic sanction to the lenient position and, in *Responsa Pri Tvu'a* (Nowydwor: 1795–96), §1, noted that tavern keepers were established (*huḥzeku*) in most of the towns of Poland and that no one even chirped or opened their mouth [against this practice]; fol. 3a. See also the novellae of R. David Solomon Eibenschutz to *Shulḥan Arukh, Yore De'a*, §124 [=*Sefer Levushei Sered*, part III] (Hrubieszow: 1819), fol. 96. Ber of Bolechow (1723–1805) drew his living completely from trade in gentile wine, and didn't even raise the question of a need for some sort of license; M. Wischnitzer, ed., *Zikhronot*

R. Dov mi-Boliḥov (5483–5565) (Berlin: 1922; reprint, Jerusalem: 5729) [and English translation, *The Memoirs of Ber of Bolechow (1723–1805)* (London: 1922)—*tr.*].

[7] See *Tosafot, Avoda Zara*, fol. 2b, s.v. "Asur," and *Tosafot, Sanhedrin*, fol. 63b, s.v. "Asur."

[8] See my article and book cited above, n. 2, and the bibliography cited therein.

[9] Communities were still accused of converting gentiles on occasion. See, for example, the passages from the *pinkas yashan*, or first record book, of the Jewish community in Lithuania published by I. Halperin, "The Beginnings of the Lithuanian Jewish Council and Its Relations with the Council of the Four Lands" [in Hebrew], *Zion* 3 (1937–38), pp. 51–57, reprinted in Halperin, *Yehudim ve-Yahadut be-Mizraḥ Eyropa*, pp. 48–54. Accepting converts is listed as one of three well-known canards leveled against the Jews (p. 53). See also *Pinkas ha-Medina o Pinkas Vaad ha-Kehilot ha-Rishonot bi-Mdinat Lita*, ed. Simon Dubnow (Berlin: 1925), §§410 and 438; Halperin, ed., *Pinkas Vaad Arba Araẓot*, pp. 71, 171, 172; idem, *Takanot . . . Mehrin*, §267 and n. 13, ad loc. It is hard to know how literally to take these testimonies, but one way or the other, Jewish institutions warned against converting gentiles. R. Solomon Luria was typical in this (*Yam shel Shlomo* [Stettin: 1861–62], *Yevamot*, IV, §49):

> Now that we live in a land not our own and as slaves under their hands, should a Jew aid such a convert he would be committing treason, and be guilty of a capital crime. . . . Would that Israel remain safe among the nations during our exile, and may there not be many strangers, not of our people [who seek to convert]. One should be very cautious.

R. Samuel Edels (MaHaRSHA') paraphrased the Talmudic maxim "God exiled the Jews among the nations so as to increase the number of converts" as follows: "That is, to spread word of the faith among the other nations"; *Ḥidushei Agadot* [Lublin: 1626–27], *Pesaḥim*, fol. 87b. This change is also reflected in the new meaning associated with the word "ger," which had once meant "convert." For example, a Sephardic source, R. Jacob Sasportas, *Responsa Ohel Yaakov*, §3, sees former *conversos* who return to Judaism as the true "gerei ẓedek" (righteous converts), while R. Benjamin Wolf ben Mattathiah states that "contemporary *gerim* are those who were expelled from a distant land"; *Tohorat ha-Kodesh*, II, fol. 41a.

[10] R. Moses Rivkes, *Be'er ha-Gola, Ḥoshen Mishpat*, §425. Such statements were first stated in a theoretical context, as by R. Eliezer ben Elijah Ashkenazi, *Maasei ha-Shem* (Venice: 1582–83), fol. 134d–135a, in commenting on the prayer "Pour Out Thy Wrath" in the Passover Haggada (possibly following Azariah de' Rossi, *Me'or Einayim* [Mantua: 1573], chapter 55). What is new in Ashkenazi and those who followed him is that they

included belief in the Exodus from Egypt as one of the factors distinguishing between the various nations for halakhic purposes.

[11] The halakhists cited above, n. 5, admitted that at least according to one approach cited by Jacob ben Asher (*Arbaa Turim, Yore De'a*, §123, citing RaSHBaM, RaSHI, and ultimately the *Ge'onim*), all trade might be allowed on the grounds that contemporary gentiles no longer performed ritual libations. These halakhists did not, however, want to arrive at such a radical conclusion, and therefore limited the license to acceptance of wine in payment for a debt. Once, however, Jews began to engage in the wine trade outright, this argument served as the basis for a general license; cf. Margalioth, *Responsa Pri Tvu'a*, §1.

[12] R. Moses Isserles, *Darkhei Moshe ha-Arokh, Yore De'a* (Sulzbach: 1691–92), §151. [Isserles intentionally distorts the Christian name for strings of rosary beads (used to count off the number of times the "Pater noster" prayer was recited) into "Ptor Havalim" or "unravel vanities"—*tr.*] Isserles's words, which bear witness to the fact that such trade in Christian objects was customarily allowed, were cited and explained by R. Sabbetai Kohen, *Siftei Kohen, Yore De'a*, §151.7, who links them with Isserles's position (*Darkhei Moshe ha-Arokh, Tur Oraḥ Ḥayim*, §157) concerning the permissibility of accepting an oath taken by a contemporary Christian. In the latter case, Isserles had suggested that gentiles, as opposed to Jews, were not forbidden to believe in a composite God [*shituf*], and therefore Christian Trinitarianism was not idolatrous. The radical nature of Isserles's position was soon noted by R. Ephraim b. Jacob ha-Kohen, *Responsa Shaar Efrayim* (Sulzbach: 1688), §24 [who tried to re-interpret it in order to lessen its impact—*tr.*].

[13] R. Benjamin Aaron b. Abraham Slonik, *Responsa Mas'at Binyamin* (Vilna: 1893; photographically reprinted, Jerusalem: 1967–68), §86. For the most part, the halakhists tended to allow such a practice on the grounds of the medieval reasoning; see *Darkhei Moshe, Yore De'a*, §151, cited in n. 12, above.

[14] *Avoda Zara*, fol. 26a; *Tosafot, ibid.*, fol. 26b, s.v. "La-afukei"; *Tosafot, Gitin*, fol. 70a, s.v. "Rav Shimi"; *Arbaa Turim, Yore De'a*, §154, and R. Joseph Caro, *Beit Yosef*, ad loc.; Sirkes, *Responsa Bayit Ḥadash ha-Ḥadashot*, §2. On other uses of this concept, see *Enẓiklopediya Talmudit*, s.v. "Eyva." A parallel concept is "darkhei shalom"; it appears as a reason, for example, to support the gentile poor along with the Jewish poor; *Gitin*, fol. 61a; Maimonides, *Mishne Tora, Laws of Kings*, X, 12; *Arbaa Turim, Yore De'a*, §151; *Shulḥan Arukh, Yore De'a*, §151.12. The wording here is quite significant. According to Maimonides, "the sages commanded . . . ," while for the later codifiers, "it is permitted to support." Cf. R. David ha-Levi, *Turei Zahav, Yore De'a* §151.9.

[15] The Talmud rules that if a Jew be invited by a fellow townsman who is an idolator to the latter's son's wedding, "even if the Jew eats and drinks his own food" he is considered "a participant in idolatry though in a pure fashion"; *Avoda Zara*, fol. 8a; *Arbaa Turim, Yore De'a*, §152. R. Joshua Falk

specifically notes in *Prisha*, ad loc., that in this case permission to participate is not granted "on grounds of enmity." The comment of R. David ha-Levi, *Turei Zahav* (*Yore De'a*, §152.1), is typical: "The Torah commands that there be enmity between us in order to keep their daughters at a distance [i.e., to prevent intermarriage], so how would it be possible to permit attendance at the wedding on the grounds of [preventing] enmity!" The view of R. Ya'ir Ḥayim Bacharach (*Responsa Ḥavot Ya'ir* [Lemberg: 1895–96], §66) is similar:

> Were we to permit such a thing in order [to prevent] enmity, [then the same logic would suggest that] we drink from their cup and eat of their bread, and all the regulations aimed at creating social distance which the holy Sages issued . . . in order to keep us from assimilating among the nations and learning their ways would become moot.

The essence of Bacharach's ruling is that the argument of "preventing enmity" applies only when it serves to allow an action that is necessary in its own right. It was not intended, however, to revoke the basic goal of socio-religious separation. Here the halakhists clearly expressed the sociological distinction between different forms of contact.

[16] Glückel of Hameln relates that noblemen and ladies attended her daughter's wedding; David Kaufmann, ed., *Zikhronot Marat Glikel me-Hamil* [The (Yiddish) Memoirs of Glückel of Hameln] (Frankfurt am Main: 1896), p. 146 [*The Memoirs of Glückel of Hameln, 1646–1724, Written by Herself*, tr. Marvin Lowenthal (New York: 1932), p. 97]. Other examples are reported by H. Schnee, *Die Hoffinanz und der moderne Staat* (Berlin: 1952–55), III, pp. 225–31.

[17] Dubnow, *Pinkas . . . Lita*, §§133 and 947. The first *takana* dates from 1628, and amounts to no more than a general warning. The second, dated 1752, lays a cloud of suspicion on the morality of female peddlers, suggesting that "their children are close to bastards," and seeks totally to eradicate this profession. But the *takana* clearly reflects the economic interests of its authors. It complains, among other things, that peddling "limited the livelihood of many burghers and merchants in all the other communities"—that is, that the peddlers were crossing over from the commercial territory of one community to that of another. Still, one should not see these *takanot* concerning moral probity as nothing more than camouflage for the attempt by a class to protect its economic interests. The Council of the Four Lands, for instance, was already warning women against being alone with males in 1607, with no reference to female peddlers per se; Halperin, *Pinkas Vaad Arba Araẓot*, §51. R. Joshua Falk wondered about "the custom which has become established that [Jewish women] take to the road even with a gentile wagon-driver, and with no more than a young boy or girl with them to protect them." He did find a justification for the practice; *Prisha, Arbaa Turim, Even ha-Ezer*, §22.4. See also Halperin, *Takanot . . . Mehrin*, §279. For a warning on this matter

in Eisenstadt, see B. Wachstein, *Urkunden und Akten zur Geschichte der Juden in Eisenstadt und den Siebengeminden* (Vienna: 1926), p. 149.

[18] *Responsa Ḥavot Ya'ir*, §§66 and 73. R. Me'ir Stern, author of the first *responsum*, notes that his father-in-law had forbidden the practice to his congregants, and he had followed in his footsteps while serving as the rabbi of Fulda. However, he knew that he did not have the power to change the local practice, and hence struggled to find a justification for what had become established custom. R. Ya'ir Ḥayim Bacharach himself goes even further in recognizing the reality of the situation. He rejected all the halakhic justifications, recognized that economic necessity lay at the heart of the practice, and accepted it *on that basis*. From these *responsa* we see that the problem arose at the latest in the second half of the seventeenth century.

[19] R. Me'ir Stern and R. Ya'ir Ḥayim Bacharach mention the stricture against being alone with an idolator (i.e., a gentile) on the grounds that all idolators were suspected of being murderers (*Avoda Zara*, fol. 22b). This stricture applied as much to men as to women. But even they admitted that no one paid attention to this ban, and it was clearly no longer observed.

[20] For Italy, see R. Samuel Aboab, *Responsa Dvar Shmu'el*, §49. For Moravia, see R. Moses Isserles, *Responsa*, §124, fol. 484a–488b. Though dealing in particular with Moravia, the *responsum* also includes other lands. In the sources cited above, n. 5, there is evidence for a breakdown in observance also in the Polish border cities that came under Isserles's personal jurisdiction. Sirkes, *Responsa Bayit Ḥadash ha-Ḥadashot*, §29, cited the general view that local gentiles were merely "following in the paths of their fathers" and were therefore not true idolators. But Isserles gives the real reason for the spread of the practice: "In those places where Jews have become accustomed to practice lenience, [they do so] because [they see it as] a matter of life and death [*mipnei ḥayei nefesh*]: they have nothing else to drink but wine"; *Responsa*, fol. 486b.

[21] *Sefer ha-Ora*, p. 148; *Tosafot, Avoda Zara*, fol. 57b, s.v. "La-Afukei."

[22] See Isserles, *Responsa*, §124, a responsum that was omitted from several of the later editions. In his sermons, MaHaRaL states explicitly that rabbis had endorsed the license to drink *stam yeinam*. See the homily on study and observance (Torah and *mizvot*) that was republished in the introduction to R. Nathan Nata [ben Reuben David] Spira, *Maamar Yayin ha-Meshumar* (Venice: 1659–60). The minutes of the Frankfurt rabbinical assembly in 1603 also refer to this phenomenon: "If someone holding the title of 'rabbi' or 'ḥaver' transgresses this *takana* and mocks the stricture against gentile wine, he is to be considered a scholar who desecrates the name of heaven in public"; Markus Horovitz, *Die Frankfurter Rabbinerversammlung von 1603 (Beilage zur Einladungsschrift der israelitischen Religionsschule)* (Frankfurt am Main: 1897), p. 23. [Horovitz's publication of the Hebrew minutes of this rabbinic synod is very rare. Two German versions of the minutes were published from archives by M. Stern: "Der Hochverratsprozess gegen die deutschen Juden im Anfange des 17. Jahrhunderts," *Monatsblätter für Vergangenheit und Gegenwart des Judentums*, Bernhard Koenigsberger, ed. (Berlin: 1890–91),

and the text in question, decision no. 4, appears on pp. 125–28. See also Markus Horovitz, *Rabanei Frankfurt* (Jerusalem: 1972), p. 29—*tr.*]

[23] See *Arbaa Turim, Yore De'a*, §123; R. Joseph Caro, *Beit Yosef*, ad loc.; R. Joshua Falk, *Prisha*, ad loc., §3. The medieval development still requires clarification. See my article and book cited above, n. 2.

[24] In Moravian communities, a special blessing (*mi she-berakh*) was customarily recited for "all the righteous and abstinent ones who refrain from drinking wine which our Sages, of blessed memory, have forbidden"; see Halperin, ed. *Takanot . . . Mehrin*, p. 89, n. 8. As a result of MaHaRaL's efforts, we find rigorous religious supervision of winemaking—something that became an important source of income for rabbis and their agents; see Halperin, ed., *Takanot . . . Mehrin* (§§272–77, 565, 571, 619, and 642), and Krokhmal, *Responsa Ẓemaḥ Ẓedek*, cited above, n. 5. Even in this period, the middle of the seventeenth century, we can still see signs of tension between the supervisory institutions and the lay community. Supervisory agents were required to take an oath that they would not deviate from the halakhists' instructions. Krokhmal suspected that laymen intentionally misinformed the halakhists in matters of *stam yeinam* (*Ẓemaḥ Ẓedek*, §75).

[25] See the homily on study and observance (Torah and *miẓvot*) cited above, n. 22.

[26] R. Nathan Nata Spira wrote his *Maamar Yayin ha-Meshumar* expressly for this purpose. For other examples, see chapter 20.

[27] See I. Heinemann, "The Dispute over Nationality in the Aggada and in Philosophy during the Middle Ages," in Yitzhak Baer et al., eds., *Sefer Dinaburg* (Jerusalem: 1949), pp. 132–50.

[28] For examples and a summary of this approach, which is to be found throughout the *Zohar*, see F. Lachower and I. Tishby, eds., *Mishnat ha-Zohar* [The Wisdom of the Zohar] (Jerusalem: 1949), I, pp. 290ff.

[29] I believe that a systematic analysis and comparison of the sources from the two periods would demonstrate this difference in approach. This, of course, cannot be accomplished in the present context.

[30] See for example the rules about what is permitted and what forbidden in trading with gentiles on their holy day: *Yore De'a*, §148. The last paragraph dismisses all restrictions on the grounds that "in our day, they [i.e., the gentiles] are not expert in the nature of idolatry." But Sabbetai Kohen (*SHaKH*, §12) comments that the bans on entering the home of the idolator on his holy day and on greeting him (§9) remained in force.

[31] G. Scholem, "The Sabbatean Movement in Poland" [in Hebrew], in I. Halperin, ed., *Beit Yisra'el be-Folin mi-Yamim Rishonim ve-ad li Ymot ha-Ḥurban* (Jerusalem: 1954 and 1953), II, p. 69.

Chapter 4. Contact with the Surrounding Society

[1] The 1264 charter issued by Boleslav the Pious (a model for those that followed) obligated Christians to come to the aid of Jews living in their midst: *Beit Yisra'el be-Folin,* II, p. 233; and cf. ibid., I, pp. 3f. That Jews shared this attitude to their neighbors is evidenced, for instance, by the halakhic ruling that it is permitted to extinguish a fire "on the Sabbath, even if the fire is in the home of an idolator; and this is the customary practice"; ReMA', *Shulḥan Arukh, Oraḥ Ḥayim,* §334.26. Natural disasters that upset the social balance could lead, of course, to conflict and inter-group violence, especially when a subgroup was ethnically distinct, etc. The history of the Jewish Diaspora is replete with instances of this. In our period, for example, we find the testimony of Rabbi Jacob Reischer, *Responsa Shvut Yaakov,* II, (Offenbach: 1718–19), §84, about the events of 5473 (1712–13), a year of plague:

> In most places where our people lived, [gentiles] would close the Jewish street and prevent anyone from entering or leaving. Only with great effort and as a result of truly enormous *shtadlanut* [Jewish appeals to the authorities] would they allow food to enter. In some places [Jews] were forced to flee and hide themselves in the forests and caves. Jews who were on the roads or in the fields were literally in danger of being killed. . . .

Sometimes, however, catastrophe led to the opposite reaction. After the burning of the ghetto in Frankfurt in 1711, the homeless, including the communal rabbi, Naphtali ha-Kohen, found refuge in the homes of gentiles. (We might note that the rabbi was himself suspected of causing the fire by his experimenting with practical Kabbala.) See I. Kracauer, *Geschichte der Juden in Frankfurt an Main. 1150–1824* (Frankfurt am Main: 1925–27), II, p. 122; M. Horovitz, *Frankfurter Rabbinen,* II, p. 70 [*Rabanei Frankfurt,* pp. 73f.—*tr.*]. An example of a humane attitude at a time of trouble is found in R. Menaḥem Mendel Krokhmal, *Responsa Ẓemaḥ Ẓedek,* §93: A Christian blacksmith tried to keep a Jew and his apprentice from continuing on their journey during a snowstorm. But we should note that the Jew did not want, under any circumstances, to stay with the gentile or to spend the Sabbath outside his own home.

[2] The Council of the Four Lands ruled in 5367 (1606–7) that it was undesirable to have "holders of *arenda* [leasehold contracts] who live in the villages in isolation. . . . Rather, two householders should hold the *arenda* [in partnership] and live there with their wives"; Halperin, ed., *Pinkas Vaad Arba Araẓot,* p. 17. Cf. a similar ruling in Lithuania, dated 5392 (1631–32); Dubnow, ed., *Pinkas . . . Lita,* §259. In 5388 (1627–28) *arendars* were requested at least to seek instruction of the local rabbinical judge with regard to how to behave in their isolated residences; ibid., §132. We find an attempt

to remove the Jew symbolically from his isolation in R. Moses Isserles's ruling, citing R. Moses ben Jacob of Coucy, *Sefer Mizvot Gadol* (Venice: 1546–47), that "people who dwell in settlements [i.e., small villages] and who do not have access to a quorum for prayers, should at least recite the morning and evening prayers at the hour when communal prayers are said [in the larger centers]; *Oraḥ Ḥayim*, §90.9.

[3] Attracting or dissuading new settlers amounted, at times, to a conflict between one's personal interests and one's Jewish values. For economic reasons, the first settler might wish to remain alone. Although the Jewish legal principle of *ḥezkat ha-yishuv* (residence monopoly) certainly did not give an individual the right to keep another out (see chapter 9), in practice the original settler was often able to do exactly that, and the local ruler would help him in this. Rabbi Joseph Stadthagen saw in this desire of individuals to prevent others from settling in their areas the "sin of his generation," for "everyone seeks his own advantage"; A. Berliner, *Religionsgespräch* (Berlin: 1914), p. xxviii. Still, the establishment of many Jewish communities as a result of the settlement of a Court Jew, a very common phenomenon in our period specifically in Germany, proves that events tended to move in the opposite direction. See H. Schnee, *Die Hoffinanz,* III, pp. 223–24, as well as numerous other examples in the first two volumes.

[4] Individuals placed great store by such visits, to the extent that, in order to extract tax payments from recalcitrants, the communities were able to threaten them with withholding such services. The *takanot* of Moravia forbade communities from expelling villagers from the synagogue during the blowing of the *shofar* and during prayers because they had not paid all their local institutional dues; Halperin, ed., *Takanot . . . Mehrin,* §521.

[5] The Council of Lithuania decided in 1626–27 to send special emissaries to supervise tax collection. The emissaries were to serve also as judges; Dubnow, ed., *Pinkas . . . Lita,* §125. Rabbi Judah Loeb Pukhovitser describes the two aspects and ascribes the positive to the past and the negative to the present:

> It may be that it was a *minhag kadmonim* (ancient custom) that great rabbis would travel each year to their settlements to teach isolated individuals and *arendars* the laws and the religious customs of our holy Torah, such as how to sell the farm in order not to profane the Sabbath . . . and the laws of prayer and blessings. . . . This is no longer true. I have seen evil in that most of those who travel in the countrysides [*glilot*] and settlements [do so] for the sake of their livelihood, in order to fill their containers with grain and food and their knapsacks with money, and they do not teach [the local Jews] anything.

Kne Ḥokhma (Frankfurt an der Oder: 1681), fol. 8c; and see also ibid., fol. 8d, which describes the itinerant scholars who held no post. The obligation of rabbis to supervise villagers religiously and to make sure that their ritual slaughter, wine, and so forth were proper, is spelled out in many *takanot*; Halperin, ed., *Takanot . . . Mehrin*, §§274 and 478; Dubnow, ed., *Pinkas . . . Lita*, §§137 and 261.

[6] See above, chapter 3, nn. 17–18.

[7] The sources cited above in chapter 3 with regard to Jewish women being alone with (non-Jewish) men prove that women traveled in the company of gentiles. In his autobiography R. Jacob Emden describes an instance of such travel with non-Jews; *Megilat Sefer* (Jerusalem: 1979), p. 83. For Jews lodging in gentile homes even on the Sabbath, see R. Menaḥem Mendel Krokhmal, *Responsa Ẓemaḥ Ẓedek*, §§35 and 42. On more than one occasion, halakhists discussed the proper way of observing the ritual when traveling Jews ate their meals in gentile homes; ReMA', *Oraḥ Ḥayim*, §193.3; R. Moses Mat, *Mate Moshe* (Cracow: 1590–91, but references are to the annotated edition of M. Knoblowicz, London: 1958), §350, p. 130 (which mentions "a festive meal accompanying the ceremony of redemption of the firstborn in the house of a gentile attended by important people"); and R. Joseph Yuspa Hahn (Nordlingen), *Yosef Omeẓ* [or: *Yosif Omeẓ*] (Frankfurt am Main: 1722–23, but references are to the edition of Frankfurt am Main: 1927–28; reprinted photographically, Jerusalem: 1964–65), §163, pp. 36f.

[8] R. Joseph Hahn, *Yosef Omeẓ*, loc. cit., testified that as a child he was "with my teacher, the head of the rabbinical court here, the great sage . . . Rabbi Hertz, of blessed memory, at the spa in Wiesbaden and we always said the blessings. . . . We had a separate room which no gentile entered." Cf. F. Baer, *Das Protokollbuch der Landjudenschaft des Herzogtums Kleve* (Berlin: 1922), p. 64.

[9] On such types, see chapters 6–9.

[10] In Lithuania it was felt necessary to warn that "no one hit [i.e., mock] the gentile nations, and of course that no one hit an individual gentile" (Dubnow, ed., *Pinkas . . . Lita*, p. 13, §69; and cf. ibid., p. 35, §145, for evidence of Jews having gentile maidservants in their homes). For real examples of such relationships see, on the one hand, R. Menaḥem Mendel Krokhmal, *Responsa Ẓemaḥ Ẓedek*, §101, and, on the other hand, the story told by Solomon Maimon, *Geschichte des eigenen Lebens* (Berlin: 1935), p. 27 [*Solomon Maimon: An Autobiography*, ed. J. Clark Murray (London: 1888), p. 41].

[11] For examples of the activities of Jewish doctors, see the *Responsa Bayit Ḥadash ha-Ḥadashot*, §2; [Bernard] Dov Weinryb, *Texts and Studies in the Communal History of Polish Jewry* [Hebrew title: *Te'udot le-Toldot ha-Kehilot be-Folin*] (New York: 1950), p. 27; and Louis Lewin, "Jüdische Ärzte in Grosspolen," *JJLG* 9 (1911), pp. 367–420. The study of languages with non-Jewish teachers was not an innovation of the Haskala period as is sometimes assumed. Individuals—*shtadlanim* (intercessors), owners of large businesses, and the like—had often needed to know the local language or the official language of the government. There is evidence of such study in places

where the influence of the Haskala was not yet felt. See Ber of Bolechow, *Zikhronot,* pp. 46 and 103. [English: *The Memoirs of Ber of Bolechow,* pp. 79f., 164].

[12] Baer, *Protokollbuch,* p. 64; Lewin, "Jüdische Ärzte," p. 378; G. Kisch, "Der erste Deutschland promovierte Jude," *Monatsschrift für Geschichte und Wissenschaft des Judentums* 78 (1934), pp. 350–63.

[13] It is well known that Christian master craftsmen did not, as a rule, accept Jewish apprentices, but arrangements of this sort undoubtedly occurred on occasion, as in the case of Aaron Isaacs (Isak). See Aron Isak, *Avtobiografie* [Autobiography], ed. Nahum Stiff (Shtif) (Berlin: 1922), p. 10 [=*Denkwürdigkeiten des Aron Isak, 1730–1817,* ed. Z. Holm (Berlin: 1930), p. 36].

[14] Concerning friendships, see above, chapter 3. In religious ceremonies, there was a tendency, well known to sociologists of religion everywhere, to exclude outsiders—i.e., those who were not members of the group conducting the ceremony. Several *ḥumrot* (stringent measures), which can be traced, only with difficulty, to halakhic principles, were instituted on the basis of this feeling of segregation. See the case noted above, n. 7, concerning saying the introduction to the Grace After Meals in the house of a gentile. We get a similar impression from the restrictions placed on the use of [Christian] ritual objects. Though Jews were not enjoined from deriving any use from such objects, they were forbidden to use them for Jewish religious purposes. Concerning wax candles "from their houses of prayer," Rabbi Solomon Luria declared that "it would be loathsome [*me'usim*] to use them for [Jewish] ritual purposes . . . even though they were no longer dedicated to [Christian] religious purposes"; *Responsa of the MaHaRSHaL* (Jerusalem: 1968–69), §85. Already during the Middle Ages Judah ben Samuel he-Ḥasid (c. 1150–1217) had attacked the use of non-Jewish tunes in religious rituals (*Sefer Ḥasidim,* ed. Judah Wistinetzki and Jakob Freimann [Frankfurt am Main: 1924], §348), and the question arose again in our period. In *Responsa Bayit Ḥadash ha-Yeshanot,* §127, R. Joel Sirkes limits the prohibition to "tunes which are specifically a part of the idolatry" [i.e., which are part of the Christian church service], but Rabbi Joseph Hahn, *Yosef Omeẓ,* §602, p. 134, forbade singing even "the *zmirot* [hymns sung during and after the meals] on Friday and Saturday nights" to the tunes of gentile musicians. . . . "Certainly these tunes should not be used in the synagogue." The converse was also to be found; e.g., "One should not allow a gentile to eat from food that was dedicated to a religious purpose"; *Sefer Ḥasidim,* §728; R. Joseph Caro, *Beit Yosef, Oraḥ Ḥayim,* end of §167, citing the *Kolbo*; R. Abraham Ḥayim Schor, *Torat Ḥayim* (Lublin: 1624; and often reprinted), *Sanhedrin,* fol. 102a. Such questions were treated casuistically in order to establish the limit between what was considered merely a technicality incident to performing the commandment (*hakhana tekhnit*) and what was considered actually an integral part of the performance (*hekhsher miẓva*). E.g., R. Solomon Luria, *Yam shel Shlomo, Gitin,* chapter 2, §38, permits sending a bill of divorce by means of a gentile messenger for it amounts

to no more than "the act of a monkey . . . and indeed it is the custom in German and French lands to send bills of divorce and contracts of marriage through a gentile." R. David ha-Levi makes a similar distinction with regard to the preparation of flour for *maẓot; Turei Zahav, Oraḥ Ḥayim*, §460.1.

[15] This situation is demonstrated in several of the incidents cited in this and the previous chapter. R. Menaḥem Mendel Krokhmal expressed some suspicion of burghers who relied on nonexistent customs: "I am very cautious about taking the word of ordinary burghers who claim to be relying on a local custom. In fact, with regard to several matters I have investigated their claims of a local custom and [discovered] they were lying." *Responsa Ẓemaḥ Ẓedek*, §75.

Chapter 5. The Attitude toward the Environment

[1] For Poland see Moses Schorr, *Rechtsstellung und innere Verfassung*, pp. 7–8; M. Balaban, "The Legal Status of the Jews and their Communal Organization" [in Hebrew], in I. Halperin, ed., *Beit Yisra'el be-Folin*, I, pp. 44–46. For Germany see, e.g., Selma Stern, *Der preussische Staat und die Juden*, I, pp. 14–33.

[2] R. Ya'ir Ḥayim Bacharach reports that his brother-in-law, then rabbi of Mannheim, once declared to Karl Ludwig, Duke of Pfalz, that Jews bribed Christian judges on the assumption that the latter automatically favored their own co-religionists. Thus, in bribing the judge, the Jews were trying only "to balance the scales of justice and to return those scales to the true"; *Responsa Ḥavot Ya'ir*, §136. The belief that Jewish law was divinely inspired in contrast to the merely human and conventional laws of other nations inevitably elevated the value of the former and lowered that of the latter. This view was strengthened by frequent warnings by communal authorities against Jews bringing their internal squabbles before non-Jewish courts [*arka'ot shel goyim*]. Even cases in which the gentile courts found for the Jew and against the Christian did not affect this view in any fundamental sense since it was based on principles of faith rather than on any empirical observation. Already in the twelfth century, the *Sefer Ḥasidim* had noted that "there are places where gentile courts are just while Jewish [courts] are not" (ed. Wistinetzki and Freimann, §1301), and an anonymous scholar of the seventeenth century expressed the opinion that the judgments of gentile courts were superior at least to those issued by lay (i.e., non-rabbinic) Jewish courts; see R. Judah Loeb Pukhovitser, *Kne Ḥokhma*, fol. 25d. But such comments were, more than anything, exhortations to Jewish judges to adjudicate properly and in accordance with the Torah; they did not contradict the basic assumption that the Jewish system of justice was superior to that of the gentiles.

[3] *Bekhorot*, fol. 13b, and *Tosafot*, ad loc. (s.v. "Rav Ashi"). For the development of halakhic thought on these issues, see *Enẓiklopediya Talmudit*, V, pp. 327–33.

[4] Solomon Luria, *Yam shel Shlomo, Bava Kama*, chapter 10, §20.

[5] *Bava Kama*, fol. 113a–b; *Avoda Zara*, fol. 26a–b.

[6] This question was treated often. Cf. the supra-commentaries, especially that of Israel Isser ben Mordekhai Isserlein to *Oraḥ Ḥayim*, §448.3, in his *Pitḥei Tshuva* (published together with Abraham Danzig, *Sefer Ḥayei Adam ha-Shalem* [Vilna: 1874–75]), II, fol. 47b–48a. Rabbi Shlomo Yosef Zevin summarizes the matter nicely in *Ha-Mo'adim ba-Halakha*, 3rd revised edition (Jerusalem: 1953–54), pp. 245–55 [*The Festivals in Halacha*, tr. Sh. Fox-Ashrei (Brooklyn and Jerusalem: 1982), pp. 89–110—*tr.*]. The question of the legal nature of a gentile's acquisition also arose in connection with the firstborn male offspring of ritually pure farm animals (*bekhor behema tehora*). According to biblical law such offspring were sacred. Because of the extreme difficulties of raising these animals under contemporary circumstances, it had become customary to offer part-ownership in them to gentiles, and thus eliminate the obligation of sanctification. The correct manner of doing so was the subject of many *responsa*. Cf. *Yore De'a*, §320.3–8, and *Pitḥei Tshuva*, ad loc., as well as *Enẓiklopediya Talmudit*, loc. cit. above, n. 3.

[7] *Tosafot, Kidushin*, fol. 3a (*s.v.* "Ve-Isha"). There is a similar ruling concerning another type of acquisition that, according to R. Tam, was not instituted for gentiles. Cf. Isaac ben Moses of Vienna *Or Zarua, Bava Batra*, §168; *Enẓiklopediya Talmudit*, V, pp. 332–37.

[8] Maimonides, *Mishne Tora, Laws of Theft and Loss*, I, 10. Maimonides is followed in this by all other authorities (cf. *Ḥoshen Mishpat*, §359a) except for R. Eliezer ben Samuel of Metz, *Sefer Yere'im ha-Shalem* (Vilna: 1891–92; photographic reprint, Tel-Aviv: s.a.), fol. 50a–b.

[9] Maimonides, *Mishne Tora, Laws of Theft and Loss*, XI, 4–5; ibid., 3 (concerning loss); *Ḥoshen Mishpat*, §§266.1 and 348.2.

[10] Isaac ben Moses *Or Zarua, Bava Kama*, §415; *Responsa of MaHaRaM* [*Meir ben Barukh*] *of Rothenburg* (Prague: 5468 [1608]), §953. The question was again raised in a practical context by R. Ya'ir Ḥayim Bacharach in his *Responsa Ḥavot Ya'ir*, §171. Initially Bacharach speaks of a "tugar" (Turk), but by the end of the *responsum* he uses the more usual term "goy" (gentile) once more. R. Bacharach was not only a halakhic expert; as is well known, he was also possessed of broad erudition and was familiar with current events. See D. Kaufmann, *R. Jair Chajjim Bacharach (1638–1702) und seine Ahnen* (Trier: 1894). Still, Bacharach's views in this matter were no different than those of the medieval halakhists. See below, n. 15.

[11] See the perceptive comments of the Christian scholar A. Künen cited in David Hoffmann, *Der Schulchan-Aruch und die Rabbinen über das Verhältniss der Juden zu Andersgläubigen*, 2nd enlarged edition (Berlin: 1894), pp. vi–vii.

[12] R. Eliezer Ashkenazi (1512–85) was apparently the first Ashkenazic

scholar to express this view. See his commentary to the Passover Haggada, *Maasei Miẓrayim* [usually printed as part II of the author's *Maasei ha-Shem*], on the passage "Pour out thy wrath" (*Shfokh ḥamatkha*) [in the edition of Zolkiew: 5562 (1801–2), the passage appears on fol. 25d]. But in this regard he was not a typical Ashkenazi thinker, and it seems reasonable to assume that he was influenced by R. Azaria de' Rossi and other Italians. See de' Rossi's *Me'or Einayim*, especially chapter 55. For R. Eliezer Ashkenazi's biography, see J. Perles, *Geschichte der Juden in Posen* (Breslau: 1865), pp. 40–41.

13 The major advocate of this position was R. Moses Rivkes. See his *Be'er ha-Gola* to *Ḥoshen Mishpat*, §425.5. He cites R. Eliezer Ashkenazi (see above, n. 12) as well as the views of the Tosafists quoted by R. Moses Isserles [ReMA'], *Oraḥ Ḥayim*, §156, with regard to partnership. The development of a positive attitude to Christianity is clearly seen, for example, in *Be'er ha-Gola, Ḥoshen Mishpat*, §§266.1.2 and 348.2.3–4. Cf. also Azriel Shoḥet, "The German Jews' Integration within their Non-Jewish Environment in the First Half of the Eighteenth Century" [in Hebrew], *Zion* 21 (1956), pp. 229–34.

14 I was not able to determine when this custom began, nor were bibliographers with whom I consulted able to shed much light on this question. There is a lengthy warning to this effect on the verso of the second title-page of R. Ezekiel Landau, *Responsa Noda bi-Yhuda*, first collection (1775–76), but this is certainly not the first such instance.

15 R. Ya'ir Ḥayim Bacharach (cited above, n. 10) is an excellent representative of this. He himself states that contemporary gentiles were "not to be treated in all things as pagans seeing that they believe in the Creator of heaven and earth, may His name be blessed. They are not to be included in the negative proscriptions concerning gentiles found in the Talmud and later codes"; *Responsa Ḥavot Ya'ir*, §1, fol. 5b. This statement was issued in the context of a polemic within the Jewish community and was certainly not intended for publication. Note that Bacharach also ruled that from a halakhic point of view it was permissible to profit from a gentile's error.

16 See, e.g., Halperin, *Pinkas Vaad Arba Araẓot*, p. 124 (a warning to counterfeiters of coins that they would be handed over to the government authorities); Dubnow, ed., *Pinkas . . . Lita*, §§26, 69, 163, 637, 665, 830; Halperin, ed., *Takanot . . . Mehrin*, §§260, 263, 264, 265. R. Moses Rivkes attests generally to the communal leadership's concern in this regard; *Be'er ha-Gola, Ḥoshen Mishpat*, §425. See also the *pinkas yashan* of Lithuanian Jewry in Halperin, "Beginnings of the Lithuanian Jewish Council"; Majer Balaban, "Die krakauer Judengemeinde—Ordnung von 1595 und ihre Nachträge," *JJLG* 10 (1912–13), p. 328; Weinryb, *Texts and Studies*, p. 14.

17 R. Joel Sirkes issued such a ruling in his *Responsa Bayit Ḥadash*, §44 (despite the opposition of some who sided with the felon), and summarized his view in his commentary to *Tur Yore De'a*, §157. See also R. David ha-Levi, *Turei Zahav*, ad loc., §8, who emphasizes the authority of the community and carefully defines the issue to suit contemporary needs. There is no doubt

that he meant his ruling to be applied in practice. In a case cited by R. Joseph ben Gershon Katz, *Responsa She'erit Yosef*, ed. Asher Ziv (New York: 1983–84), §32bis, the leaders of the community paid off the government in order to protect those who had purchased the stolen property. Afterward, however, they sued the guilty parties. See the end of chapter 10.

[18] See the sources cited above, n. 16.

[19] We no longer find, in our period, a position such as the one espoused by R. Moses of Coucy in *Sefer Miẓvot Gadol*, Positive Commandment §74. The author argued that profiting from a gentile's error or loss should no longer be permitted on the following grounds: "Now that the exile has gone on too long, it is time for Jews . . . to grasp truth which is the 'seal' [*ḥotemet*] of the Holy One, blessed be He. One should not lie to Jews or to gentiles, nor fool anyone in any matter. . . ."

[20] R. Solomon Luria explains the prohibition against stealing from a gentile "on the grounds that one should distance oneself from anything which is detestable [*ki'ur*] or the like. Eat and drink from your own, and do not let theft and larceny become a habit"; conclusion to the text cited above, n. 4. R. Ẓvi Ashkenazi responds to the above question of Solomon Luria as follows (*Responsa Ḥakham Ẓvi* [Amsterdam: 1711–12], §26):

> Have we not been commanded to eschew detestable actions? Even if the intention of the thief was not actually to keep the stolen object but only temporarily to anger [the victim], or even if the thief intended ultimately to help the victim by paying him fines amounting to double the value of the stolen object [cf. *Bava Meẓi'a*, fol. 61b] and not to actually steal . . . we were nevertheless commanded not to let theft become a habit. . . . The Torah commands us not to cause suffering even to dumb animals . . . and we are commanded not to destroy a tree, that is a plant. And all of this is not for the sake of the object of our action [i.e., the animal or plant] but for our own sakes, in order to implant in our souls true opinions and good, upright qualities.

Chapter 6. Economic Structures

[1] For Poland and Lithuania, see the terms of the *kiyumim* issued by King Boleslav for Kalisch (1264), which served as a model for those which followed; Halperin, ed., *Beit Yisra'el be-Folin*, II, p. 231; Balaban, "Medieval Jewish History" [in Hebrew], in Halperin, ed., *Beit Yisra'el be-Folin*, I, pp. 3ff.; and Isaac Schipper, "The Economic History of the Jews of Poland and Lithuania from Ancient Times to the Division of the State" [in Hebrew], in Halperin, ed., *Beit Yisra'el be-Folin*, I, pp. 173ff. For Prussia, see Ismar Freund, *Die Emanzipation der Juden in Preussen unter besonder Berücksichtigung des Gesetzes vom 11 März 1812* (Berlin: 1912), II, p. 3. For specific cities, see

Louis Lewin, *Geschichte der Juden in Lissa* (Pinne: 1904), pp. 350f.; Löwenstein, *Geschichte der Juden in der Kurpfalz* (Frankfurt: 1895), p. 77.

[2] As is well known, the texts of the *kiyumim* were copied from place to place, albeit with certain changes. See Balaban, "Medieval Jewish History," pp. 3ff.

[3] See Georg Caro, *Sozial- und Wirtschaftsgeschichte der Juden im Mittelalter und der Neuzeit* (Leipzig: 1908 and 1920), I, pp. 396–453; II, pp. 116–218; and Isaac Schipper, *Toldot ha-Kalkala ha-Yehudit* [History of the Jewish Economy] (Tel-Aviv: 1935 and 1936). The contrast between the Middle Ages and the modern period is not, of course, absolute. On occasion, one can find investments in the medieval period quite similar to the modern type; Schipper, "The Economic History of the Jews of Poland," p. 162. But the overall pattern was as we have suggested.

[4] There are many descriptions of the economic activities of Jews in various countries and cities in the scholarly literature. I shall mention a few of these here and more below. I. Schipper, "The Economic History of the Jews of Poland" (above, n. 3), pp. 155–99; R. Kestenberg-Gladstein, "The Economic History of the Jews in Non-Metropolitan Bohemia in the Seventeenth and Eighteenth Centuries" [in Hebrew], *Zion* 12 (1947), pp. 49–65 and 160–85; S. Stern, *Der preussische Staat und die Juden*, I, pp. 119–39; Marcus Breger, *Zur Handelsgeschichte der Juden in Polen während des 17. Jahrhunderts* (Breslau: 1932); Berthold Altmann, "Jews and the Rise of Capitalism: Economic Theory and Practice in a Westphalian Community," *Jewish Social Studies* 5 (1943), pp. 163–86.

[5] There is an extensive literature on this matter. See, e.g., Werner Sombart, *Der moderne Kapitalismus* (Leipzig: 1902); F. Lütge, *Deutsche Sozial- und Wirtschaftsgeschichte* (Berlin: 1952; 3rd edition, Berlin and New York: 1966), from chapter 4 on.

[6] This is the well-known thesis of Sombart in his *Die Juden und das Wirtschaftsleben* (Leipzig: 1911; *The Jews and Modern Capitalism*, London: 1913; reprinted with an introduction by Bert Hoselitz, Glencoe: 1951) and in his above-mentioned magnum opus in which he changed many of his earlier positions. On the question itself, see below.

[7] See chapters 14, 15, and 19.

[8] In medieval Poland there was nothing to prevent Jews from acquiring land, and the original versions of the *kiyumim* even promised that Jews would have the right to permanent ownership of unredeemed pawns. Ph. Bloch, *Die Generalprivilegien der polnischen Judenschaft* (Posen: 1892); *Zeitschrift der Historischen Gesellschaft für die Provinz Posen* 5, pp. 7ff.; M. Balaban, "Medieval Jewish History," p. 5. The historical literature has ascribed the absence of Jewish land acquisition to opposition from government and the other landowners. But the sociological analyst cannot be content with such explanations; he must also enquire as to why that which was theoretically possible did not actually occur.

[9] Scholars have recognized that the Jewish economy rested on credit. The implications of this fact will be analyzed in the coming chapters.

[10] I. Schipper, "The Economic History of the Jews of Poland," p. 178; Kestenberg-Gladstein, "Bohemian Jewry," pp. 61–65.

[11] At the most authorities would permit the settlement of certain craftsmen deemed vital to the Jews, such as butchers and tailors. But the mass of craftsmen were nothing more than a secondary phenomenon in the economic development of the Jewish communities.

Chapter 7. Sociological Aspects of Jewish Capitalism

[1] In the scientific literature the term "capitalism" is used to refer to modern, free capitalism. However Max Weber, in clarifying and debating this issue, distinguished between various types of premodern capitalism or, to be more precise, between forms of capitalism that existed in other historical frameworks. He referred to these by various terms (*Staatskapitalismus, Pariakapitalismus, Abenteuerkapitalismus*) without being exact about the meaning of the words. His main intent was to distinguish between modern capitalism, on the one hand, and all other forms of investment on the other. Weber emphasized that Judaism had participated in nonmodern capitalism, but argued that it contributed only indirectly to the formation of modern capitalism. In this regard his views have been confirmed by later research and analysis. See his *Gesammelte Aufsätze zur Religionssoziologie* (Tübingen: 1920), I, p. 181; III, p. 260; *Wirtschaft und Gesellschaft*, pp. 636, 812; *Wirtschaftsgeschichte* (Munich and Leipzig: 1923), pp. 289ff.

[2] In Poland a furious, but futile, battle was waged against the Jews. See M. Breger, *Zur Handelsgeschichte der Juden in Polen*, pp. 2–5, 8–10; I. Schipper, "The Economic History of the Jews of Poland," pp. 165–68. From H. Schnee, *Die Hoffinanz und der moderne Staat*, III, p. 179, and I, p. 46, it is clear that during the sixteenth century Christians still dominated among the burghers in Germany.

[3] The notion that geographic dispersion was one of the objective characteristics that prepared the Jewish community for its special economic role was already suggested by Sombart, *Die Juden und das Wirtschaftsleben* (Leipzig: 1911), p. 198 [*The Jews and Modern Capitalism* (Glencoe: 1951), pp. 169ff.—*tr.*].

[4] Sombart also mentioned their civil status—which he called "semi-citizenship"—as one of the objective characteristics that prepared the Jews for capitalistic activity; *Die Juden und das Wirtschaftsleben*, p. 207 [*The Jews and Modern Capitalism*, pp. 176ff.—*tr.*]. He did not, however, explore the ways in which this status actually led to specific types of economic activity.

Sombart saw this status as paving the way for free capitalism, something that has no basis whatsoever in fact.

[5] R. Simone (Simḥa) Luzzatto listed the absolute political neutrality of the Jew as one of the main factors for rulers tolerating Jews; *Maamar al Yehudei Veneẓiya*, p. 92 [*Discorso circa il stato de gl'Hebrei et in particolar dimoranti; nell'inclita Città di Venetia* (Venice: 1638; reprinted Bologna: 1976), pp. 21f.—*tr.*]. There is evidence that this was not merely apologetics on his part.

[6] For the Court Jew see H. Schnee's thorough and detailed treatment, *Die Hoffinanz und der moderne Staat*. This work is not free of anti-Semitic tendencies and distortions, but its description of the events is superior to anything previously written by Jews. See S. Stern, *Jud Süss* (Berlin: 1929); idem, *The Court Jew* (Philadelphia: 1950); M. Grunwald, *Samuel Oppenheimer und sein Kreis* (Vienna: 1913).

[7] At various points in his study, Schnee notes the similarity between Court Jews in Germany and the Jews who served the magnates of eastern Europe, but he never explains the principle involved. See for instance his summary, III, pp. 171–73.

[8] See M. Wischnitzer, "Die jüdische Zunftverfassung in Polen und Litauen im 17. und 18. Jahrhundert," *Vierteljahrschrift für Sozial- und Wirtschaftsgeschichte* 20 (1928), pp. 433–51, and cf. chapter 16.

[9] This had nothing to do with an attitude to wealth per se. For instance, Ḥ. H. Ben-Sasson, "Wealth and Poverty in the Teaching of the Preacher, Reb Ephraim of Lenczyca" [in Hebrew], *Zion* 19 (1954), p. 148, n. 18, found that even someone who detested wealth and what was associated with it had a negative attitude to the work of artisans. Indeed, contemporary works of ethics (*musar*) never praised those who labored with their hands in the manner in which they did the honest businessman who followed the ideal occupation (see chapter 8 below). The antithesis between labor and trade is explicit in R. Isaiah Horowitz, *Shnei Luḥot ha-Brit*, at the start of the treatment of *Ḥulin* (Amsterdam edition, I, fol. 111a). After comparing different phraseology in two biblical passages concerning work on weekdays and rest on the Sabbath, Horowitz distinguished between two types of work (*mle'khet ha-maase*):

> The first type is an occupation which occurs between a man and his fellow, such as trade, and the second type is the work which one does on one's own, such as a craft (*asiyat mla'kha*). As for the second type . . . , it were better that it be done of itself, as we saw in the case of the *ḥasidim rishonim* [early righteous ones] who devoted themselves primarily to holy study and their work was accomplished of itself. On the other hand, it is more meritorious to engage directly in trade than to have an agent do it for one. . . .

Workers' guilds sometimes cited the classic texts that praised labor; see Israel Halperin, "The Minute Book of the 'Ḥavura' of Craftsmen in Luboml" [in

Hebrew], *Yedi'ot ha-Arkhiyon ve-ha-Muze'on shel Tnu'at ha-Avoda* [Newsletter of the Archive and Museum of the Labor Movement] (5695 [1934–35]), p. 11, reprinted in his *Yehudim ve-Yahadut be-Mizraḥ Eyropa*, pp. 182 and 184. But this attitude was never raised programmatically until the early *maskilim* began to consider the problem of productivization.

[10] See above, chapter 6, n. 11.

[11] This applies especially to western Europe during the mercantilist period when authorities carefully controlled Jewish trade, forcing Jews to engage in certain types of commerce and forbidding them others. See, e.g., Selma Stern, "The Jews in the Economic Policy of Frederick the Great," *Jewish Social Studies* 11 (1949), pp. 129–52. But in fact residence privileges everywhere specified which economic activities were permitted the Jews, and there was an ongoing struggle with the guilds and merchants over the particulars.

[12] See Breger, *Zur Handelsgeschichte der Juden in Polen*, pp. 3–5; Schipper, "The Economic History of the Jews of Poland," p. 177. In fact the situation was now sometimes reversed: Gentiles lent money to Jews for their business needs. See, e.g., Weinryb, *Texts and Studies*, pp. 42f. and 62, as well as the sources cited there. Moneylending was one of the activities of the Court Jews, but not the most important. See Stern, *The Court Jew*, chapters 1 and 2.

[13] For coinage see Dubnow, ed., *Pinkas . . . Lita*, §§81, 92, 662, pp. 308–11; Halperin, ed., *Pinkas Vaad Arba Araẓot* pp. 41, 124, 416, 418, etc.; Halperin, ed., *Takanot . . . Mehrin*, §§260 and 477.

[14] See Schnee, *Hoffinanz und der moderne Staat*, III, p. 199. Sombart attributed the entire rationalist inspiration of capitalism to Jews but his proofs relate only to marketing methods, whereas the decisive turning point, as M. Weber has demonstrated in his analyses, came in the area of production processes—in which Jews did not take an active part. See Max Weber, *Wirtschaftsgeschichte* (1923), pp. 289ff. (which includes bibliographic references to the author's earlier works).

[15] See *Arbaa Turim, Ḥoshen Mishpat*, §156. The views of the two major authorities of the second half of the sixteenth century, Rabbi Moses Isserles and R. Mordecai Jaffe, *Levush* [*Ir Shushan*], *Ḥoshen Mishpat*, §156.5, lean only slightly in the direction of permitting monopolization. That the matter was still an open question is indicated by the fact that the third major legist of the day, R. Solomon Luria (MaHaRSHaL), decided in absolute terms in favor of free competition (*Yam shel Shlomo, Kidushin*, chapter 3, §2 [Stettin: 1860–61 edition, fol. 29b], and cf. his *Responsa*, §35 [Jerusalem: 1968–69 edition, pp. 103b–108b], which dates probably from the second quarter of the sixteenth century since Luria [1510?–74] says he wrote it "in the days of [his] youth"). Luria was not the only one to decide against monopolies: "I found a similar judgment," he noted, "in the writings of a certain former communal rabbi and jurist. That sage declared: 'In these regions we have never been in the habit of allowing [people to claim someone as their] exclusive client [*maarufya*]' " (*Yam shel Shlomo*, ibid. [Stettin edition, fol. 31a]). The litigant had claimed: "Moreover, it is the local custom concerning taxes and liquor

that first someone buys the monopoly for a fixed period and then another may jump in and offer more money and buy the monopoly . . . and many greater men than I have done this" (ibid., fol. 29c). Even R. Joseph ha-Kohen of Cracow, who disagreed with Luria's ruling, never denied that this was the custom (*Responsa She'erit Yosef*, §17). Rather, he argued that the custom was not supported by any rabbinic authority and was therefore not binding. The event being litigated occurred in Lithuania, but it seems that even in Rabbi Joseph ha-Kohen's area there was no *takana* to the contrary.

[16] The first communal ordinance to this effect that has survived is from 5356 (1596; Halperin, ed., *Pinkas Vaad Arba Arazot*, p. 11), and it mentions an even earlier ordinance. A Lithuanian ordinance concerning *ḥazaka* has been preserved from 5383 (1623), but here also there is an assumption of earlier such ordinances (Dubnow, ed., *Pinkas . . . Lita*, §§73, 87; Sirkes, *Responsa Bayit Ḥadash*, §60). The ordinances differ on minor details: the *Pinkas Vaad Arba Arazot* allows competition upon the death of the lessor while *Pinkas . . . Lita* maintains the *ḥazaka* even during the lifetime of his heir. The heirs of the lessee have no *ḥazaka*, even according to *Pinkas . . . Lita*. R. Benjamin Aaron Slonik testifies about an ordinance in his region, apparently Russia, according to which no Jew could acquire a leasehold within half a year of another Jew's lease coming to an end; *Responsa Mas'at Binyamin*, §27. *Responsum* §62 of R. Meir b. Gedaliah [MaHaRaM] of Lublin shows that this ordinance spread. For regions outside of Poland, see Halperin, ed., *Takanot . . . Mehrin* §259, and for Metz, Bacharach, *Responsa Ḥavot Ya'ir*, §42 (and the author's objections). The change occurred, apparently, in the last third of the sixteenth century. The transition from free competition to monopolization in Jewish society was paralleled by a similar development in sixteenth- and seventeenth-century Europe generally; see Lütge, *Deutsche Sozial- und Wirtschaftsgeschichte*, pp. 227ff. This matter deserves detailed study in its own right.

[17] R. Moses Isserles [ReMA'], *Ḥoshen Mishpat*, §156.7; R. Mordecai Jaffe, *Levush* [*Ir Shushan*], ad loc.; and cf. R. Joshua Falk, *Prisha, Arbaa Turim, Ḥoshen Mishpat*, §156. I will treat this matter more fully in my discussion of the composition of the community, below, chapter 11.

[18] Maimonides, *Laws of Neighbors*, VI, 10; *Shulḥan Arukh, Ḥoshen Mishpat*, §156.7. On the application of this rule in practice, see below, chapter 11.

[19] This narrowing of vision is apparent, for instance, in the halakhic ruling that merchants of a city cannot prevent merchants from another city from importing their goods if these are cheaper or of better quality than the local product. This exception did not apply, however, if the customers were non-Jews. (R. Moses Isserles, *Ḥoshen Mishpat*, §156.7, citing medieval authorities.) In the present context it is unfortunately impossible to examine the medieval transition from the Talmudic treatment, which assumed a self-supporting Jewish economy, to the later positions outlined here.

[20] As is well known, the farming of taxes and customs was forbidden in

Poland for this reason; Halperin, ed., *Pinkas Vaad Arba Arazot*, p. 1. As R. Joel Sirkes explains (*Responsa Bayit Ḥadash*, §61): "There was a great deal of danger since the gentiles in most locales began to cry out that the Jews were taking over and ruling them and lording it over them as if they were kings"; cf. *Pinkas Vaad Arba Arazot*, p. 2, Halperin's note. This theme is quite common.

[21] Partnerships with gentiles were forbidden, for example, for this reason; Halperin, ed., *Pinkas Vaad Arba Arazot*, p. 148, and cf. ibid., p. 124, and the sources cited by Halperin, nn. 3–4. It is significant that the ordinance referred to business matters as "Jewish secrets [*mistorin*]" that one may not reveal to a gentile (and cf. Dubnow, ed., *Pinkas . . . Lita*, §793). Typical was the reasoning of R. Me'ir ben Gedaliah of Lublin (*Responsa MaHaRaM*, §62) who argued that if a Jew was not able to maintain his lease another Jew might sublet it, "for if no Jew leases it, the lord will rent it out to a gentile or keep it for himself."

[22] The defendant in the *responsum* by R. Solomon Luria cited above, n. 15, was also concerned "lest Jewish money fall into gentile hands." The expression, clearly emotive, is a variation on the Talmudic phrase: "The Torah cares for the money of the Jews" (*Yoma*, fol. 39a).

[23] For stratification within Jewish society, see chapter 19.

Chapter 8. Religion and Economic Activity

[1] See Halperin, ed., *Pinkas Vaad Arba Arazot* p. 486, §§12–13; Dubnow, ed., *Pinkas . . . Lita*, §§137–38; R. Joel Sirkes, *Bayit Ḥadash, Yore De'a*, §117; R. Sabbetai ha-Kohen, *Siftei Kohen, Shulḥan Arukh, Yore De'a*, §117.3; R. David ha-Levi, *Turei Zahav*, ad loc., §§2, 4; R. Benjamin Aaron Slonik, *Responsa Mas'at Binyamin*, §25; R. Menaḥem Mendel Krokhmal, *Responsa Ẓemaḥ Ẓedek*, §60; R. Gershon Ashkenazi, *Responsa Avodat ha-Gershuni* (Frankfurt am Main: 1698–99), §13; R. Ezekiel Landau, *Responsa Noda bi-Yhuda*, second collection, *Yore De'a*, §§62–63.

[2] A complete historical picture is presented in the *takanot* (rulings) of R. Meshullam Phoebus (Halperin, ed., *Pinkas Vaad Arba Arazot*, pp. 483–87, and the parallel source cited in *Kvod Ḥakhamim* of R. Judah Loeb Pukhovitser [Venice: 1700], fol. 89a–90b. On the dating of the *takanot* and the relation between the two sources, see Halperin, ed., *Pinkas Vaad Arba Arazot*, pp. 487f.). These matters are scattered throughout Dubnow, ed., *Pinkas . . . Lita*, §§137, 281, 358, 530, 713, 740, 775, 912, 966, and in the rulings of contemporary *poskim* (jurists): R. David ha-Levi, *Turei Zahav, Oraḥ Ḥayim*, §450.6; ibid., §244.7; R. Berechiah Berakh, *Zera Berakh* (Amsterdam: 1661–62, introduction to part II (Hamburg: 1687); R. Judah Loeb Pukhovitser, *Kne Ḥokhma*, fol. 3d, and idem, *Derekh Ḥokhma* (Frankfurt an der Oder: 1682–83), §10, fol. 17d–18a; R. Menaḥem Mendel Krokhmal, *Responsa Ẓemaḥ Ẓedek*, §35; and R. Ezekiel Landau, *Drushei ha-ẒLaḤ*, fol.

8d, in which the author fixes the conditions under which it would be permitted to sell barley to gentile travelers. It seems to me that this sermon, and several others in the collection, were given not in Prague but in Yampol. See Ḥ. H. Ben-Sasson, "Statutes for the Enforcement of the Observance of the Sabbath in Poland" [in Hebrew], *Zion* 21 (1956), pp. 183–206.

[3] See R. Jacob Israel Emden, *Responsa She'ilat Yaavez̧* (Altona: 1738–39 and 1769–70), II, §§60–61; R. Ezekiel Landau, *Responsa Noda bi-Yhuda*, second collection, *Oraḥ Ḥayim*, §38.

[4] These three principles, all deriving from the Talmud and the early legists, constantly preoccupied the halakhists cited above. See, for example, the *Arbaa Turim, Oraḥ Ḥayim*, §§243–46, and the accompanying commentaries.

[5] In the *takanot* (rulings) of R. Meshullam Phoebus (Halperin, ed., *Pinkas Vaad Arba Araz̧ot*, p. 485) we find a recommendation that a gentile collecting taxes for a Jewish tax-farmer do so "outside the Jew's house." The version in R. Judah Loeb Pukhovitser, *Kvod Ḥakhamim*, states: "It is absolutely forbidden for a Jew to be with the gentile during the collection of the taxes . . . , although he may stand at a distance in order to make sure that the gentile doesn't steal" (§6). We find, in §9, a stringency forbidding the Jew to answer any of the gentile's questions concerning the business, and, in §12, a ruling that liquor to be sold on the Sabbath must be removed from the Jew's house before the Sabbath commences. R. Ezekiel Landau made his ruling permitting the operation of a factory on the Sabbath conditional on the Jew's refraining from coming to the workplace on that day, and R. Jacob Emden made the same precondition (above, n. 3). The latter writer dealt with this matter in great detail in a *responsum* written to someone who was studying surgery at a university. He forbade doing so for other reasons, but at the end of the *responsum* expressed his opinion that even participating without actually doing any work "is forbidden in and of itself and because of the sanctity of the [holy] day"; *She'ilat Yaavez̧*, I, §41.

[6] Halperin, ed., *Pinkas Vaad Arba Araz̧ot*, p. 484; Pukhovitser, *Derekh Ḥokhma and Kne Ḥokhma*, (above, n. 2).

[7] The *takanot* of R. Meshullam Phoebus (Halperin, ed., *Pinkas Vaad Arba Araz̧ot*, pp. 484f.); Pukhovitser, *Kvod Ḥakhamim*, fol. 89b–90a; R. David ha-Levi, *Turei Z̧ahav, Oraḥ Ḥayim*, §244.7.

[8] Krokhmal, *Responsa Z̧emaḥ Z̧edek*, §35. The case involved Jewish teamsters from Nikolsburg who were transporting goods in their wagons while accompanied by their non-Jewish assistants. They were themselves to spend the Sabbath at an inn, but wanted to send their horses and gentile assistants ahead on the Sabbath, intending to catch up with them on the next day. Another jurist had permitted the plan through "sale" or "abandonment" of the animals. R. Krokhmal's response is interesting from several points of view. He did not find the plan to be absolutely forbidden, for this *heter* [license] was no different in essence from others that were used in other fields. In fact he agreed to allow the procedure if what was involved "was a public *miz̧va* such as the transporting of citrons [needed for the holiday of Tabernacles]."

On the other hand, Krokhmal forbade following this practice on a regular basis, in part because of the direct, personal contact between the Jewish wagoners and the actions of their assistants. "Moreover, they and the others with them [apparently: other Jewish travelers] commit other sins": on Sabbath eve they use their utensils and clothes, and the next day, on the Sabbath, they hand everything over to the drivers to take with them "because they are in a rush to go after the wagons after the close of the Sabbath. . . . Thus they sin and lead others to sin." The view of R. Jacob Emden concerning someone studying at a university is quite similar; see above, n. 5.

[9] Permission to trade in non-kosher meat under certain circumstances is already found in the Mishna. See Tractate *Shviit*, VII, §§3–4: "One who comes across various forms of impure meat is permitted to sell them." The argument against trading in nonkosher food "lest one eat" is cited in the name of R. Solomon ben Adret (RaSHBA') by R. Joseph Caro, *Beit Yosef*, §117, and by R. Sabbetai Kohen, *Siftei Kohen, ad loc.*, §2. There were legists, however, who felt that the rule against such trade was biblical (*de-oraita*) in origin. See R. Yom Tov Lipmann Heller, *Tosfot Yom Tov* (Prague: 1614–17), *Shviit*, VII, 3, and R. Ezekiel Landau, *Responsa Noda bi-Yhuda*, second collection, *Yore De'a*, §62. Later scholars did not accept this view and thus left some latitude in the law.

[10] See the sources cited above, n. 1, which leave no doubt that the rabbis involved were trying to rationalize lenient practices (*heterim*) already in existence. Rabbi Ezekiel Landau, who was not sure about the *heter* given for trading in the pelts and flesh of rabbits, advised the rabbi who had addressed this question to him simply to ignore what his congregants were doing. Landau noted that he himself did the same thing (ibid.). This was also the practice of R. Gershon Ashkenazi in a quite similar case. See his *Responsa Avodat ha-Gershuni*, §13.

[11] Halperin, ed., *Pinkas Vaad Arba Arazot*, p. 486. R. Joel Sirkes declared that those who raised pigs as food for the gentile workers on estates they leased "had never prospered . . . and of them it was said: 'Cursed be they who raise pigs . . .' "; *Bayit Ḥadash, Arbaa Turim, Yore De'a*, end of §117.

[12] See Halperin, ed., *Pinkas Vaad Arba Arazot*, p. 486, n. 5, and the sources cited there. R. Benjamin Aaron Slonik, *Responsa Mas'at Binyamin*, §36, mentions that some scholars had ruled that even someone who collected a pig in payment of a debt was to sell it immediately, even if this meant a monetary loss, but Slonik himself rejects this extreme position.

[13] R. David ha-Levi, *Turei Zahav, Yore De'a*, §117.4, notes that "this has been the custom . . . and the sages have not objected"; he himself therefore supports the practice. In his comments to *Oraḥ Ḥayim*, §450.6, ha-Levi even uses this *heter* [license] as the basis for another, new *heter*. His manner of citing R. Joel Sirkes (*BaḤ*) is characteristic. Whereas Sirkes had ruled that Jews who allowed the breeding of pigs on their estates were transgressing a law of the Torah, ha-Levi merely mentions that "my teacher and father-in-law, of blessed memory, ruled that those who lease towns and villages from

the [gentile] nobleman . . . are acting improperly [*lo yafe hem osim*]." Rabbi ha-Levi's biographers have not dealt at all with the fact that his work represents the acme of the tendency in Polish Jewish law to justify existing practice.

[14] R. David ha-Levi, *Turei Zahav, Yore De'a*, §117.2. Here, too, ha-Levi opposes the view of his father-in-law, Sirkes.

[15] The *heter* based on the formulation of the loan as a partnership derives from *Tosafot, Bava Kama*, fol. 102a, and especially R. Moses of Coucy, *Sefer Miẓvot Gadol*, Positive Commandment §82 (Venice: 1546–47, fol. 167c). The second *heter*, involving the gentile, is based on Rabenu Jacob Tam's view that gentiles cannot formally become legal agents of Jews. Hence the gentile emissary is, from a formal point of view, acting on his own, and the Jewish borrower is paying interest to a gentile and not to the Jew who was the ultimate source of the loan; *Responsa* of R. Meir of Rothenburg, ed. Moses Bloch (Budapest: 1895), II, fol. 106c, §796. The first of these licenses was accepted by later legists (*Shulḥan Arukh, Yore De'a*, §177.5); the latter was rejected (*Shulḥan Arukh, Yore De'a*, §169.7). In any case, these are only examples of the many *heterim* that were followed in the Middle Ages, and which we cannot treat in detail here. For a discussion of the legal-halakhic aspects, see E. E. Hildesheimer, *Das jüdische Gesellschaftsrecht* (Leipzig: 1930), pp. 89–131.

[16] The pamphlet on the laws of usury compiled by R. Joshua Falk (below, n. 20) includes laws concerning credit transactions of various types: for example, cases in which a capitalist lends a villager money with the intention that the latter will use the money to buy certain goods and then resell the goods to the lender at a fixed price; Halperin, ed., *Pinkas Vaad Arba Araẓot*, p. 21.

[17] To mention only one prominent example, the rabbis meeting at the Lublin (*Grominice*) fair in 1607 (see below, n. 20) ruled that a lender had to trust the individual to whom he had lent, or with whom he had invested, money. Hence, if the borrower swore that he had suffered a loss on the money and was therefore not obliged to repay the loan, the capitalist had to believe him and was not allowed to insist on especially onerous and embarrassing oaths such as swearing specifically "between the recitation of *Ashrei* and *La-Mnaẓe'aḥ* [i.e., Psalms 145 and 20, recited toward the end of the morning service] in public and in the synagogue." The rabbis labeled such a demand a "trick" (*taḥbula*); Halperin, ed., *Pinkas Vaad Arba Araẓot*, p. 19. And yet it is exactly this "trick" that Rabbi Isaiah Horowitz recommends to his sons, adding even that the Torah scroll should be "naked" (i.e., without its cover), making the condition even more impracticable; R. Isaiah Horowitz, *Shnei Luḥot ha-Brit*, Tractate *Ḥulin, Inyan Masa u-Matan be-Emuna*, fol. 114b.

[18] Halperin, ed., *Pinkas Vaad Arba Araẓot*, p. 20. For one example, see R. David ha-Levi, *Turei Zahav, Yore De'a*, §177.3, which involves a question of *ribit de-ribit* (compound interest) on *MaMRaME*.

[19] Contemporary sources often express the fear that the laws regarding interest may become "an object of derision"; see the opening of *Kuntres ha-*

SMa', Halperin, ed., *Pinkas Vaad Arba Araẓot*, p. 18; *Shnei Luḥot ha-Brit*, loc. cit.; Pukhovitser, *Derekh Ḥokhma*, fol. 54a.

[20] The pamphlet was reprinted often. Halperin's edition in the *Pinkas Vaad Arba Araẓot*, pp. 18–23, does not include the halakhic reasoning. My citations are drawn from Falk, *Kuntres . . . Baal ha-SMA'* [*Sefer Me'irat Einayim*] (Cracow: 5654 [1893–94]).

[21] Halperin, ed., *Pinkas Vaad Arba Araẓot*, p. 23.

[22] In the year 5399 (1638–39) the *Pinkas . . . Lita*, §367, recommends two methods of circumvention in addition to the *heter iska* developed by R. Menaḥem of Cracow, which we shall discuss below. Rabbi David ha-Levi, *Turei Zahav, Yore De'a*, §173.9, and *Oraḥ Ḥayim*, §246.5, attests to yet other methods of *heter*. The first of these was a sort of compound fiction. The borrower announced that he had cash in some other location. Although ha-Levi opposed this approach, there were other scholars who accepted it; see *Responsa Beit Yaakov*, §112, where the author declares that "the custom is clearly to allow this." In Moravia there was yet another type of common *heter*. See Halperin, ed., *Takanot . . . Mehrin*, §289, and Halperin's note ad loc.

[23] *Kuntres . . . Baal ha-SMA'*, p. 16. The text of the contract was included in Samuel b. David ha-Levi's collection of model contracts, *Naḥalat Shiv'a* (Amsterdam: 1667, and often reprinted), §40.

[24] The leaders of the Jewish community of Poznan and the head of its rabbinical court ruled in 1676 that an individual *shtar iska* was required for each loan; Weinryb, *Texts and Studies*, Hebrew section, p. 143. For the objections of ethicists, see, e.g., the writings of R. Judah Loeb Pukhovitser, in particular his *Derekh Ḥokhma*, fol. 54a. We shall discuss the reasoning behind the opposition from kabbalistically inclined ethicists to this entire issue below, chapter 20.

[25] R. Moses Yekutiel Kaufmann, in the last section of his *Leḥem ha-Panim*, attests that his father-in-law, the author of the *Magen Avraham*, gave his "imprimatur" to the use of the abbreviated formula for this reason. Rabbi Ezekiel Landau actually begs his congregants to use the abbreviated formula; *Drushei ha-ẒLaḤ*, fol. 16b–d and 52a–b. In his day there were already those who objected on principle to the *heter iska*; ibid., fol. 52a. The sources also attest to many examples of people simply ignoring the entire question.

[26] It is not insignificant that the *Mishna* (Tractate *Bava Metzi'a*, chapter *Eizehu Neshekh*) and Maimonides (*Laws of Lenders and Borrowers*, chapters 5–10) both treat the issue of interest as part of civil law, while Rabbi Jacob ben Asher treats it within the context of ritual law (*isur ve-heter*); *Arbaa Turim, Yore De'a*, §§159ff. This shift was noted already by the traditional commentators (Falk, *Prisha*, and Sirkes, *Bayit Ḥadash*, at the start of §160).

[27] See Halperin, ed., *Pinkas Vaad Arba Araẓot*, pp. 545f., and the bibliography cited there.

[28] This is clear from all of the sources. See the index to Halperin, ed., *Pinkas Vaad Arba Araẓot*, as well as Halperin, ed., *Takanot . . . Mehrin*, and

Dubnow, ed., *Pinkas . . . Lita*; Weinryb, *Texts and Studies*, Hebrew section, pp. 11 and 31, etc.

29 See the *takanot* in the sources cited above, especially the *takanot* of Moravia, which stress the need to collect debts immediately.

30 Sombart, basing himself on the writings of Jewish scholars, tried to prove that the *MaMRaMe* derived from the Talmudic legal tradition; *Die Juden und das Wirtschaftsleben*, pp. 81f. [*The Jews and Modern Capitalism*, pp. 87f.—*tr.*] and passim. M. Cohen expressed this same opinion in his article in the *Jüdisches Lexicon*, III, p. 1351. But the halakhists themselves state the opposite—and this, despite the fact that they always try to establish Talmudic precedents for their rulings. Cf. Sirkes, *Responsa Bayit Ḥadash*, §32, where the author clearly decides that "the only basis for collecting a debt through a *MaMRaMe* contract is the agreement among communal leaders that it should have the same power as [Talmudically] binding contracts."

31 R. David ha-Levi, *Turei Zahav, Ḥoshen Mishpat*, §207.18.

32 See Halperin, ed., *Takanot . . . Mehrin*, §§225–36; Halperin, ed., *Pinkas Vaad Arba Araẓot*, pp. 45f.; R. Menaḥem Krokhmal, *Responsa Ẓemaḥ Ẓedek*, §15.

33 No contemporary ethical treatise overlooks this issue entirely. Note, for example, R. Abraham b. Sabbetai Horowitz, *Yesh Noḥalim* (Amsterdam: 1701), fol. 31a; R. Isaiah Horowitz, *Shnei Luḥot ha-Brit*, Tractate *Ḥulin*, *Inyan Masa u-Matan be-Emuna*, fol. 113b–114b; R. Judah Loeb Pukhovitser, *Kvod Ḥakhamim*, fol. 57a ff.; Ezekiel Landau, *Drushei ha-ẒLaḤ*, fol. 13b and passim; R. Joseph Hahn, *Yosef Omeẓ*, §§340–45.

34 Again to cite only a few examples, see the comments of R. Jacob Horowitz on *Yesh Noḥalim*, fol. 20b; R. Sheftel Horowitz, *Vavei Amudim*, the introduction to *Shnei Luḥot ha-Brit*, fol. 17c–d; R. Joseph Hahn, *Yosef Omeẓ*, pp. 116f. and 306–15.

35 For an analysis of this rejectionist view, see Ḥ. H. Ben-Sasson's Hebrew article "Wealth and Poverty in the Teaching of the Preacher, Reb Ephraim of Lenczyca."

36 Sombart's description of Judaism, *Die Juden und das Wirtschaftsleben*, pp. 231ff. [*The Jews and Modern Capitalism*, pp. 187ff.—*tr.*], is one-sided but not completely in error. The main criticism of his argument lies in his claim for a psychological link between the "spirit" of Judaism and the "spirit" of capitalism. Though Sombart (as he admits in his introduction) wrote his work in the wake of Weber's analysis of Protestantism, he did not follow Weber's method. Like most of those who have participated in the debate surrounding Weber's work, Sombart treated only the economic teachings of, and/or the psychological preparedness engendered by, the religion. Weber's new approach was only slowly understood, and misapprehensions of his ideas are still to be found in the sociological and historical literature. See T. Parson's review of H. H. Robertson, *The Rise of Economic Individualism. A Criticism of M. Weber and His School*, in *The Journal of Political Economy*, 1935, pp. 688ff.

[37] The basic link between wealth and the possibility of fulfilling the religious ideals is found everywhere in the classical sources. In the present context it is sufficient to mention that there are many discussions in the halakhic and ethical literature as to the amount one is obligated to expend for charity and in fulfillment of the other commandments. See, e.g., *Shulḥan Arukh, Yore De'a*, §249, and *Oraḥ Ḥayim*, §656, and the commentaries ad loc.

[38] See below, chapters 16 and 17.

[39] The notion that society was composed of various "orders," each of which had a different level of obligation with regard to Torah study, was widely accepted. See *Shulḥan Arukh, Yore De'a*, §246.1; R. Joel Sirkes, *Bayit Ḥadash [BaḤ], Oraḥ Ḥayim*, §156; MaHaRSHA', *Ḥidushei Agadot, Brakhot*, fol. 35b. Rabbi Judah Loeb Pukhovitser deals with this question at length in his works and tries to come to some conclusion regarding the exact amount of time that each "order" is required to devote to the study of Torah. See *Kne Ḥokhma*, fol. 19d; *Derekh Ḥokhma*, fol. 52c–d. Even so, the basic assumption remains that whatever time one devotes to making a living is justified only by the force of circumstances. See below, chapter 16. And cf. Azriel Shoḥet, "Study Societies in Palestine, Poland-Lithuania, and Germany during the Sixteenth through Eighteenth Centuries" [in Hebrew], *Ha-Ḥinukh*, 5716 (1955–56), pp. 404–18.

Part II. Communal Institutions and Structure

Chapter 9. The Form and Structure of the Kehila

[1] Already R. Meir of Rothenburg expressed doubts as to whether it was possible to issue a *din tora* on matters relating to communal governance; *Responsa of MaHaRaM* (Berlin: 1891; reprinted Jerusalem: 1967–68), p. 205, §128 [English translation: Irving A. Agus, *Rabbi Meir of Rothenburg*, 2nd edition (New York: Ktav, 1970), §581, p. 540], and cf. Ephraim E. Urbach, *Baalei ha-Tosafot. Toldoteihem, Ḥibureihem ve-Shitatam* [The Tosaphists: Their Biographies, Writings, and Methodology] (Jerusalem: 1955), pp. 410 and 420, and my comments in *Kiryat Sefer* [*Kirjath Sefer*] 31 (5716 [1955–56]), pp. 9–16. Similar remarks are found in R. Israel Isserlein, *Trumat ha-Deshen* (Fürth: 1777–78), §§345, 346, as well as in our own period (sometimes based on the views of earlier authorities) in Krokhmal, *Responsa Ẓemaḥ Ẓedek*, §19; Bacharach, *Responsa Ḥavot Ya'ir*, §81; and cf. also Katz, *Responsa She'erit Yosef*, §9.

[2] The main sources are: Mishna, *Bava Batra* I:5; Tosefta, *Bava Meẓi'a*, chapter 11. The source for the notion of dividing the costs was *Bava Batra*,

fol. 7b, 11b, etc. Concerning the *etrog*, see *Shulḥan Arukh, Oraḥ Ḥayim*, §658.9, and R. Arye Judah Leib ben Samuel Ẓvi Hirsch, compiler, *She'elot u-Tshuvot Ge'onei Batra'i*, ed. Elijah b. Moses Gershon [Elias Gerson], 1st edition (Turka: 1763–64) §37. Concerning the teacher, see *Shulḥan Arukh, Yore De'a*, §245.7; ReMA', *Shulḥan Arukh, Ḥoshen Mishpat*, §163.3; R. Aaron Samuel Kaidanover, *Responsa Emunat Shmu'el* (Lemberg: 1884–85), §26. On the costs of negotiating with the government, see R. Joseph Katz, *Responsa She'erit Yosef*, §38; MaHaRaM of Lublin, §102; R. Aaron Samuel Kaidanover, *Responsa Emunat Shmu'el*, §120. Parallel problems were raised by the need to hire men to fill out the public-prayer quorum on the High Holy Days (*Shulḥan Arukh, Oraḥ Ḥayim*, §55.21–22), the hiring of someone to blow the *shofar* (R. Ya'ir Ḥayim Bacharach, *Responsa Ḥavot Ya'ir*, §186), and the laying of pipe to bring water to a Jewish quarter (Krokhmal, *Responsa Ẓemaḥ Ẓedek*, §34).

[3] Where the *Shulḥan Arukh, Ḥoshen Mishpat*, §163.1, cited the *Braita* to the effect that residents of a city may force each other to contribute to a specific list of common expenses, R. Moses Isserles went further and extended the right of communal taxation "to all municipal needs." But this generalization was overly broad, and ReMA' felt obliged immediately to withdraw to the casuistic approach and listed a number of specific examples. R. Joseph Katz (*Responsa She'erit Yosef* §38) required the *kehila* to bear the costs if the damage was of public, rather than private, concern. R. Ya'ir Ḥayim Bacharach, *Responsa Ḥavot Ya'ir*, §81, offered an almost rationalist argument when he stated that

> those *takanot* are for the purpose of maintaining the group, and all benefit equally. For example, we might think it unfair if a tax were imposed specifically on money of gentiles deposited with Jews or on property beyond the city limits since [the assessors obviously know] who currently is holding gentile deposits or has property beyond the city limits. But things have a way of evening out: sometimes a given burgher will be engaged in one sort of business and sometimes in another. Moreover, there will be other *takanot* which will obligate other individuals. No two people have exactly the same interests; and under this assumption the decision was made to approve and accept the *takanot en bloc*.

[4] When R. Menaḥem Mendel Krokhmal issued a ruling (*Responsa Ẓemaḥ Ẓedek*, §37) derived from medieval Spanish Jewish practice, he was aware that objections might be raised on the grounds that that custom had not been current among his addressees, the Jews of Vienna. Nevertheless, he declared "that since the Viennese community does not have an opposing tradition, we treat it as if this custom was indeed accepted here too." But note that in a case where local custom was clearly defined, the very same author ruled that "one cannot cite [the custom of] one area as precedent for [practice in] another," and rejected the arguments of those who cited customs of "other

large communities" in support of efforts to introduce change; ibid., §2. The ReMA' uses the expressions "And this is the custom" and "People customarily do so" referring to the Ashkenazic-Polish tradition generally, and "This is the custom in our city" in reference to the traditions of Cracow itself. The ReMA' ruled that any practice followed three times was to be considered an "established custom" (*minhag kavua'*); *Shulḥan Arukh, Ḥoshen Mishpat*, §163.3, regarding taxation. He similarly concludes his halakhic discussion of several other matters by ruling that the matter should be decided according to custom. It should be emphasized that in this ReMA' was referring to *custom* and not to *takanot*. It is certain that some communities already had written *takanot* by his time, but their importance was not yet recognized. See n. 5, below.

[5] The oldest surviving set of *takanot* from Ashkenazic Jewry is the one from Cracow, 1595, but these mention earlier *takanot* that were also committed to writing. See Majer Balaban's comments to his edition of this text, "Die krakauer Judengemeinde—Ordnung von 1595 und ihre Nachträge," *JJLG* 10, p. 296–360, and 11, pp. 88–114.

[6] See Y. F. Baer, "The Origins of the Organization of the Jewish Community in the Middle Ages" [in Hebrew], *Zion* 15 (1949–50), p. 39. On the degree of rabbinical participation in the governance of the community, see the end of this chapter. The Cracow *takanot* are not signed by the rabbi, and he is mentioned only with regard to halakhic matters in the narrow sense—i.e., the laws of *kashrut*, marriage, and divorce. On the other hand, Rabbi Isaiah Horowitz was obliged, by the terms of his contract, to be a signatory to the communal *takanot*; M. Horovitz, *Frankfurter Rabbinen*, pp. 58f. [Hebrew version: *Rabanei Frankfurt*, p. 64—*tr.*]. This was the custom elsewhere as well. The leaders of the Jewish community of Tiktin were trying to strengthen the force of the ancient communal *takanot* when they stated that these were "established by ancients, great rabbis, brilliant scholars of the region . . . together with the contemporary leaders of the area"; Halperin, ed., *Pinkas Vaad Arba Araẓot*, p. 118. In the *takanot* of Moravia the power of the *takanot* is made dependent upon the signature of a rabbi or scholar (*ḥaver*) of the city; Halperin, ed., *Takanot . . . Mehrin*, §§176, 286, and 335. The notion of "*ḥaver* of the city" in these texts is not completely clear (see Halperin, p. 51, n. 8), but it obviously refers to someone who bears a certain measure of halakhic authority (see §378).

[7] These expressions are found in all the sources. Parallel to them is *gezel de-rabim* (stealing from the public), which is used to refer to actions that should be avoided because they harmed the public good. See, for instance, Balaban, "Die krakauer Judengemeinde," *JJLG* 10, p. 356, and the parallel expressions in Weinryb, *Texts and Studies*, Hebrew section, p. 30, etc. The very use of the term *rabim* sometimes implies the notion of the public (as opposed to private), as for instance in the ruling of R. Abraham Horowitz: "For the *rabim* [the public (interest)] is always primary and the interests of individuals are always disregarded in favor of those of the *rabim*"; *Yesh Noḥalim*, fol. 33a.

[8] Moses Isserles (*Responsa*, §73) expressed clearly the notion that members of a community (*bnei ha-ir*) might impose *takanot* only in accordance with the *din* [law]. On the other hand, they did not, and would never, have the power to institute new *takanot* merely on the basis of their own judgment. It is true that in the specific case in question, Isserles supported the community's ruling, but he categorically opposed its claim to "the power to decide and rule as [it] wished." Similarly, the author of *Responsa Ḥavot Ya'ir*, R. Ya'ir Ḥayim Bacharach, denied (§81) the right of communal representatives to impose a bylaw once they knew their ruling would harm an individual. He cited the wording of R. Meir of Rothenburg: "Are they allowed to be thieves because they are the majority?" This phrase is repeated often in similar cases; see Isserles, *Darkhei Moshe, Ḥoshen Mishpat*, §4.

[9] The council of Jewish communities of Lithuania decided explicitly that doubts concerning the interpretation of a *takana* were to be decided by the *Rav Av Bet Din* (head of the local rabbinical court) together with "the *baalei ha-takanot* who had issued the ruling"; Dubnow, ed., *Pinkas . . . Lita*, §753, and cf. §758. Many of the questions concerning the *kehila* focus on how to interpret communal *takanot*. See, for example, Krokhmal, *Responsa Ẓemaḥ Ẓedek*, §33; R. Jacob Reischer, *Responsa Shvut Yaakov*, III, §83.

[10] See Baer, "The Jewish Community in the Middle Ages," pp. 24f.

[11] See Baron, *The Jewish Community*, III, pp. 106ff.

[12] See H. Tchernowitz, *Toldot ha-Poskim* [English title: *History of the Jewish Codes*] (New York: 1946–47), III, pp. 37–91, and his citations from Rabbis Solomon Luria and Moses Isserles, establishing them as guardians of the Ashkenazic tradition. In my opinion, it must still be clarified whether these jurists actually followed through on their statements of principle in all areas. In the field of communal governance that interests us, the contradiction between their declared intent and reality is clear.

[13] The legitimacy, for instance, of *piskei baalei batim* [lay legal decisions] even in cases of capital offenses, which we shall treat in the next chapter, was established on the basis of Sephardic sources. Similarly R. Moses Isserles's acceptance of government-appointed rabbis (assuming that members of the *kehila* agreed) was based on proofs drawn from the Sephardic scholars R. Solomon ben Adret (RaSHBA'), R. Isaac bar Sheshet [RIBaSH], and R. Jacob ben Asher (*Baal ha-Turim*); *Responsa*, §123. For further examples of this, see below.

[14] For the number of *parnasim* in Poland, see Balaban, "Legal Status," p. 46, where the numbers three to five are mentioned. In Hamburg there were initially four and in 1725 the number was raised to six; M. Grunwald, "Die Statuten der 'Hamburg-Altonaer Gemeinde' von 1726," *Mitteilungen der Gesellschaft für Jüdische Volkskunde* 11 (1903), p. 19. In Frankfurt and Metz there were twelve; see Isidor Kracauer, *Geschichte der Juden in Frankfurt an Main*, I, p. 410, and Simḥa Assaf, *Mekorot le-Toldot ha-Ḥinukh be-Yisra'el* [Sources for the History of Jewish Education] (Tel-Aviv: 1954), I, p. 151. Terminology is not uniform even within Ashkenazic Jewry. In addition to

those titles that I mentioned, one finds also "ksherim" in Poznan and "ikorei kahal" in Moravia (see Halperin, ed., *Takanot . . . Mehrin*, index, s.v.) and Lithuania (Dubnow, ed., *Pinkas . . . Lita*, index, s.v.), and others. Here I intended to indicate only the nature of the offices and not their titles. The smallest communities aside, there was at least a universal division between an administrative body, an advisory and representative body, and a group of paid functionaries.

[15] See the *takanot* of Hamburg, cited in the previous note, §§62 and 63; the *takanot* of Frankfurt of 1674–75 [Jewish National and University Library, MS Hebrew 4° 662, "Pinkas Kahal Frankfurt de-Main"; cf. M. Nadav, "The *Pinkas* of the Jewish Community of Frankfurt on the Main" (in Hebrew), *Kiryat Sefer* (*Kirjath Sefer*) 31 (1955–56), pp. 507–16]. Almost the entire burden of government was placed upon the council of *parnasim* known as the *ḥavruta*, while the *parnas ha-ḥodesh* had only certain specific tasks, such as the direct contact with the state authorities. In Moravia, the institution of the *parnas ha-ḥodesh* apparently did not exist at all. The head of the *kahal* was elected for a year or more, and he and his associates, called "tovim," conducted the affairs of the community; cf. Halperin, ed., *Takanot . . . Mehrin*, especially §§176ff. The same is true in Eisenstadt as is clear from the community's records; cf. Wachstein, *Urkunden*, p. 44. The authority of the head of the *kahal* was so limited that the *shamash* was not obligated to obey him unless all the *tovim* were present; ibid., p. 369.

[16] This is evident from even a quick survey of the *takanot* of Cracow; Balaban, "Die krakauer Judengemeinde." Balaban summarizes the situation in Poland as a whole in "The Legal Status of the Jews and Their Communal Organization," pp. 44–49. For certain actions, the *takanot* of Cracow require the *parnas ha-ḥodesh* to consult with one of his colleagues (Balaban, "Die krakauer Judengemeinde," *JJLG* 10, p. 321). But even here, he must decide whether there is some pressing need or not, and this decision was his alone.

[17] In Hamburg, *parnasim* who missed meetings were fined, as was the *parnas ha-ḥodesh* if he refused to carry out a decision that was reached in his absence; Grunwald, "Statuten der 'Hamburg-Altonaer Gemeinde,' " §63. For Frankfurt, see MS "Pinkas Kahal Frankfurt de-Main" (above, n. 15), §18. In this case, since the council existed apart from the *parnas ha-ḥodesh*, it could collect the fine; usually it was the *parnas ha-ḥodesh* who levied fines and ordered other punishments. The *takanot* of Cracow mention, at one point, "a large fine of the *parnas ha-ḥodesh*," without, however, specifying the amount or how it was to be collected. This may therefore have been simply rhetorical; Balaban, "Die krakauer Judengemeinde," *JJLG* 10, p. 391.

[18] The *takanot* of Cracow repeatedly label anyone who does not do what is incumbent upon him a "transgressor of the *takanot*" and someone who is "excluded from the *mi she-berakh*"—that is, someone who is not included in the public prayer recited every Sabbath on behalf of "those who faithfully

serve the community's needs." A similar prayer was recited also on each eve of the New Moon when the office of *parnas ha-ḥodesh* passed from one incumbent to another; ibid., p. 359.

[19] Concerning the formula of this oath, see Halperin, ed., *Takanot . . . Mehrin*, §178. This is not the same as the oath of loyalty to the secular government customarily taken by holders of Jewish communal office in Poland; Schorr, *Rechtsstellung*, p. 13. In Hamburg the *parnasim* were required to take an oath quite apart from any link to the government; (above, n. 15), §52.

[20] In practical terms, therefore, individuals could move from a "lower" to a "higher" office. See, for example, Grunwald, "Statuten der 'Hamburg-Altonaer Gemeinde,' " §9, for Frankfurt; Halperin, ed., *Takanot . . . Mehrin*, §345.

[21] The *takanot* of Cracow empower the *parnas ha-ḥodesh* to delegate tasks to the other *parnasim* and the *tovim*, but this seems to be referring only to his right to request help on an ad hoc basis, and not to permanent appointments of subordinates; Balaban, "Die krakauer Judengemeinde," *JJLG* 10, p. 322. Lower-level functionaries, such as synagogue beadles (*gaba'im*), were essentially independent.

[22] The *takanot* of Cracow present a complex picture. The budget of the Poznan community of 1638 mentions ten *shamashim*, one scribe, and twelve guards (six Jewish and six gentile); Weinryb, *Texts and Studies*, Hebrew section, pp. 57f. The varying status of the jobs is reflected in the differing titles (*shamash*; synagogue *shamash*; assistant *shamash*) and, especially, in the differences in salary. A chief *shamash* received 150 gold coins, an assistant *shamash* 35, and a synagogue *shamash* 18.

[23] Balaban, "Die krakauer Judengemeinde," *JJLG* 10, p. 394; and *cf.* Weinryb, *Texts and Studies*, Hebrew section, p. 167, and Wachstein, *Urkunden*, pp. 508–21. In Poznan in 1644–45 a lawsuit was brought to decide whether the income from a certain service belonged to the *ḥazanim* and *shamashim* or to the communal scribe; Weinryb, *Texts and Studies*, Hebrew section, p. 168. R. Berechiah Berakh (b. Eliakim Getzel) criticizes these functionaries in his *Zera Berakh ha-Shlishi* (Frankfurt an der Oder: 1731), *Brakhot*, fol. 12d.

[24] Balaban, "Die krakauer Judengemeinde," *JJLG* 10, p. 395; Halperin, ed., *Takanot . . . Mehrin*, §§221–22.

[25] Balaban, "Die krakauer Judengemeinde," *JJLG* 10, pp. 321 and 326. Characteristically, no sanction was brought against the *shamash* in such a case; he was simply warned, in exactly the same terms as one of the officials, of "the penalties for abrogating the *takana*." The *rashim* and *tovim* obligated themselves before the provincial and local *shamashim* to meet at a given time. The *shamashim* thus became responsible for the fulfillment of the promise; see L. Lewin, *Die Landessynode der grosspolnischen Judenschaft* (Frankfurt am Main: 1926), p. 67.

[26] See L. Lewin, "Der Schtadlan im Posener Ghetto," *Festschrift zum achtzigsten Geburtstage . . . Wolf Feilchenfeld*, Bernhard Koenigsberger and Moritz Silberberg, eds. (Pleschen-Schrimm: 1907), pp. 31–39. A knowledge of written and spoken Polish is mentioned in a document cited there, p. 32, and this is understood elsewhere as well. Weinryb, *Texts and Studies*, p. 168; Halperin, ed., *Pinkas Vaad Arba Araẓot*, index, s.v. "Shtadlan," and especially pp. 311–12; Dubnow, ed., *Pinkas . . . Lita*, "Index," and also Halperin, ed., *Takanot . . . Mehrin*.

[27] The *shtadlan* was paid 300 gold coins in Poznan in 1637–38 and the communal rabbi 230; Weinryb, *Texts and Studies*, Hebrew section, pp. 57f. The *shtadlan* of the Council of the Four Lands was guaranteed an income of over 400 gold coins plus expenses in 1729–30; Halperin, ed., *Pinkas Vaad Arba Araẓot*, p. 313. In the eighteenth century the rabbi's salary rose to more than that of the *shtadlan*; Perles, *Geschichte der Juden in Posen*, and see below, n. 30. There is also evidence of one-time grants to a *shtadlan* for special services to the *kehila*; Weinryb, *Texts and Studies*, Hebrew section, p. 99.

[28] The Cracow *takanot* (Balaban, "Die krakauer Judengemeinde," *JJLG* 10, p. 328) explicitly state that the *shtadlan* was appointed "in order to lighten the burden of the *rashim*, who cannot personally go with everyone, for our people have great needs and are unable to care for themselves." That the *shtadlan* was to function only as an agent of those who sent him is also stated in the other sources we have cited.

[29] Balaban, "Die krakauer Judengemeinde," loc. cit., and Lewin, "Der Schtadlan im Posener Ghetto," p. 29.

[30] In 1760–61 the Council of Lithuania urged that *shtadlanim* should be provided with "a fixed and adequate livelihood in order that they not have to collect [from individuals]"; Dubnow, ed., *Pinkas . . . Lita*, §1014, p. 271. The same year, a levy was added to the poll tax in order to pay the salary of the provincial *shtadlan* (ibid., pp. 301f.). The text is not completely clear, but it is evident that the amount of his salary was no longer fixed, nor was it completely guaranteed. In the face of this development we need not be surprised to learn that the *shtadlan* in Cracow was assigned a percentage of the burial tax (Weinryb, *Texts and Studies*, English section, p. 83, n. 28) and a cantor's salary was to be taken from the fees paid by women who used the ritual bath in Posen (Lewin, "Der Schtadlan im Posener Ghetto," p. 37). We might note that everything stated here with respect to the *shtadlan* applies specifically to Poland, Lithuania, and Moravia where, apparently, there was no provincial *shtadlan*. In the German communities, the *parnas* served as the *shtadlan* and performed this task on a voluntary basis. See Baer, *Protokollbuch*, p. 89. The *shtadlan* was paid in Germany only occasionally (e.g., Bacharach, *Responsa Ḥavot Ya'ir*, §154) and never as a permanent office.

[31] On these aspects of the rabbinate, see chapter 17.

[32] R. Menaḥem Mendel Krokhmal mentions the custom whereby all taxpayers participated in the election; *Responsa Ẓemaḥ Ẓedek*, §§1–2. In most

places, the community at large elected a body of electors: in Poznan there were 32, in Lissa 71. Lewin, *Landessynode*, p. 67; L. Lewin, *Geschichte der Juden in Lissa*, p. 75.

33 Many such letters of rabbinical appointment have been preserved. See, e.g., Wachstein, *Urkunden*, pp. 450ff. The custom of sending such a *shtar rabanut* to the rabbi is mentioned for the year 1672–73 in Dubnow, ed., *Pinkas . . . Lita*, §694.

34 In Moravia there were some communities that, prior to 1648–49, forbade appointing a rabbi for a term of more than one year. Provincial *takanot* overturned this practice; Halperin, ed., *Takanot . . . Mehrin*, §291. In Lithuania the question was raised as to whether the rabbi's contract lapsed automatically at the end of its term or whether it had to be formally canceled. At first, the council found in favor of the community (Dubnow, ed., *Pinkas . . . Lita*, §48, for the year 1622–23), but later decided in favor of the rabbi (ibid., §726).

35 For a treatment of educational institutions, see chapter 18.

36 For a description of the ceremony welcoming a rabbi, see Krokhmal, *Ẓemaḥ Ẓedek*, §16: "He arrived on Wednesday . . . and was received with much honor. On the Sabbath he preached before a large congregation and gave a nice sermon. Most members of the community came to honor him at the party which the congregation, may God protect and guard it, prepared. They sent him gifts and all rejoiced and were happy, he in them and they in him." This rabbi stayed in his position only three days. The custom of delivering a sermon upon assuming office is also mentioned in Dubnow, ed., *Pinkas . . . Lita*, §882.

37 In the fifteenth century rabbis still took advantage of their Talmudic prerogative to excommunicate anyone who acted brazenly before them. The communities now limited this right and offered instead to protect their rabbi themselves; cf. Halperin, ed., *Pinkas Vaad Arba Araẓot*, p. 50. The arrangement that the Frankfurt community established with Rabbi Isaiah Horowitz, author of the *Shnei Luḥot ha-Brit*, is typical. According to this, he was forbidden to use his power of excommunication against his opponents unless the *parnasim* had refused to defend his honor. See Horovitz, *Frankfurter Rabbinen*, I, pp. 59f. [Hebrew: *Rabanei Frankfurt*, cf. p. 323]. Wachstein, *Urkunden*, p. 397, provides an example of a punishment handed down against the *parnasim* for offending the rabbi. Of course, such protection was not forthcoming in all places to a satisfactory extent, and some rabbis were forced to suffer insults by their opponents; e.g., *She'elot u-Tshuvot ha-BaḤ ha-Ḥadashot*, §42.

38 On the rabbinate of the previous centuries, see Moshe Frank, *Kehilot Ashkenaz u-Vatei ha-Din Shelahen* [Ashkenazic Communities and their Courts] (Tel-Aviv: 1938), pp. 19ff.

39 See chapter 19.

40 The *takanot* of Hamburg require the rabbi to be present during the entire election procedure; M. Grunwald, "Statuten der 'Hamburg-Altonaer Gemeinde,' " §45ff., *MGJV* 11 (1903), p.17f. R. Benjamin Aaron Slonik,

Responsa Mas'at Binyamin (first edition, Cracow: 1632–33; references are to the edition of Jerusalem: 1967–68, which restores *responsa* censored in earlier versions), §7, reports that elections in Satanow were once held only because of pressure from the rabbi.

[41] See chapter 10 below concerning the methods of enforcement available.

[42] The *takanot* of Cracow, which, in general, do not grant the rabbi any authority in communal affairs, still require local rabbis to annul such a decree of excommunication by declaring its initiators themselves to be excommunicated; Balaban, "Die krakauer Judengemeinde," *JJLG* 10, p. 391.

[43] For an example of opposition to the increased influence of rabbis, see Halperin, ed., *Pinkas Vaad Arba Araẓot*, p. 325. A clear tendency to advance the authority of rabbis is to be seen in the *takanot* of Moravia of 1649–50, authored by, among others, R. Menaḥem Mendel Krokhmal. This tendency is manifest also in his *responsa*. In typical fashion he ends a response concerning communal leadership with the following words: "And the most proper way in such matters is to do everything in accordance with the opinion of a 'righteous teacher and scholar' [i.e., a rabbi] who will mediate peace within the community and establish a proper norm [*tikun*] which will meet with everyone's approval, and the entire people will rest peacefully"; *Responsa Ẓemaḥ Ẓedek*, §2. In 1714 the new rabbi of Poznan was appointed for six years, in 1717 for ten years, and in 1796 for nineteen years. This tendency is evidenced in the histories of both rabbis and communities. In Metz in 1766 the rabbi agreed not to leave office in less than twelve years while the congregation obligated itself to keep him for six years; N. Netter, *Vingt siècles d'histoire d'une communauté juive* (Paris: 1938), p. 131.

[44] On rabbis engaging in commerce in Poland, see Halperin, ed., *Pinkas Vaad Arba Araẓot*, p. 325, n. 1. For Moravia, see Halperin, ed., *Takanot . . . Mehrin*, §§150 and 336 as well as in nn. 5–6 ad loc.

[45] R. Moses Isserles had ruled that one should not delay the start of the public prayers "for an important individual who had not yet come"; *Shulḥan Arukh, Oraḥ Ḥayim*, §124.3. But the author of the *Magen Avraham* comments on this: "We now customarily wait for the communal rabbi [*av bet din*]"; ibid., §7. A popular joke gives evidence of the custom of waiting for the rabbi. The Mishnaic statement that "the world stands [*omed*] on three things—on truth [*emet*] and peace [*shalom*] . . ." was understood as meaning that people stand waiting for the rabbi before ending the recital of the prayer "Hear O Israel" with the word *emet* and the recital of the *amida* prayer with the words *ose shalom*. The source of this witticism is one of the rabbinate's most trenchant critics, R. Berechiah Berakh (b. Eliakim Getzel), *Zera Berakh ha-Shlishi, Brakhot*, fol. 24.

Chapter 10. The Kehila's Range of Activities

[1] A loyalty oath taken before the "judge of the Jews"—that is, the government representative—was customary in Poland; M. Schorr, *Rechtsstellung*, p. 13, and Balaban, "Legal Statutes," p. 46.

[2] In R. Joel Sirkes, *Responsa Bayit Ḥadash* (Ostrog: 1834), §43, we find the community's leaders warned that if they did not try someone suspected by the authorities of criminal activity, they would be subject "to all the punishments decreed by the king." R. Menaḥem Mendel Krokhmal, *Responsa Ẓemaḥ Ẓedek*, §§18–19, provides typical examples of the fact that even military officers passing through a city would, as a matter of course, use the Jewish communal leaders as intermediaries in transmitting demands to the members of the community at large.

[3] There are many examples of such a procedure. See, e.g., Halperin, ed., *Takanot . . . Mehrin*, §§114, 250, 259; Wachstein, *Urkunden*, p. 364, and cf. also his introduction, p. xviii. The custom began in medieval times, and the charter to the Jews of Halle in 1713 still specified that two-thirds of every fine imposed by the leaders of the community was to go to the royal fisc; Benjamin Hirsch Auerbach, *Geschichte der israelitischen Gemeinde in Halberstadt* (Halberstadt: 1866), p. 40. The same was true in the edict issued to the Jews of Prussia in 1714; J. Freund, *Die Emanzipation der Juden in Preussen*, II, p. 12.

[4] Halperin, ed., *Takanot . . . Mehrin*, §177, fined anyone who accepted a Jewish communal appointment from the government "twenty *thäler* to the Jewish provincial authority and twenty *thäler* to the government, may its honor be exalted."

[5] Resorting to the secular authorities in order to collect taxes from those who refused to pay was already permitted in the Middle Ages. See Ephraim E. Urbach, *Baalei ha-Tosafot*, p. 418. At the end of the period, R. Joseph ben Solomon Colon states: "It is standard practice to use the judges of the gentiles to force anyone who refuses to pay his due" (*Responsa* [first edition, Venice: 1519; new edition, Jerusalem: 1988], §1.17, pp. 43b–44a), and his view was cited as authoritative by R. Moses Isserles, *Shulḥan Arukh, Ḥoshen Mishpat*, §4. Cf. also ibid., §163.1.

[6] For the origins of these methods of collection, see Baer, "Jewish Community in the Middle Ages," p. 33. In our period, there are many sources that testify to this custom. See R. Moses Isserles, *Shulḥan Arukh, Ḥoshen Mishpat*, §163.3; Balaban, "Die krakauer Judengemeinde," *JJLG* 10, p. 351; Perles, *Juden in Posen*, p. 69, n. 15; Krokhmal, *Responsa Ẓemaḥ Ẓedek*, §§24 and 102; Bacharach, *Responsa Ḥavot Ya'ir*, §§57 and 58. This last source comments on the mixture of the two systems: First the assessors evaluated the property, and whoever felt that he had been overassessed could swear to what he felt was a more accurate evaluation. The opposite procedure was followed in the case mentioned in *Responsa Ẓemaḥ Ẓedek*, §24. There, if the

assessors felt that the self-declared value was too low, they could require the individual to take an oath.

[7] See Baer, "Jewish Community in the Middle Ages," p. 34, and, for the start of our period, R. Moses Isserles, *Shulḥan Arukh, Ḥoshen Mishpat,* §163.3.

[8] See for example Ḥayim Ze'ev Margalioth, *Dubno Rabati. Toldot ha-Ir Dubno ve-Haatakot mi-Pinkas ha-Kahal shelah mi-Shnat [5]475 va-Hal'a u-me-Maẓevot she-al Kivrei Gdolei ha-Ir ha-Zot ve-Nikhbadeha* [Greater Dubno. The History of (the Jewish Community of) the City of Dubno, Excerpts from Its Communal Register from 1714–15 on, and Epitaphs of This City's Great (Rabbis) and Honored (Leaders)] (Warsaw: 1910), p. 45; R. Aaron Samuel Kaidanover, *Responsa Emunat Shmu'el,* §29.

[9] It was typical to discover after the death of the taxpayer that his property was worth more than the figure at which it had been assessed; e.g., the situations cited in *Responsa Ẓemaḥ Ẓedek* and *Responsa Ḥavot Ya'ir,* above, n. 6. In the case cited in *Responsa Ẓemaḥ Ẓedek,* §24, the subjective honesty of the taxpayer was not in doubt. While Krokhmal decided for the taxpayer's estate and against the community on formal grounds, it seems likely that there were actually objective difficulties in accurately assessing the value of the man's property, in part because his business was based on credit—that is, he was a capitalist who invested in other people's business ventures or lent money at interest. The *kehila* tried to pressure the individual into assessing his own property fairly in the first place, as we see in a *takana* quoted by R. Ya'ir Ḥayim Bacharach, *Responsa Ḥavot Ya'ir,* §57: A taxpayer whose initial self-assessment was questioned and who was therefore required to take an oath as to its accuracy could not, at that point, add more than 5 percent to his original estimate.

[10] The *takanot* of Cracow already include a consumption tax; Balaban, "Die krakauer Judengemeinde," *JJLG* 10, p. 356. See Balaban, "Legal Status of the Jews and Their Communal Organization," p. 54. In 1714–15 the *parnasim* of Eisenstadt declared it "an accepted and fit practice in all communities and lands to establish levies . . . on all food and drink consumed to aid the community," and they testified that this had been the practice in their community "from the day it was established"; Wachstein, *Urkunden,* p. 222. On the method of allocating the tax, see *Ḥoshen Mishpat,* §163.4. Practical questions regarding this matter are cited in Krokhmal, *Responsa Ẓemaḥ Ẓedek,* §§18 and 34; Israel Klausner, *Toldot ha-Kehila ha-Ivrit be-Vilna* [History of the Jewish Community of Wilno] (Wilno: 1938), I, pp. 156–63; B. D. Weinryb, "Outlines of the Economic and Financial History of the Jews in Poland and Lithuania in the Seventeenth and Eighteenth Centuries" [in Hebrew], *Tarbiẓ* 10 (1938–39), pp. 90–104 and 201–31, now reprinted in his *Meḥkarim u-Mkorot le-Toldot Yisra'el ba-Et ha-Ḥadasha* [Studies and Documents in Modern Jewish History] (Jerusalem: 1975), pp. 68–120; idem, "Beiträge zur Finanzgeschichte der jüdischen Gemeinden in Polen," part I: *Monatsschrift für*

Geschichte und Wissenschaft des Judentums 82 (1938), pp. 248–63, and part II: *Hebrew Union College Annual* 16 (1941), pp. 187–214.

[11] For example, R. Joseph b. Gershon Katz of Cracow ruled on absolute halakhic grounds in favor of the poor. The case involved a communal levy to defray a slaughtering tax imposed on the Jews by the authorities. Katz ruled that the levy was to be raised as a direct tax on individual wealth rather than as a consumption tax on meat. *Responsa She'erit Yosef*, §70.

[12] The responses of R. Menaḥem Mendel Krokhmal in the two cases cited above, n. 10, from his *Ẓemaḥ Ẓedek*, are typical. His ruling was not the logical result of his deliberations but the product of his desire to assuage the feelings of both parties. A query addressed to R. Ya'ir Ḥayim Bacharach states clearly that tax law could not be based directly on formal halakhic principles:

> for in matters of assessments and the like, the community unquestionably has the right to proceed as it sees fit, and it need not listen to anyone who seeks to find the legal principles involved. . . . They [i.e., the authors of the query] would like to discover our Sages' views and be aided by them. . . . Having done so, however, they may do as they wish, approximating the view of the Torah (*ya'asu ke-fi reẓonam karov le-din tora*).

Responsa Ḥavot Ya'ir, §57, and cf. ibid., §81, at the start of the response. See also R. Solomon Luria, *Responsa*, §4, who, in dealing with a question of customs levies, admits that such matters were known to be "difficult to base on *din tora* and [were settled] rather through compromise and common sense" (*raḥok hu le-karvo le-din tora ela al-yedei pshara u-svara*).

[13] See the summaries in Balaban, "Legal Status of the Jews and their Communal Organization," p. 54; Schorr, *Rechtsstellung*, pp. 14 and 16; Weinryb, *Te'udot*, pp. 59f., 83, and 103, and the sources cited there.

[14] Supervision of tax farmers was customary in Moravia; Halperin, ed., *Takanot . . . Mehrin*, §§253–56. Supervision of the economic activities of individuals is found, for example, in Balaban, "Die krakauer Judengemeinde," *JJLG* 10, p. 326; Lewin, *Die Landessynode*, pp. 88, 89; Dubnow, ed., *Pinkas . . . Lita*, §637.

[15] Communal life was treated primarily under the rubric of the laws of partnership in the *Shulḥan Arukh*, and this derives ultimately from Talmudic tradition. See Baer, "The Jewish Community in the Middle Ages," p. 8.

[16] On the basis of the laws of partnership, R. Joseph Katz decided, *Responsa She'erit Yosef*, §38, that the expenses involved in appealing to the government against the activities of a Christian tax collector should be borne by the entire community. R. Ya'ir Ḥayim Bacharach argues (*Responsa Ḥavot Ya'ir*, §81) that someone who quits a community is not held responsible for further dues on the grounds that the partnership had been dissolved. The *takanot* of Moravia (Halperin, ed., *Takanot . . . Mehrin*, §207) state explicitly

that, from a purely halakhic point of view, an individual wishing to leave a community need not pay his share of any communal debts that had not yet fallen due (and see Halperin's comment, p. 70, n. 7). But in practice, the authors of the *takana* continue, "custom overrides the Halakha." The individual must "pay up everything fully and immediately, and he may not argue that he will pay when the community does." This was also the norm elsewhere; see Balaban, "Die krakauer Judengemeinde," *JJLG* 10, p. 352; Bacharach, *Responsa Ḥavot Ya'ir*, §§156–57. There were cases in which a community tried actually to prevent the individual from leaving a place, something that had no basis in the laws of partnership; Perles, *Juden in Posen*, p. 96; Weinryb, *Text and Studies*, Hebrew section, pp. 10f.; etc.

[17] R. Ya'ir Ḥayim Bacharach justifies the communal custom of collecting the estimated equivalent of the tax burden for the coming two or three years from anyone leaving the community with the theory that "there was no fixed time limit to their partnership"; *Responsa Ḥavot Ya'ir*, §157, and cf. §81.

[18] The custom of empowering the community has its source in the medieval period; see Baer, "The Jewish Community in the Middle Ages," p. 97. This *takana* is cited by R. Moses Isserles as law; *Shulḥan Arukh, Ḥoshen Mishpat*, §4. Application of the law in practice is exemplified in R. Joseph Katz, *Responsa She'erit Yosef*, §38. It should be mentioned that in the end the individuals won their suit against the *kehila*; above, n. 16.

[19] On the contradiction between the conception of the *kehila* as a partnership and the view of it as a municipal organism, see Baer, "The Jewish Community in the Middle Ages," especially at the end of the article. This contradiction continues even in our own days, if in a new form.

[20] R. Benjamin Aaron Slonik notes (*Responsa Mas'at Binyamin*, §33) that the power of contemporary lay leaders was greater than that accorded them in the Talmudic period:

> In our time, in these lands, the custom of the communities is to appoint leaders and *parnasim*, and to give them authority [literally: a stick and whip] over all the members of the community. They can impose their will in all communal matters. . . . Those leaders have the power to sell a synagogue. . . . Even if members of the community object, it is of no relevance.

Similarly R. Ya'ir Ḥayim Bacharach derives the power of the *parnasim* to issue *takanot* from the fact "that they were elected by a majority of the congregation," and he attributes this view to the *rishonim* [early sages] R. Eliezer ben Joel ha-Levi of Bonn [RaAViYaH, 1140–1225] and his school, who did in fact justify the right of the community to impose its will on the individual but who did not use this reasoning; *Responsa Ḥavot Ya'ir*, §81.

[21] See chapter 9, n. 8.

[22] Dubnow, ed., *Pinkas . . . Lita*, §364:

> The communal leaders [*manhigim*] shall serve as judges in matters of arguments, fights and quarrels, *arendas* [leases of land, chattels, or the right to farm a tax or operate a mint], the liquor tax, fines and punishments, while the judges [*dayanim*] of the *kehila* shall judge matters involving money. The leaders shall not become involved in money cases, and the judges shall not become involved in matters which do not belong to them.

A similar division is found in Halperin, ed., *Takanot . . . Mehrin*, §67. This was the normal practice everywhere; Balaban, "Die krakauer Judengemeinde," *JJLG* 10, p. 324; Krokhmal, *Responsa Ẓemaḥ Ẓedek*, §24; Halperin, ed., *Takanot . . . Mehrin*, §199, e.g., and see n. 23, below. See also Simḥa Assaf, *Batei ha-Din ve-Sidreihem aḥar Ḥatimat ha-Talmud* [Jewish Courts and Their Procedures after the Talmudic Period] (Jerusalem: 1923–24), pp. 46–51.

[23] See Halperin, ed., *Takanot . . . Mehrin*, §67; Balaban, "Die krakauer Judengemeinde," *JJLG* 10, p. 330; Wachstein, *Urkunden*, p. 415. Lewin, *Die Landessynode*, pp. 72f., provides a negative formulation of the rights of the communal rabbi.

[24] The authority and jurisdiction of judges is clearly spelled out in Balaban, "Die krakauer Judengemeinde," *JJLG* 10, pp. 326, 331, and 332; Weinryb, *Texts and Studies*, Hebrew section, p. 165. See the citation from Dubnow, *Pinkas . . . Lita*, above, n. 22. Halperin, ed., *Takanot . . . Mehrin*, also assumes the existence of permanent judges at least in some *kehilot*; see §§64, 157, etc. And see also the nn. below.

[25] "Laymen judge by common sense"; R. Solomon Luria, *Responsa*, §93, and cf. §4. See also R. Moses Isserles, *Responsa*, §33, who mentions a litigant who considered it an advantage to use lay judges who decide "according to their own judgment." See also the words of the anonymous scholar cited by R. Judah Loeb Pukhovitser, *Kne Ḥokhma*, fol. 25d–26a, whose main point was that "laymen's judgments have no rules, and the lay judge may well decide the same case in opposite fashions on two different occasions." Similarly R. Ezekiel Landau, *Drushei ha-ẒLaḤ*, §3, fol. 2, and §8, fol. 16a.

[26] Such courts were justified by R. Moses Isserles in his commentary to *Shulḥan Arukh, Ḥoshen Mishpat*, §8.1 (following R. Joseph Caro who in turn cited R. Solomon ben Adret). Cf. also R. Mordecai Jaffe, *Levush* [*Ir Shushan*], *Ḥoshen Mishpat*, §8.1. A formal justification was also included in the remarks of R. Solomon Luria cited in the previous note. Cf., Sirkes, *Responsa Bayit Ḥadash*, §58.

[27] The question was treated explicitly in Sirkes, *Responsa Bayit Ḥadash*, §51. That authority justified charging a fee and found no fault with the practice unless judges began to issue multiple judgments and insisted on retrying the same case in order to get more fees.

[28] See *Tosafot, Ktubot*, fol. 105a, s.v. "*gozrei gzerot*," as well as the comments of R. Joel Sirkes, *Responsa Bayit Ḥadash*, cited above, n. 27.

[29] See the sources cited above, n. 26.

[30] R. Moses Isserles, *Responsa*, §33, still feels that he must justify the superiority of a rabbinic court "which knows the law" over a merchants' court. His contemporaries accepted the lay court as an unfortunate necessity. R. Judah Loeb Pukhovitser and the anonymous sage he quoted in *Kne Ḥokhma* (later seventeenth century), and R. Ezekiel Landau (eighteenth century) all project a quite different attitude; cf. above, n. 25.

[31] *Drushei ha-ẒLaḤ*, sermon 8.

[32] Balaban, "Die krakauer Judengemeinde," *JJLG* 10, pp. 332f.; Dubnow, ed., *Pinkas . . . Lita*, §67; and cf. Assaf, *Batei ha-Din ve-Sidreihem*, pp. 15f. But this stipulation may refer only to lay courts.

[33] It is sufficient to cite the general testimony of R. Moses Isserles in this matter (*Responsa*, §109):

> A gift or sale arranged before a non-Jewish court is certainly binding . . . and indeed, if we wanted to invalidate the courts of the gentiles in these countries with regard to land ownership, the entire status quo would be overturned and the [position] of the [Jews of these] countries would be destroyed, for we would not leave any real estate in its owners' hands over which there would not be repeated squabbles and quarrels.

[34] This appears often in the sources; cf. *Shulḥan Arukh, Ḥoshen Mishpat*, §26; R. Solomon Luria, *Yam shel Shlomo, Bava Kama*, chapter 8, §65. RaSHI's formulation (Exodus 21:1) probably influenced this development: "He who brings a case between Jewish litigants before gentile [judges] thereby desecrates the name [of God] and honors the name of idols." Maimonides' statement (*Mishne Tora, Laws of Sanhedrin*, §26.7) that such an individual was considered "to have lifted his hand against the Torah of Moses" was understood in a similar fashion by R. Joseph Caro, *Shulḥan Arukh*, loc. cit., and by R. Moses Isserles, *Responsa*, §88. Cf. also Assaf, *Batei ha-Din*, pp. 11f.

[35] See *Shulḥan Arukh, Ḥoshen Mishpat*, §26.2; R. Solomon Luria, *Yam shel Shlomo, Bava Kama*, chapter 8, §65; and R. Moses Isserles, *Responsa*, §108. According to the latter, there was an "established custom in our city" that one had to seek permission from the *parnasim* to sue a fellow Jew in a gentile court, even if the contract between them expressly permitted such a step. R. Solomon Luria disagreed with this position; *Yam shel Shlomo*, loc. cit. In Moravia at the end of the seventeenth century, appealing an internal court ruling to the government authorities was allowed, but the *kehilot* tried to prevent such moves; Halperin, ed., *Takanot . . . Mehrin*, §467.

[36] In contrast to the explanation offered by Assaf, *Batei ha-Din*, p. 17, it was the power of the *kehila*, rather than a lack of familiarity with the Polish language, that led Polish Jews to avoid gentile courts. Even in Poland, however, Jews did use the gentile courts on occasion. R. Nathan Hannover's description (upon which Assaf relies, ibid., p. 19) should be treated as a typical idealization. Azriel Shoḥet has collected interesting details concerning the situation in

Germany in his *Im Ḥilufei ha-Tkufot, Reshit ha-Haskala bi Yahadut Germanya* [Beginnings of the Haskala among German Jewry] (Jersualem: 1960), pp. 72–88.

[37] See the remarks of the *Shulḥan Arukh* and R. Solomon Luria, *Yam shel Shlomo,* as cited above, nn. 34–35. For examples of licenses to resort to the general authorities and to gentile courts, see Halperin, *Pinkas Vaad Arba Araẓot,* index, s.v. "arka'ot."

[38] See chapter 12.

[39] Solomon Luria deals with this question in a theoretical fashion in *Yam shel Shlomo, Yevamot,* X, §20, as does R. Meir b. Gedaliah of Lublin in his *Responsa,* §138. Aside from one citation from R. Menaḥem of Marsburg cited by Luria, both writers rely entirely on Sephardic jurists. The changed historical reality also suggests that Ashkenazic commentators were dealing with practical, and not merely theoretical, questions when they discussed the right of the *kehila* to judge capital crimes; see R. Joshua Falk, *Prisha,* and R. Joel Sirkes, *Bayit Ḥadash,* to *Arbaa Turim, Ḥoshen Mishpat,* §2, as well as Falk's *Sefer Me'irat Einayim [SMA'], Shulḥan Arukh, Ḥoshen Mishpat,* §2.4. See also n. 40, below.

[40] In Posen the *kehila* had the right to impose the death penalty; see Perles, *Juden in Posen,* pp. 22–24. The *responsum* of MaHaRaM of Lublin cited in the previous note deals with a Jewish murderer who was caught by the gentile authorities. It was because of the involvement of the government that MaHaRaM urged that the accused be condemned to death lest the gentiles say that Jews treat such matters leniently. His *responsum,* §120, similarly speaks of a case in which the ruler "gave them [the Jews] permission to execute [an informer]."

[41] R. Meir of Lublin, *Responsa,* §138, includes testimony concerning a maiming at the order of R. Shalom Shakhna. Apparently R. Solomon Luria was referring to that incident in the above citation. On the basis of the results of that action, Luria decided that the death penalty was to be preferred to maiming. Granted our evidence that such incidents actually occurred, we should take the threats mentioned in the rabbinic decisions as warnings that were to be taken seriously; see Weinryb, *Texts and Studies,* Hebrew section, pp. 66 and 71; Perles, *Juden in Posen,* p. 97, n. 85. In my opinion we should similarly understand R. Moses Isserles, *Responsa,* §11, as a true death sentence.

[42] In the case cited in MaHaRaM of Lublin, *Responsa,* §138, the author of the question (identified as the rabbi and sage, head of a *yeshiva* and head of a court, our teacher and rabbi, Rabbi Samuel, may his Rock protect and save him—perhaps referring to MaHaRSHA', R. Samuel Edels) sought to prevent the sentence from being executed by Jews though he did consider the possibility of a sentence of maiming, and even MaHaRaM urged in the end that the sentencing be handed over in this case to a gentile court. Similar advice is offered by R. Jacob ben Samuel, *Responsa Beit Yaakov* (Dyhernfurth [?]: 1695–96), §2.

[43] See *Shulḥan Arukh, Ḥoshen Mishpat,* §2, and the commentaries ad loc. The Halakha relies on the Talmudic statement (*Yevamot,* fol. 90b) that "a court may order lashes and punishments not decreed in Scriptures"—i.e., not in accordance with the legal norms for capital punishment. Under the conditions of the Diaspora, the exception became the norm.

[44] Court procedures and methods of operation were summarized by Assaf, *Batei ha-Din,* especially pp. 25ff. See also his *Ha-Onshin Aḥarei Ḥatimat ha-Talmud* (Jerusalem: 1922).

[45] For the medieval period in Ashkenaz, see Baer, "The Jewish Community in the Middle Ages," p. 30. On the development of the *ḥerem,* see Assaf, *Ha-Onshin,* [Criminal Jurisdiction since the Conclusion of the Talmud] pp. 31f. The subject of the *ḥerem* and its development and function over the generations deserves separate treatment. Meanwhile, see J. Wiesner, *Der Bann in seiner geschichtlichen Entwicklung auf dem Boden des Judenthumes* (Leipzig: 1864).

[46] For cases of disqualification from holding public office, see Dubnow, ed., *Pinkas . . . Lita,* index, s.v. "Haavarat minui"; Halperin, ed., *Takanot . . . Mehrin,* §§182, 183; Krokhmal, *Responsa Ẓemaḥ Ẓedek,* §102; etc. Keeping people from attending synagogue services was very common.

[47] See *Shulḥan Arukh, Yore De'a,* §334.2, as well as in the formulae for *ḥaramot,* as in Halperin, ed., *Pinkas Vaad Arba Araẓot,* p. 1; Balaban, "Die krakauer Judengemeinde," *JJLG* 11, p. 90.

[48] A decree to this effect is found in Dubnow, ed., *Pinkas . . . Lita,* §546.

[49] As is well known, it was difficult to find someone who would agree to be called to the reading of the "portion of admonition" [Lev.26: 14–41 and Deut.28: 15–68; see *Shulḥan Arukh, Oraḥ Ḥayim,* §428.6—*tr.*] "and therefore they had to put it in the sexton's contract that he would be called for the 'portion of curses' or else they would have to pay a poor man to be called for it"; Krokhmal, *Responsa Ẓemaḥ Ẓedek,* §56.

[50] It is sufficient here to mention the various excommunications attributed to Rabenu Gershom "Light of the Exile" (*Me'or ha-Gola*); L. Finkelstein, *Jewish Self-Government in the Middle Ages,* 2nd revised edition (New York: 1964), pp. 20ff. Every commitment to a marriage was strengthened with a declaration of *ḥerem* against anyone who sought to revoke it; see chapter 14.

[51] Halperin, ed., *Pinkas Vaad Arba Araẓot,* pp. 1 and 62f. A *ḥerem* was declared in Buda against the appointment as rabbi of anyone who had relatives in the community; R. Gershon Ashkenazi, *Responsa Avodat ha-Gershuni,* §12.

[52] R. Sheftel Horowitz praised the great sages of Poland for excommunicating those who purchased their rabbinical office with money, but added: "But because of our many sins, their remedy has caused further problems, since some do not accept the strictures and, because of our many sins, transgress these *ḥaramot* and the curses written in the book, and lead many others to sin"; *Vavei ha-Amudim,* end of chapter 21, *Shnei Luḥot ha-Brit,* Amsterdam edition, fol. 32a. This is the implication of R. Joel Sirkes's protest

against the decree of excommunication issued by "the heads and leaders of the land" in Lublin in 1621–22 concerning "coin clipping"; *Responsa Bayit Ḥadash ha-Ḥadashot*, §43, and Halperin, ed., *Pinkas Vaad Arba Arazot*, pp. 42–45. Sirkes agrees with the intent of the prohibition and seeks only to insure that it be enforced with rational means: a monetary fine, exile from the kingdom or even handing the transgressor over to the government. He was opposed to the *ḥerem* because he feared that the punishment for the sin would rest on the entire community because of individuals who could not "restrain themselves . . . from profiting and making their own and their families' livelihood from counterfeiting which, because of our sins, has begun in our generation." The leaders of Lithuanian Jewry followed Sirkes's proposal when, in 1633–34, they canceled all *ḥaramot* even though the essence of the bans was retained; see *Pinkas Vaad Arba Arazot*, p. 44, n. 2. The dilemma of the "double-edged swords" involved in requiring an oath and in using the decree of excommunication was not new; see *Tosafot, Gitin*, fol. 35a, s.v. "demoria"; R. Solomon Luria, *Yam shel Shlomo*, IV, §34.

[53] We should not conclude, from complaints about those who transgressed the *ḥaramot*, that the bans had no force. A ruling such as that of the R. Joshua Falk, *Sefer Me'irat Einayim, Ḥoshen Mishpat*, §34.5.10, citing [Alexander Suslin ha-Kohen of Frankfurt] *Ḥidushei Aguda*, to the effect that transgressors of *ḥaramot* should not be disqualified as witnesses since "if so, not one in a thousand would be qualified," should not be taken as accurate testimony. This is one of those value judgments that are quoted from one author to another; see Halperin, ed., *Pinkas Vaad Arba Arazot*, p. 42, n. 3, who did not notice that Falk was quoting. R. Berechiah Berakh (b. Eliakim Getzel) seems to deny the force of the *ḥerem* when he advises an individual excommunicated by the community to ignore it and respond in kind; *Zera Berakh ha-Shlishi, Brakhot*, fol. 3a. Aside from the fact that this author was quite exceptional, we are speaking here of a case in which he considered the content of the ban to be a distortion of justice. His advice therefore relied upon the halakhic ruling that anyone excommunicated improperly may himself excommunicate those who had issued the original ruling; *Shulḥan Arukh, Yore De'a*, §334.39.

[54] R. Joel Sirkes, cited above, n. 52, also complained that the Council of the Four Lands did not include the sages of the day in their decisions. But this did not mean that the actual decree of excommunication was issued without the participation of the rabbis.

[55] See, for example, *Responsa* of R. Meir of Lublin, §58; R. Gershon Ashkenazi, *Responsa Avodat ha-Gershuni*, §2; R. Ephraim ha-Kohen, *Responsa Shaar Efrayim*, §63.

[56] The limits of the obligation to save a fellow Jew from a gentile were not, of course, clearly spelled out. R. Solomon Luria ruled that a Jew who had stolen from gentiles need not be ransomed by his relatives; *Yam shel Shlomo, Kidushin*, I, §28. On the other hand, R. Ya'ir Ḥayim Bacharach criticized members of a community who asked him whether they had to redeem

the body of a Jew who had been hanged as a thief. He replied that they should have saved him while he was still alive, since by Jewish law a thief does not deserve the death penalty; *Responsa Ḥavot Ya'ir*, §139.

[57] E.g., Halperin, ed., *Takanot . . . Mehrin*, §260, which ends its warning to anyone engaged in counterfeiting with the words: "And certainly, if he is caught in the tower of evil [Eccles. 9:12], no man will come to his aid." Similarly R. Ezekiel Landau admonishes that people not buy property from rebellious peasants, "and if anyone transgresses this, his blood shall be upon his head, and all of the house of Israel is free [of responsibility], and no one is obligated to make any effort whatsoever on his behalf"; *Drushei ha-ẒLaḤ*, fol. 56d.

[58] See Halperin, ed., *Takanot . . . Mehrin*, §265.

[59] Typical is the treatment by R. Joel Sirkes in his *Responsa Bayit Ḥadash*, §44, and cf. also §43. It is clear that Sirkes sought to negate the view that one should not adopt this policy as a matter of first recourse for he states that the entire congregation had been placed in danger. See also the summary in R. David ha-Levi, *Turei Zahav, Yore De'a*, §157.1.8:

> So also in our day, anyone who sins and rebels against his king should be handed over, and the same applies to other crimes which an individual commits repeatedly [*she-eḥad muḥzak bahem*] such as counterfeiting or other things which involve danger [to the community]—it is obvious that we hand such a person over. It is proper that he be handed over even if the government hadn't yet singled him out by name for, in a sense, through his bad, criminal activities he is "pursuing" [*rodef*] the rest of Israel [i.e., he is considered a would-be murderer whom it is permitted to kill in self-defense].

Cf. also R. Jacob ben Samuel, *Responsa Beit Yaakov*, §107.

Chapter 11. The Composition of the Kehila

[1] The two leading jurists at the start of our period, R. Moses Isserles and R. Mordecai Jaffe, authorized *kehila* members to block new settlers even by resorting to the secular authorities; *Ḥoshen Mishpat*, §156. A concrete example of this practice is provided by the *takanot* of Cracow (Balaban, "Die krakauer Judengemeinde," *JJLG* 11, p. 90), as well as by Wachstein, *Urkunden*, pp. 35–38.

[2] Balaban, "Die krakauer Judengemeinde," *JJLG* 10, p. 354; Weinryb, *Texts and Studies*, Hebrew section, p. 13.

[3] Isserles, *Ḥoshen Mishpat*, §156.7.

[4] Beggars were quickly sent packing. Dubnow, ed., *Pinkas . . . Lita*, §§88, 91, 378, 666; Lewin, *Landessynode*, p. 92; Wachstein, *Urkunden*, pp. 153f., 158, and 167. On the other hand, refugees who had been expelled from their

homes were treated better; Lewin, *Landessynode*, p. 82; Dubnow, ed., *Pinkas . . . Lita*, §§460 and 516; Halperin, ed., *Takanot . . . Mehrin*, §270; and cf. below, chapter 12.

[5] Balaban, "Die krakauer Judengemeinde," *JJLG* 11, pp. 90, 92, and 99; Lewin, *Landessynode*, p. 69; Weinryb, *Texts and Studies*, Hebrew section, pp. 7–8; Dubnow, ed., *Pinkas . . . Lita*, §§756 and 875; Halperin, ed., *Takanot . . . Mehrin*, §§268, 284, and 383. Concerning the saying of *kadish*, see R. Mordecai Jaffe, *Levush [ha-Tkhelet], Oraḥ Ḥayim*, §133; Slonik, *Responsa Mas'at Binyamin*, §73; R. Gershon Ashkenazi, *Responsa Avodat ha-Gershuni*, §63; Landau, *Responsa Noda bi-Yhuda*, second collection, *Oraḥ Ḥayim*, §8; and the special pamphlet concerning *kadish* in the *Responsa Kneset Yeḥezkel* of R. Ezekiel b. Abraham Katzenellenbogen (Altona: 1731–32), fol. 53b–54b at the end of *Yore De'a*.

[6] Balaban, "Die krakauer Judengemeinde," *JJLG* 10, p. 352; Weinryb, *Texts and Studies*, Hebrew section, p. 5; R. Menaḥem Mendel Krokhmal, *Responsa Ẓemaḥ Ẓedek*, §77.

[7] Legal documents registering such acceptances have survived from Eisenstadt; Wachstein, *Urkunden*, pp. 3f.

[8] R. Gershon Ashkenazi, *Responsa Avodat ha-Gershuni*, §32; Kaidanover, *Responsa Emunat Shmu'el*, §42; Wachstein, *Urkunden*, pp. 51–58. A protocol of Alsace for the year 1776–77, §10, forbids accepting any such advance. This implies that up until that time it was customary to do so; *Blätter für jüdische Geschichte und Literatur* 2.

[9] R. Moses Isserles, *Ḥoshen Mishpat*, §156.7 (end); Balaban, "Die krakauer Judengemeinde," *JJLG* 11, p. 89; Weinryb, *Texts and Studies*, Hebrew section, p. 6.

[10] Balaban, "Die krakauer Judengemeinde," *JJLG* 11, p. 353; Krokhmal, *Responsa Ẓemaḥ Ẓedek*, §37; Bacharach, *Responsa Ḥavot Ya'ir*, §157 (end); Halperin, ed., *Takanot . . . Mehrin*, §§205–7; Baer, *Protokollbuch*, p. 127.

[11] Weinryb, *Texts and Studies*, Hebrew section, p. 10; Perles, *Juden in Posen*, p. 86.

[12] Balaban, "Die krakauer Judengemeinde," *JJLG* 10, p. 354, and 11, p. 91; Kaidanover, *Responsa Emunat Shmu'el*, §42.

[13] Balaban, "Die krakauer Judengemeinde," *JJLG* 10, pp. 339, 345; Weinryb, *Texts and Studies*, Hebrew section, pp. 19ff.; Perles, *Juden in Posen*, pp. 61 and 94.

[14] See above, chapter 9.

[15] Halperin, ed., *Takanot . . . Mehrin*, §§176, 179, 317, etc. For appointments to the national council, see *ibid.*, §§98, 131. R. Benjamin Aaron Slonik seems to indicate that in his day elections were virtually always held on the intermediate days (*ḥol ha-mo'ed*) of Passover; *Responsa Mas'at Binyamin*, §7. The Frankfurt *takanot* of 1623 declared a fine of 1000 ducats for anyone who sought to hold his office beyond the appointed time; I. Kracauer, *Geschichte der Juden in Frankfurt an Main*, I, p. 410.

[16] Johann Jakob Schudt mockingly reports in his *Jüdische Merkwürdig-*

keiten (Frankfurt an Main: 1714–18) that the election of their *parnasim* aroused so much passion among the Frankfurt Jews that one might have thought that they were choosing a new Emperor. Slonik, *Responsa Mas'at Binyamin*, §7, provides an accurate historical representation.

[17] In Moravia the title "morenu" (our teacher) could be granted only by the provincial rabbi in conjunction with two other rabbis; Halperin, ed., *Takanot . . . Mehrin*, §142. In Lithuania it was to be granted "by the two sages, the rabbis of our province"; Dubnow, ed., *Pinkas . . . Lita*, §882. This was also the case in Alsace; *Takanot* of 1776–77, §9, in *Blätter für jüdische Geschichte und Literatur* 2. And cf. below, in our treatment of educational institutions.

[18] In Poznan the *takana* read: "The rabbi of the community may not be a local" nor may he have "ties to members of our community." Lewin, *Landessynode*, pp. 72, 79, and 91; and see R. Gershon Ashkenazi, *Responsa Avodat ha-Gershuni*, §2; R. Ephraim Kohen, *Responsa Shaar Efrayim*, §§67–68. On the basis of such a *takana*, R. Ya'ir Ḥayim Bacharach was at first disqualified for his rabbinic post in Worms; D. Kaufmann, *R. Jair Chajjim Bacharach und seine Ahnen*, p. 54.

[19] See R. Ephraim Kohen, *Responsa Shaar Efrayim*, §§67–68, and below, chapter 15.

[20] Halperin, ed., *Takanot . . . Mehrin*, §§126, 152, 345; Dubnow, ed., *Pinkas . . . Lita*, §§914, 961; MS "Pinkas Kahal Frankfurt de-Main" (above, chapter 9, n. 15), §38.

[21] Halperin, ed., *Takanot . . . Mehrin*, §345; Balaban, "Legal Status and Communal Organization," p. 47; *Takanot* of Frankfurt, loc. cit., §§9, 38.

[22] See Halperin, *Pinkas Vaad Arba Araẓot*, p. 548, and the indices to that work as well as to Dubnow, ed., *Pinkas . . . Lita*, and Halperin, ed., *Takanot . . . Mehrin*, s.v. "skhum."

[23] For *takanot* in this vein, see Halperin, ed., *Takanot . . . Mehrin*, §§187 and 189; Baer, *Protokollbuch*, p. 95; the *Takanot* of Frankfurt (above, chapter 9, n. 15), §38.

[24] For rabbinic treatments of disputes over the extent of this linkage, see *Responsa She'erit Yosef*, §18; Krokhmal, *Responsa Ẓemaḥ Ẓedek*, §§1 and 2.

[25] Halperin, ed., *Takanot . . . Mehrin*, §§184, 188, etc.; Krokhmal, *Responsa Ẓemaḥ Ẓedek*, §2; Weinryb, *Texts and Studies*, Hebrew section, p. 239. See also below, chapter 18, concerning educational institutions.

[26] The methods of election have been summarized often. See Balaban, "Legal Status and Communal Organization," p. 47; Baer, *Protokollbuch*, pp. 94f.

[27] For the meaning of "fate" in elections, see R. Joseph Steinhardt, *Responsa Zikhron Yosef* (Fürth: 1772–73), §1. For the selectors taking an oath, see R. Judah Loeb Pukhovitser, *Divrei Ḥakhamim*, fol. 35a; Halperin, ed., *Takanot . . . Mehrin*, §34 (concerning provincial elections).

[28] See below, chapter 15.

Chapter 12. Inter-communal Relations

[1] The Lithuanian *takanot* state explicitly how much should be spent on behalf of a Jew who, "God forbid, was arrested and accused of theft"; Dubnow, ed., *Pinkas . . . Lita,* §296. The case is one of joint action on the part of a number of communities, but we can extrapolate from this to the obligation of each individual *kehila* to act on behalf of a *yishuv* Jew who belonged to a specific community. The participation of the *kehila* extended also to "expenses involved in interceding with the authorities to obtain revenge for murder"—that is, appealing to the government to bring a Jew's murderer to justice.

[2] Hence the need to fix the rights of communities and of specific office-holders within them to provide these services to *yishuv* Jews in the area; see, e.g., Dubnow, ed., *Pinkas . . . Lita,* §368. A description of villagers bringing presents to a rabbi is found in R. Berechiah Berakh (b. Eliakim Getzel), *Zera Berakh ha-Shlishi, Brakhot,* fol. 22b. For cases of rabbis going out to the villages only in their own interest, see R. Judah Loeb Pukhovitser, *Kne Ḥokhma,* fol. 8c: As opposed to earlier times when rabbis traveled to the villages to teach isolated Jews, "nowadays it is different. I have seen an evil. Most of them travel to the countryside and villages for the sake of their own profit, in order to fill their containers with grain and food, and their knapsacks with silver. They teach [the village Jew] nothing. . . ." See also above, chapter 4, n. 5.

[3] For Poland, see the summary and examples given by Balaban, "Legal Status," pp. 59f. For further examples, see Halperin, ed., *Pinkas Vaad Arba Araẓot,* pp. 180 and 280. The quarrel in the latter case was between the city of Cracow and the surrounding province—that is, the organization of the smaller communities. The Council of the Four Lands established as a principle "that settlements, villages and towns which do not have a synagogue of their own and are within two miles of a major community are subject to that latter community also with respect to taxes and business"; ibid., p. 228. See also Perles, *Juden in Posen,* p. 73, concerning a dispute between Posen and Schwersenz.

[4] Fritz (Yitzhak) Baer described such a provincial organization in exemplary fashion in his *Protokollbuch.* See also B. Altmann, "The Autonomous Federation of Jewish Communities in Paderborn," *Jewish Social Studies* 3 (1941), pp. 159–88.

[5] See Baer's insightful remarks on this question in "Gemeinde und Landjudenschaft," *Korrespondenzblatt des Vereins zur Gründung und Erhaltung einer Akademie für die Wissenschaft des Judentums* 2 (1921), pp. 21ff.

[6] The *kehilot* would fine their members for unacceptable behavior even when this had occurred beyond the boundaries of the *kehila* itself. Note, for example, that the *kehila* of Posen forbade a member of the community to return to the Frankfurt fair because he had behaved improperly there on a previous occasion; Weinryb, *Texts and Studies,* Hebrew section, p. 23.

[7] This understanding, which was implicit in the actions of the *kehilot*, also found expression in the *takanot*. For example, the sages and leaders of Ashkenaz decided at a meeting in Worms in 1541–42 that no rabbi or teacher had the right to issue decrees concerning another community; R. Aaron Simeon b. R. Jacob, *Or ha-Yashar* (Amsterdam: 1728–29), fol. 5a–b. Similarly, see the Cracow *takana* that ruled that if a decree of excommunication was issued elsewhere, the local rabbis were required to issue a counter-ban; Balaban, "Die krakauer Judengemeinde," *JJLG* 10, p. 301. Though the rules applying to strangers temporarily living in a place differed from those for members of the local community, no one ever questioned the notion that the former were subject to local jurisdiction.

[8] For economic matters, see above, chapters 6–8; for family and education, see chapters 14–15 and 18.

[9] This was the case already in the Middle Ages: see Finkelstein, *Jewish Self-Government in the Middle Ages*, pp. 36–81. In our period, such a convention was held at Frankfurt. See n. 30 in this chapter.

[10] For examples, see Perles, *Juden in Posen*, pp. 86, 90. Posen (Poznan) appears once as extending aid and once as receiving it; Weinryb, *Texts and Studies*, Hebrew section, p. 158. After a fire in Eisenstadt in 1795 a circular was published asking for donations. "At first," it stated, "we thought to send messengers . . . who would 'run and jump through' the cities as many perfect ones did before us." After further consideration, however, the community satisfied itself with issuing the circular; Wachstein, *Urkunden*, p. 212.

[11] On activity outside the sphere of authority of the Council of the Four Lands for the redemption of captives after the events of 1648–49, see Heinrich Graetz, *Geschichte der Juden von den ältesten Zeiten bis auf die Gegenwart*, 4th edition, X, p. 72.

[12] R. Joseph Colon, *Responsa*, §4, pp. 8f. On the historical context of the debate, see Graetz, *Geschichte der Juden*, 4th edition, VIII, p. 269. MaHaRaM of Lublin relied on this ruling in his *Responsa*, §40, concerning the expulsion of the Jews of Silesia and the saving of the Jews of Zuelz. On the time of that event, see Halperin, ed., *Pinkas Vaad Arba Araẓot*, p. 451.

[13] See, for example, "The 'Ḥavaya de-Rabanan' Circulars Against the Sect of Sabbetai Ẓvi," issued by the three communities of Amsterdam, Hamburg, and Frankfurt in 1724–25 and published by Y. D. Wilhelm and G. Scholem, *Kiryat Sefer* 30 (1954–55), p. 99–104. The three circulars were issued "in the name of the nobles, officials, *parnasim* and leaders of our community . . . , in association with the great sage, court president and head of the academy in our community, and his court. . . ." (The Frankfurt circular was issued by "the holy society [*ḥevra kadisha*], . . . in association with our father, our teacher and rabbi, the great sage, president of the court. . . ." In Frankfurt, the term "holy society" was used to refer to the board of *parnasim*.)

[14] See Simon Dubnow, *Toldot ha-Ḥasidut* [History of Hasidism] (Tel-Aviv: 1930–32), pp. 115–17, 119, 144–46. Individuals such as R. Jacob Sasportas, R. Moses Ḥagiz, R. Jacob Emden, and R. Elijah, the Gaon of Vilna,

were also important in pursuing "deviants" not as representatives of any organization but only on the basis of their personal authority, which was recognized spontaneously by the people at large (and not only the members of a single community). See I. Tishby's introduction to his edition of R. Jacob Sasportas, *Sefer Ẓiẓat Novel Ẓvi* (Jerusalem: 1954), pp. 13f.

[15] See the last three chapters of the present work.

[16] See, for instance, the controversy over a bill of divorce (*get*) issued in Prague in 1549–50. The controversy involved two rabbinic "factions," one of which questioned the validity of a *get* issued by the other. Those who had issued the *get* sought to excommunicate the critics, while the critics were supported by a number of Italian rabbis. The critics argued that the *get* should have been submitted to other rabbis in Prague before being issued, "for this is the custom of every master [*more ẓedek*], even if he were a halakhic expert, to send a *get* to all the masters in the city [for prior review] and if even one of them questions it and finds fault with it, the *get* would not be issued until the matter was resolved"; *Responsa* of ReMA', §55, and cf. §§56–59. It is clear that in this period there was no hierarchy of authority among the rabbis of Prague.

[17] For example, see the dispute between MaHaRaM of Lublin and R. Mordecai Jaffe, author of the *Levushim*, on the one hand, and their contemporaries on the other, concerning a bill of divorce drawn up in Vienna by R. Joshua Falk on behalf of a man who was dangerously ill (*get shkhiv mera*). MaHaRaM of Lublin, who ruled that the *get* was invalid, was related to the husband involved. MaHaRaM argued that the husband had been misled by his wealthy mother-in-law. MaHaRaM sought to nullify the *get* and treat the divorcee as if she were still legally married, thus affording the husband, who was quite young, an opportunity to insist on conditions that would save what his family felt was owing him. The matter was discussed widely in the halakhic literature of the time; see the sources listed by Halperin, ed., *Pinkas Vaad Arba Araẓot*, p. 27. We should note that MaHaRaM's view is difficult to sustain from a purely halakhic point of view, and was in fact rejected by all the major sages of the time with the exception of R. Jaffe.

[18] The text of the *ḥerem*, which is cited by Mordecai ben Hillel, *Sefer Mordekhai*, end of *Gitin*, §455, was appended to bills of divorce in this period. It seems that it was customary to mention the *ḥerem* at the end of the ceremony of divorce; see R. Joseph Colon, *Responsa*, §37.2; Samuel ben David Moses ha-Levi, *Naḥalat Shiv'a*, fol. 75b–76a. Those opposed to appeal cited the *ḥerem* of Rabenu Tam in all disputes. The text of the *ḥerem* is also reproduced in Finkelstein, *Self-Government*, pp. 105f.

[19] See the example cited in n. 16.

[20] See chapter 9. The rabbi who issued the famous bill of divorce of Cleves, R. Israel Lipschütz, understood that his opponents suspected him of hurrying to issue the *get* in order to derive monetary profit from it; cf. his *Or Yisra'el* (Cleves: 1769–70), fol. 8b.

[21] This is always the argument upon which critics of a rabbinic decision

rely. See the sources cited above, and the issue of the Cleves bill of divorce. For the appeal of the Mannheim court, see Aaron Simeon ben Jacob Abraham, *Or ha-Yashar* (Amsterdam: 1768–69), fol. 4a; for the appeal of the Frankfurt court, ibid., fol. 5a; and cf. the self-justification issued by R. Natan Maz, chief judge of Frankfurt, in R. Markus (Mordekhai ha-Levi) Horovitz, *Responsa Mate Levi* (Frankfurt am Main: 1890–91), I, p. 60.

[22] The men of Frankfurt argued thus, that as "the leaders of all the Ashkenazic lands" they were obligated to deal with the matter. Otherwise, "God forbid, all of Israel might fall into error"; Horovitz, *Responsa Mate Levi*, loc. cit. On the other hand, their opponents argued that there were rabbinic courts closer to Cleves than Frankfurt, and if anyone were obliged to intervene, it was they; cf. *Or ha-Yashar*, fol. 25a, and see n. 23 below.

[23] This position was still maintained by most of the disputants in the affair of the Cleves *get*, which arose at the dawn of the Haskala period, in 1766–67. Even when those who supported the *get* and the man who had issued it based themselves on the autonomy of *kehilot*, they never argued that the matter could not be brought for clarification before other courts. The judges of Frankfurt were attacked because they claimed that they were uniquely authorized to deal with the matter. Quite correctly, R. Ezekiel Landau saw this as an unprecedented claim and an insult to the major contemporary scholars; *Or ha-Yashar*, fol. 55b. It is not impossible that the position of the Frankfurt judges already contains an indication of the tendency to separatism. It was the lay leaders of the community who prevented their rabbis from bringing the issue before a court of great contemporary rabbinic scholars. Their rationale was quite odd: "For their sages judge on behalf of the Emperor"; loc. cit., fol. 85a. The fact is that the writings of the great scholars of Poland were burned in the streets of Frankfurt, and contemporaries rightly wondered "what had raised their ire . . . concerning the words of those scholars any more than in the case of the other rulings of contemporary scholars which reached them"; loc. cit., fol. 109b. It may be assumed that we are here witnessing the beginnings of a feeling of disparagement toward the Jews of Poland that would later become quite common. See chapter 24.

[24] See above, chapter 11.

[25] For example, note the following two rulings of ReMA', *Ḥoshen Mishpat*, §156.7: "If city dwellers flee to a village [*yishuv*] for fear of some danger, the residents of that settlement may not prevent [the refugees] from earning their livelihood there until the danger has passed"; and "If someone is being ejected from a city because he does not hold the *ḥezkat yishuv*, he may not be expelled until he has collected his debts. During that period, he is entitled to earn enough for his livelihood." We also find a *takana* that shows that in Lithuania the first of these *halakhot* was applied in practice with regard to the refugees from the pogroms of 1648–49: "For the duration of the period during which they live with us, no one may deny them the right to engage in any business they wish in order to earn enough for their livelihood";

Dubnow, ed., *Pinkas . . . Lita*, §§460, 484–85, 503, 516. The wording of these *takanot* is reminiscent of the ruling of the ReMA'.

[26] See above, chapter 11, n. 4.

[27] See *Shulḥan Arukh, Ḥoshen Mishpat*, §14.1, and *cf.* Luria, *Yam shel Shlomo, Bava Kama*, X, §10, as well as the sources cited, especially R. Joseph Colon, *Responsa*, §21, pp. 50f., and R. Israel Isserlein, *Trumat ha-Deshen*, part II, *Psakim*, §65, fol. 10a.

[28] See Frank, *Kehilot Ashkenaz*, p. 55; Assaf, *Batei ha-Din ve-Sidreihem*, pp. 29f. The use of sequestration is still found in our period, but it was essentially limited to the political sphere—that is, in a place where the jurisdictions of administrative units such as national councils overlapped, or in cases where it was necessary to force recalcitrants to accept the authority of the communal organizations; see Halperin, ed., *Pinkas Vaad Arba Araẓot*, and *idem, Takanot . . . Mehrin*, indices, s.v. "*ikul*" (sequestration).

[29] R. Tam's opinion—that in our time "the wisest and most important scholar of the day" is considered the *bet din gadol*—is well known; cf. R. Moses of Coucy, *Sefer Miẓvot Gadol*, Positive Commandment §97, and S. Albeck, "Rabenu Tam's Attitude to the Problems of his Time" [in Hebrew], *Zion*, 1953–54, p. 111.

[30] For the decisions of this congress, see Horovitz, *Die Frankfurter Rabbinerversammlung*, pp. 20–30. Horovitz blurred the clear intent of these decisions.

Chapter 13. Supra-Kehila Organizations

[1] The term "medina" may also refer to the members of what we called in the last chapter a "provincial *kehila*"—that is, members of small communities spread throughout a single state who come together into a single *kehila*. Here we use the term to refer to a supra-communal organization. Our treatment will focus here on the structure of the *medinot*; for a treatment of the factors that led to their dissolution at the end of our period, see chapters 21–23. On the broad methodological questions involved in treating Jewish communal institutions in the abstract, see my "Concept of Social History."

[2] The situation was not completely identical in the two regions. In Poland representatives of the communities gathered in provincial congresses, which in turn sent representatives to a national congress. In Moravia, on the other hand, the representatives of all *kehilot* gathered together in one central congress that chose the provincial heads who also served as heads of the *medina*; See Halperin, ed., *Takanot . . . Mehrin*, §§24, 25, 30, 34, 42, and in Halperin's introduction, p. 12. This method of choosing district heads through a general assembly is indicative of the relatively greater power of the *medina* in Moravia as compared with that of parallel institutions elsewhere.

[3] The *pinkas* of Lithuania makes no mention of representation for the

secondary communities in the central organization. Hence the only guarantee for the rights of these communities lay in the shared judiciary, which was defined as standing above the interests of the parties that appeared before it; see J. Klausner, *Toldot ha-Kehila ha-Ivrit be-Vilna* (Wilno: 1937–38), part I, pp. 138f. and 149f.

[4] Concerning the Council of the Four Lands and the chronology of its establishment, see Halperin, ed., *Pinkas Vaad Arba Araẓot*, pp. 17–24; concerning the *medina* of Lithuania, see S. Dubnow, "Introduction" to *Pinkas . . . Lita*; concerning Moravia, Halperin, Introduction to *Takanot . . . Mehrin*; on the unification of the seven communities in the territory of the Graf Esterhazy, see Wachstein, *Urkunden*, pp. 553ff.

[5] Cf. my treatment of the creation of the "provincial *kehila*" in Germany above, chapter 12.

[6] For Lithuania, see Dubnow, ed., *Pinkas . . . Lita*, §§159 and 224. The leaders of the *medina* are here elected directly by the principal communities. In Greater Poland, the leaders of the community of Poznan together with the representatives of the communities formed the leadership of the *medina*; see Lewin, *Landessynode*, pp. 77 and 85. *Kehila* electors even chose the heads of the Council of the Four Lands; see Halperin, ed., *Pinkas Vaad Arba Araẓot*, pp. 257f., etc. At their head stood the Council *parnas*, elected by majority vote; ibid., p. 387. In Moravia, the local *kehila* elected only a representative to a congress. That body in turn chose the heads of the *medina* and the assessors from among its members; Halperin, ed., *Takanot . . . Mehrin*, §§24–49, and Halperin's Introduction, p. 13.

[7] In Halperin, ed., *Takanot . . . Mehrin*, we find a fixed list of permissible expenditures for the heads of the *medina*; §58, and see also §89 in which an attempt is made to stop a head of the *medina* from charging the organization for private expenses. *Parnasim* were also reimbursed for expenses in Poland; Halperin, ed., *Pinkas Vaad Arba Araẓot*, pp. 109f. For Lithuania, see Dubnow, ed., *Pinkas . . . Lita*, §907. That eligibility for office in the supra-communal organization depended on the size of one's tax contribution is stated explicitly in Moravia; see Halperin, ed., *Takanot . . . Mehrin*, §126. Elsewhere, it can be deduced a fortiori from the rules concerning local communal offices.

[8] All of this is clear from the sources and is summarized in the treatments mentioned above, n. 4.

[9] See above, chapter 8, concerning the congress of Lublin in 1607. There it is stated that the heads of the *yeshivot* made all decisions. But R. Joshua Falk, who summarized the decisions, did not fail to mention that he had committed these matters to writing "at the command of the heads of the *medinot*, and they agreed to ratify and carry out [these decisions], and so they recorded in their minute book [*pinkas*] as they know"; Halperin, ed., *Pinkas Vaad Arba Araẓot*, p. 23. *Idem, Takanot . . . Mehrin*, §24, defines the function of the heads of the *medina* as follows: "They shall have a stick and lash with which to excommunicate and punish the sinners and rebels, and they shall exercise their authority forcefully." Similar phrases are found in many texts.

[10] The *parnasim* of Poznan and the leaders of Greater Poland felt it necessary to make it a precondition of employment for their *av bet din*

> that he did not have the right to speak [against] or protest *takanot* established by a majority of the *parnasim, tovim* and the community. . . . [This applied] both to prior rulings and to those passed after [his appointment]. On the contrary, the *av bet din* was obliged to implement and support them. Similarly in all areas of communal concern, the *av bet din* was not entitled to protest anything agreed upon by the majority of the *parnasim, tovim* and the community. . . .

Lewin, *Landessynode*, p. 73. R. Joel Sirkes, author of *Bayit Ḥadash*, protested openly against "the heads and leaders of the land who gather together at the Lublin fair" because they issued a decree of excommunication without consulting with the great halakhic scholars; Halperin, ed., *Pinkas Vaad Arba Araẓot*, pp. 42f. Cf. chapter 10, n. 52.

[11] See the previous note and Halperin, ed., *Pinkas Vaad Arba Araẓot*, p. 1. In Moravia, the *takanot* were approved by the *rav ha-medina*; Halperin, ed., *Takanot . . . Mehrin*, §§311 and 337. Moreover, the *rav ha-medina* was empowered to interpret the *takanot* should there be some doubt as to what they meant; ibid., §292. In Lithuania, the rabbis of the principal *kehilot* signed the decrees of meetings in which they participated; see Dubnow, ed., *Pinkas . . . Lita*, Introduction, pp. xxif., and the *takanot* cited there.

[12] A typical example is provided by the agreement between the community of Poznan and the Jews of the surrounding *medina*. These latter protested the practice of having Poznan judges involved in adjudicating their cases, but readily accepted the judgment of the city's *av bet din* [chief rabbi]; Lewin, *Landessynode*, p. 81.

[13] Halperin, ed., *Takanot . . . Mehrin*, §§64, 65, 68, and 75.

[14] For all of this, see the indices to Halperin, ed., *Pinkas Vaad Arba Araẓot*; Dubnow, ed., *Pinkas . . . Lita*; and Halperin, ed., *Takanot . . . Mehrin*. On the status of the *ne'eman*, see in particular *Pinkas . . . Lita*, §§578 and 798. The *rosh medina* would often utilize a community *shamash* to carry out tasks, and was allowed to hire a special *shamash* for the *medina* only when necessary; *Pinkas . . . Lita*, §§157–58.

[15] For an example of the demand for such a report, see Dubnow, ed., *Pinkas . . . Lita*, §128: "When the leaders of the people gather together in the *medinot* of Lithuania, the *rashei medina* of each town must bring a report, signed by their *av bet din*, as to the number of maidens married off in accordance with this *takana* in the period since the previous council." Dubnow, ed., *Pinkas . . . Lita*, §§210 and 211, deals with matters touching directly on the *medina*, such as the collection of taxes.

[16] E.g., Halperin, ed., *Pinkas Vaad Arba Araẓot*, pp. 1 and 42f. See also the indices to that work; to Dubnow, ed., *Pinkas . . . Lita*; and to Halperin, ed., *Takanot . . . Mehrin*.

[17] E.g., Halperin, ed., *Pinkas Vaad Arba Araẓot,* pp. 222 and 254f.

[18] A good example of this "*medina* consciousness" is to be found in the wording of the oath of office taken by leaders of the Moravian *medina;* Halperin, ed., *Takanot . . . Mehrin,* §115. On the emotive terms used with regard to the central organization, see Lewin, *Landessynode,* p. 45. The use of the term "sanhedrin" is found in Nathan Nata Hannover, *Yeven Meẓula* [The Miry Pit] (Berlin: 1923), p. 62 [*Abyss of Despair,* tr. Abraham J. Mesch (New York: 1950; and reprinted with a foreword by William B. Helmreich, New Brunswick: 1983), p. 120—*tr.*]. See below, n. 24.

[19] For permanent arrangements by which the *medina* would be involved in recording false accusations, see Dubnow, ed., *Pinkas . . . Lita,* §§9, 110, 273, and others listed in the index, s.v. "alilot"; Halperin, ed., *Takanot . . . Mehrin,* §271. This would also appear to be the meaning of the letter sent by the Council of the Four Lands to the community of Tiktin in 1626–27: "and if they will join the Council, their portion will be the same as all other districts with regard to *bilbulim* as well"; Halperin, ed., *Pinkas Vaad Arba Araẓot,* p. 55. On the other hand, there was litigation between the Council of the Four Lands and the *medina* of Lithuania as to the degree of mutual responsibility of each in countering unwarranted decrees on the part of the non-Jewish authorities; Halperin, ed., *Pinkas Vaad Arba Araẓot,* p. 114.

[20] Halperin, ed., *Pinkas Vaad Arba Araẓot,* p. 424.

[21] Halperin, ed., *Takanot . . . Mehrin,* §§64, 69–74, gives detailed procedures for summoning individuals to the court of "the *rosh medina* accompanied by one other rabbi," which was authorized to judge district members. District courts in Lithuania and Poland operated somewhat less formally; see the next note.

[22] Halperin, ed., *Takanot . . . Mehrin,* §§64, 65, and 72; Dubnow, ed., *Pinkas . . . Lita,* §§12–13, 113–15, and 426.

[23] Halperin, ed., *Takanot . . . Mehrin,* §§214–15. See Assaf, *Batei ha-Din ve-Sidreihem,* pp. 74–84. Assaf understood Dubnow, ed., *Pinkas . . . Lita,* §426, as suggesting the existence of an appeals court in Lithuania, and also saw such institutions in Poland and even in Germany, but there is clear evidence only for Moravia.

[24] In Halperin, ed., *Takanot . . . Mehrin,* §§70, 82, and 149, the expression "bet din gadol" is used with clear reference to *Sanhedrin,* fol. 31a. This is also true in R. Nathan Nata Hannover's reference to Polish Jewry's "amud ha-din" (the pillar of justice), *Yeven Meẓula,* p. 61.

[25] Halperin, ed., *Pinkas Vaad Arba Araẓot,* pp. 22f.; idem, *Takanot . . . Mehrin,* §10. See also Assaf, *Mekorot le-Toldot ha-Ḥinukh,* I, p. 111. The fact that the *takana,* though of Polish origin, was accepted in Moravia as well, proves that, for the reasons I have suggested, they found the ruling useful.

[26] Halperin, ed., *Takanot . . . Mehrin,* §§3, 5; Dubnow, ed., *Pinkas . . . Lita,* §484; and see chapter 23, concerning education.

[27] Halperin, ed., *Pinkas Vaad Arba Araẓot,* p. 1; idem, *Takanot . . .*

Mehrin, §256. It was the district head who supervised the implementation of the *takana*, but he presumably called upon the *kehilot* for help.

[28] See chapter 8; Halperin, ed., *Takanot . . . Mehrin*, §221.

[29] The *takana* on this matter added to its warning: "And there is no sin nor guilt in the matter, for our Sages of blessed memory have already expressed it beautifully for us in their sweet language when they said: 'Let us be grateful to swindlers.' " [The reference is to R. Eliezer's remark, *Ktubot*, fol. 68a, that the existence of so many who pretend poverty in order to live off charity was actually a good thing for society since it saved Jews who regularly ignored the poor from being considered sinners in accordance with the biblical verse "He will cry out to the Lord against you, and you will incur guilt."—*tr.*] Dubnow, ed., *Pinkas . . . Lita*, §88, and *cf.* §§378 and 666.

Chapter 14. The Family

[1] This chapter and the next are an expansion of my Hebrew article "Marriage and Sexual Life among the Jews at the End of the Middle Ages," *Zion* 10 (1944–45), pp. 21–54. Whereas that article restricted itself to the situation in western Europe, we will now treat the situation of Ashkenazic Jewry generally.

[2] *Shulḥan Arukh, Yore De'a*, §248.4; ReMA', *Even ha-Ezer*, §86.2. Cf. also R. Samuel of Fürth, *Beit Shmu'el* (Dyhernfurth: 1688–89), ibid., §86.19. The *takanot* of Cracow represent wives as normally involved in their husbands' businesses (Balaban, "Die krakauer Judengemeinde," *JJLG* 10, pp. 351, 356); those not in trade were exceptions (ibid., 11, p. 102; and cf. R. Ẓvi Ashkenazi, *Responsa Ḥakham Ẓvi*, §124; R. Jonah Landsofer, *Responsa Me'il Ẓdaka* [Prague: 1756], §15). The "woman of valor" who supported her husband was not as common in this period as in nineteenth-century eastern Europe, but there were some instances. See the remarks of R. Jacob Emden, *Megilat Sefer*, ed. David Cahana (Warsaw: 1896–97), p. 157. He hoped that his wife would remove the burden of earning a living from his shoulders. And see the *Likutei Dinim* in Benjamin Wolf b. Mattathiah, *Tohorat ha-Kodesh*, part II, fol. 3a.

[3] The *takanot* of Frankfurt forbade sons to assist their fathers in peddling or clothes selling unless the father had himself ceased to work; MS "Pinkas Kahal Frankfurt de-Main" (above, chapter 9, n. 15), §71.

[4] See *Shulḥan Arukh, Yore De'a*, §§240.5, and 251.3.

[5] See my remarks in "Marriage and Sexual Life," p. 25.

[6] There is ample evidence for the presence of Jewish servants in the homes of the wealthy. See, for example, Halperin, ed., *Takanot . . . Mehrin*, §§203 and 205; Dubnow, ed., *Pinkas . . . Lita*, §28; Bacharach, *Responsa Ḥavot Ya'ir*, §105. On teachers, see below, chapter 18.

[7] See Abraham H. Freimann, *Seder Kidushin ve-Nisu'in aḥarei Ḥatimat ha-Talmud. Meḥkar Histori-Dogmati be-Dinei Yisra'el* [Post-Talmudic Be-

trothal and Marriage. A Historico-Dogmatic Investigation of Jewish Law] (Jerusalem: 1944–45; reprint, 1964), pp. 28–30.

[8] For example, *Zikhronat Marat Glikel me-Hamil,* pp. 271f. [English: *The Memoirs of Glückel of Hameln,* p. 149].

[9] All of this is explained in Samuel ha-Levi, *Naḥalat Shiv'a,* §8, and see Katz, "Marriage and Sexual Life," p. 38.

[10] Solomon Maimon correctly summarized the traditional attitude in this matter: according to "strict rabbinic morality," it was forbidden for him to look at a girl or to speak with her. See *Geschichte des eigenen Lebens,* p. 40 [*Solomon Maimon. An Autobiography,* tr. J. Clark Murray, p. 59; abridged version, ed. Moses Hadas (New York: 1947), p. 20—tr.]. The laws that establish these rules are found in *Shulḥan Arukh, Even ha-Ezer,* §21. The sin of "spilling one's seed in vain" is stressed in the "The Gate of Holiness" section of Elijah ben Moses de Vidas, *Reshit Ḥokhma* (Venice: 1578–79), chapter 17, and R. Joseph Yuspa Hahn, *Yosef Omeẓ,* §§195–96, pp. 286f. R. Joseph ben Solomon Calahora (known as R. Joseph Darshan, i.e., the preacher) of Poznan devoted an entire work, his *Yesod Yosef* (Frankfurt an der Oder: 1679), to the theme.

[11] *Shulḥan Arukh, Even ha-Ezer,* §1. R. Solomon Luria fixed the maximum age at which a Torah scholar might marry as twenty-four; *Yam shel Shlomo, Kidushin,* chapter 1, §57. See Katz, "Marriage and Sexual Life," p. 38.

[12] For the marriage age of males, see *Shulḥan Arukh, Even ha-Ezer,* §1, citing Talmudic sources. In Lithuania, poor girls were given assistance toward a dowry from the age of fifteen; Dubnow, ed., *Pinkas . . . Lita,* §§42, 93, and 128, and similarly Balaban, "Die krakauer Judengemeinde," *JJLG* 10, p. 345. See also Katz, "Marriage and Sexual Life," p. 35, n. 98.

[13] The Halakha fixed the fees of *shadkhanim* according to local custom; ReMA', *Shulḥan Arukh, Ḥoshen Mishpat,* §185.10. All of their activities were regulated by communal *takanot*; Halperin, ed., *Pinkas Vaad Arba Araẓot,* p. 50; idem, ed., *Takanot . . . Mehrin,* §§170–73 and 353; Dubnow, ed., *Pinkas . . . Lita,* §§34 and 36. The *takanot* assign different fees for arranging a match depending upon the distance involved.

[14] See Samuel ha-Levi, *Naḥalat Shiv'a,* §8. In Germany the standard engagement contract (*shtar shidukhin*) stated that "the bride's father shall house and feed the couple exactly as all other members of his household for an entire year after the marriage, and then provide free lodging in his house for a further two years." In Poland, the father would promise two years of board and then a further two years of free lodging. In Dubnow, ed., *Pinkas . . . Lita,* §232, we hear of five years. Solomon Maimon mentions that in Lithuania wealthy families tended to support their sons-in-law for six to eight years. See also R. Joseph Hahn, *Yosef Omeẓ,* p. 282. These years of support were not merely to allow the son-in-law to study the Torah; they also provided an opportunity to introduce him into the business world. Although the *takanot* did restrict the extent to which the young man could engage in business during

this period (Halperin, ed., *Pinkas Vaad Arba Araẓot*, p. 47 and n. 3; Balaban, "Die krakauer Judengemeinde," *JJLG* 11, p. 102), they did not prevent him from learning about it (see Assaf, *Mekorot le-Toldot ha-Ḥinukh*, I, p. 79, and *Zikhronot Marat Glikel me-Hamil* [English: *The Memoirs of Glückel of Hameln*, p. 37—*tr.*]. For a definition of the years of support as years of training for business, see R. Jacob Reischer, *Responsa Shvut Yaakov*, II, §142.

15 Balaban, "Die krakauer Judengemeinde," *JJLG* 10, p. 345; Halperin, ed., *Pinkas Vaad Arba Araẓot*, pp. 45 and 215; idem, ed., *Takanot . . . Mehrin*, §§174–75; Dubnow, ed., *Pinkas . . . Lita*, §§41–42, 93, 128, and 366; R. Aaron Samuel Kaidanover, *Responsa Emunat Shmu'el*, §29. Wealthy householders might give dowries to their female domestics; Netter, *Vingt siècles*, p. 105, and Taglicht, *Nachlässe der wiener Juden*, p. 24.

16 Balaban, "Die krakauer Judengemeinde," *JJLG* 10, pp. 329 and 339; Weinryb, *Texts and Studies*, Hebrew section, pp. 19–22.

17 For an example see Taglicht, *Nachlässe der wiener Juden*, p. 9.

18 The author of "Di beshreibung fun Ashkenaz und Polak," *YIVO Filologishe Shriften* 3, mentions that the bridegroom gave his dowry for positions as cantor, rabbi, or beadle. The same sort of arrangement is indicated by the ruling of Dubnow, ed., *Pinkas . . . Lita*, §913, that "it is forbidden to appoint anyone as city rabbi [*rav av bet din*] because of a match. . . ."

19 R. Ephraim of Lenczyca, *Ir Giborim* (Lublin: 1884), *Meẓora*, p. 21, mentions that members of the Nadler family who were suspected of some blemish had to give large dowries.

20 See Katz, "Marriage and Sexual Life," pp. 33f.

21 See, for example, R. Ezekiel Katzenellenbogen, *Responsa Kneset Yeḥezkel*, §77, fol. 98c–99b.

22 Not for nothing did the moralists warn repeatedly against delaying marriage in the hope of attracting a better match; R. Moses of Brisk, *Ḥelkat Meḥokek, Shulḥan Arukh, Even ha-Ezer*, §2.1, and the ethical will of R. Jonah Landsofer, §23, *Ẓavaot ve-Derekh Tovim* (Zhitomir: 1874–75), pp. 16f.

23 See Katz, "Marriage and Sexual Life," pp. 33f., and the sources cited there.

24 For the battle waged by the *kehilot* and other institutions against secret marriages, see Freimann, *Seder Kidushin ve-Nisu'in*, pp. 210ff. This tendency is expressed well by R. Jacob Reischer, *Responsa Shvut Yaakov*, II, §112: "Every female domestic will aspire to marry a son of her wealthy employer and give herself to him in order to induce him to marry her. But since she has acted improperly . . . so too we must act improperly with her."

25 *Shulḥan Arukh, Even ha-Ezer*, §2.2.

26 *Shulḥan Arukh, Oraḥ Ḥayim*, §240.1, and R. Abraham Abele Gombiner, *Magen Avraham*, ad loc.

27 See Katz, "Marriage and Sexual Life," p. 42.

28 See *Shulḥan Arukh, Oraḥ Ḥayim*, §240.1. This matter is repeated constantly in the ethical works. There are substantial differences of approach even in this period. See, for example, R. Joseph Hahn, *Yosef Omeẓ*, §193,

and, on the other hand, R. Berechiah Berakh b. Eliakim Getzel, *Zera Berakh ha-Shlishi, Brakhot*, fol. 14a.

[29] See Katz, "Marriage and Sexual Life," p. 42.

[30] Ibid., p. 39.

[31] Ibid., idem.

[32] Ibid., p. 43.

[33] Samuel ha-Levi, *Naḥalat Shiv'a*, §16.

[34] R. Jonah Landsofer, *Responsa Me'il Ẓdaka*, §33. The author of *Mishmeret ha-Kodesh*, in the section "Likutei Dinim," considers whether someone who studied the Torah full time and was supported by his wife was obligated to divorce her if they had no children. He permitted maintaining the marriage and advised consistency only for someone totally dedicated to fulfilling the commandment of "be fruitful and multiply."

[35] The situation was especially severe in the absolutist states from the first quarter of the eighteenth century on, for the rulers limited the number of marriage licenses given to Jews; Baer, *Protokollbuch*, p. 59.

[36] See Katz, "Marriage and Sexual Life," p. 45. For beggars suspected of licentious behavior, see Dubnow, ed., *Pinkas . . . Lita*, §88. For female domestics, see R. Joseph Hahn, *Yosef Omeẓ*, p. 286; R. Ezekiel Landau, *Drushei ha-ẒLaḤ*, fol. 4a, 33b, 45b, and 52a; Wachstein, *Urkunden*, pp. 148f. The *takanot* of Frankfurt required the expulsion of "any woman who had become pregnant out of wedlock" within a half-year and also forbade arranging a marriage for someone born out of wedlock; MS "Pinkas Kahal Frankfurt de-Main" (above, chapter 9, n. 15), §§29–30.

[37] See Katz, "Marriage and Sexual Life," pp. 46f.; R. Meir of Lublin, *Responsa of MaHaRaM of Lublin*, §45; R. Judah Loeb Pukhovitser, *Divrei Ḥakhamim*, fol. 23b.

Chapter 15. The Extended Family

[1] *Shulḥan Arukh, Even ha-Ezer*, §15.

[2] *Shulḥan Arukh, Ḥoshen Mishpat*, §33.

[3] Cf. *Ktubot*, fol. 52b; *Tana de-Vei Eliyahu*, chapter 27. Meir Ish-Shalom (Friedmann), ed., *Seder Eliyahu Raba ve-Seder Eliyahu Zuta* (Vienna: 1902; reprint, Jerusalem: 1959–60), pp. 143f.

[4] *Shulḥan Arukh, Yore De'a*, §251.3–5.

[5] See below, at the end of this chapter.

[6] See chapter 14, n. 15.

[7] In the wills and estates of the wealthy we find that poor relatives are given preference. In other words, it was assumed to be obvious that not all members of the family would be rich. See Taglicht, *Nachlässe der wiener Juden*, p. 39; Horovitz, *Frankfurter Rabbinen*, IV, p. 64.

[8] See my "Marriage and Sexual Life," p. 30. On commercial ties between relatives, see below.

[9] See R. Ephraim of Lenczyca's drastic portrayal in *Ir Giborim,* fol. 11ff. (*Meẓora*). The history of the struggle between the Drach and Kam families in Frankfurt provides an interesting example of this phenomenon; I. Kracauer, *Juden in Frankfurt an Main,* II, pp. 49ff. See also R. Gershon Ashkenazi, *Responsa Avodat ha-Gershuni,* §49.

[10] A case reported in *Ktubot,* fol. 52b, can be used to exemplify the extension of the notion of family for purposes of restricting relatives from judging each other. In the case, R. Yoḥanan at first agrees to hear a case involving a (distant) relative based on Isaiah's admonition (58:7, cited above) not to ignore one's own kin. Later he regrets his act and feels that he had acted improperly. See also *Shulḥan Arukh, Ḥoshen Mishpat,* §33.2 and 6, for listings of relatives forbidden to bear witness against each other. A good example of increased severity concerning in-laws is provided by a ruling concerning *meḥutanim*—that is, the fathers of the bride and groom. By Talmudic law, the two are allowed to testify against each other because, as is explicitly stated, their relationship does not bind them very closely; *Sanhedrin,* fol. 28b. There were those who tended to forbid them from serving as a judge in a case involving the other, at least if there was a choice; cf. the comments of R. Moses Isserles, *Shulḥan Arukh, Ḥoshen Mishpat,* §33.6. MaHaRaM of Lublin went further, forbidding this absolutely "for reason dictates that one should compare the father of the groom and the father of the bride to close friends, for there is no case of greater friendship and fellowship"; *Responsa,* §63. The *Takanot . . . Mehrin,* ed. Halperin, include a similar ruling (§133):

> After the marriage, the father of the groom and the father of the bride may not sit together [on any body] dealing with matters of the *medina.* Similarly, they are considered as partial [and therefore may not] sit in judgment together nor may they judge one another. This applies also to local communal matters.

[11] The *takanot* stress in particular that the members of a given administrative body not be related to each other; Dubnow, ed., *Pinkas . . . Lita,* §§68 and 276; Halperin, ed., *Takanot . . . Mehrin,* §§27, 30, 35, 43, 49, 132, 133, 184, etc.; Weinryb, *Texts and Studies,* Hebrew section, p. 165; Wachstein, *Urkunden,* p. 144. The degree of permissible relatedness was always defined by analogy to the laws governing witnesses.

[12] R. Benjamin Aaron Slonik (*Mas'at Binyamin, Responsum* §7) deals with this issue in a case in which a group wished to expand the notion of partiality to those who selected the electors. Similar also was the dispute in Eisenstadt treated by R. Meir ben Isaac, author of *Responsa Panim Me'irot;* Wachstein, *Urkunden,* pp. 144f. Poznan provides an example of the degrees of forbidden kinship changing in response to changing conditions; Weinryb, *Texts and Studies,* p. 165. A desire to find a compromise is seen in the definition offered in *Takanot . . . Mehrin,* ed. Halperin, §§132–33. Different standards were adopted for different organizations.

[13] See Lewin, *Landessynode*, pp. 75 and 91. The rule applied to relatives as well as to other types of interested parties; R. Gershon Ashkenazi, *Responsa Avodat ha-Gershuni*, §2; R. Ephraim ha-Kohen, *Responsa Shaar Efrayim*, §67; and cf. R. Ya'ir Ḥayim Bacharach, *Responsa Ḥavot Ya'ir*, Frankfurt edition, fol. 230b.

[14] R. Ephraim ha-Kohen bears explicit testimony to this; *Responsa Shaar Efrayim*, cited above, n. 13. See also, Lewin, *Urkunden*, pp. 106f.

[15] The Lithuanian Council of 1622–23 left the matter in the hands of the *kehilot*, ordering that they take the degree of relatedness into account; Dubnow, ed., *Pinkas . . . Lita*, §8. In 1624–25 an edict was issued forbidding accepting merchandise from relatives from Poland, but the text of the *takana* indicates that here too there was an even stronger tendency to allow trade with relatives; *Pinkas . . . Lita*, §172. In *Takanot . . . Mehrin*, ed. Halperin, such degrees of relatedness are ignored; see, e.g., §§283, 284, and 649.

[16] This custom was based upon the Talmudic ruling in *Nedarim*, fol. 65b; R. Moses Mat, *Mate Moshe*, part III.2 (*"Be-Maalat ha-Ẓdaka"*), chapter 6, p. 334, citing *Sefer Mordekhai* (Mordecai ben Hillel) and R. Solomon ben Adret. See Weinryb, *Texts and Studies*, Hebrew section, p. 38, where the rich are obligated to lend money to poor relatives. See also ibid., pp. 157f. and 197. See R. Menaḥem Mendel Krokhmal, *Responsa Ẓemaḥ Ẓedek*, §111, which requires relatives to spend at least up to a certain amount on bringing a (non-Jewish) murderer to trial. Only to the extent that there was some fear that relatives would not be able to support such expenditures did he impose this obligation on the community.

[17] Typical was the behavior of relatives with regard to the bankrupt; *Zikhronat Marat Glikel me-Hamil*, pp. 216ff. [English: *The Memoirs of Glückel of Hameln*, pp. 117ff.]. Relatives among the creditors felt no hesitation at seizing his property.

Chapter 16. Confraternities and Social Life

[1] The *takanot* of Moravia encourage members of communities too small to maintain a local *yeshiva* to "set aside fixed times for Torah and for community study of . . . a daily portion in the Study House." The head of the *kahal* was made responsible for enforcing this ruling. Halperin, ed., *Takanot . . . Mehrin*, §16.

[2] The *takanot* of Cracow fixed different "prices" for honors in each of the three synagogues—the Old, the New (named for R. Moses Isserles, the ReMA'), and the High. There is no doubt that this is a reflection of the different social status associated with each of these synagogues; Balaban, "Die krakauer Judengemeinde," *JJLG* 10, p. 347.

[3] The *minyanim* weakened the total control of the *kehila* over religious life and competed with it for the donations customarily given during prayer

service; hence, the usual opposition of the *kehila* to them. For their part, halakhists recognized the legal right of the *kehila* to forbid private *minyanim*; R. Abraham Gombiner, *Magen Avraham, Shulḥan Arukh, Oraḥ Ḥayim*, §154.23. Events in Cracow over the years 1722–27 provide an interesting illustration of the tendency toward separate prayers as well as of the *kehila*'s interest in blocking it; Weinryb, *Texts and Studies*, Hebrew section, pp. 189–96. The founders of the "Shiv'a Kru'im" (literally: seven are called) Society based their request on "the obligation spelled out in the words of the rabbis of blessed memory that every Jewish male must say the blessings over the Torah at least once every thirty days"; pp. 189 and 196. In fact, this obligation is not found in the works of the medieval jurists (*rishonim*). It appears as a suggestion in R. Joseph Hahn, *Yosef Omeẓ*, §506, and R. Joseph Darshan sees it as a method of atoning for nocturnal emission (*keri*); *Yesod Yosef* (1679), p. 8. Apparently, however, the practice became widespread and served as a justification for splitting off from the main synagogue. R. Ezekiel Landau, who opposed the *minyanim*, has left us a good description of the situation: "This problem began with the elite . . . and if I had the power, I would forbid all of them, no matter who was involved, unless they have a [legal] privilege to this effect"; *Drushei ha-ẒLaḤ*, fol. 30b. In Frankfurt, the closing of R. Nathan Adler's private *minyan* led to a general ban on private *minyanim*; Dubnow, *Toldot ha-Ḥasidut*, p. 439. In Eisenstadt, the community was still waging this battle in 1803; Wachstein, *Urkunden*, pp. 185f. For prayer groups with their own, innovative, liturgical practices, see R. Isaiah Horowitz, *Shnei Luḥot ha-Brit, Psaḥim*, fol. 143b, who mentions that a "holy *ḥavura*" had recently begun to gather in Prague for the purpose of reciting the evening prayer at the proper time. The *kabalat shabat* ceremony on Friday evenings was similarly first introduced in such separate groups; R. Ezekiel Katzenellenbogen, *Responsa Kneset Yeḥezkel, Kuntrus ha-Kadishim* at the end of *Yore De'a*, fol. 52a.

4 Summaries of what is known about the development of the *Ḥevra Kadisha* or burial society are provided by Max Grunwald, *Encyclopaedia Judaica* (German; Berlin: 1930), pp. 430–38, s.v. "Chewra Kadischa," and by Salo Baron, *The Jewish Community*, I, pp. 352–54, and III, pp. 89–91. The latter includes a lengthy bibliography. Baron errs in trying to prove the existence of this sort of confraternity in early Askenazic communities from RaSHI's comments on *Mo'ed Katan*, fol. 27b, and those of the Tosafists to *Ketubot*, fol. 17a, and R. Eliezer ben Joel ha-Levi (*Mavo le-Sefer Ra'AViYaH* [Introduction to the Book of Ra'AViYaH], ed. Victor [Avigdor] Aptowitzer [Jerusalem: 1938], II, pp. 561ff.). These sources are dealing with an institution of the Talmudic period. An explicit reference to the establishment of such a society in Frankfurt at the end of the sixteenth century, at the earliest, is found in R. Joseph Hahn's remarks in *Yosef Omeẓ*. See Marcus Horovitz, "Die Wohltätigkeit bei den Juden im alten Frankfurt," *Israelitische Monatsschrift* (Supplement to *Jüdische Presse*) 27 (1896), pp. 17–27. See also

R. Joseph Hahn, *Yosef Omeẓ*, p. 328, who attests to the involvement of the entire congregation in funerals in the previous generation, stating that the practice had changed owing to population growth.

[5] There are many confraternities of this sort, especially in Germany. B. H. Auerbach found twelve of them in Halberstadt; *Geschichte der israelitischen Gemeinde in Halberstadt*, pp. 128f. Among these was one that provided heating wood to the poor. The same was true in Frankfurt; cf. A. Sulzbach, "Ein alter Frankfurter Wohltätigkeitsverein," *JJLG* 2 (1904), pp. 241–66; S. Unna, "Statuten-Entwurf eines alten Vereins in Frankfurt a/M aus dem Jahre 1822," *JJLG* 21 (1930), pp. 265–71. This confraternity dedicated itself to providing ritual fringes for anyone needing them.

[6] M. Hendel, *Mlakha u-Vaalei Mlakha be-Am Yisra'el* [Crafts and Craftsmen among the Jewish People] (Tel Aviv: 1955–56), pp. 311–13, provides a good bibliography on artisans' associations.

[7] Hendel, *Mlakha u-Vaalei Mlakha*, chapters 3–4, provides a summary of the associations' activities, though without a detailed scientific analysis.

[8] See the *takanot* of the confraternities mentioned above in n. 5.

[9] The basic laws on this matter are found in the *Shulḥan Arukh, Even ha-Ezer*, §23, and in the commentaries ad loc. Thus, even on days when they permitted women to play cards, the *takanot* of Cracow forbade such an activity by mixed groups of men and women; Balaban, "Die krakauer Judengemeinde," *JJLG* 11, p. 89. The ethical works repeated this prohibition endlessly. See, for example, *Keiẓad Seder ha-Mishna*, in Assaf, *Mekorot le-Toldot ha-Ḥinukh*, I, p. 95; R. Joseph Darshan, *Yesod Yosef* (Berlin: 1738–39 edition), fol. 2b; and the remarks of R. Ezekiel Landau, quoted in the next note.

[10] R. Joseph Hahn, *Yosef Omeẓ*, §132. A typical expression of this approach is found in R. Ezekiel Landau's sermon (*Drushei ha-ẒLaḤ*, fol. 18a):

> Some people customarily have a friendly meal, now in this one's house and then in another's. I have already demonstrated that eating and drinking themselves should be limited to the necessary minimum. As [the Sages] said: "A piece of bread with salt and a measure of water"—he who obeys this regimen "is blessed" [Mishna *Avot* 6.4]. But of course, this is not for everyone, and [our] generation is weak. Still, to actually seek out the artifices of this world is a criminal sin, and 'the lion roars over a container of meat.' The evil desire is the father of the 'cub of fire' [a reference to the temptation to worship idols; cf. *Sanhedrin*, fol. 64a; *Yoma*, fol. 69b—*tr.*], and from this [devotion to the things of this world] one comes to looking at women, and nothing good ever derives from that, and one breaks the covenant of language [i.e., one speaks improperly] and the covenant of sexual purity.

The situation in Prague of 1770 may already reflect a degree of secularization; cf. end of chapter 8.

[11] Community *takanot* and the ethical works are constantly preoccupied

with Jews engaging in card playing and other games of chance. See, for example, Balaban, "Die krakauer Judengemeinde," *JJLG* 11, pp. 88f.; Dubnow, ed., *Pinkas . . . Lita*, §51; Halperin, ed., *Takanot . . . Mehrin*, §280; R. Solomon Luria, *Yam shel Shlomo, Beiẓa*, I, §34; R. Judah Loeb Pukhovitser, *Derekh Ḥokhma*, fol. 49a; R. Isaiah Horowitz, *Shnei Luḥot ha-Brit*, fol. 93d; R. Joseph Hahn, *Yosef Omeẓ*, §§817–18, 907–8; R. Ezekiel Landau, *Drushei ha-ẒLaḤ*, fol. 35d. For a bibliography on this matter, see Halperin's note to *Takanot . . . Mehrin*, p. 92.

[12] See Leopold Löw, *Die Lebensalter in der jüdischen Literatur* (Szegedin: 1875), pp. 89–92, 214; Israel Abrahams, *Jewish Life in the Middle Ages* (London: 1896), p. 143. Abrahams's list is far from complete. I too have sought only to provide a few examples. See R. Joseph Hahn, *Yosef Omeẓ*, §657; Balaban, "Die krakauer Judengemeinde," *JJLG* 11, pp. 98f.; and n. 13 below.

[13] See R. Solomon Luria, *Yam shel Shlomo, Bava Kama*, VII, §37; R. Joseph Hahn, *Yosef Omeẓ*, §§132–34; *Shulḥan Arukh, Oraḥ Ḥayim*, §670.2; and R. Abraham Gombiner, *Magen Avraham*, ad loc., §4.

[14] The economic motive is explicit, for instance, in Dubnow, ed., *Pinkas . . . Lita*, §327; Halperin, ed., *Pinkas Vaad Arba Araẓot*, p. 90. The social motive is clear from the fact that the number of guests allowed at such parties varied with the tax burden paid by the specific host.

[15] Dubnow, ed., *Pinkas . . . Lita*, §§463–70.

[16] See the citations from R. Solomon Luria, *Yam shel Shlomo*, and R. Joseph Hahn, *Yosef Omeẓ*, above, n. 13.

[17] See Leopold Löw, *Gesammelte Schriften*, ed. Immanuel Löw (Szegedin: 1889–1900), II, p. 151.

[18] The *takanot* of the burial society of Szegedin obligated the members to hold the meal each year "as is the custom among the Jews everywhere in order to symbolize the eating of the Leviathan [in messianic days]"; Immanuel Löw and Solomon Klein, *A Szegedi Chevra 1787 töl 1887* (Szegedin: 1887), p. 105.

[19] Dubnow, ed., *Pinkas . . . Lita*, §§641 and 817. The burial society required supervision to prevent the treasurers from demanding arbitrary fees for graves and burial services (Halperin, ed., *Pinkas Vaad Arba Araẓot*, pp. 185 and 246; *Pinkas . . . Lita*, §972 [and cf. Israel Klausner, *Toldot ha-Kehila ha-Ivrit be-Vilna*, I, pp. 116f.]; and Halperin, ed., *Takanot . . . Mehrin*, §243), and to prevent them from passing arbitrary decisions (ibid., §244). See R. Moses Sofer, *Responsa of the ḤaTaM Sofer, Yore De'a*, §329, a *responsum* of 1804–5 that bears witness to conditions that the author had witnessed already at the end of the eighteenth century.

[20] See, for example, Klausner, *Toldot . . . Vilna*, I, p. 110, and in Heinrich Flesch, "Aus den Statuten der mährischen Beerdigungsgesellschaften," *Jahrbuch der Gesellschaft für Geschichte der Juden in der Čechoslovakischen Republik* 5 (1933), pp. 157–74.

[21] In Vilna, elections for the burial society were held on the day after

those for the *kehila* as a whole—probably in order to preserve offices in the burial society for those who were not chosen for communal office; Klausner, *Toldot . . . Vilna*, I, p. 110.

[22] The *takanot* of 1621 required members of the burial society in Metz to come to classes devoted to Torah and Mishna on weekdays and to a sermon on the Sabbath; Abraham Cahen, "Le rabbinat de Metz pendant la période française (1567–1871)," *Révue des Etudes Juives* 7 (1883), pp. 110f. See also the Viennese *takanot* of 1763, in B. Wachstein, "Die Gründung der Wiener Chewra Kadischa im Jahre 1763," *Mitteilungen zur jüdischen Volkskunde* 32–33; revised and printed separately (Leipzig: 1910).

[23] See, for example, Halperin, ed., *Pinkas Vaad Arba Arazot*, p. 471.

Chapter 17. Religious Institutions

[1] A typical example is the ruling of the Frankfurt assembly of rabbis of 1603 against those "who dress in the clothes of non-Jews in order to hide the fact that they are Jews while the Torah cries out: 'And I shall separate you from the nations' "; Horovitz, *Die Frankfurter Rabbinerversammlung vom Jahre 1603*, p. 26. Similar rulings are found in Halperin, ed., *Pinkas Vaad Arba Arazot*, p. 17, and Dubnow, ed., *Pinkas . . . Lita*, §339. The use of Yiddish was understood as a given, but it was justified on principle, apparently, only by those who clung to it after it had begun to disappear. As is well known, customs are ascribed religious value even if they have no religious significance. Even R. Ya'ir Ḥayim Bacharach, who discovered that he was the unintentional source of a certain custom (*Responsa Ḥavot Ya'ir*, §238), warns his readers not to abandon traditional custom; loc. cit., §§225 and 234.

[2] The communal organizations tried to ensure that only authorized figures would rule on halakhic issues; Halperin, ed., *Takanot . . . Mehrin*, §380; Dubnow, ed., *Pinkas . . . Lita*, §591; and the decisions of the Alsatian provincial leaders of 1772–73, *Blätter für jüdische Geschichte und Literatur* 2, §9. In fact it was quite unusual to see teachers ruling on what was ritually permitted or forbidden even in the outlying settlements. See Assaf, *Mekorot le-Toldot ha-Ḥinukh*, I, pp. 169 and 171, and IV, p. 127 (where the practice was permitted!); R. Ya'ir *Ḥayim Bacharach, Responsa Ḥavot Ya'ir*, §186. In any case, no religious ruling or act was ever revoked on the grounds that it had come from an unauthorized figure. A decision was evaluated on its own merits as to whether or not it conformed to the Halakha. See the comments of R. Samuel Edels (MaHaRSHA'), *Ḥidushei Agadot, Kidushin*, fol. 13a, who distinguishes between marriages and divorces: "Anyone who knows a little something is allowed to take care of marriages; not so bills of divorce."

[3] See, for example, Bacharach, *Responsa Ḥavot Ya'ir*, §186. Even in disputes between major halakhists it sometimes happened that one side totally rejected his opponent's view. Thus, for example, the view of MaHaRaM of Lublin was rejected in favor of the consensus opinion of almost every contem-

porary rabbi concerning a bill of divorce issued in Vienna; see chapter 12, n. 17.

[4] I know of no example of this sort of legist from our period. R. Moses Sofer lived after our period, and he should be seen as someone who embodied traditional values that were already beginning to be questioned in practice. See R. Shlomo Sofer, *Ḥut ha-Meshulash* (Mukachevo [Munkácz]: 1895), fol. 24f. See the remarks of J. Ben-David, "Beginnings of Modern Jewish Society in Hungary During the First Half of the Nineteenth Century" [in Hebrew], *Zion* 17 (1952), especially pp. 122ff. From other periods one can note, among others, R. Abraham ben David (RA'BaD) of Posquières as one who strengthened his halakhic authority with the certainty of the mystic; see G. Scholem, *Reshit ha-Kabala* (Jerusalem: 1948), p. 71 [and see now the much expanded English *Origins of the Kabbalah* (Philadelphia: 1987), p. 206—*tr.*].

[5] This is already clear in Maimonides who, in *Mishne Tora, Hilkhot De'ot* [*Laws concerning Opinions*], §6.7–8, obligates every man to admonish others. But in *Hilkhot Tshuva* [*Laws of Repentance*], 4.2, Maimonides ruled that "every community in Israel must appoint a great sage, old and pious from youth and beloved to the people, who will admonish them and lead them to repent."

[6] "And now the custom is to deliver a sermon on *Shabat ha-Gadol* and on *Shabat Shuva*"; R. Abraham Gombiner, *Magen Avraham, Oraḥ Ḥayim*, §429.1. The rabbinical appointment letter of R. Simeon Wertheimer of Eisenstadt, dated 1691–92, states that he must "preach in our congregation exactly as is customary elsewhere on *Shabat ha-Gadol* and on *Shabat Tshuva*"; Wachstein, *Urkunden*, p. 453.

[7] We have, for example, R. Ezekiel Landau's sermons for the days of *Sliḥot* (penitential prayers) and festivals, as well as his eulogies; see *Drushei ha-ẒLaḤ*. From R. Jonathan Eybeschutz we have a sermon for the seventh of Adar as well as for special events such as when the community learned that the Jews of Prague had been expelled; see his *Yaarot Dvash* (2 volumes: Carlsruh: 1778–79 and 1781–82).

[8] For Cracow, see Balaban, "Die krakauer Judengemeinde," *JJLG* 11, pp. 93 and 97; Weinryb, *Texts and Studies*, Hebrew section, p. 185. For Poznan, see Perles, *Geschichte der Juden in Posen*, pp. 81f. For Nikolsburg, see Halperin, ed., *Takanot . . . Mehrin*, p. 284.

[9] Already R. Moses Mat (end of the sixteenth century) describes preachers "who wander in the land and everywhere stand before the congregation and preach . . . in order to be honored and be given presents"; *Mate Moshe*, part I.4 ("Be-Hanhagat Lomdeha"), p. 33. In the seventeenth and eighteenth centuries, the wandering preacher was found everywhere in Jewish Poland and Lithuania; see Halperin, ed., *Pinkas Vaad Arba Araẓot*, s.v. "drashot" and "darshanim"; Dubnow, ed., *Pinkas . . . Lita*, §§130 and 596; as well as Wachstein, *Urkunden*, p. 154.

[10] Typical is the definition offered in the Nikolsburg regulations, which allow for "three preachers. . . . They must be great scholars, and at least two of them must be well known as capable of speaking about matters of *agada*

[i.e., non-halakhic matters] which draw the hearts of listeners and of offering moral exhortations . . . and the third preacher who does not have this ability shall speak in public in the Beit ha-Midrash Synagogue"; Halperin, ed., *Takanot . . . Mehrin*, p. 284. See also R. Moses Mat, *Mate Moshe*, part I.2 ("Be-Eykhut ha-Limud"), p. 18, who describes preachers expert only in aggadic matters but not in Halakha.

[11] See Dubnow, ed., *Pinkas . . . Lita*, loc. cit. (above, n. 9), as well as §88 where the itinerant preachers are mentioned alongside beggars and are suspected of major sins. The Council of the Four Lands sought to limit even the printing of collections of sermons; Halperin, ed., *Pinkas Vaad Arba Araẓot*, p. 74, and idem, "*Imprimaturs* of the Council of the Four Lands" (in Hebrew), *Kiryat Sefer* 11 (1934–35), pp. 108f. This was even before the Sabbatean movement.

[12] See Dubnow, ed., *Pinkas . . . Lita*, loc. cit. above, n. 9. R. Berechiah Berakh b. Eliakim Getzel, author of *Zera Berakh ha-Shlishi*, received a letter of recommendation from a *parnas* of the Council of the Four Lands that authorized him "to preach without having to ask permission of any rabbi or [local] leader"; Halperin, ed., *Pinkas Vaad Arba Araẓot*, pp. 477f. On the limitation of the right to preach in Poznan, see Lewin, *Die Landessynode*, p. 102. For Eisenstadt, see Wachstein, *Urkunden*, p. 154.

[13] See Dinur, *Be-Mifne ha-Dorot*, pp. 99 and 133. Dinur ascribes an overly revolutionary intent to the preachers. The fact that lay leaders and rabbis supported the preachers and made efforts to publicize their books proves that there was no real confrontation between the two groups. For their part, the preachers, and even the overtly antiestablishment among them, expected the leaders and rabbis to mend their ways. The most radical critic of the leadership, R. Berechiah Berakh b. Eliakim Getzel, uses the image of the shepherd and his dog. The shepherd, that is, the rabbi, watches over his sheep while the preacher, "in holy matters likened to the dog," is nothing but his helper; *Zera Berakh ha-Shlishi, Brakhot*, fol. 20b–21a.

[14] For testimonies in this regard concerning R. Judah the Pious, see Graetz, *Geschichte der Juden*, 4th ed., X, pp. 307 and 463.

[15] Preachers emphasized the need for new insights in their sermons, and when they criticized each other, it was on the quality of these insights, a judgment for which, of course, there could be no universally accepted criterion. See, for example, R. Ephraim of Lenczya, *Ir Giborim*, Introduction, fol. 2b. Asked to define the sermon in halakhic terms, Rabbi Jacob Reischer required a measure of originality; *Responsa Shvut Yaakov*, II, §146, fol. 43a–b.

[16] Studies on Jewish homiletics have concentrated so far on the ideational content of sermons, but there is also good reason to investigate their formal development. The sermons of R. Ezekiel Landau, and especially those of R. Jonathan Eybeschutz from the end of our period, provide good examples of perfected structure.

[17] See for example the words of R. Ephraim of Lenczyca referred to above, n. 15: "One does not learn either ethical ways of behaving or the proper way

of performing some commandment. Hence what has the reader availed himself?" See also R. Sheftel Horowitz, *Vavei ha-Amudim*, fol. 10a. Typical are the remarks of R. Ezekiel Landau to his congregants (*Drushei ha-ẒLaḤ*, fol. 8a):

> I see that over the years you liked my *pshatim* [novel exegeses], while I would have preferred that you had liked my ethical entreaties, for that is the main purpose of a sermon. What does it matter to me if you forget the *pshatim*. . . . This is almost a net loss and quite far from the profitable. I beg of you, I cry and plead and implore of you, to accept my ethical exhortations and may my words enter into your hearts.

[18] Aesthetics affected the cantor just as they did the preacher. The congregation wanted to derive pleasure from the cantor's melodies, while the moralists decried any phenomenon that was not directed at the "service of the heart"; see R. Benjamin Aaron Slonik, *Responsa Mas'at Binyamin*, §6; R. Joseph ben Moses Kossman, *Nohag ke-Ẓon Yosef* (Hanau: 1717–18), fol. 17b–18b. *Takanot* against itinerant cantors are to be found in Margalioth, *Dubno Rabati*, p. 40; Perles, *Geschichte der Juden in Posen*, pp. 122f.

[19] As is well known, the kabbalists who participated in the *kloyz* in Brody used the Lurianic liturgy even before the rise of Hasidism; Dubnow, *Toldot ha-Ḥasidut*, p. 121. R. Nathan Adler of Frankfurt changed the way in which the liturgy was pronounced from Ashkenazic to Sephardic so that it would fit with the kabbalistic schema; ibid., p. 435.

[20] See *Shulḥan Arukh, Oraḥ Ḥayim*, §90.9–11.

[21] In Cracow the *kehila* issued regulations that applied to all synagogues in the city; Balaban, "Die krakauer Judengemeinde," *JJLG* 10, pp. 344 and 347–49, and cf. Weinryb, *Texts and Studies*, Hebrew section, pp. 189–96. These documents, dating from the years 1722–28, prove that synagogues were theoretically subject to *kehila* authority at the beginning of the eighteenth century, though we can also see signs of the breakdown of this control in practice. R. Menaḥem Mendel Krokhmal expresses the ideal of bringing all worshipers together in a single place in his *Responsa Ẓemaḥ Ẓedek*, §94.

[22] There is evidence for a *beit midrash* of young men during the time of R. Solomon Luria in R. Moses Mat, *Responsa Mate Moshe*, §241. Similar evidence from the time of R. Ezekiel Landau is found in *Responsa Noda bi-Yhuda*, 2nd collection, *Oraḥ Ḥayim*, §§11 and 15, and his *Drushei ha-ẒLaḤ*, fol. 33b. For Eisenstadt in 1803, see Wachstein, *Urkunden*, p. 186.

[23] See *Shulḥan Arukh, Oraḥ Ḥayim*, §90.14, and R. Menaḥem Mendel Auerbach, *Ateret Zkenim*, ad loc. "One should always try to arrive at the synagogue early even if he won't be among the first ten, for the earlier one comes the closer one is to the source [literally: the root] of holiness, and those who come later suck from the farthest leaves. . . ." Typical was the position taken by litigants when a synagogue was closed because of a quarrel over a cantor: "It would be better that he continue to function lest we lose a single

[opportunity to say] 'amen, yehei shmei raba' [the *kadish* prayer], *kdusha* and *barkhu*"; R. Solomon Luria, *Responsa*, §20; *Shulḥan Arukh, Oraḥ Ḥayim*, §55.1, 125.1–2, and R. Joseph Hahn, *Yosef Omeẓ*, §7.

[24] The qualifications required of the cantor were partly linked to his ethical and religious behavior and partly to his ability to inspire a sense of spirituality and devotion in the worshipers; see *Shulḥan Arukh, Oraḥ Ḥayim*, §53.

[25] See *Shulḥan Arukh, Oraḥ Ḥayim*, §§60.5, 61.1–3, 93.1–3, 95, and 98. These concerns are repeated in the ethical tracts with slightly different emphases.

[26] "In a place where there is no regular quorum in the synagogue, members may compel each other to attend by issuing fines, such that the *tamid* not be canceled"; R. Moses Isserles, *Shulḥan Arukh, Oraḥ Ḥayim*, §55.22. In line with this, the Moravian *takanot* obligate members of small communities in particular "to pass by-laws among themselves backed up by large fines so that there will always be public services morning and night"; Halperin, ed., *Takanot . . . Mehrin*, §17.

[27] For the custom and its source, see Assaf, *Batei ha-Din ve-Sidreihem*, pp. 25f. For our period, see R. Moses Mat, *Mate Moshe*, §66; R. Ephraim b. Jacob ha-Kohen, *Shaar Efrayim, Responsum* §112.

[28] In a similar fashion, communities were much stricter about maintaining the required quorum for public prayer on the Days of Awe than during the rest of the year; see *Shulḥan Arukh, Oraḥ Ḥayim*, §55.22, and R. Ya'ir Ḥayim Bacharach, *Ḥavot Ya'ir, Responsum* §186. The *takanot* of Gaya for 1679–80 are more strict concerning someone who absents himself from the synagogue on Mondays and Thursdays than on other weekdays; see H. Gold, *Die Juden und Judengemeinden Mährens in Vergangenheit und Gegenwart* (Brünn: 1929), p. 31.

[29] A few examples will suffice: R. Moses Isserles, *Shulḥan Arukh, Oraḥ Ḥayim*, §232.2; R. Abraham Horowitz, *Yesh Noḥalim*, fol. 27a; R. Joseph Hahn, *Yosef Omeẓ*, §§6, 487–88; Halperin, ed., *Takanot . . . Mehrin*, §630.

[30] See above, at the end of chapter 16.

[31] The Moravian *takanot* require that people close their stores immediately after the beadle's call to prayer, but they also indicate that not everyone actually did so; Halperin, ed., *Takanot . . . Mehrin*, §630, and similarly, R. Benjamin Wolf b. Mattathiah, *Tohorat ha-Kodesh*, I, fol. 29a. R. Ezekiel Landau complains that neither male nor female domestics always manage to hear even the *kidush*; *Drushei ha-ẒLaḤ*, fol. 49b.

[32] *Shulḥan Arukh, Oraḥ Ḥayim*, §151.

[33] *Shulḥan Arukh, Oraḥ Ḥayim*, §§51.4 and 66.104.

[34] R. Abraham Horowitz, *Yesh Noḥalim*, fol. 31b; the comments of R. Jacob Hurwitz, ibid., fol. 15a; R. Joseph Hahn, *Yosef Omeẓ*, §14.

[35] One's synagogue seat was considered an economic good and could be used as collateral for a loan and the like; Halperin, ed., *Takanot . . . Mehrin*, §§235 and 240, and idem, *Pinkas Vaad Arba Araẓot*, p. 46. In general, one

who became impoverished was stripped of his synagogue seat, especially if he went bankrupt. For a fight over a synagogue seat, see R. Joel Sirkes, *Responsa Bayit Ḥadash*, §6. Benjamin Wolf b. Mattathiah mentions that the wealthy would string ribbons around their seats in the synagogue "boastfully and grandly as a way of marking them off"; *Tohorat ha-Kodesh*, I, fol. 7b.

[36] R. Moses Isserles, *Shulḥan Arukh, Yore De'a*, §249.13 (citing R. Solomon ben Adret, but cf. *Sefer Ḥasidim*, §§706 and 1527); R. Menaḥem Mendel Krokhmal, *Ẓemaḥ Ẓedek, Responsum* §50; R. Aaron Samuel Kaidanover, *Emunat Shmu'el, Responsum* §35.

[37] See Halperin, ed., *Takanot . . . Mehrin*, index, s.v. *"aliya,"* for an especially rich source in this matter. See also below, chapter 19.

[38] E.g., Dubnow, ed., *Pinkas . . . Lita*, §§183, 315, 317, and 323; Halperin, ed., *Takanot . . . Mehrin*, §§298 and 703.

Chapter 18. Educational Institutions

[1] On principle, the respect and fear owed to one's father and to one's mother were considered equal, but in cases of conflict the honor owed to the father took precedence; *Shulḥan Arukh, Yore De'a*, §§240.1 and 240.14. As *SHaKH* explains, basing himself on the Talmud, *Kidushin*, fol. 31a: "For the mother is also obligated to honor the father"; *Shulḥan Arukh, Yore De'a*, §240.16. The hierarchic structure of the Jewish family finds expression in many sources. Sigmund Mayer makes specific reference to it in his memoirs, *Ein jüdischer Kaufmann* (Leipzig: 1926), p. 76. During his youth, Mayer was still able to observe the traditional family in its pristine form, and the changes that occurred during his lifetime gave him considerable insight into the theoretical underpinnings of the Jewish family. That the father's authority was derived from his role as representative of the tradition is clear from the theoretical limits which were imposed on him. For example, were the father to demand something that went counter to the tradition, the son was considered free of any obligation to obey. For other circumstances in which the obligatory respect for parents was superseded by other values, see *Shulḥan Arukh, Yore De'a*, §240.12–17.

[2] The Passover eve ritual, as is known, is constructed so as to involve the child actively; cf. *Shulḥan Arukh, Oraḥ Ḥayim*, §472.15–16 and §473.6–7.

[3] See Assaf, *Mekorot*, I, pp. 64, 82, 92, etc.

[4] Our period is characterized by a tendency to stringency as compared with the Middle Ages, with regard to the question of whether a minor could be counted for a quorum (ten males for public prayer; three or ten for the Grace after Meals); see *Shulḥan Arukh, Oraḥ Ḥayim*, §§55.4 and 199.10. This is also true with regard to a minor serving as cantor (for the evening prayers; see ibid., §53.10) and being called to the reading of the Torah (ibid., §282.3, and R. Abraham Gombiner, *Magen Avraham*, ad loc., n. 6: "And in our day it is not customary to call a minor to the reading of the Torah except

for *maftir*"—i.e., the last portion, for which age was irrelevant). But such formal restrictions do not mean that the child was not included in the activities of the adults. We hear about the bringing of very young children to the synagogue (and not always in positive terms) in, for example, R. Joseph Yuspa Hahn, *Yosef Omeẓ*, §§62–63, cited in Assaf, *Mekorot*, IV, p. 101. Hahn complained specifically about the very youngest of children, but he agreed that "those who know when to respond 'amen' and 'May His great name be exalted' and how to recite the *kdusha* and know how to stand in awe without playing and making noise must be brought by their fathers to the synagogue and other religious ceremonies."

[5] As we shall see later in this chapter, even in the *yeshivot* there was no organization or public activity for the students. For a report about the participation of *yeshiva* students in a controversy that broke out among local scholars, see R. Moses Isserles, *Responsa*, §63.

[6] See the *takanot* of Cracow cited in Assaf, *Mekorot*, I, p. 101; Dubnow, ed., *Pinkas . . . Lita*, §401 (Assaf, ibid., p. 107). This last source is very instructive. It describes a donor who established a trust dedicated in part to maintenance of "a scribe who will be obliged to teach writing to the children of the poor." This scribe was not, apparently, identical with the *melamed* or regular teacher. For the children of the wealthy studying other languages, see Assaf, ibid., I, pp. 163, 205, 209; IV, p. 111.

[7] According to the *takanot* of Cracow, a poor youth incapable of learning Talmud was to be given at age fourteen "to a craft or to be a servant in someone's home"; Assaf, ibid., I, p. 102; and similarly, Halperin, ed., *Takanot . . . Mehrin*, §14, and Dubnow, ed., *Pinkas . . . Lita*, §351.

[8] See the description offered by R. Joseph Stadthagen cited in Assaf, *Mekorot*, I, pp. 171–73. The omnipresence of the *ḥeder* is clear: though there were, of course, places that found it difficult to maintain a permanent teacher (Assaf, *Mekorot*, I, pp. 154 and 162), complaints were about the low quality of the teachers, rather than that there were none at all. Dubnow, ed., *Pinkas . . . Lita*, §528, requires any community of ten householders to maintain a permanent teacher. Halperin, ed., *Takanot . . . Mehrin*, §13, mentions that in smaller communities the teacher was also the cantor and sexton; cf. also Assaf, *Mekorot*, IV, p. 127.

[9] The obligation to hire a teacher was outlined in *Shulḥan Arukh, Yore De'a*, §245.4, and see also Halperin, ed., *Takanot . . . Mehrin*, §14; and *Takanot Trebitsch*, §49, cited in Assaf, *Mekorot*, IV, p. 239. This customary arrangement also underlies the *takanot* about how parents were to pay the teachers; see, e.g., the *takanot* of Cracow in Assaf, *Mekorot*, I, p. 99. There is evidence for the wealthy hiring private tutors in *Yosef Omeẓ* cited in Assaf, loc. cit., p. 83, and in Bacharach, *Responsa Ḥavot Ya'ir*, cited ibid., p. 126. See also Isidore Fishman, *The History of Jewish Education in Central Europe from the End of the Sixteenth to the End of the Eighteenth Century* (London: 1944), pp. 22ff.

[10] *Shulḥan Arukh, Yore De'a*, §245.7, clearly states that the community

is obliged to retain an elementary teacher, but when R. Moses Isserles ruled on the allocation of the consequent tax burden (*Shulḥan Arukh, Ḥoshen Mishpat*, §163.3 [end]), he expressed the obligation in quite conditional terms: "In a place where the townspeople retain an elementary teacher and the parents of the children are not able to pay for the lessons and the community must pay for them, the tax should be allocated on the basis of wealth." Indeed, even in Isserles's own city, the community took direct charge of education only for the children of the poor; see the *takanot* of Cracow in Assaf, *Mekorot*, I, p. 101, to which parallels can be found in many other contemporary sources. In Poznan, taxes were levied for the education of the poor; Assaf, *Mekorot*, I, p. 114. In Poznan as well as in Frankfurt we hear of *gaba'ei talmud tora* appointed by the community (Assaf, *Mekorot*, I, p. 116), whereas in Cracow (*Mekorot*, I, pp. 98–104) and Minsk (*Mekorot*, IV, pp. 153–61), there was an organized *ḥevra* under the auspices of the *kehila*. Other communities whose *takanot* are known to us would lean to one or another of these arrangements, and we need not go into detail here. For examples of direct support given to the individual from charity funds, see Halperin, ed., *Takanot . . . Mehrin*, §14, as well as the *takanot* of Metz cited in Assaf, *Mekorot*, I, p. 152. For a poor student being added to the lessons of a wealthy one in Tiktin, see Assaf, *Mekorot*, IV, p. 87. We might note that the term "talmud tora" was not used in this period to describe a specific educational institution. This usage seems to have developed only in the nineteenth century. Fishman, *History of Jewish Education*, p. 24, errs in this.

11 In Hamburg, new teachers moving into the city had to register with the *parnasim* but were not required to pass an examination; Assaf, *Mekorot*, I, p. 189. In Nikolsburg a non-resident could serve as a teacher in the city for a maximum of two years; ibid., p. 140. Those who wanted to teach Talmud with the commentary of the Tosafists had to pass an examination; ibid., §8. One also had to hold the title of *ḥaver* in order to teach there; ibid., p. 142. As for the meaning of this title, see below in this chapter. In Amsterdam every elementary teacher had to be examined by a rabbi; ibid., p. 190.

12 Assaf, *Mekorot*, I, p. 100, and see the index, s.v. "beḥina."

13 Assaf, *Mekorot*, I, pp. 98–101, 138–39, and passim.

14 Assaf, *Mekorot*, I, pp. 98, 101, 139; IV, pp. 78f. and throughout the *takanot* cited there.

15 For a summary of the sources, see Assaf's introduction, *Mekorot*, IV, pp. 6–10; Fishman, *History of Jewish Education*, pp. 77f.

16 This is clear from the *takanot* of Cracow (Assaf, *Mekorot* I, p. 101), Worms (ibid., p. 117), and many other sources. See also Fishman, *History of Jewish Education*, pp. 93f.

17 See Y. F. Baer, "RaSHI and the Historical Conditions of His Time" [in Hebrew], *Tarbiẓ* 20 (1949–50), pp. 320–32.

18 R. Judah Loew's criticisms of educational methodology at the primary level were collected by Assaf, *Mekorot*, I, pp. 45ff. Those of other contemporaries are cited ibid., pp. 61, 67, 87, 154, and 169.

[19] Assaf, *Mekorot*, I, pp. 101, and passim.

[20] In addition to the sources listed in n. 18, above, see the critique offered by R. Isaac Wetzlar, *Liebes Brief* (1749), cited in Assaf, *Mekorot*, IV, p. 114.

[21] See the sources cited above, nn. 18 and 20, and especially the remarks of R. Moses b. Aaron Moravchik, "*Keizad Seder Mishna?*" [*How to Organize Learning*] *(Lublin: 1634–35), reprinted in Assaf, Mekorot*, I, p. 88.

[22] The fact that *yeshiva* students wandered over great distances is evidenced from what we shall see below about the manner of their support. See the description offered by R. Nathan Nata Hannover cited in Assaf, *Mekorot*, I, p. 112, and Dubnow, ed., *Pinkas . . . Lita*, §§46, 49, 484, etc.

[23] The maximum number of pupils accepted in the *yeshiva* depended on the local community, but the decision as to who would be accepted remained totally in the hands of the rabbi. This is explicitly stated in Halperin, ed., *Takanot . . . Mehrin*, §6, and it is implicit in many other sources. See the rabbinical contract issued in Cracow in 1699–1700 cited in Assaf, *Mekorot*, I, p. 160, and in the *takanot* of Tiktin, ibid., IV, p. 87.

[24] See Assaf, *Mekorot*, I, pp. 111 (R. Nathan Nata Hannover, *Yeven Meẓula*), 113 (Worms), 64 (Frankfurt), and 87 (Tiktin, where no more than three locals might be included among the ten students allowed), and similarly Halperin, ed., *Takanot . . . Mehrin*, §443.

[25] Assaf, *Mekorot*, I, p. 160, and IV, p. 61; Dubnow, ed., *Pinkas . . . Lita*, §§557 and 709; Perles, *Juden in Posen*, p. 124.

[26] Assaf, *Mekorot*, I, pp. 78f., 110, 119, 149, and 161, and IV, pp. 63 and 88; Dubnow, ed., *Pinkas . . . Lita*, §401. Sometimes the proceeds of communal fines were assigned to the "fund"; Balaban, "Die krakauer Judengemeinde," *JJLG* 10, p. 358, and Netter, *Vingt siècles*, p. 133.

[27] Dubnow, ed., *Pinkas . . . Lita*, §§46, 141, 459, 484, 513, 528, and 630; Halperin, ed., *Takanot . . . Mehrin*, §§1–6, 385, and 443. The Councils would try to prevent the students' being sent out to the settlements too early. In Lithuania they suggested that the smaller settlements be required to "provide for the needs of the youths from the 15th of *Shvat* to the beginning of *Nisan* [one and a half months] and from the 15th of *Av* to the middle of *Elul* [one month]"; Dubnow, ed., *Pinkas . . . Lita*, §354. Presumably, this was a suggestion that was difficult to fulfill; cf. Halperin, ed., *Takanot . . . Mehrin*, §§3 and 388.

[28] On the *ḥilukim* see Assaf, *Mekorot*, in the indices to volumes I and IV, and especially the comments of R. Ephraim of Lenczyca, MaHaRaL of Prague, and R. Isaiah Horowitz, author of *Shnei Luḥot ha-Brit*. The justification in terms of sharpening the wits is cited ibid., I, p. 63 and passim. On the nature of "ḥilukim" see H. Ehrentreu, "Über den 'Pilpul' in den alten Jeschibot," *JJLG* 3 (1905), pp. 206–19. More work remains, however, to be done on the nature of this style of study, and we have offered only a very general description.

[29] See R. Nathan Nata Hannover, cited in Assaf, *Mekorot*, I, p. 111; and cf. also ibid., IV, pp. 81, 119, and 124.

[30] See Assaf, *Mekorot*, I, p. 78; Dubnow, ed., *Pinkas . . . Lita*, §354.

[31] See e.g., Assaf, *Mekorot*, I, pp. 118–20, concerning Worms. See MaHaRSHA', *Ḥidushei Agadot, Kidushin*, fol. 30b; Landau, *Drushei ha-ẒLaḤ*, fol. 51b. It would appear that the custom of pairs of individuals all studying in one large study hall was unknown in our period. See below, chapter 20.

[32] Dubnow, ed., *Pinkas . . . Lita*, §§592–94, 881, 978, and 1004; Halperin, ed., *Takanot . . . Mehrin*, §§134–42, 511. In Frankfurt and Poznan, the communal rabbi was required to obtain the agreement of the "members of the *yeshiva*"—that is, the Torah scholars who served as rabbis and judges (*morei horaa*). Markus Horovitz, *Frankfurter Rabbinen*, I, p. 59; Lewin, *Landessynode*, p. 59. Halperin cites efforts in Tiktin to strengthen communal control over the granting of titles and to correspondingly limit the authority of the *rashei yeshiva* to do so; *Pinkas Vaad Arba Araẓot*, p. 463. For Eisenstadt see Wachstein, *Urkunden*, p. 164. The same situation held in Lithuania according to the sources cited above, and by the end of our period it was necessary to defend the local rabbi's authority in this matter by ruling that, in his absence, the lay communal leaders could not issue the title of "morenu"; *Pinkas . . . Lita*, §978, dated 1760–61.

[33] The *takanot* of Moravia make it clear that serving as a *rosh yeshiva* gave a rabbi a higher status than that of his fellows; Halperin, ed., *Takanot . . . Mehrin*, §§69, 137, 141, 161, 211, etc.

[34] Financial difficulties were significant. See the sources cited above, nn. 27 and 28. R. Judah Loeb Pukhovitser, *Derekh Ḥokhma*, §71, complains about householders who refuse to maintain students beyond the 15th of Shvat.

[35] Of course there were those who complained about this long intersession, but they were unable to effect change; see the remarks of MaHaRaL of Prague, R. Isaiah Horowitz, and others, cited in Assaf, *Mekorot*, I, pp. 48 and 65. The extent of student wandering from one *yeshiva* to another can be gauged from the *takanot* of Moravia which, from 1680–81 on, allowed communities to maintain *yeshivot* on alternate years or for only half the year, such that students were forced to travel from place to place; Halperin, ed., *Takanot . . . Mehrin*, §§388, 443, 569, 598, and 622.

[36] Halperin, ed., *Takanot . . . Mehrin*, §§468 and 508 (1696–97 to 1708–9); R. Judah Loeb Pukhovitser, cited in Assaf, *Mekorot*, I, p. 164; R. Berechiah Berakh b. Eliakim Getzel, *Zera Berakh ha-Shlishi, Brakhot*, fol. 30b.

Chapter 19. Stratification and Mobility

[1] Jewish tradition also contained such organic metaphors, as, for instance, in the words of Resh Lakish (*Ḥulin*, fol. 92a): "The people is like a grape vine. The branches are comparable to householders; the grape clusters are comparable to the unlearned; and the tendrils are to be compared with the

empty-headed in Israel." See also the discussion ad loc. as well as the passage in *Leviticus Raba* (30:12) in which the four species used on Tabernacles are compared to four types of Jews who, when bound together, atone for one another. Such images were cited and interpreted often in the homiletic literature; see, for instance, R. Ephraim of Lenczyca, *Olelot Efrayim*, part II, fol. 26 (Jerusalem: 1988–89, pp. 207f.)

2 See above, chapters 6 and 16.

3 This was especially common in the small German states of the seventeenth and eighteenth centuries where residence rights were dependent upon obtaining a charter (*kiyum*) from the authorities. For a similar situation in Bohemia, see R. Kestenberg-Gladstein, "Differences of Estates within Pre-Emancipation Jewry," *Journal of Jewish Studies* 5 (1954), pp. 156–66; 6 (1955), pp. 35–49.

4 This was the approach taken, in theory and in practice, toward the Court Jews. As R. Samuel Oppenheimer wrote to his sons in his will (Taglicht, *Nachlässe der wiener Juden*, p. 15):

> Second, it is my wish to be helpful to our brethren, the children of Israel, who are spread and scattered throughout the world. Since you [i.e., the sons] have connections at court, you must take care to work diligently for the good of the community . . . and not to be lazy in this regard. And may a thread of grace descend upon you for having worked for the general good. Kindness to others, whether to one or to many and whether they be rich or poor, is no trivial matter. . . .

Similar praise is showered upon R. Jacob Isaac Speyer in the Metz memorial book; Netter, *Vingt siècles*, p. 103. See Selma Stern, *Court Jew*, p. 194.

5 See above, chapter 11.

6 Kestenberg-Gladstein (above, n. 3) gives examples of this situation among Bohemian Jewry. Similar conditions undoubtedly applied in other places in the German lands. It should be noted that the distinction between resident and stranger was created not only by the licensing methods of the secular governments. The same distinction applied even where the residence privilege was obtained directly through the Jewish ruling institutions; cf. chapter 12.

7 The factual basis for this analysis is provided above, chapter 11.

8 See n. 9, below.

9 The instability of wealth was one of the most common motifs in the ethical literature of these generations, as the following citations illustrate:

> Does any man have a guarantee that his wealth will remain forever? . . . As we see with our own eyes, the world turns on its head—those who were on the bottom rise above, and *vice versa*. This is the nature of the world, that nothing remains stable; rather everything is in constant

> flux and change. In an instant the rain passes and is over. By its nature, [the world] is meant to change and is acquired through change.

R. Abraham Horowitz, *Yesh Noḥalim*, fol. 1b–2a. [The last sentence is a play on a rabbinic maxim. Cf. *Bava Meẓi'a*, fol. 45b.—*tr.*] Similarly R. Ezekiel Landau: "Who has not seen great wealthy men, burghers who became completely impoverished?" (*Drushei ha-ẒLaḤ*, fol. 36c); and "We see that wealth is not preserved forever, and in general the children of the wealthy are not themselves wealthy" (ibid., fol. 36c–d, and cf. R. Joseph Stadthagen, *Divrei Zikaron* (Amsterdam: 1705), fol. 1a; R. *Ẓvi Ashkenazi, Responsa Ḥakham Ẓvi*, §144). Worries about the instability of wealth as well as faith in the possibility of rapid advance fill the consciousness of Glückel of Hameln; see especially pp. 74–79 (English, pp. 42–45), and cf. the passages cited in this regard by Ḥ. H. Ben-Sasson, "Wealth and Poverty in the Teaching of Reb Ephraim of Lenczyca," pp. 153, 156, 162–64. Schnee, *Die Hoffinanz und der moderne Staat*, showed that most Court Jews rose from low status.

[10] The laws affecting Priests are spelled out, in the order mentioned in the text, in *Shulḥan Arukh, Even ha-Ezer*, §6; *Oraḥ Ḥayim*, §128; *Yore De'a*, §305; and *Oraḥ Ḥayim*, §135.

[11] A clear example of this is provided by the family of R. Isaiah Horowitz, author of *Shnei Luḥot ha-Brit*. His father, R. Abraham Horowitz, took a clear stand against the privileges of pedigree, arguing that "the son brings honor to the father and not *vice versa*"; *Yesh Noḥalim*, fol. 3b. On a practical level he argued against paying attention to pedigree in choosing mates; ibid., fol. 42a. R. Isaiah himself took a similar stand, arguing that the only use of pedigree was to encourage sons to emulate their parents; *Shnei Luḥot ha-Brit*, fol. 346a, comment on Leviticus 26:42: "I shall remember my covenant with Jacob." But R. Isaiah's son, R. Sheftel Horowitz, the third generation in the dynasty, already exhibits a clear tendency to emphasize his pedigree. He began the will that he left for his sons with a listing of his pedigree. True, he tried to rationalize this by noting that the chaos created by the pogroms of 1648–49 required every family to behave in this fashion, but his rhetoric, and especially the ending, demonstrate the positive value that he ascribed to pedigree in its own right ("and you must command your children, and they theirs, forever, for God allows His presence to rest only upon the pedigreed of Israel"; end of *Yesh Noḥalim*, fol. 43b). He also saw in his pedigree a basis for a practical, legal claim. He warned his children against arguing with their congregations about anything "except whether you have the privilege of having rabbinical students, should the community not wish to allow this. . . . Proclaim your suffering publicly—that you wish to maintain a *yeshiva*, for this is your ancestral heritage"; ibid., fol. 44b. We might also note that R. Sheftel's book, *Vavei ha-Amudim*, is built for the most part of quotations from his father's book as well as those of other members of the Horowitz family (*Beit Avraham, Emek ha-Brakha*, and *Shefa Tal*). The tendency to establish dynasties of Torah scholars is clear and unquestionable here. There

are hints of a similar tendency in the Middle Ages in the writings of Rabenu Yitzḥak, the Tosafist, who was a great-grandson of RaSHI and a relative of Rabenu Tam and R. Samuel ben Meir [RaSHBaM]; see E. E. Urbach, *Toldot Baalei ha-Tosafot*, p. 195. From the latter period we can point to the family of R. Moses Sofer, who founded a true Torah dynasty.

[12] The halakhic authorities disagreed over whether pedigree should influence the choice of a cantor; see R. Jacob ben Asher, *Tur Oraḥ Ḥayim*, §53; *Prisha*, ad loc., citing R. Solomon Luria; *Responsa* of R. Solomon Luria, §20; R. Moses Mat, *Responsa Mate Moshe*, §60; R. David ha-Levi, *Turei Zahav, Shulḥan Arukh, Oraḥ Ḥayim*, §53.3. Even those who argued for pedigree felt only that it should be given some weight, not that it should provide an absolute advantage.

[13] See chapter 9, n. 39. Complaints about the purchase of rabbinical office do not mean that someone unworthy could attain the position through wealth. The complainants objected to *any* linkage between the selection of a rabbi and monetary considerations. In the eighteenth century, however, the nature of the complaint changed. By that time we find the office purchased not from the *kehilot* but from the government authorities. See Dubnow, ed., *Pinkas . . . Lita*, §913; R. Jacob Emden's remarks in Halperin, ed., *Pinkas Vaad Arba Arazot*, p. 407; R. Berechiah Berakh b. Eliakim Getzel, *Zera Berakh ha-Shlishi, Brakhot*, fol. 29b–c. Appointment of rabbis through influence with the government was also to be found in Germany at that time; S. Stern, *Der preussische Staat und die Juden*, I, p. 150.

[14] Thus, for example, R. Samuel Edels (MaHaRSHA') and his *yeshiva* were supported by the scholar's wealthy mother-in-law; see Samuel Abba Horodezky, *Shem mi-Shmuel* (Drohobycz: 1895), p. 15.

[15] It was not only the most radical critics of the rabbis who made such claims; see above, n. 13. R. David ha-Levi, for example, distinguished between rabbis who depended on their rabbinical salary for their daily livelihood and "those wealthy ones who took large fees for issuing bills of divorce and arranging *ḥalizot* [the ceremony that freed a widow from marrying her levir]"; *Turei Zahav, Even ha-Ezer*, §154: *Seder ha-Get*, n. 2. Testimony about heads of *yeshivot* who became wealthy from the presents they received appears in R. Joel Sirkes, *Responsa Bayit Ḥadash*, §52: "A *rosh yeshiva* may accept and derive his living from presents while he is poor, and he may continue to do so until he becomes wealthy." In my opinion the notion of wealth here should not be limited to the relatively modest amounts which, in formal terms, prevented one from accepting charity; there is no indication of such a restricted interpretation in the *responsum*. Quite to the contrary, the thrust of the *responsum* is that wealth would earn the *rosh yeshiva* respect and obedience from his community. This is similar to R. Nathan Nata Hannover's remarks in *Yeven Mezula* about how one should honor a *rosh yeshiva* with presents; see Assaf, *Mekorot*, I, p. 110: "They would offer large salaries to their *rosh yeshiva* so that he could conduct the *yeshiva* without [monetary] worries, and he could make learning his profession." Cf. also ibid., p. 112.

[16] "Whoever cannot study because he lacks the necessary background or because he is too distracted, shall support others who can"; *Shulḥan Arukh, Yore De'a,* §246.1. "This shall be counted as if he had studied himself"; *Tur, Yore De'a,* §246. "One individual can arrange with another that the one will study Torah while the other earns a living, and they will divide the merit between them"; ReMA', ad loc. This idea was cited by many ethical and homiletical works. See, for example, R. Judah Loeb Pukhovitser, *Derekh Ḥokhma,* fol. 25c; R. Ezekiel Landau, *Drushei ha-ẒLaḤ,* fol. 49b and 51d.

[17] See S. Stern, *The Court Jew,* pp. 226–29, and Schnee, *Die Hoffinanz und der moderne Staat,* III, pp. 191f.

[18] Throughout her memoirs we find Glückel of Hameln assessing the economic worth of her contemporaries. In this she is typical of the openness with which the financial position of everyone was assessed in this society. On the amount of dowries, see the assumption by R. Ezekiel Katzenellenbogen, *Responsa Kneset Yeḥezkel,* §79, that "certainly everyone in the community must know how much dowry and support he gave him."

[19] Typical is the warning by R. Abraham Horowitz: "Take care to honor scholars each in accordance with his status and position. . . . Our rabbis of blessed memory said that Rabbi [Judah] would honor the wealthy [and that] Rabbi Akiva would honor the wealthy, and so must you . . ."; *Yesh Noḥalim,* fol. 34a. Similar is the wording of a *takana* relating to the rules of precedence governing the calling of judges and rabbis to the Torah at the fair of Thorn: "And so with respect to other honors—each must go in order of his importance"; Lewin, *Die Landessynode,* p. 109.

[20] Dubnow, ed., *Pinkas . . . Lita,* §602; Halperin, ed., *Takanot . . . Mehrin,* §§104–5, 340, 342, 391 ("Arguments, quarrels, and disputes multiply when people say that they are not called to the Torah at the point appropriate to their status. . . . Representatives should not be called to the Torah at all in order not to arouse envy among them"), 410, 425, 433, 453, 471, 488, and 499.

[21] Halperin, ed., *Takanot . . . Mehrin,* §434, can provide us with a good example of the complexity of such casuistry.

> Those communities which do not have a rabbi or *rosh medina* may not give the sixth *aliya* to anyone who does not hold the title of *morenu.* A person with this title who is a taxpayer has precedence over someone with this title who is not, except for a *dayan* [judge] who has precedence over someone with the title *morenu* who is not a taxpayer. But a *rosh medina* is similar to the judge of the community and has precedence over him.

Here we see three bases of stratification in conflict: learning (*morenu*), wealth (taxpayers), and political power (judge and *rosh medina*). See also §§513 and 526 (where age also enters into it: "and if the head of the community is forty years old").

[22] In 1739 Polish authorities fixed rules for the seating of rabbis who were district representatives, after disputes broke out "about who would sit where and who would serve as chair"; Halperin, ed., *Pinkas Vaad Arba Arazot*, pp. 324f.

[23] See chapter 17.

[24] See, for example, Dubnow, ed., *Pinkas . . . Lita*, §881 and p. 295; Halperin, ed., *Takanot . . . Mehrin*, §§323, 377, 439, 469, 476, 494, and 587.

[25] See chapter 14.

Part III. The Beginnings of Breakdown

Chapter 20. The Impact of Historical Events

[1] On the rabbinate, see chapter 9; on artisans, chapters 3 and 16.

[2] See chapter 18.

[3] Our period is especially rich in literary creativity in the fields of Halakha, homiletics, and Kabbala. The research of G. Scholem and his students in the area of Kabbala proves that, despite the high incidence of formulaic repetitiveness in its writings, this spiritual discipline also left room for fresh development, innovation, and creativity. If scholars have not been able to identify substantial development in the other areas, and especially in the area of Halakha, this may indicate only that they have not yet applied the correct methodology to the problem. See my review of E. E. Urbach, *Baalei ha-Tosafot*, pp. 10ff.

[4] See Dubnow, ed., *Pinkas . . . Lita*, §§452, 460, 484–85, 505, and 516, and chapter 12, n. 25. On the participation of *kehilot* outside Poland and Lithuania, see also Heinrich Graetz, *Geschichte der Juden*, 3rd ed., X, pp. 72–74.

[5] R. Nathan Nata Hannover is especially noteworthy for his realistic understanding of events in his *Yeven Mezula*, but even his conclusions are limited to the merely ethical; cf. *Yeven Mezula* (Cracow: 5656 [1895–96]), pp. 5–6 and 60. See also the remarks of R. Sabbetai Katz, *Megilat Eyfa* (reprinted in the documentary appendix to Halperin, ed., *Beit Yisra'el be-Folin*, II, p. 253), and especially those of R. Berechiah Berakh b. Isaac Eisik, *Zera Berakh*, II, Introduction. That latter work provides a detailed list of contemporary sins that in his view caused the tragic events. As for the imposition of penitential prayers and fasts—see Halperin, ed., *Pinkas Vaad Arba Arazot*, p. 78, and the literature cited there. For sumptuary legislation, see Dubnow, ed., *Pinkas . . . Lita*, §§463–67.

[6] In 1665 Zvi canceled the fast of the tenth of Tevet, and in 1666 he canceled even that of the ninth of Av. He declared these to be henceforth holidays, days of rejoicing, and added to them the twenty-third of Tamuz as a *shabat shabaton*—i.e., a supreme Sabbath. See R. Jacob Sasportas, *Sefer*

Ẓiẓat Novel Ẓvi, pp. 2, 49, 76–77, 129–30; and cf. Graetz, *Geschichte der Juden*, 3rd ed., X, pp. 210, 217–18. See also G. Scholem, *Shabtai Ẓvi ve-ha-Tnu'a ha-Shabta'it bi-Ymei Ḥayav* [Sabbetai Ẓvi and the Sabbatean Movement during his Lifetime] (Tel-Aviv: 1967), index, s.v. *"bitul ẓomot"* [English edition: *Sabbatai Ṣevi*, index, s.v. "Fasts, abolishment of"—*tr.*].

[7] This is clear from contemporary testimonies. It is sufficient to mention here only Nathan of Gaza's letter, *Sefer Ẓiẓat Novel Ẓvi*, pp. 7–12. Cf. Scholem, *Shabtai Ẓvi*, pp. 217–35 [English: *Sabbatai Ṣevi*, pp. 267–90—*tr.*].

[8] In what follows I am summarizing the research of G. Scholem and his students and trying to place it within the general context of a description of the traditional society. It seems to me, however, that this more general framework demands a somewhat changed estimation of the role of the Sabbatean heresy within the overall pattern. See G. Scholem, "Redemption through Sin" [in Hebrew], *Kneset* 2 (1937) [English version, tr. Hillel Halkin, in Scholem, *The Messianic Idea in Judaism and other Essays on Jewish Spirituality* (New York: 1971), pp. 78–141]; idem, "The Sabbatean Movement in Poland" [in Hebrew]; idem, *Major Trends in Jewish Mysticism*, 3rd ed., pp. 287ff., as well as the extensive bibliography offered there, pp. 434–36 and 439–40.

[9] For a detailed exposition, see Meir Balaban, *Le-Toldot ha-Tnu'a ha-Frankit* [Toward a History of the Frankist Movement] (Tel Aviv: 1933–34 to 1934–35), as well as the analysis offered by Scholem, "The Sabbatean Movement in Poland," pp. 64ff.

[10] See Scholem, "The Sabbatean Movement in Poland," pp. 61–64, and especially the remarks of Joseph Weiss, "The Beginnings of Hasidism," *Zion* 16 (1950–51), pp. 49–58.

[11] See Scholem, "The Sabbatean Movement in Poland," p. 41.

[12] See now Scholem's incisive remarks, *Shabtai Ẓvi*, pp. 3–7 [*Sabbatai Ṣevi*, pp. 1–8—*tr.*].

[13] Scholem did not take the importance of this strengthening of communications between various sections of the people into consideration in his analysis of the difference between the impact of Sabbateanism and that of all preceding movements.

[14] See Scholem, "The Sabbatean Movement in Poland," and now in his book, *Shabtai Ẓvi*, pp. 1f. and 69–74 [*Sabbatai Ṣevi*, pp. 1f. and 86ff.—*tr.*].

[15] See especially Scholem, *Major Trends*, pp. 284ff., 295–99; idem, *Sabbetai Ẓvi*, pp. 18–52 [*Sabbatai Ṣevi*, pp. 22–66—*tr.*].

[16] See the remarks of R. Jacob Sasportas, *Ẓiẓat Novel Ẓvi*, pp. 14f., 18, and 98; and see Tishby's summary, ibid., pp. xxx—xxxi.

[17] See the remarks of Yitzhak Fritz Baer in his German study, *Galut*, pp. 90–92 [Hebrew edition, pp. 95–98; English edition, pp. 106–8].

[18] See Scholem, *Major Trends in Jewish Mysticism*, pp. 273–78; I. Tishby, *Torat ha-Ra ve-ha-Klipa be-Kabalat ha-ARI* (Jerusalem: 1941–42), pp. 113f. We should also mention that S. R. Hirsch already defined the kabbalistic approach characteristic of this period as "magical mechanism"; *Igrot Ẓafon*.

Neunzehn Briefe über Judenthum (Altona: 1836), p. 92 [English translation: *The Nineteen Letters of Ben Uziel* (New York: 1899), p. 187].

[19] A good example of this is provided by comparing R. Abraham Horowitz's *Emek Brakha* (Amsterdam: 1728–29; new edition, Jerusalem: 1969–70) with the annotations added by Horowitz's son, Isaiah, author of *Shnei Luḥot ha-Brit*. While the father explained the laws of the blessings in halakhic fashion, the son added a kabbalistic rationale in each case. In the father's remarks, the various precepts are ranked in accordance with their halakhic importance; for the son, all were equivalent.

[20] G. Scholem, "Tradition und Neuschöpfung im Ritus der Kabbalisten," *Eranos Jahrbuch* 19 (1950), pp. 121–80 [English translation: Gershom G. Scholem, *On the Kabbalah and Its Symbolism* (New York: 1965), chapter 4: "Tradition and New Creation in the Ritual of the Kabbalists"]. R. Sheftel Horowitz remarked concerning his father, R. Isaiah, that "he had established more than four hundred new laws"; *Vavei Amudim*, Introduction to *Shnei Luḥot ha-Brit*, fol. 2b. R. Ezekiel Landau says in his typically critical fashion: "I say that because of his great, holy piety, this scholar fulfilled the maxim 'He who loves the commandments will not be sated by the commandments' [cf. *Midrash Raba*, Ecclesiastes 5: 8–9]"; *Noda bi-Yhuda*, 2nd collection, *Yore De'a*, §123.

[21] *Shulḥan Arukh, Oraḥ Ḥayim*, §60.4, and R. Abraham Gombiner, *Magen Avraham*, n. 3: "[*Kavana* is required] specifically with a biblical commandment. Obligations instituted by the rabbis do not require *kavana*." For another type of distinction that eased the requirement for *kavana*, cf. *Shulḥan Arukh, Oraḥ Ḥayim*, §475.4, and *Magen Avraham*, n. 14.

[22] Scholem, *Major Trends*, pp. 276–78; Tishby, *Torat ha-Ra*, loc. cit., above n. 18.

[23] The emergence of this kabbalistic elite is observable already in the first generation of popularization. R. Jacob Horowitz, brother to R. Isaiah and a kabbalist like him, waged a polemical battle against those who claimed that one was obligated to observe only that which is found in the Talmud

> while whoever does not wish to observe [what is commanded in the Zohar] and the other books of the pietists . . . commits no sin. In fact, though he may not be punishable at the hands of man, [such a transgressor] is guilty in the eyes of heaven. . . . Our holy rabbis and those who follow them, of blessed memory, did not make these obligatory and punishable for the entire community of Israel, great and small, exactly for this reason—because the majority of the community is incapable of living up to these [demands]. . . . But for someone capable of standing in the palace of the king . . . the yoke hangs around his neck.

See his comments to *Yesh Noḥalim*, fol. 26a.

[24] See R. Isaiah Horowitz, *Shnei Luḥot ha-Brit, Shvu'ot*, fol. 182b; *Vavei ha-Amudim, Amud ha-Tora*, chapter 5, fol. 10a–b; R. Judah Loeb Pukhovitser,

Kne Ḥokhma, fol. 13f.; *Mishmeret ha-Kodesh*, fol. 2b–c. There are complaints about the spread of Kabbala among the masses (e.g., R. Berechiah Berakh b. Isaac Eisik, *Zera Berakh*, II, Introduction), but these were directed only at unworthy students. Study of the Kabbala continued to be perceived as an exalted level of Torah study.

[25] R. Judah Loeb Pukhovitser views the establishment of houses of study for those who study the Torah "li-shmah" as superior to support for *yeshiva* students; *Derekh Ḥokhma*, fol. 26a. We have detailed information concerning the *kloyz* in Brody, at least some of whose members were engaged in kabbalistic study; see N. M. Gelber, *Toldot Yehudei Broyde* [History of the Jews of Brody] [=*Arim ve-Imahot be-Yisra'el* (Major Jewish Communities), ed. J. L. Maimon, VI] (Jerusalem: 1955), pp. 62ff. From several points of view, one can see the Gaon of Vilna as this type of reclusive scholar; see Israel Klausner, *Vilna bi-Tkufat ha-Gaon* (Jerusalem: 1942), pp. 16–20. See now also A. Shoḥet, "Study Societies in the Sixteenth through Eighteenth Centuries in Palestine, Poland-Lithuania, and Germany" [in Hebrew], *Ha-Ḥinukh* (5716 [1955–56]), pp. 404–18.

[26] See the comments of the ReMA' to *Shulḥan Arukh, Yore De'a*, §246.1: "A man may strike a deal with another to the effect that the one engage in Torah study and the other provide a livelihood, and they divide the reward."

[27] This concept appears repeatedly in the writings of R. Judah Loeb Pukhovitser with regard to the Talmudic remark, *Ktubot*, fol. 111b, which shows the *am ha-areẓ* how to cleave to the *shkhina* (divine presence) through cleaving to the *talmid ḥakham*.

> The reason for this would seem to be what is written in Elijah di Vidas's *Reshit Ḥokhma* and in Abraham Azulai's *Ḥesed le-Avraham* that one can cleave to the *shkhina* only through the aspect of the soul called *neshama*, and not with the *neshama* unless with the aspect of the soul called *ru'aḥ*, and not with the *ru'aḥ* unless with the aspect of the soul called *nefesh*. Now only the scholars of the Law accede to *ru'aḥ* and *neshama* . . . and therefore if he cleaves to a scholar and the scholar cleaves to the *shkhina*, he too is linked to the *shkhina* and can live.

Kvod Ḥakhamim, fol. 46b, and cf. *Derekh Ḥokhma*, fol. 25b.

[28] Here are a few examples. R. Moses Isserles mentions that drinking whiskey in a gentile's house was customarily permitted "in these lands" even on a regular basis; *Shulḥan Arukh, Yore De'a*, §114.1). Even R. Abraham Horowitz only suggested, in this matter, that his children be among those who adopt a stringent position (*yihyu beyn ha-maḥmirin*); *Yesh Noḥalin*, fol. 35b. But R. Benjamin Wolf b. Mattathiah saw this as a "serious criminal matter" even though he knew that "most of our brother Jews" do it; *Tohorat ha-Kodesh*, part II, fol. 40b. Trading in gentile wine (*stam yeinam*) was the basis of the livelihood for many in the eighteenth century; R. Judah Loeb Margalioth, *Responsa Pri Tvu'a*, §1. But the author of *Mishmeret ha-Kodesh*

warns that it is forbidden; cf. under Laws of Purifying Utensils. Taking interest in accordance with the formula known as *heter iska* was accepted by both rabbis and laymen; see above, chapter 8. But R. Benjamin Wolf b. Mattathiah suggests "not to accept any formula as allowing the charging of interest"; *Tohorat ha-Kodesh*, II, fol. 29b. So also the author of *Mishmeret ha-Kodesh*; see under the Laws of Interest. As we have seen, R. Joel Sirkes saw it as absolutely permissible to take a fee for acting as a judge. R. Isaiah Horowitz customarily accepted such fees in his youth but changed his policy in his later years; see the testimony of his son in *Vavei Amudim*, fol. 32a. Following him, R. Judah Loeb Pukhovitser argued against allowing it; *Divrei Ḥakhamim*, fol. 49a. R. Berechiah Berakh b. Eliakim Getzel condemns rabbis guilty of this crime to be cast into boiling liquids; *Zera Berakh ha-Shlishi, Brakhot*, fol. 14b. Such examples demonstrate the absence of any realistic contact between the ethicists and life as it was. In this they differed from the scholarly leadership of earlier generations.

Chapter 21. Historic Turning Points

1 In using the expression "portatives Vaterland" Heine was referring to the Bible, to which he attributed the power to preserve the Jewish people; *Geständnisse, Sämtliche Werke* (Leipzig and Vienna: 1898), VI, p. 58.

2 For an example of the transmission of the concept of communal institutions from place to place, see the memoirs of Aron Isak, *Denkwürdigkeiten 1730–1817*. Neither a scholar nor a Hasid, this man whose relation to Judaism was merely traditional became the "founder of the [Jewish] community of Sweden" as he calls himself, because he was the first Jew to come there, and he attracted an entire group of people looking for a livelihood or merely for adventure. Even though these people were from the margins of Jewish society and the period (the second half of the eighteenth century) was the beginning of the breakdown of traditional society, they organized themselves in accordance with the Jewish organizational model of their homeland, Germany. Within a brief period they had a synagogue and a cemetery, had attracted a rabbi, and had many quarrels concerning these institutions.

3 See above, especially in the chapters concerning the *kehila* and the supra-*kehila* institutions (chapters 9–13), where I was forced to distinguish between various types of organization. I could have made similar distinctions in other regards, but the purpose of the present study was to emphasize the common characteristics of the sub-units within the Ashkenazi-Polish world.

4 We shall treat the actual connection between the general European phenomenon and the development within Jewish society in chapters 23 and 24.

5 Gershom Scholem commented on the parallel between Sabbateanism and the deviant sects within the Pravoslavic church, but he did so very cautiously; "The Sabbatean Movement in Poland," p. 59. Even if there were proof of direct contact between the two movements, the most one can see here

is fertilization and not influence in the sense of the direct penetration of ideas or the transmission of means of expression from one camp to the other.

[6] See Dubnow, *Toldot ha-Ḥasidut*, pp. 8–24. B. Dinur developed this approach systematically and with great emphasis, in his article "The Beginnings of Hasidism and Its Social and Messianic Elements" [in Hebrew], *Zion* 8–10, now reprinted in his volume *Be-Mifne ha-Dorot*, pp. 83–227.

[7] R. Judah Loeb Pukhovitser, *Derekh Ḥokhma*, §71; R. Berechiah Berakh b. Eliakim Getzel, *Zera Berakh ha-Shlishi, Brakhot*, fol. 30b. The phenomenon is not restricted to Poland. A *takana* of Moravia warned similarly in 1708–9: "Rabbis shall not accept students for a fee"; Halperin, ed., *Takanot . . . Mehrin*, §505.

[8] Dubnow, ed., *Pinkas . . . Lita*, §§914 and 961. For instances of rabbinical office purchased from gentile authorities, see ibid., §913; R. Berechiah Berakh b. Eliakim Getzel, *Zera Berakh ha-Shlishi, Brakhot*, fol. 29b–c; Halperin, ed., *Pinkas Vaad Arba Araẓot*, p. 407; and cf. Dinur, *Be-Mifne ha-Dorot*, pp. 100–110; Assaf, "Toward a History of the Rabbinate in Germany, Poland, and Lithuania" [in Hebrew], reprinted in his *Be-Ohalei Yaakov* (Jerusalem: 1946–47), pp. 27–65.

[9] In 1666–67, the *takanot* of Lithuania insisted on eleven years of study after marriage for the title *morenu*, and two years for the title *ḥaver*. The latter title was given to "a respected and famous man of proper morals" (i.e., to someone without knowledge of the Torah) only on rare occasions; Dubnow, ed., *Pinkas . . . Lita*, §§592f. A regulation of 1694–95 seems to mean that the title *ḥaver* required two years of study or the passage of six years without study after marriage, and the title *morenu* required eight years with continuing study or ten years without; ibid., §881. At this point the *takanot* were still trying to withhold the privileges associated with these titles from those who received them by reason of mere longevity, but during the first half of the eighteenth century all such distinctions disappeared. Note the language of the *takana* of 1760–61, ibid., §1004:

> The title *morenu* should not be given to any bridegroom during the marriage ceremony. Nor should the title be given to anyone who does not set aside time to study each day or, in the case of a wealthy individual, he must be at least ten [!] years after marriage and have donated at least a thousand *thäler* and must be familiar with books.

There is also a tendency to take the right to grant such titles out of the hands of rabbis, or at least to make this dependent on the prior agreement of the lay leaders; ibid., at the end of the *takana*, and §978; and cf. Halperin's comment, *Pinkas Vaad Arba Araẓot*, p. 463; and Wachstein, *Urkunden*, p. 164. In Moravia as well, the title of *morenu* became a mere honorific (Halperin, ed., *Takanot . . . Mehrin*, §461), but it seems that matters did not reach quite as low a state there as in Lithuania. As late as 1721–22 we find the Moravian authorities reconfirming *takanot* that maintained standards regarding these titles; *Takanot . . . Mehrin*, §651. One might note that the granting of titles was one of the legitimate sources of income for rabbis; *Pinkas Vaad Arba Araẓot*, p. 249; Wachstein, *Urkunden*, pp. 18f.

Chapter 22. The Transition to Hasidism

[1] G. Scholem, "The Two First Testimonies on the Relations between Hasidic Groups and the Baal Shem Tov," *Tarbiẓ* 20 (1948–49), pp. 228–40.

[2] Ibid., pp. 232f.

[3] B. Dinur, "The Beginnings of Hasidism and Its Social and Messianic Foundations," *Be-Mifne ha-Dorot*, pp. 159ff.; Joseph Weiss, "Beginnings of Hasidism."

[4] Cf. Dinur, "Beginnings of Hasidism."

[5] Though there is not yet an adequate biography of the BESHT based on a critical evaluation of the traditions and testimonies concerning him, the ecstatic nature of his personality is not in doubt; cf. G. Scholem, *Major Trends*, pp. 349–50. [See now G. Scholem, "The Historical Figure of R. Israel Baal Shem Tov" (in Hebrew), *Molad* 144–45 (Av-Elul, 5620), reprinted in an expanded, corrected version in Scholem, *Dvarim be-Go* (Explications and Implications. Writings on Jewish Heritage and Renaissance) (Tel Aviv: 1975), pp. 287–324.—*YK*]

[6] On this, see S. Dubnow, *Toldot ha-Ḥasidut*.

[7] Students of Hasidism differ greatly over the religious meaning of the movement and its basic tendencies. It is, of course, not for me to decide the basic issue: Was the movement a mystical or a contemplative one? The use of clearly defined terminology introduced into the discussion by Scholem and his students is gradually bringing about the identification of the various religious trends within Hasidism. But when it comes to distinguishing Hasidism from the movements that preceded it, none of these distinctions are crucial. See G. Scholem, *Major Trends*, p. 325; idem, "Devekuth, or Communion with God," *Review of Religion* 14 (1949–50), pp. 115–39 [reprinted in *The Messianic Idea in Judaism*, pp. 203–27, and, in an edited Hebrew version, in *Dvarim be-Go*, pp. 325–50]; Joseph Weiss, "Beginnings of Hasidism."

[8] This attitude is implicit in the entire Hasidic approach. It can be seen clearly, for example, in the words of R. Jacob Joseph of Polonnoye, author of the *Toldot Yaakov Yosef* (Korets: 1779–80), commenting on the Talmudic debate between R. Yoḥanan and Resh Lakish (*Sanhedrin*, fol. 111a) over the verse in Isaiah 5:14: "Assuredly Sheol has opened wide its gullet and parted its jaws in a measureless gape." Whereas Resh Lakish interpreted the verse to mean that one who failed to observe even a single commandment was doomed to hell, R. Yoḥanan understood it to mean that one who had observed only a single commandment would be saved from hell. R. Jacob Joseph comments (*Ben Porat Yosef*, Introduction [Korets: 1780–81]):

> If one arrives at the unification of Him, may He be blessed, through a single commandment he is saved from hell, whereas the other authority [i.e., Resh Lakish] states that even had one fulfilled all of the commandments and omitted only one, that particular commandment being the one through which he could have achieved *dvekut* (which is the intended goal), that person is not saved from hell. Thus, each states his view but they do not disagree.

There are many similar statements in R. Jacob Joseph's works; cf. e.g., *Toldot Yaakov Yosef, Va-Yishlaḥ,* where the author argues that the single commandment upon which Habakkuk saw the entire Torah as depending was "faith which is *dvekut.*"

[9] This attitude is clear in many places in the writings of R. Jacob Joseph of Polonnoye. To cite one example (*Toldot Yaakov Yosef, Va-Yakhel,* Exodus 35):

> For it is known what is written in the Zohar, that the scholar is called "Sabbath" while the masses are called "workdays" [*yemei ha-maase*]. . . . There is a [necessary] connection and link between the workdays and the Sabbath; indeed, one cannot exist without the other. In the same way, the masses of people cannot be saved [*eyn takana la-hamonei ha-am*] without the scholar who at least will lend them a supporting arm. It goes without saying, therefore, that if they were to spurn the *Ẓadik,* they would be entirely lost.

(In this work, the "scholar" [*talmid ḥakham*] is that true scholar who has achieved *dvekut* or communion with God.) See also *Toldot Yaakov Yosef,* at the end of the commentary to the portion *Ẓav.*

[10] See *Toldot Yaakov Yosef, Breshit,* who notes the mutual interdependence of the masses and the scholar but rejects the notion that they are equal. This idea occurs often in his writings.

[11] Some students of the movement have consequently tended to argue that the erosion of the distinction between sacred and profane was the essence of Hasidic teaching. See especially S. Schechter, "The Chassidim," *Studies in Judaism,* 1st series (Philadelphia: 1896), pp. 25f., and G. Scholem, *Major Trends in Jewish Mysticism,* p. 347.

[12] The *mitnagdim,* the opponents of Hasidism, complained specifically about this in the Brody circular: "And they pray after the time designated for the recital of the *Shma* and the *Tfila*"; Dubnow, *Toldot ha-Ḥasidut,* p. 120. On the motives for this change, see Graetz, *Geschichte,* 2nd ed., XI, p. 105.

[13] Dubnow, *Toldot ha-Ḥasidut,* pp. 120f. (who cites proof that members of the Brody *kloyz* had in fact done so). See also Benjamin Wolf b. Mattathiah, *Tohorat ha-Kodesh,* I, fol. 36a, who reports in the name of "a great man and pious man that it is permissible for anyone in our land to pray according to

the Sephardic rite." The author himself feels that this should be allowed only if there were ten people "who were worthy of deciding for themselves."

[14] The circulars of the *mitnagdim* expressed their fear of a split created by the new customs: "They build altars for themselves to separate themselves from the holy congregation; they form separate prayer groups"; Dubnow, *Toldot ha-Ḥasidut,* p. 120, and cf. p. 116, as well as Dov Baer ben Samuel, *Shivḥei ha-BESHT* [In Praise of the Baal Shem Tov], Samuel A. Horodezky, ed., 2nd edition (Tel-Aviv: 1959–60), p. 95 [*In Praise of the Baal Shem Tov,* tr. and ed. Dan Ben-Amos and Jerome R. Mintz (Bloomington, Ind.: 1970), p. 111].

[15] Chone Shmeruk (Szmeruk) recently investigated "The Social Implications of Hasidic Slaughter" [in Hebrew] *Zion* 20 (1955), pp. 47–72. Shmeruk erred in his description of the order and development of events. It was not the *mitnagdim* who first forbade eating meat from animals slaughtered by Hasidim. Rather, it was the Hasidim who refrained from eating meat slaughtered by non-Hasidim on the grounds that the slaughter was not *kosher* unless performed with honed knives. The Brody circular of 1742–43 complained about the Hasidim: "They insist that the slaughtering knives be honed, something not found in the Talmud or any of the early or late authorities"; Dubnow, *Toldot ha-Ḥasidut,* p. 120. This is also seen in the words of R. Abraham Katzenellenbogen in 1783–84: "The Hasidim have banded together . . . and find fault with our sacred practices and criticize our knives . . . and in their haughtiness they invalidate, and do not wish to eat of, meat slaughtered with *kosher* knives"; ibid., p. 155. Note especially the words of R. Shneor Zalman of Lyady in his *Shulḥan Arukh, Yore De'a* (5611 [1850–51]), fol. 23a: "Hence, God forbid that we [i.e., the Hasidim] find fault with communities which are not rigorous in this regard . . . and God forbid that you [i.e., the *mitnagdim*] go harshly with those communities which are." He is not trying to justify the Hasidic practice in response to perceived opposition, as Shmeruk would have it (p. 67), but rather to allow for both methods. The ban issued by the *mitnagdim* was a reaction to that of the Hasidim. The question is: Why did the Hasidim introduce this innovation? Shmeruk stressed a link between the use of honed knives and the belief in transmigration connected with ritual slaughter. Though I do not feel that his argument is convincing, there is no question that he did demonstrate that the Hasidim were interested in total control over the realm of ritual slaughter, and their insistence on this new stringency of honed knives was a means toward this end.

[16] Hasidism's attitude to Torah study is quite complicated, and has not yet been analyzed systematically. The *mitnagdim* claimed that the Hasidim mocked such study; see, e.g., the Brody circular, Dubnow, *Toldot ha-Ḥasidut,* p. 120.

[17] See G. Scholem, *Major Trends,* p. 334.

[18] Solomon Maimon, *Geshichte des eigenen Lebens,* pp. 97–110 [*An Autobiography,* pp. 151–75; Hadas's edition, pp. 49–55—tr.].

[19] There were, of course, a number of functionaries at the *Ẓadik*'s court —his familiars and messengers, agents and *shamashim*, and the like—but these were not intermediaries.

[20] Typical is the tradition mentioned by R. Jacob Joseph of Polonnoye, author of *Toldot Yaakov Yosef*, who remembered that "it was easier for him [i.e., the BESHT] to deliver a halakhic discourse than to say one *Shmone Esre* [the basic prayer of supplication at each service]"; *Shivḥei ha-BESHT*, ed. Horodezky, p. 65.

[21] Young men, that is youths still living with their in-laws, like Solomon Maimon, seem to have been the most likely, because of their age and economic position, to be attracted by Hasidism. Maimon himself says: "Young people forsook their parents, wives, and children and went in groups to visit these great leaders"; *Geshichte des eigenen Lebens*, p. 100 [*An Autobiography*, p. 154]. Similarly the *takanot of* Cracow (1786) mention "young men" as bearers of Hasidism; Dubnow, *Toldot ha-Ḥasidut*, III, pp. 450f.

[22] See, for example, the remarks of R. Nathan, R. Naḥman of Bratslav's chief assistant, after the latter's death (Nathan b. Naphthali Herz of Nemirov, *Yemei MaHaRaNaT* [New York: 1969–70], fol. 46a):

> And afterwards I came to my home with a broken heart, depressed as an orphan with no father. . . . God, may He be blessed, caused it that I was forced to undergo seven days of mourning, for just before I came home my little brother died in my father's house. . . . And similarly last year when the *Ẓadik*, the rabbi of Berditchev, died, the same thing happened to me, that I was forced to conduct seven days of mourning because of the same sort of event, and may this also be for the good [*ve-gam zu le-tova*]. Blessed be God who makes everything good at its appointed time, for it was certainly proper to conduct the seven days of mourning over holy *Ẓadikim* such as these.

[23] See, e.g., *Toldot Yaakov Yosef, Breshit*, which weighs the possibility of exempting someone who achieved *dvekut* from the commandment of procreation. The language of the text proves that consideration of the question had been prompted by real personal experience. See also Dov Baer b. Samuel, *Shivḥei ha-BESHT*, pp. 80 and 164.

[24] Dov Baer b. Samuel, *Shivḥei ha-BESHT*, pp. 109, 111f.; Dubnow, *Toldot ha-Ḥasidut*, pp. 300f.

Chapter 23. The Emergence of the Neutral Society

[1] For details, see chapter 24.

[2] See chapter 4, n. 12.

[3] See chapter 7. I am returning to the question of the Court Jew here in

order to examine the extent of his influence on the process of disintegration.

[4] See the bibliography listed in chapter 7, n. 6.

[5] See S. Stern, *The Court Jew*, pp. 179 and 219, and the summary in Schnee, *Hoffinanz*, III, p. 220.

[6] S. Stern, *The Court Jew*, pp. 183f.; Baer, *Protokollbuch*, pp. 89f.

[7] See the summary and examples in E. Priebatsch, "Die Judenpolitik des fürstlichen Absolutismus im 17 und 18 Jahrhundert," *Festschrift Dietrich Schäffer* (1915), pp. 608ff.; S. Stern, *The Court Jew*, pp. 181f.

[8] *Cf.* Priebatsch, "Die Judenpolitik," loc. cit. Concerning the right to impose the ban, see Baer, *Protokollbuch*, pp. 109f.; S. Stern, *Der preussische Staat und die Juden*, II, index, s.v. "Bann." Though they were not consistent in empowering communities to issue the ban, it was always understood that the state authorities would oversee its use. For examples of appeals of sentences issued by Jewish courts, see Wachstein, *Urkunden*, pp. 384–86.

[9] S. Stern, *The Court Jew*, pp. 196–99, tried to present the actions of Court Jews on behalf of their community as a sort of struggle for communal autonomy. But the examples she cites actually prove that it was the personal influence of the Court Jew rather than any argument from historic right that decided the issue. In one case the king threatened to expel the Jews, and in another the Jews threatened to emigrate! The rabbinic leadership was certainly distressed at the narrowing of the Jewish judicial prerogative, but even the rabbis made peace with the situation. Typical is the attitude of R. Ezekiel Landau toward the transfer of bankruptcy proceedings to a secular court. He accepts it on the grounds of "dina de-malkhuta" [i.e., the law of the land that Talmudic Halakha recognized as binding] and asks his followers only to turn to a Jewish court to arrange those matters which the government did not take over; *Drushei ha-ẒLaḤ*, fol. 32c.

[10] For a description of such social encounters, see S. Stern, *The Court Jew*, pp. 234f.; Schnee, *Hoffinanz*, III, pp. 224–28, as well as many examples scattered through the earlier volumes. Stern incorrectly attributes tremendous importance to these meetings.

[11] A typical expression of this relationship is to be found in the words of one of the Gomperz who, in a private letter, declared himself ready to give his lifeblood for his king; Baer, *Protokollbuch*, p. 74, n. 66. Samuel Oppenheimer expressed similar sentiments in his will; Taglicht, *Nachlässe*, p. 15.

[12] Schnee noted many cases of conversion among the sons and daughters of Court Jews; see the summary in *Hoffinanz*, III, pp. 216–20. But most of the cases occurred during the second half of the eighteenth century. For the implications of this phenomenon, see below.

[13] This inclusion was initiated by Lessing in *Nathan der Weise* (1778) [English translation by Bayard Quincy Morgan: *Nathan the Wise* (New York: 1955)—*tr.*] and Christian Wilhelm Dohm in *Über die bürgerliche Verbesserung der Juden* [On the Civil Improvement of the Jews] (Berlin: 1781–83). Mendelssohn himself mentioned both of them as the first who included the Jews in the notion of toleration: "die Bestimmung der Menschen und die

Gerechtsame der Menschheit in Zusammenhange gedacht," *Moses Mendelssohns gesammelte Schriften*, ed. G. B. Mendelssohn (Leipzig: 1843–44), III, p. 180.

[14] See Hans Weil, *Die Entstehung des deutschen Bildungsprinzips* (Bonn: 1930), especially chapter 5.

[15] This approach is evident, for example, in R. Ya'ir Ḥayim Bacharach, *Ḥavot Ya'ir*, §139, who attributes gentile hostility toward Jews to "the masses and not the sages among them or the authorities." An even more extreme position is taken by R. Jacob Emden at the end of *Seder Olam Raba ve-Zuta u-Mgilat Taanit* (Hamburg: 1756–57).

[16] See Weil, *Entstehung des deutschen Bildungsprinzips*, loc. cit., and Henri Brunschwig, *La crise de l'état prussien à la fin du XVIIIe siècle, et la genèse de la mentalité romantique* (Paris: 1947), pp. 36–46 [*Enlightenment and Romanticism in Eighteenth-Century Prussia* (Chicago: 1974), pp. 26–40—tr.].

[17] See my dissertation, *Die Entstehung der Judenassimilation in Deutschland und deren Ideologie*, pp. 223ff.; Brunschwig, *Crise de l'état prussien*, pp. 101ff. [*Enlightenment and Romanticism*, pp. 85f.].

[18] See my dissertation, pp. 233ff.

[19] See Mendelssohn, *Gesammelte Schriften*, III, p. 47.

[20] See Weil, *Entstehung des deutschen Bildungsprinzips*. The change to a humanistic and rationalist approach to the Jewish question can also be seen in the public-opinion shift between the debate with Lavater (1770) and the debate over Dohm's pamphlet (1782). See my dissertation, p. 260. During Mendelssohn's own life, this decade was marked by a shift from relative indifference concerning the situation of the Jews, which there was not much hope of changing, to at least limited promotion of internal change and demands for rights from the outside world; see ibid., p. 72.

[21] On these salons, see Graetz, *Geschichte*, 3rd ed., XI, pp. 139ff.; H. Landsberg, *Henrietta Herz, ihr Leben und ihre Zeit* (Weimar: 1913); S. W. Baron, *Die Judenfrage auf dem Wiener Kongress auf Grund von zum Teil ungedruckten Quellen dargestellt* (Vienna and Berlin: 1920), pp. 117ff.

[22] D. Friedländer, *Sendschreiben an . . . Probst Teller . . . von einigen Hausvätern jüdischer Religion* (Berlin: 1799; [reprinted with Hebrew translation by Miriam Di-Nur, Jerusalem: 1975—*tr.*]); and cf. my dissertation, pp. 262f.

[23] As is known, Graetz saw this period as one of "mass baptism" (*Massentaufe*); see *Geschichte*, 3rd ed., XI, p. 155. But in his note ad loc., pp. 579f., S. Neumann already showed that Graetz had no proof for this.

[24] An example of such a group of Jewish *maskilim* is described in the next chapter.

Chapter 24. The Haskala's Vision of the Future

[1] The views of Dohm and of the participants in the public debate over his book, *Über die bürgerliche Verbesserung der Juden*, were unanimous in this regard. See n. 2, below.

[2] See for example, Naphtali Herz Wessely's remarks (*Divrei Shalom ve-Emet* [Words of Peace and Truth] [Berlin: 1782], chapter 3):

> Know that we are not responsible for this matter. . . . Rather, [it is the fault of] the nations who, for more than a thousand years now . . . have issued senseless edicts. . . . Then [the Jews came to] despise everything under the sun . . . and in the bitterness of their souls, they abandoned and left the laws and teachings intended to teach the science of leadership and the knowledge of what occurs in the heavens and on earth, as for instance how to calculate the paths of the stars, and to study those corrective measures needed for the working the land, and to sail the oceans and to build cities and towers and to know the laws of the nations and the ways of royal government. For they [i.e., the Jews] said, "What do we have to do with all of these? The local people are our enemies. They will not listen to our advice, and they will pay no heed to our accomplishments. We have no fields or vineyards in the land. Let us leave off all such studies and occupy ourselves with commerce and trade in order to make our living."

This is paralleled by Mendelssohn's argument in his introduction to R. Menasseh ben Israel's *Vindiciae Judaeorum*:

> Jetzt ist es gerade Aberglaube und Dummheit, die uns vorgerückt werden. . . . Unfähigkeit zu Künsten, Wissenschaften und nützlichen Gewerben, hauptsächlich in Diensten des Krieges und des Staates. . . . Man bindet uns die Hände und macht uns zum Vorwurfe, dass wir sie nicht gebrauchen.

Manassah Ben Israel Rettung der Juden aus dem Englischen übersetzt nebst einer Vorrede von Moses Mendelssohn. Als ein Anhang zu des Hrn. Kriegsraths Dohm Abhandlung: Über die bürgerliche Verbesserung der Juden (Berlin and Stettin: 1782); *Gesammelte Schriften*, III (1843), pp. 182–83.

[3] Ibid., pp. 189f.

[4] See the citation above, n. 2. In a letter to Herz Homberg (*Gesammelte Schriften*, V, p. 680), Mendelssohn provides something of a program for Jewish intellectual achievement aimed at obtaining government recognition.

[5] The Königsberg community effectively promised the King of Prussia to do just this in 1808; see Freund, *Emanzipation der Juden in Preussen*, II, pp. 401f., and cf. pp. 403f. The same motif reappears over and over again in contemporary publications.

[6] Mendelssohn, *Gesammelte Schriften*, III, pp. 194 and 281ff.

[7] That this was a compromise is clear. It was really suggested only in Mendelssohn's introduction to Menasseh Ben Israel's *Vindiciae Judaeorum* as a response to Dohm's remarks; *Gesammelte Schriften*, III, p. 193. When Mendelssohn outlined his views systematically in *Jerusalem*, he omitted the matter of self-governance completely.

[8] On the establishment of the Königsberg society, see *Ha-Me'asef* (5544 [1783–84]), fol. 2–3. On the name change, see ibid. (5546 [1785–86]), pp. 210f. The name change suggests that fostering the Hebrew language had henceforth become secondary to a more all-inclusive fostering of the Enlightenment. On the Berlin society, see Ludwig Lesser, *Chronik der Gesellschaft der Freunde in Berlin* (Berlin: 1842), pp. 9ff.

[9] Lesser, *Chronik*, pp. 10f. The Berlin society had a sort of branch in Königsberg, and it is reasonable to assume that the activities of the latter paralleled those of the mother group. There was also a similar society in Breslau; ibid., p. 43.

[10] The Berlin society had a sort of club for its meetings; ibid., p. 29. This purely social unit eventually came to function almost independently of the society; loc. cit. and p. 26.

[11] *Sulamith* (1807), pp. 129–30; L. Löw, *Lebensalter*, pp. 90–92.

[12] See Akiva E. Simon, "Pedagogic Philanthropism and Jewish Education" [in Hebrew], *Mordecai M. Kaplan Jubilee Volume on the Occasion of his Seventieth Birthday* (New York: 1953), pp. 147–87.

[13] Naphtali Herz (Hartwig) Wessely, *Divrei Shalom ve-Emet*, chapters 1–3.

[14] Wessely, *Divrei Shalom ve-Emet*, chapters 1 and 5.

[15] R. David ben Nathan (Tevele), the rabbi of Lissa, understood the issue clearly. He directed his arguments primarily at Wessely's claim that without secular studies a Jew was incapable of achieving human perfection. See L. Lewin, "Aus dem jüdischen Kulturkampfe," *JJLG* 12 (1918), pp. 165–98, and especially p. 187. R. David Tevele's sermon was published in part in Assaf, *Mekorot*, I, pp. 236–38. Cf. also a summary of R. Ezekiel Landau's remarks on the same issue, ibid., pp. 238f., and my dissertation, p. 250.

[16] Over the years 5544–45 (1783–85), Wessely published three pamphlets in defense of his proposal, and in them he went on to explain and develop his earlier words further. The pamphlets were afterward published together with *Divrei Shalom ve-Emet*.

[17] On the development of educational institutions at this level, see Mordekhai Eliav, *Ha-Ḥinukh ha-Yehudi be-Germanya* [Jewish Education in Germany] (Jerusalem: 1960–61). I have followed his conclusions in my presentation.

[18] See my "Marriage and Sexual Life," pp. 50f.

[19] Katz, "Marriage and Sexual Life."

[20] See Brunschwig, *La crise de l'état prussien*, especially pp. 252ff.

[21] This notion is developed in his *Jerusalem*, *Gesammelte Schriften*, III,

pp. 339ff. [English: *Jerusalem or On Religious Power and Judaism*, tr. Allan Arkush (Hanover and London: 1983), pp. 117ff.—*tr.*]. On Mendelssohn's attitude towards the tradition in general, see Isaac Heinemann, "Unity in Moses Mendelssohn's Philosophy of Religion" [in Hebrew], *Meẓuda* [*Metsudah*], ed. Simon Rawidowicz, VII (London and Waltham: 1954), pp. 197–219.

[22] Homburg, letter to Mendelssohn (which the latter answered in 1783); *Schriften*, V, p. 669. S. Ascher, *Leviathan oder über Religion in Rücksicht des Judentums* (Berlin: 1792), pp. 184ff.

[23] See Ascher's remarks, *Leviathan*, pp. 184ff., and regarding his views: Max Wiener, *Jüdische Religion im Zeitalter der Emanzipation* (Berlin: 1933), pp. 40–41.

[24] The use of halakhic material in a manner different from its original intent is typical of the entire transition period and continued in the era of the Reform conferences. This was correctly emphasized by Wiener, *Jüdische Religion*, pp. 91–97. Here, too, the conservatives were the first to correctly understand the implications of things. For example, R. Moses Sofer justified his refusal to enter into a literary debate with the reformers as follows: "I am unwilling to publish anything in this matter, for they will simply respond with further arguments of this sort . . . and the decision as to which of the arguments is correct will fall to those who sit in coffeehouses and music halls drinking liquor"; *Responsa of HaTaM Sofer*, VI (Vienna: 1863–64), §85. This *responsum* was written in 1818–19 as part of the debate over the modifications in the prayer service in the reform Temple in Hamburg.

[25] It seems that sections were first omitted from the traditional liturgy at the instigation of Israel Jacobson in Westphalia. See Auerbach, *Geschichte der israelitischen Gemeinde in Halberstadt*, p. 217, and cf. R. Menaḥem Mendel Steinhardt, *Divrei Igeret* (Roedelheim: 1811–12).

[26] The debate over the Hamburg Temple in 1818 centered on, among other things, the omission of the traditional notes in the reading of the Law. Aaron Chorin mentioned that in his synagogue in Arad he had instituted reading of the Law without the notes; see Eliezer Liebermann, ed., *Noga ha-Ẓedek* (published together with *Or Noga*, Dessau: 1818), p. 24.

[27] Similar is G. Scholem's argument in "Thoughts on *Wissenschaft des Judentums*" [in Hebrew], *Luaḥ ha-Areẓ (5705)* (Tel-Aviv: 1944), pp. 98ff.

[28] For Mendelssohn's well-known remarks on Yiddish, see his *Gesammelte Schriften*, V, p. 605.

[29] See his debate with Michaelis, in Dohm, *Verbesserung der Juden*, II, p. 74.

[30] See in Wessely, *Divrei Shalom ve-Emet*, chapter 7.

AFTERWORD: *Tradition and Crisis* and the Study of Early Modern Jewish History

[1] Shmuel Ettinger's review appeared in *Kirjath Sepher* 35 (1959–60), pp. 12–18. Ḥ. H. Ben-Sasson's review appeared as "Concepts and Reality in the History of Late Medieval Jewry," in *Tarbiẓ* 29 (1959–60), pp. 297–312. See also Katz's reply to the latter: "On Halakha and Sermons as Historical Sources," *Tarbiẓ* 30 (1960–61), pp. 62–68, and Ben-Sasson's final "Reply," ibid., pp. 69–72. Relevant also is Katz's "Martyrdom in the Middle Ages and in 1648–1649," in S. W. Baron et al., eds., *Yitzhak F. Baer Jubilee Volume on the Occasion of His 70th Birthday* (Jerusalem: 1960), pp. 318–37. All of these appeared in Hebrew. Katz's pieces were reprinted in his collected essays, *Halakha ve-Kabala. Mehkarim be-Toldot Dat Yisra'el al Medoreha ve-Zikatah ha-Ḥevratit* [English title: Halakhah and Kabbalah. Studies in the History of Jewish Religion, Its Various Faces and Social Relevance] (Jerusalem: Magnes Press, 1984).

[2] See Michael Meyer, "When Did the Modern Period in Jewish History Begin?" *Judaism* 17 (1975), pp. 329–38. Standard bibliographies and survey histories clearly reflect the regnant periodization scheme. See, for example, *Bibliographical Essays in Medieval Jewish Studies* (The Study of Judaism, No. 2) (New York: 1976) and *A History of the Jewish People*, edited by Ḥ. H. Ben-Sasson (Cambridge, MA.: 1976; translation from the original 3-vol. Hebrew edition of 1969).

[3] Heinrich Graetz, *Geschichte der Juden*, 3rd ed., vol. 9 (Leipzig: 1891), p. 1. Not surprisingly, these categories were substantially modified by Graetz's Hebrew translator/editor S. P. Rabinowicz (*Divrei Yemei Yisra'el* 8 [Warsaw: 1907/8], ch. IV, pp. 91–159), who naturally emphasized this period of Polish Jewish efflorescence to his east European audience.

[4] This was exactly the same terminology adopted by Ḥ. H. Ben-Sasson in *his* study of the social values of Polish Jewry of that era: *Hagut ve-Hanhaga. Hashkefoteihem ha-Ḥevratiyot shel Yehudei Folin be-Shilhei Yemei ha-Beinayim* [Thought and Leadership. The Social Views of Polish Jewry at the End of the Middle Ages] (Jerusalem: 1959).

[5] Theodore K. Rabb, *The Struggle for Stability in Early Modern Europe* (New York: 1975), p. 12. For a brief overview of the *Annales* school and its accomplishments, see Stuart Clark, "The *Annales* historians," in Quentin Skinner, ed., *The Return of Grand Theory in the Human Sciences* (Cambridge: Cambridge University Press, 1985), pp. 177–98.

[6] See, for example, A. Teller, ed., *Guide to the Sources for the History of the Jews in Poland in the Central Archives* [= Polish Jewry: Bibliographical Series, 4] (Jerusalem: Center for Research on the History and Culture of Polish Jews, Central Archives for the History of the Jewish People, Hebrew University of Jerusalem, 1988).

[7] Gershon Hundert and G. Bacon, *The Jews in Poland and Russia: Bib-*

liographical Essays (Bloomington: 1984) gives an excellent introduction to the field. A good sampling of current research is found in the proceedings of a 1984 conference published as *The Jews in Poland,* ed. Chimen Abramsky, Maciej Jachimczyk, and Antony Polonsky (Oxford: Basil Blackwell, 1986), the first five chapters of which deal with our period. The Institute for Polish-Jewish Studies at Oxford University publishes an annual review: *Polin. A Journal of Polish-Jewish Studies* (1986–).

[8] On the charters, see Jacob Goldberg, *Jewish Privileges in the Polish Commonwealth. Charters of Rights Granted to Jewish Communities in Poland-Lithuania in the Sixteenth to Eighteenth Centuries* (Jerusalem: Israel Academy of Sciences and Humanities, 1985), summarized in "The Privileges Granted to Jewish Communities of the Polish Commonwealth as a Stabilizing Factor in Jewish Support," in Abramsky et al., *The Jews in Poland,* pp. 31–54. The applicability to Polish Jewry of sociological theory concerning minority trading societies is discussed in Gershon Hundert, "An Advantage to Peculiarity? The Case of the Polish Commonwealth," *AJS Review* 6 (1981), pp. 21–38.

[9] The issue of Jews' awareness of, and polemics against, contemporary strains of Christian thought was the basis for much of the debate between Katz and Ben-Sasson in the articles listed above, n. 1. For the results of the new archivally based historiography, see M. J. Rosman, *The Lords' Jews: Magnate-Jewish Relations in the Polish-Lithuanian Commonwealth during the 18th Century* (Cambridge, MA: Harvard University Press, 1990) and Gershon David Hundert, *The Jews in a Polish Private Town: The Case of Opatów in the Eighteenth Century* (Baltimore: Johns Hopkins University Press, 1992). Hillel Levine, *Economic Origins of Antisemitism: Poland and Its Jews in the Early Modern Period* (New Haven: Yale University Press, 1991) uses the techniques of comparative history to describe the structural and cultural limits on Jewish entrepreneurial activity in Poland, the failure of modernization there, and the consequent intensification of anti-Jewish sentiment. On magnate-Jewish relations, see also Hundert, "Security and Dependence: Perspectives on 17th-Century Polish-Jewish Society Gained Through a Study of Jewish Merchants in Little Poland" (Ph.D. dissertation, Columbia University, 1978); idem, "Jews in Polish Private Towns. The Jewish Community in Opatów and the Town's Owners in the Eighteenth Century," *Studies on Polish Jewry* [=Paul Glikson Memorial Volume], ed. E. Mendelsohn and C. Shmeruk (Jerusalem: Center for Research on the History and Culture of Polish Jews, The Hebrew University of Jerusalem: 1987), pp. xvii–xxxviii; idem, "Jews, Money and Society in the Seventeenth-Century Polish Commonwealth: The Case of Kraków," *Jewish Social Studies* 43 (1981), pp. 261–74; idem, "The Role of Jews in Commerce in Early Modern Poland-Lithuania," *Journal of European Economic History* 16 (1987), pp. 245–75. See also Daniel Tollet's summary essay, "Merchants and Businessmen in Poznan and Cracow, 1588–1668), in Abramsky, ed., *Jews in Poland,* pp. 22–30. Rosman, "Jewish Perceptions of Insecurity and Powerlessness in 16th–

18th Century Poland," *Polin* 1 (1986), pp. 19–27, provides a useful caveat, reminding us of Polish Jews' sense of the precariousness of their situation. Jacob Goldberg surveys changing attitudes in "The Changes in the Attitude of Polish Society toward the Jews in the 18th Century," *Polin* 1 (1986), pp. 35–48; idem, "Poles and Jews in the 17th and 18th Centuries—Rejection or Acceptance?" *Jahrbücher für Geschichte Osteuropas* 22 (1974), pp. 148–282.

[10] Rosman, *The Lords' Jews*, chap. 7. In his study of "Miedzyboz and Rabbi Israel Baal Shem Tov," in Gershon David Hundert, ed., *Essential Papers on Hasidism: Origins to the Present* (New York: New York University Press, 1991), pp. 209–25, Rosman analyzes the first Polish archival records relating directly to the BESHT and his earliest followers. The texts confirm that early Hasidism was not, as had been argued, a broadly based anti-establishment movement.

[11] Salo W. Baron, *Social and Religious History of the Jews*, 2nd ed., revised and enlarged; vol. 13, 14, and 16 (New York: 1969 and 1976). Baron's extensive bibliographical footnotes provide a rich source of information for all researchers.

[12] Raphael Mahler, *A History of Modern Jewry: 1780–1815* (London: 1971), which is an abridgment of a larger Hebrew work. See also his *Hasidism and the Jewish Enlightenment: Their Confrontation in Galicia and Poland in the First Half of the Nineteenth Century* (Philadelphia: 1985). Bernard D. Weinryb, *The Jews of Poland: A Social and Economic History of the Jewish Community in Poland from 1100 to 1800* (Philadelphia: Jewish Publication Society, 1973), provides useful data on legal status and intergroup relations during our period, but despite its title, the work does not attempt either a social or an economic history of the community.

[13] Jonathan I. Israel, *European Jewry in the Age of Mercantilism* (1550–1750), 2nd ed. (Oxford: 1989).

[14] Some of the excitement as well as the professional frustration of those years is reflected in Jacob Katz's autobiography *Be-Mo Einay* [With my own eyes] (Jerusalem, 1989), which, unfortunately, has not yet been translated into English.

[15] *Scripta Hierosolymitana* 3 (1956), pp. 292–312.

[16] Ettinger, "Review," p. 14.

[17] Henry Waserman, "Comments on Jewish Historiography in Israel in Light of Ḥ. H. Ben-Sasson's Work *Reẓef u-Tmura*," *Kivunim* 34 (February 1987), pp. 101–15. [I would like to thank Dr. David Ruderman of Yale University for bringing this article to my attention.—BDC] Waserman traces this position back to nineteenth-century debates about the philosophy of history, but he also attributes Ettinger's critique to a fear that Katz's comparative typologies would threaten the perceived uniqueness of the Jewish historical experience. While this latter idea is an intriguing one, it does not appear in Ettinger's review or, to my knowledge, in any of his other writings, and must be set aside for the moment. For a brief overview of the general issue of the nomothetic as opposed to idiographic approaches, see Robert F. Berkhofer, Jr.,

A Behavioral Approach to Historical Analysis (New York: 1969), pp. 245–48, and the many sources cited there.

[18] Shlomo Deshen, *The Mellah Society: Jewish Community Life in Sherifian Morocco* (Chicago: 1989), p. 2. Perhaps the most clearly articulated application of social science methodology to Jewish modernization is Calvin Goldscheider and Alan S. Zuckerman, *The Transformation of the Jews* (Chicago and London: University of Chicago Press, 1984). The preface and first two sections provide useful insights for the student of the pre-modern period as well.

[19] Clifford Geertz, *The Interpretation of Cultures* (New York: 1973), esp. chaps. 1 and 4. A useful description of this approach and its assumptions is given in Peter Burke, *The Historical Anthropology of Early Modern Italy* (Cambridge: Cambridge University Press, 1987), pp. 3–7. Convenient surveys of the shift in social theory are provided by Charles Y. Glock and Phillip E. Hammond, eds., *Beyond the Classics? Essays in the Scientific Study of Religion* (New York: Harper and Row, 1973) and Quentin Skinner, ed., *The Return of Grand Theory in the Human Sciences* (see n. 5 above).

[20] Dov Noy, "Is There a Jewish Folk Religion?" in Frank Talmage, ed., *Studies in Jewish Folklore* (Cambridge, MA: Association for Jewish Studies, 1980), pp. 273–85. Katz made considerable use of material first published in the *Mitteilungen für jüdische Volkskunde*, the major scholarly journal of the pre-Holocaust era devoted to Jewish folklore, but his interest was largely in establishing "official" practice. On the development of Jewish folkloristics as a field of research, see Dov Noy, "Eighty Years of Jewish Folkloristics: Achievements and Tasks," in Talmage, ed., *Studies in Jewish Folklore*, pp. 1–11. A sign of increased academic recognition of the importance of folklore as a source for Jewish history is the creation of the Folklore Research Center at the Hebrew University in Jerusalem. Herman Pollack's examination of *Jewish Folkways in Germanic Lands (1648–1806): Studies in Aspects of Daily Life* (Cambridge, MA: MIT Press, 1971) provides a useful introduction to customs associated with "life cycle," child rearing, and ritual.

[21] To date, almost the only person to explore the history of Ashkenazic women in our period is Chava Weissler; see her "The Religion of Traditional Ashkenazic Women: Some Methodological Issues," *AJS Review* 12 (1987), pp. 73–94. Weissler has focused on the *tkhines* (Yiddish supplicatory prayers intended largely, though not exclusively, for women) as an only partially satisfactory key with which to unlock their world; "The Traditional Piety of Ashkenazic Women," in *Jewish Spirituality from the Sixteenth-Century Revival to the Present*, ed. Arthur Green (New York: 1987), pp. 245–75; " 'For Women and for Men Who Are Like Women'; The Construction of Gender in Yiddish Devotional Literature," *Journal of Feminist Studies in Religion* 5, No. 2 (Fall 1989), pp. 3–24; and "Prayers in Yiddish and the Religious World of Ashkenazic Women," in *Jewish Women in Historical Perspective*, ed. Judith Baskin (Detroit: Wayne State University Press, 1991), pp. 159–81. The extensive sources and bibliography on which Judith Baskin was able to base her

own article on "Jewish Women in the Middle Ages," *Jewish Women in Historical Perspective*, pp. 94–114, suggests that diligent research can provide material for the early modern period as well.

[22] Susan Starr Sered bemoans "the shocking paucity of information concerning the religious lives of Jewish women in past centuries" in her study of *Women as Ritual Experts: The Religious Lives of Elderly Jewish Women in Jerusalem* (New York and Oxford: Oxford University Press, 1992). Her bibliography, which provides a useful introduction to the state of the field, contains not even a single entry about the religious lives of women in the society and period covered by *Tradition and Crisis*.

[23] Azriel Shoḥet, *Im Ḥilufei ha-Tkufot: Reshit ha-Haskala bi-Yahadut Germaniya* (Jerusalem: 1960). The work has not been translated into English, but its central thesis was briefly reiterated by Chimen Abramsky in "The Crisis of Authority within European Jewry in the Eighteenth Century," in *Studies in Jewish Religious and Intellectual History Presented to Alexander Altmann on the Occason of His 70th Birthday*, ed. Siegfried Stein and Raphael Loewe (Alabama: 1979), English section, pp. 13–28.

[24] *Kirjath Sepher* 37 (1961/62), pp. 150–55.

[25] Cambridge, MA: 1973. See especially pp. 34 ff. The same line of argumentation was recently reiterated by Immanuel Etkes in a Hebrew article, "The Question of the Forerunners of the Haskala in Eastern Europe," *Tarbiẓ* 57 (1988–89), pp. 95–114. Etkes uses this ideological criterion to distinguish between the Haskala movement with its reformist program aimed at Jewish society and the broader social phenomena of "leaving the ghetto" and assimilating into the outside society. See also his "Immanent Factors and External Influences in the Development of the Haskalah Movement in Russia," in Jacob Katz, ed., *Toward Modernity: The European Jewish Model* (New Brunswick and Oxford: Transaction Books, 1987), pp. 13–32.

[26] Jacob Katz, "Traditional Society and Modern Society," in Shlomo Deshen and Walter P. Zenner, eds., *Jewish Societies in the Middle East: Community, Culture and Authority* (Lanham, MD: University Press of America, 1982), pp. 35–47. The quotes appear on p. 36 f. The article appeared originally in Hebrew in *Megamot* 10 (1960), pp. 304–11.

[27] Todd M. Endelman, *The Jews of Georgian England, 1714–1830: Tradition and Change in a Liberal Society* (Philadelphia: Jewish Publication Society, 1979).

[28] In his article on "The Concept of Social History," Katz singled out Salo Baron's comprehensive overview *The Jewish Community: Its History and Structure to the American Revolution* (Philadelphia: 1942) as an example of the failure of the older eclectic approach to Jewish society, an approach that gave examples of institutions from different times and places rather than an abstract paradigm of a type (p. 309). The rationale for this older approach was forcefully articulated by Gerson Cohen, who argued for "the basic homogeneity of social organization and religious orientation throughout the far-flung Jewish settlements in the Rabbinic age." According to Cohen, "the

Talmudic community structure served as the model for all subsequent Jewish communal life" because it performed functions for both Jews and Gentiles that "changed little throughout the many centuries before the emancipation of the Jews." Gerson D. Cohen, "The Talmudic Age," in Leo W. Schwarz, ed., *Great Ages and Ideas of the Jewish People* (New York: 1956), p. 148.

[29] *Jewish Social Studies* 21 (1959), pp. 249–51.

[30] On the debate between Katz and Ben-Sasson, see above, n. 1. Haym Soloveichik deals with the methodological problems of halakhic history in "Can Halakhic Texts Talk History?" *AJS Review* 3 (1978), pp. 152–96, and "Religious Law and Change: The Medieval Ashkenazic Example," *AJS Review* 12 (1987), pp. 205–22.

[31] Most of these studies appeared in Hebrew articles that have been conveniently collected in his *Halakha ve-Kabala* (above, n. 1). *Goy shel Shabat* (Jerusalem: 1983) has appeared in English as *The "Shabbes Goy": A Study in Halakhic Flexibility* (Philadelphia: Jewish Publication Society, 1989).

[32] See *"Shabbes Goy,"* p. 6 f. and chapter 13: "The Limits of Halakhic Flexibility," especially p. 236 f.; *Halakha ve-Kabala*, "Introduction."

[33] Naḥum Rakover, *A Bibliography of Jewish Law: Modern Books, Monographs and Articles in Hebrew* (Jerusalem: 1975) lists 12,098 entries on every subject from "Foundations and Nature of *Halakhah*" to "Jewish Law: State of Israel." Phyllis Holman Weisbard and David Schonberg, *Jewish Law: Bibliography of Sources and Scholarship in English* (Littleton, CO: F. B. Rothman, 1989) lists what is available in English. Menachem Elon, *Ha-Mishpat Ha-Ivri* (Jerusalem: 2nd ed., 1978), is both a practical guide and an encyclopedic overview of rabbinic law; an English translation is currently in preparation. Meanwhile, see his comprehensive article, "Mishpat Ivri," in *EJ* 12. Aaron M. Schreiber, *Jewish Law and Decision-Making: A Study through Time* (Philadelphia: 1979) includes translations of several important texts cited extensively by Katz. An English translation of the excellent *Enẓiklopediya Talmudit* is being issued as *Encyclopedia Talmudica* (Jerusalem: 1969–). For current research, see the *Jewish Law Annual* as well as Bernard Jackson, ed., *Modern Research in Jewish Law* (Leiden: Brill, 1980).

[34] Biographical treatments include Simon Hurwirtz, *The Responsa of Solomon Luria (MaHaRSHaL)* (New York: 1938); Elijah Judah Schochet, *Bach: Rabbi Joel Sirkes: His Life, Works and Times* (Jerusalem: 1971), and see his translation of Sirkes's important responsum §43 as *A Responsum of Surrender* (Los Angeles: University of Judaism Press, 1973); idem, *TaZ. Rabbi David Halevi* (New York: 1979); Byron L. Sherwin, *Mystical Theology and Social Dissent: The Life and Works of Judah Loew of Prague* (London and Toronto: Associated University Presses, 1982); Nisson E. Shulman, *Authority and Community: Polish Jewry in the Sixteenth Century* (Hoboken, NJ: 1986) on Benjamin Aaron Slonik; Lawrence Kaplan, "Rationalism and Rabbinic Culture in Sixteenth-century Eastern Europe: Rabbi Mordecai Jaffe's *Levush Pinat Yikrat*" (unpublished Ph.D. dissertation, Harvard University, 1975), partially summarized in "R. Mordekhai Jaffe and the Evolution of Jewish Culture in

Poland in the Sixteenth Century," in Bernard Dov Cooperman, ed., *Jewish Thought in the Sixteenth Century*, pp. 266–82. Jacob J. Schacter, "Rabbi Jacob Emden: Life and Major Works" (unpublished Ph.D. dissertation, Harvard University, 1988) has now supplanted Mortimer J. Cohen, *Jacob Emden: A Man of Controversy* (Philadelphia: 1937). Schacter is currently preparing an English translation of Emden's autobiography. For an overview of the scholars of this period, see Y. Horowitz, "Aḥaronim," in *EJ Decennial Book 1973–1982* (Jerusalem: 1982).

[35] Naḥum Rakover, *Ha-Kehila: Irgun ve-Hanhaga, Takanot u-Finkasei Kahal* [The Community: Organization and Government, *Takkanot* and *Pinkasim*] (Jerusalem: Merkaz Zalman Shazar and the Israeli Historical Society, 1977).

[36] "On Power and Authority: Halakhic Stance of the Traditional Community and Its Contemporary Implications," *Kinship and Consent: The Jewish Political Tradition and Its Contemporary Uses*, ed. Daniel J. Elazar (Washington: University Press of America, 1983), pp. 183–213. Though they do not deal directly with our period, Gerald J. Blidstein, "Individual and Community in the Middle Ages: Halakhic Theory," in Elazar, ed., *Kinship and Consent*, pp. 215–56; M. P. Golding, "The Juridical Basis of Communal Association in Medieval Rabbinic Legal Thought," *JSS* 28 (1968), pp. 67–78; and Samuel Morell's exploration of "The Constitutional Limits of Communal Government in Rabbinic Law," *JSS* 33 (1971), pp. 87–119, will go a long way to placing the *kehila* described by Katz into its proper juridical and legal context.

[37] See, most especially, Elazar and Cohen, *The Jewish Polity: Jewish Political Organization from Biblical Times to the Present* (Bloomington: 1985), especially pp. 160–203. The volume is marred by slipshod bibliographic guides at the end of each section. Cohen's basic approach is outlined in "The Concept of the Three *Ketarim*: Its Place in Jewish Political Thought and Its Implications for a Study of Jewish Constitutional History," *AJS Review* 9 (1984), pp. 27–54.

[38] Jacob Katz, "Post-Zoharic Relations between Halakhah and Kabbalah," in *Jewish Thought in the Sixteenth Century*, ed. Bernard Dov Cooperman (Cambridge, MA: Harvard University Press, 1983), pp. 283–307; idem, "Halakhah and Kabbalah as Competing Disciplines of Study," in Green, ed., *Jewish Spirituality* (above, n. 21), pp. 34–63. Hebrew versions of these, as well as several other articles dealing with the relationship between the exoteric and the esoteric in Jewish thought, are republished in his *Halakha ve-Kabala*, section I.

[39] Isadore Twersky provides "road-maps" to the study of this complex issue in "Talmudists, Philosophers, Kabbalists: The Quest for Spirituality in the Sixteenth Century," in Cooperman, ed., *Jewish Thought in the Sixteenth Century*, pp. 431–59, and "Law and Spirituality in the Seventeenth Century: A Case Study in R. Yair Ḥayyim Bacharach," in I. Twersky and B. Septimus, eds., *Jewish Thought in the Seventeenth Century* (Cambridge, MA: Harvard

University Press, 1987), pp. 447–67. Robert (Reuven) Bonfil's study of "Halakhah, Kabbalah and Society: Some Insights into Rabbi Menaḥem Azariah da Fano's Inner World," in Twersky and Septimus, eds., *Jewish Thought in the Seventeenth Century*, pp. 39–62, opens with a methodological discussion of the issue itself, one which "touches on history in its widest sense." Each of these articles includes an extensive bibliography.

[40] Gershon David Hundert's most welcome anthology of *Essential Papers on Hasidism: Origins to the Present* (above, n. 12), contains many of the most important interpretative and survey articles on the history of Hasidism. The composite article on "Hasidism" in *EJ* 7, pp. 1390–1432, is likewise especially useful. All three of the articles contained in Bezalel Safran, ed., *Hasidism: Continuity or Innovation?* (Cambridge, MA: Harvard University Press, 1988), play down social confrontation and stress conceptual continuity in the movement's early history.

[41] Jacob Katz, *Exclusiveness and Tolerance* (Oxford: Oxford University Press, 1961; New York: Schocken, 1962).

[42] *Bonim Ḥofshim vi-Yhudim: Kishreihem ha-Amitiyim ve-ha-Medumim* (Jerusalem: 1967–68) [English translation: *Jews and Freemasons in Europe, 1723–1939*] (Cambridge, MA: Harvard University Press, 1970). Some of the main points were first presented in "Freemasons and Jews," *Journal of Jewish Sociology* 9 (1967), pp. 137–48; see also "The Fight for Admission to Masonic Lodges," *Year Book of the Leo Baeck Society* 9 (London: 1966), pp. 171–209.

[43] Alexander Altmann's definitive *Moses Mendelssohn* (Philadelphia: Jewish Publication Society, 1973) will long remain a model for biographical treatment. On figures from the east, see, for example, N. Rezler-Bersohn, "Isaac Satanow, An Epitome of an Era," *Year Book of the Leo Baeck Society* 25 (1980), pp. 81–99; David Fishman, "Science, Enlightenment and Rabbinic Culture in Belorussian Jewry 1772–1804," unpublished Ph.D. dissertation (Harvard University, 1985); idem, "A Polish Rabbi Meets the Berlin Haskalah: The Case of R. Barukh Schick," *AJS Review* 12 (1987), pp. 95–121.

[44] Moses Mendelssohn, *Jerusalem, or On the Religious Power and Judaism*, tr. by Allan Arkush, with an introduction and commentary by Alexander Altmann (Hanover and London: 1983).

[45] S. Lowenstein, "The Readership of Mendelssohn's Bible Translation," *HUCA* 52 (1982), pp. 179–213. Though Isaac (Eisenstein)-Barzilay's many articles on the Haskala focus primarily on the intellectual arguments presented by its proponents, mention should be made here at least of his "The Background of the Berlin Haskalah," *Essays on Jewish Life and Thought Presented in Honor of Salo Wittmayer Baron*, ed. Joseph L. Blau et al. (New York: Columbia University Press, 1959), pp. 183–97.

[46] Raphael Mahler, "The Social and Political Aspects of the Haskalah in Galicia," *Studies in Modern Jewish Social History*, ed. J. Fishman (New York: 1970), pp. 64–85 takes a Marxist approach. Deborah Hertz considers both gender and class in her statistically based study of "Seductive Conversion in

Berlin, 1770–1809," in Todd M. Endelman, ed., *Radical Assimilation in English Jewish History, 1656–1945* (Bloomington and Indianapolis: Indiana University Press, 1990), pp. 34–57. Relevant also is Zosa Szajkowski, "Marriages, Mixed Marriages and Conversions among French Jews during the Revolution of 1789," *Historia Judaica* 19 (1957), pp. 33–44.

[47] See, for example, David Sorkin, *The Transformation of German Jewry, 1780–1840* (New York: Oxford University Press, 1987) and the many articles collected in *Toward Modernity: The European Jewish Model*, ed. Jacob Katz (New Brunswick: Transaction Books, 1987).

Bibliography

Primary Sources

a. Rabbinic Works

The system of nomenclature used in traditional rabbinic literature to refer to other authorities can present a daunting challenge to the beginning student. Authorities are cited not by name but by the title of their work. Sometimes the same title is used to refer to several works by the author, even though he may have given each work a separate title. Other times the same title is used by different authors, and the only way to know which is being cited is by noting the context of the citation. To add to the confusion, many well-known authorities and works are cited by abbreviations and acronyms.

To help the student interested in pursuing the development of halakhic thought on specific historical issues, I chose to list rabbinic sources by title as well as by author. Main references are by author, but when a work's author is not obvious from its title, the title is also listed separately, with a reference to the author and, if necessary, a clarification of bibliographical ambiguities. Finally, acronyms are listed with cross-references to the appropriate author or text.

—B.D.C.

Aaron Simeon b. Jacob Abraham of Copenhagen. *Or ha-Yashar*. Amsterdam: 1768–69. Collected rabbinic opinions on the famous case of the divorce of Cleves. References are to this edition and not to the expanded edition with notes by Yekutiel Zalman Schor (*Niẓoẓei Or*), published in Lemberg (Lwow) in 1902.

Aboab, Samuel (1610–1694). *Responsa Dvar Shmu'el*. (Venice: 1701–02).

Aguda. See Alexander Suslin ha-Kohen of Frankfurt.

Alexander Suslin ha-Kohen of Frankfurt (d. 1349). *Aguda*. Cracow: 1571. Photographic reprint, 1958. Critical annotated edition, Jerusalem: 1966. The work was most widely circulated in an abbreviated digest prepared by R. Jacob Weil under the title *Ḥidushei Aguda*, and first published as an appendix to Weil's *Responsa* (Venice: 1523).

Arbaa Turim. See Jacob ben Asher.

Arye Judah Leib ben Samuel Ẓvi Hirsch, compiler. *She'elot u-Tshuvot Ge'onei Batra'i*. Ed. Elijah b. Moses Gershon [Elias Gerson]. First edition, Turka: 1763–64.

Ashkenazi, Eliezer ben Elijah (1512–85). *Maasei Miẓrayim*. Commentary to the Passover Haggada. Usually printed as part II of the author's *Maasei ha-Shem*. Venice: 1582–83.

Ashkenazi, Gershon (d. 1693). *Responsa Avodat ha-Gershuni*. Frankfurt am Main: 1698–99.

Ashkenazi, Ẓvi Hirsch ben Jacob (1660–1718). *Responsa Ḥakham Ẓvi*. Amsterdam: 1711–12.

Ateret Zkenim. See Auerbach, Menaḥem Mendel.

Auerbach, Menaḥem Mendel. *Ateret Zkenim*. Commentary on *Shulḥan Arukh, Oraḥ Ḥayim*. Published in standard editions of that work.

Bacharach, Ya'ir Ḥayim b. Moses Samson (d. 1702). *Responsa Ḥavot Ya'ir*. References are to the Lemberg edition of 1895–96. Photographic reprint, Jerusalem: 1968. First edition, Frankfurt am Main: 1698–99.

Backofen, Jacob. See Reischer, Jacob ben Joseph.

BaḤ. See Sirkes, Joel.

Bayit Ḥadash. See Sirkes, Joel.

Be'er ha-Gola. See Rivkes, Moses.

Beit Shmu'el. See Samuel of Fürth.

Beit Yaakov. See Jacob ben Samuel.

Beit Yosef. See Caro, Joseph.

Benjamin Wolf b. Mattathiah. *Tohorat ha-Kodesh. Seder Yom ve-Seder Layla ve-Seder Hanhagot Beyt-ha-Kneset ve-Seder Masa u-Matan*. First edition, Amsterdam: 1732–33. References are to the 2nd edition of Blizurka: 1806.

Berechiah Berakh b. Eliakim Getzel (c. 1670–1740). Grandson of Berechiah Berakh b. Isaac Eisik. *Zera Berakh ha-Shlishi*. Part I: commentaries and sermons on Genesis. Halle: 1714. Part II: novellae on tractate *Brakhot*. Frankfurt an der Oder: 1731.

Berechiah Berakh b. Isaac Eisik (d. 1663). *Zera Berakh*. Part I. Cracow: 1646. Part II. Hamburg: 1686–87.

Calahora, Joseph ben Solomon. Also called Joseph Darshan. *Yesod Yosef*. Frankfurt an der Oder: 1678–79. Expanded edition, Berlin: 1739. Frequently republished.

Caro, Joseph (1488–1575). *Beit Yosef*. Commentary to Jacob b. Asher, *Arbaa Turim*. Printed in all standard editions.

———. *Shulḥan Arukh*. A code of Jewish law.

Cohen. See Kohen.

Colon, Joseph b. Solomon (c. 1420–1480). *Responsa*. First edition, Venice: 1518–19. References here are to the edition of Jerusalem: 1988.

Coucy, Moses of. See Moses ben Jacob of Coucy.

Darkhei Moshe. See Isserles, Moses.

Darshan, Joseph. See Calahora, Joseph.
David ben Samuel ha-Levi (1585–1667). *Turei Zahav (TaZ).* Commentary on the four sections of the *Shulḥan Arukh.* Published in standard editions of that text.
De' Rossi, Azaria (c. 1511–c. 78). *Me'or Einayim.* Historical studies. First edition, Mantua: 1573. Critical edition, ed. David Cassel, Vilna, 1866. Photographic reprint, Jerusalem: 1969–70.
De Vidas, Elijah ben Moses. *Reshit Ḥokhma.* Moralistic work. First edition, Venice: 1578–79. Often reprinted.
Divrei Ḥakhamim. See Pukhovitser, Judah Loeb.
Divrei Zikaron. See Stadthagen, Joseph.
Dov Baer ben Samuel. *Shivḥei ha-BESHT* [In Praise of the *Baal Shem Tov*]. Ed. Samuel A. Horodezky. Berlin: 1921–22. 2nd edition, Tel-Aviv: 1960. References are to the later edition. English translation: *In Praise of the Baal Shem Tov,* ed. Dan Ben-Amos and Jerome R. Mintz. Bloomington, Ind.: 1970.
Drisha. See Falk, Joshua.
Edels, Samuel Eliezer ben Judah [MaHaRSHA'] (1555–1631). *Ḥidushei Agadot* [novellae to the non-halakhic portions of the Talmud]. First separate edition, Lublin: 1626–27. Now published as part of Edels's *Ḥidushim* [novellae] on the Talmud at the end of standard editions of the Talmud.
Eibenschutz, David Solomon (eighteenth and nineteenth centuries). *Sefer Levushei Sered.* Hrubieszow: 1819.
Eisenstadt, Abraham Ẓvi Hirsch (1813–68). *Pitḥei Tshuva* on *Yore De'a.* First edition in the *Shulḥan Arukh,* Vilna: 1836. Now regularly published in standard editions of the *Shulḥan Arukh.*
Ele Divrei ha-Brit. Altona: 1818–19. Photographic reprint, Jerusalem: 1969–70.
Elias Gerson. See Arye Judah Leib ben Samuel Ẓvi Hirsch.
Eliezer ben Samuel of Metz (c. 1115–98). *Sefer Yere'im ha-Shalem.* Explanation of the 613 commandments. Usually published in the edited version by Benjamin b. Abraham Anav. First complete edition, ed. Abraham Abba Schiff, Vilna: 1892–1902.
Elijah b. Moses Gershon. See Arye Judah Leib ben Samuel *Ẓvi Hirsch.*
Emden, Jacob Israel ben *Ẓvi (1697–1776). Responsa She'ilat Yaaveẓ.* 2 vols. Altona: 1738–39 and 1769–70.
———. Introduction to *Seder Olam Raba ve-Zuta u-Mgilat Taanit.* Hamburg: 1756–57.
Emunat Shmu'el. Responsa. See Kaidanover, Aaron Samuel.
Ephraim b. Jacob ha-Kohen (1616–78). *Responsa Shaar Efrayim.* Sulzbach: 1688.
Ephraim Solomon ben Aaron of Lenczyca (d. 1619). Also called Ephraim of Luntshitz. *Ir Giborim.* Sermons. First edition, Basle: 1580. Often reprinted. References are to the edition of Lublin: 1884.

———. *Olelot Efrayim.* Sermons. First edition, Lublin: 1589–90. Often reprinted. References are to the edition of Jerusalem: 1988–89, which includes references to the pagination of the first edition.

Even ha-Ezer. Part III of both Jacob ben Asher, *Arbaa Turim,* and Joseph Caro, *Shulḥan Arukh.* Following convention, references are to Caro's work unless Jacob ben Asher's work is indicated specifically.

Eybeschutz, David Solomon. See Eibenschutz, David Solomon.

Eybeschutz, Jonathan ben Nathan Nata (d. 1764). *Yaarot Dvash.* 2 vols. Carlsruh: 1778–79 and 1781–82.

Falk, Joshua b. Alexander ha-Kohen (c. 1555–1614). *Drisha.* A commentary on *Arbaa Turim.* Published with that text.

———. *Kuntres . . . Baal ha-SMA'.* Pamphlet concerning the laws of usury. Cracow: 1893–94. Republished often.

———. *Prisha.* A commentary on *Arbaa Turim.* Published with that text.

———. *Sefer Me'irat Einayim* [*SMA'*]. Commentary on *Shulḥan Arukh, Ḥoshen Mishpat.* Printed in standard editions of that text.

Friedmann, Meir. See Ish-Shalom, Meir.

Gombiner, Abraham Abele ben Ḥayim ha-Levi (c. 1637–83). *Magen Avraham.* Commentary on *Shulḥan Arukh, Oraḥ Ḥayim.* Regularly published with it. First edition, Dyhernfurth: 1692.

Hahn (Nordlingen), Joseph Yuspa ben Phinehas Seligmann (1570–1637). *Yosef Omeẓ.* [Also: *Yosif Omeẓ.*] Frankfurt am Main: 1722–23. References are to the edition of Frankfurt am Main: 1927–28. Photographic reprint, Jerusalem: 1964–65.

Ḥakham Ẓvi. Responsa. See Ashkenazi, Ẓvi.

Ḥelkat Meḥokek. See Moses ben Isaac Judah of Brisk.

Heller, Yom Tov Lipmann (1579–1654). *Tosfot Yom Tov.* Supracommentary to Obadiah Bertinoro's commentary to the Mishna. Prague: 1614–17. 2nd edition, Cracow: 1643–44. Often republished in rabbinic editions of the Mishna.

Ḥidushei Agadot. See Edels, R. Samuel.

Ḥidushei Aguda. See Alexander Suslin ha-Kohen of Frankfurt.

Horodezky, Samuel Abba. See Dov Baer ben Samuel.

Horovitz, Markus (Mordekhai ha-Levi). *Responsa Mate Levi.* I (1891). II, ed. Jacob Horovitz (1932). New critical edition, ed. Barukh Horovits (1979).

Horowitz, Abraham b. Shabtai (16th century). *Emek Brakha.* Amsterdam: 1728–29. New edition, Jerusalem: 1969–70.

———. *Yesh Noḥalim.* First edition, Prague: 1615. References in this text are to the edition of Amsterdam: 1701, which includes additional notes by the author's son Jacob, as well as the ethical will of Abraham's grandson, Sheftel b. Isaiah.

Horowitz, Isaiah b. Abraham (c. 1565–1630). *Shnei Luḥot ha-Brit.* Folio references, where given, are to the second edition, Amsterdam: 1697–98. Photographic reprint, New York: 1945–46.

Horowitz, Sheftel ben Isaiah. *Vavei Amudim.* Though it is an independent work, the author presented *Vavei Amudim* as nothing more than an introduction to *Shnei Luḥot ha-Brit* of his father, R. Isaiah Horowitz, *q.v.* References are to the second edition of *Shnei Luḥot ha-Brit,* Amsterdam: 1697–98. Photographic reprint, New York: 1945–46, the end of vol. II.

Ḥoshen Mishpat. Part IV of both Jacob ben Asher, *Arbaa Turim,* and Joseph Caro, *Shulḥan Arukh.* Following convention, references are to Caro's work unless Jacob ben Asher's work is indicated specifically.

Ḥut ha-Meshulash. See Sofer, Solomon.

Ir Giborim. See Ephraim Solomon b. Aaron of Lenczyca.

Isaac ben Moses of Vienna (c. 1200–c. 1270). *Or Zarua.* Halakhik compilation. Zhitomir and Jerusalem: 1861–91.

Ish-Shalom [Friedmann], Me'ir, ed. *Seder Eliyahu Raba ve-Seder Eliyahu Zuta.* Known collectively in rabbinic literature as *Tana de-Vei Eliyahu.* Vienna: 1902. Reprinted, Jerusalem: 1959–60.

Isserlein, Israel ben Petaḥia (1390?–1460). *Pitḥei Tshuva* (to *Oraḥ Ḥayim*). Vilna: 1874–75. Reprinted together with Abraham Danzig, *Sefer Ḥayei Adam ha-Shalem.* Brooklyn: 1961–62.

———. *Trumat ha-Deshen.* First edition, Venice: 1519. Reference here is to the edition of Fürth: 1777–78, which includes extra material in a supplement entitled *Psakim u-Khtavim.*

Isserles, Moses (c. 1525–72). *Darkhei Moshe.* References to this commentary on R. Jacob b. Asher's *Arbaa Turim* are complicated by a confused publishing history. The commentary to *Yore De'a* appeared in Sulzbach in 1691–92, with corrections to that edition included in Yo*ḥanan Kreminitzer, Oraḥ Mishor* (Berlin: 1722–23). The section on *Oraḥ Ḥayim* appeared in Fürth in 1759–60. [Photographic reprint: s.l. and s.a.] (A critical edition of the section on *Ḥoshen Mishpat* was prepared by Ḥayim Solomon Rosenthal and published only recently [I. Jerusalem: 1978–79. II. Jerusalem: 1982–83].) These texts are commonly referred to as *Darkhei Moshe ha-Arokh.* An abbreviated version of the entire work (*Darkhei Moshe ha-Kaẓar*) has become a standard feature of editions of the *Arbaa Turim* since 1701–2. In the footnotes I have tried to indicate when reference to the longer version is intended. Otherwise, references will be to the short version.

———. *Responsa.* First edition, Cracow: 1639–40. All references are to the critical edition of Asher Ziv, *She'elot u-Tshuvot ha-ReMA' le-Rabeinu Moshe Isserles ZaL.* Jerusalem: 1970.

Jacob ben Asher (c. 1269–c. 1340). *Arbaa Turim.* A code of Jewish law.

Jacob ben Samuel. *Responsa Beit Yaakov.* Dyhernfurth[?]: 1695–96.

Jacob Joseph ben Ẓvi ha-Kohen of Polonnoye (d. c. 1782). *Ben Porat Yosef.* Korets: 1780–81.

———. *Toldot Yaakov Yosef.* Korets: 1779–80.

Jaffe, Mordecai ben Abraham (c. 1535–1612). *Levush Malkhut* or *Levushim*

(1590–1604). Jaffe's collected works, amounting to ten volumes of novellae, commentaries, and homilies. Each volume has a separate title beginning with the word "levush" (i.e., attire); e.g., *Levush ha-Tkhelet, Levush ha-Ḥur, Levush Ateret Zahav Gdola, Levush ha-Boẓ ve-Argaman,* and *Levush Ir Shushan*—collectively intended as an alternative code of Jewish law to that of Joseph Caro.

Joseph ben Solomon. See Calahora, Joseph.

Judah ben Samuel he-Ḥasid (c. 1150–1217). *Sefer Ḥasidim.* Ed. Judah Wistinetzki and Jakob Freimann. Frankfurt am Main: 1924.

Kaidanover, Aaron Samuel (1614–76). *Responsa Emunat Shmu'el.* References are to the Lemberg edition of 1884–85. Photographic reprint, Jerusalem: 1969–70.

Katz, Ephraim. See Kohen, Ephraim b. Jacob.

Katz, Joseph ben Gershon (1510–91). *Responsa She'erit Yosef.* References are to the critical edition of the text, ed. Asher Ziv. New York: 1983–84.

Katzenellenbogen, Ezekiel ben Abraham (1667?–1749). *Responsa Kneset Yeḥezkel.* Altona: 1731–32.

Kaufmann, Moses Yekutiel (seventeenth century). *Leḥem ha-Panim.* Commentary to *Arba'a Turim. Yore De'a.* Hanau: 1715–16.

Kneset Yeḥezkel. See Katzenellenbogen, Ezekiel.

Kohen, Ephraim b. Jacob. *Responsa Shaar Efrayim.* Sulzbach: 1688. All references are to the edition of 1886. Reprinted Brooklyn: *s.a.* [together with the *Halakhot Ktanot* of R. Jacob Ḥagiz (first edition, Venice: 1704; but this edition at least 1897)].

Kohen, Sabbetai b. Meir [SHaKH]. *Siftei Kohen.* A commentary on Joseph Caro's *Shulḥan Arukh,* printed in all standard editions.

Kolbo. Anonymous medieval halakhic manual. First edition, Naples: 1485 [?].

Kossman, Joseph ben Moses. *Nohag ke-Ẓon Yosef.* Hanau: 1717–18.

Krokhmal, Menaḥem Mendel ben Abraham (1600–61). *Responsa Ẓemaḥ Ẓedek.* Amsterdam: 1675. References are to the edition of Sudylkov: 1834.

Landau, Ezekiel (1713–93). *Drushei ha-ẒLaḤ.* Warsaw: 1886. Many subsequent printings, including Jerusalem: 1965–66.

———. *Responsa Noda bi-Yhuda.* First collection, Prague: 1775–76. Second collection, Prague: 1810–11.

Landsofer, Jonah (1678–1712). *Responsa Me'il Ẓdaka.* Prague: 1756.

———. *Ẓavaa* [Ethical Will]. First published in *Sefer Derekh Tovim.* Ed. Abraham ben Reuben Deutz. Frankfurt am Main: 1716–17, and often reprinted. Reference here is to *Ẓavaot ve-Derekh Tovim* (Zhitomir: 1874–75).

Leḥem ha-Panim. See Kaufmann, Moses Yekutiel.

Levush. See Jaffe, Mordecai b. Abraham.

Levushei Sered. See Eibenschutz, David Solomon.

Liebermann, Eliezer, ed. *Noga ha-Ẓedek.* Published together with *Or Noga.* Dessau: 1818.

Lipschütz, R. Israel ben Eliezer (d. 1782). Or Yisra'el. Cleves: 1769–70.
Lublin, Meir b. Gedaliah of (1558–1616). *Responsa*. [Sometimes called *Manhir Einei Ḥakhamim* to distinguish it from the author's oft-reprinted Talmudic commentary, *Meir Einei Ḥakhamim*. The Sudylkow edition of 1834 erroneously refers to this work by the latter title.] First edition, Venice: 1619. All references are to the Brooklyn edition of 1960–61, which reproduces the Warsaw edition of 1881 and adds *responsum* 138, which was not included in the editions of 1834 or 1881. Published together with *Responsa Avodat ha-Gershuni*; see Ashkenazi, Gershon.
Luria, Solomon ben Yeḥiel [MaHaRSHaL] (1510–73 or 1574). *Responsa*. First issued in Lublin in 1573–74 to 1575–76, the *Responsa* of Solomon Luria were recently reissued in a corrected edition based on the first edition and other printed sources with useful references to standard rabbinic works. Jerusalem: 1968–69.
———. *Yam shel Shlomo*. Novellae on various tractates of the Talmud, published individually by tractate from 1636. References are to the collected edition of Stettin: 1861–62, reprinted, Brooklyn: 1984–85.
Luzzatto, Simone (Simḥa). *Discorso circa il stato de gl'Hebrei et in particolar dimoranti nell'inclita Città di Venetia*. Venice: 1638. Reproduced with an introductory essay by R. Bachi, Bologna: 1976. Hebrew edition: *Maamar al Yehudei Veneẓiya*. Jerusalem: 1950.
Magen Avraham. See Gombiner, Abraham Abele ben Ḥayim ha-Levi.
MaHaRaM of Lublin. See Lublin, Meir ben Gedaliah of.
MaHaRSHA'. See Edels, Samuel.
MaHaRSHaL. See Luria, Solomon.
Maḥzor Vitri. See Simḥa ben Samuel.
Maimonides, Moses (1135–1204). *Mishne Tora*. A code of Jewish law.
Manhir Einei Ḥakhamim. See Lublin, Meir ben Gedaliah of.
Margalioth, Judah Loeb ben Asher (1747–1811). *Responsa Pri Tvu'a*. Nowydwor: 1795–96.
Mat, Moses ben Abraham (c. 1550–c. 1606) of Przemysl. *Mate Moshe*. First edition, Cracow: 1590–91. The later editions of Frankfurt am Main: 1719–20 and Warsaw: 1876 have now been surpassed by the annotated edition of M. Knoblowicz, London: 1958, for all the typographical errors it contains, and all page references are to that edition.
Mate Moshe. See Mat, Moses ben Abraham.
Megilat Sefer. See Emden, Jacob, in section "c" (Memoirs).
Me'il Ẓdaka. See Landsofer, Jonah.
Meir ben Barukh of Rothenburg (c. 1215–93). *Responsa*. These have been published in four different collections: (1) Shorter version (*She'elot u-Tshuvot ha-Kẓarot*), Cremona: 1557. (2) Longer version (*She'elot u-Tshuvot ha-Arukot*), Prague: 1608; reprint, Sdilkow: 1835; reprint ed. Moses Bloch, Budapest: 1895. (3) Ed. Nathan Rabinowitz, Lemberg: 1860. (4) Ed. Moses Bloch, Berlin: 1891–92. These four collections were re-

published in Jerusalem in 1967–68. A comprehensive critical edition of MaHaRaM's works, including the *responsa*, was begun by Isaac Ze'ev Cahana (3 vols., Jerusalem: 1957–62), but remained incomplete at Cahana's death. A fourth volume was issued by Eliezer Klein (Jerusalem: 1977). A substantial selection of Rothenburg's *responsa* is available in English translation in Irving A. Agus, *Rabbi Meir of Rothenburg. His Life and His Works as Sources for the Religious, Legal and Social History of the Jews of Germany in the Thirteenth Century*, 2nd edition (New York: 1970), pp. 169–682.

Me'irat Einayim. See Falk, Joshua.

Mishne Tora. See Maimonides, Moses.

Mordecai ben Hillel (thirteenth century). *Sefer Mordekhai.* Commentary on Isaac Alfasi's summary of the laws of the Talmud. Reference is to the version published in standard editions of the Talmud.

Moses ben Isaac Judah of Brisk. *Ḥelkat Meḥokek.* A commentary on Joseph Caro, *Shulḥan Arukh, Even ha-Ezer* printed in all standard editions.

Moses ben Jacob of Coucy (thirteenth century). *Sefer Miẓvot Gadol* [*SMaG*]. References are to the edition of Venice: 1546–47.

Naḥalat Shiv'a. See Samuel ben David Moses ha-Levi.

Nathan ben Naphtali of Nemirov. *Yemei MaHaRaNaT.* References are to the edition of New York: 1969–70.

Noga ha-Ẓedek. See Liebermann, Eliezer.

Ohel Yaakov. See Sasportas, Jacob.

Oraḥ Ḥayim. Part I of both Jacob ben Asher, *Arbaa Turim*, and Joseph Caro, *Shulḥan Arukh.* Following convention, references are to Caro's work unless Jacob ben Asher's work is indicated specifically.

Or ha-Yashar. See Aaron Simeon ben Jacob Abraham.

Or Yisra'el. See R. Israel Lipschütz.

Or Zarua, Bava Kama, Bava Batra. See Isaac ben Moses of Vienna.

Pitḥei Tshuva, Oraḥ Ḥayim. See Isserlein, Israel.

Pitḥei Tshuva, Yore De'a. See Eisenstadt, Abraham Ẓvi Hirsch.

Prisha. See Falk, Joshua.

Przemysl, Moses of. See Mat, Moses ben Abraham.

Pukhovitser, Judah Loeb b. Joseph, of Pinsk. *Derekh Ḥokhma.* Frankfurt an der Oder: 1682–83.

———. *Divrei Ḥakhamim.* The work is composed of two parts, entitled *Daat Ḥokhma* and *Mekor Ḥokhma*, respectively.

———. *Kne Ḥokhma.* Frankfurt an der Oder: 1681.

———. *Kvod Ḥakhamim.* Venice: 1700.

RaAViYaH. See Aptowitzer, Victor, in the list of secondary sources.

RaSHI. See Solomon ben Isaac.

Reischer, Jacob ben Joseph. Also known as Jacob Backofen. *Responsa Shvut Yaakov.* I. Halle: 1708–9. II. Offenbach: 1718–19. III. Metz: 1788–89.

ReMA'. See Isserles, Moses.

Reshit Ḥokhma. See de Vidas, Elijah ben Moses.

Responsa of MaHaRaM. See Meir ben Barukh of Rothenburg.

Rivkes, Moses ben Naphtali Hirsch (d. c. 1671–72). *Be'er ha-Gola.* Commentary on Joseph Caro's *Shulḥan Arukh.* First published with that work, Amsterdam: 1660–61 to 1665–66, and often republished in standard editions of the *Shulḥan Arukh.*

Samuel ben David Moses ha-Levi (1625?–81). *Naḥalat Shiv'a.* A formulary of halakhic contracts. Amsterdam: 1667. Revised edition, Frankfurt am Main: 1681. 3rd edition, revised and expanded by the author's son, Abraham, Fürth: 1692. Often reprinted.

Samuel ben Uri Shraga Phoebus of Fürth (c. 1650–c. 1705). *Beit Shmu'el.* Dyhernfurth: 1688–89. Commentary on *Shulḥan Arukh, Even ha-Ezer,* now published in standard editions of that text.

Sasportas, Jacob (c. 1610–98). *Responsa Ohel Yaakov.* Amsterdam: 1736–37.

———. *Sefer Ẓiẓat Novel Ẓvi* [The Wilted Flower of Ẓvi]. Ed. Isaiah Tishby. Jerusalem: 1954.

Schor, Abraham Ḥayim ben Hirsch (d. 1632). *Torat Ḥayim.* Lublin: 1624. Often reprinted.

Sefer ha-Ora. See Solomon ben Isaac.

Sefer Ḥasidim. See Judah ben Samuel he-Ḥasid.

Sefer Miẓvot Gadol. See Moses ben Jacob of Coucy.

Shaar Efrayim, Responsa. Ephraim b. Jacob ha-Kohen (1616–78). Sulzbach: 1688.

SHaKH. See Kohen, Sabbetai b. Meir.

Shapira. See Spira.

She'elot u-Tshuvot Ge'onei Batra'i. See Arye Judah Leib ben Samuel Ẓvi Hirsch.

She'erit Yosef. See Katz, Joseph ben Gershon.

Shivḥei ha-BESHT. See Dov Baer ben Samuel.

Shneor Zalman of Lyady (1715–1813). *Shulḥan Arukh shel ha-Rav, Yore De'a.* 1850–51.

Shulḥan Arukh. See Caro, Joseph.

Shvut Yaakov. Responsa. See Reischer, Jacob ben Joseph.

Simḥa ben Samuel. *Maḥzor Vitri.* Ed. S. Hurwitz. Nürnberg: 1923.

Sirkes, Joel ben Samuel (1561–1640). *Responsa Bayit Ḥadash* [*BaḤ*]. Citations here are from the Ostrog edition of 1834. Since §§4, 14, and 114 were omitted from all editions after the first for fear of censorship, references to these three *responsa* are drawn from the first edition (Frankfurt an Main: 5457 [1696–97]).

———. *Responsa Bayit Ḥadash ha-Ḥadashot.* First edition, Koretz: 1784–85. References are to Jerusalem: 1958–59.

Slonik, Benjamin Aaron (b.c. 1550). *Responsa Mas'at Binyamin.* First edition, Cracow: 1632–33. All references are to the Vilna edition of 1893, photographically reprinted, Jerusalem: 1967–68. In this edition two censored *responsa* (§§29 and 86) dealing with aspects of Jewish-Christian relations were restored at the end of the volume.

SMA'. See Falk, Joshua. *Sefer Me'irat Einayim.*

SMaG, See Moses ben Jacob of Coucy. *Sefer Mizvot Gadol.*

Sofer, Moses (1762–1839). *Ḥidushei Tora Moshe Sofer. Responsa.* 6 vols. Pressburg: 1855–61. Often republished. Often known as *ḤaTaM Sofer.*

Sofer, Solomon. *Ḥut ha-Meshulash* [The Triple Cord]. Mukachevo [Munkácz]: 1895.

Solomon ben Isaac (1040–1105). *Tshuvot RaSHI* [Responsa RaSHI]. Ed. Israel Elfenbein. New York: 1943.

———, supposed author. *Sefer ha-Ora.* Ed. Solomon Buber. Lemberg: 1905. Photographic reprint, Jerusalem: 1966–67.

Spira, Nathan Nata [ben Reuben David] (d. 1662). *Maamar Yayin ha-Meshumar.* Venice: 1659–60.

Stadthagen, Joseph b. Samson (d. 1715). *Divrei Zikaron.* Amsterdam: 1705.

Steinhardt, Joseph (c. 1720–76). *Responsa Zikhron Yosef.* Fürth: 1772–73.

Steinhardt, Menaḥem Mendel b. Simeon (1768–1825). *Divrei Igeret.* Roedelheim: 1811–12.

Tana de-Vei Eliyahu. See Ish-Shalom, Meir.

TaZ. See David ben Samuel ha-Levi.

Tohorat ha-Kodesh. See Benjamin Wolf b. Mattathiah.

Tosafot. Novellae to most tractates of the Babylonian Talmud. Published in standard editions of that text.

Tosfot Yom Tov. See Heller, Yom Tov Lipmann.

Trumat ha-Deshen. See Isserlein, Israel ben Petaḥia.

Turei Zahav. See David ben Samuel ha-Levi.

Yam shel Shlomo. See Luria, Solomon.

Yore De'a. Part II of both Jacob ben Asher, *Arbaa Turim*, and Joseph Caro, *Shulḥan Arukh.* Following convention, references are to Caro's work unless Jacob ben Asher's work is indicated specifically.

Yosef Omez. See Hahn (Nordlingen), Joseph Yuspa.

Zemaḥ Zedek. See Krokhmal, Menaḥem Mendel.

Zera Berakh. See Berechiah Berakh.

Zikhron Yosef. See Steinhardt, Joseph.

Ziv, Asher. Ed. *Responsa She'erit Yosef.* See Katz, Joseph ben Gershon.

b. Communal Records

Assaf, Simḥa. *Mekorot le-Toldot ha-Ḥinukh be-Yisra'el* [Sources for the History of Jewish Education]. 2nd edition. 4 vols. Tel-Aviv: 1930–54.

Baer, Fritz. *Das Protokollbuch der Landjudenschaft des Herzogtums Kleve.* Berlin: 1922.

Balaban, Majer. "Die krakauer Judengemeinde—Ordnung von 1595 und ihre

Nachträge." *Jahrbuch der Jüdisch-Literarischen Gesellschaft* 10 (1912–13): pp. 296–360; 11 (1916): pp. 88–114.

Dubnow, Simon, ed. *Pinkas ha-Medina o Pinkas Vaad ha-Kehilot ha-Rishonot bi-Mdinat Lita* [The Register of the Jewish Provincial Council, Being the Register of the Council of the Earliest Jewish Communities in Lithuania]. Berlin: 1925.

Flesch, Heinrich. "Aus den Statuten der mährischen Beerdigungs-gesellschaften," *Jahrbuch der Gesellschaft für Geschichte der Juden in der Čechoslovakischen Republik* 5 (1933), pp. 157–74.

Grunwald, M. "Die Statuten der 'Hamburg-Altonaer Gemeinde' von 1726." *Mitteilungen der Gesellschaft für Jüdische Volkskunde* 11 (1903): pp. 1–64.

Halperin, Israel, ed. *Pinkas Vaad Arba Araẓot. Likutei Takanot, Ktavim u-Reshumot* [The Register of the Council of the Four Lands. Collected By-Laws, Writings, and Notes. Latin title: *Acta Congressus Generalis Judaeorum Regni Poloniae (1580–1764)*]. Jerusalem: 1945.

———, ed. *Takanot Medinat Mehrin. 5410–5508* [The By-Laws of (the Jewish Provincial Council of) Moravia. Latin title: *Constitutiones Congressus Generalis Judaeorum Moraviensium (1650–1748)*]. Jerusalem: 1951. Note: The editor's name is transliterated as "Halpern" on the Latin title page.

———. "The Beginnings of the Lithuanian Jewish Council and its Relations with the Council of the Four Lands [in Hebrew]." *Zion* 3 (1938): pp. 51–57.

Halpern, Israel. See Halperin, Israel.

Margalioth, Ḥayim Ze'ev. *Dubno Rabati.* See in section "e" (Secondary Sources).

Pinkas Kahal Frankfurt de-Main. Jewish National and University Library. MS Heb 4° 662.

Wachstein, Bernhard. *Urkunden und Akten zur Geschichte der Juden in Eisenstadt und den Siebengemeinden.* Vienna: 1926.

Weinryb, Bernard Dov. *Texts and Studies in the Communal History of Polish Jewry.* Hebrew title: *Te'udot le-Toldot ha-Kehilot ha-Yehiudiyot be-Folin.* New York: 1950.

c. Memoirs and Historical Accounts

Ber of Bolechow. *The Memoirs of Ber of Bolechow (1723–1805).* Ed. M. Wischnitzer. London: 1922. The original Hebrew text was published simultaneously by Wischnitzer as *Zikhronot R. Dov mi-Boliḥov (5483–5565).* Berlin: 1922. Reprint, Jerusalem: 5729.

Emden, Jacob ben Ẓvi. *Megilat Sefer.* Ed. David Cahana. Warsaw: 1896–97. Reprint, New York: 1955–56. New edition accompanied by additional critical apparatus, ed. Abraham Bik (Sha'uli), Jerusalem: 1979.

Glückel of Hameln. *Zikhronot Marat Glikel me-Hamil* [The (Yiddish) Memoirs of Glückel of Hameln]. Ed. David Kaufmann. Frankfurt am Main: 1896. English translation: *The Life of Glückel of Hameln 1646–1724, Written by Herself*. Tr. and ed. Beth-Zion Abrahams. New York: 1963. [There is also a less satisfactory translation by Marvin Lowenthal: *The Memoirs of Glückel of Hameln*. New York: 1932.]

Hannover, Nathan Nata. *Yeven Meẓula* [The Miry Pit]. Venice: 1653. Often reprinted. References in this text are to the edition of Berlin: 1923. English edition: *Abyss of Despair*, tr. Abraham J. Mesch. New York: 1950. Reprinted with foreword by William B. Helmreich, New Brunswick: 1983.

Isak, Aaron. *Avtobiografie* [Yiddish. Autobiography]. Ed. Naḥum Stiff [Shtif]. Berlin: 1922. Note that another Yiddish translation was published by Zolman Reisen as *Aharon Izik's Zikhroynos*, Warsaw: 1927.

———. *Denkwürdigkeiten des Aron Isak. 1730–1817*. Ed. Z. Holm. Berlin: 1930. German version of above.

Katz, Sabbetai. *Megilat Eyfa* [Scroll of Gloom]. First edition, Amsterdam:1650–51. Reprinted in Solomon ibn Verga, *Shevet Yehuda*, ed. M. Wiener (Hanover: 1854–55). Cited by Professor Katz from the documentary appendix to I. Halperin, ed., *Beit Yisra'el be-Folin*. (Jerusalem: 1953), II, pp. 252–55.

Maimon, Solomon. *Geschichte des eigenen Lebens. 1754–1800*. Berlin: 1935. English edition: *Solomon Maimon, An Autobiography*: tr. J. Clark Murray. London: 1888. Abridged edition by Moses Hadas, New York: 1947.

Mayer, Sigmund. *Ein jüdischer Kaufmann*. Leipzig: 1926.

d. Other Primary Sources

Ascher, S. *Leviathan oder über Religion in Rücksicht des Judentums*. Berlin: 1792.

Dohm, Christian Wilhelm. *Über die bürgerliche Verbesserung der Juden* [On the Civil Improvement of the Jews]. Berlin: 1781–83.

Friedländer, David. *Sendschreiben an . . . Probst Teller . . . von einigen Hausvätern jüdischer Religion*. Berlin: 1799. Reprinted with Hebrew translation by Miriam Di-Nur, Jerusalem: 1975.

Goethe, Johann Wolfgang von. *Aus meinem Leben. Dichtung und Warheit*. Berlin: 1970–74. English translation: *Poetry and Truth, From My Own Life*, tr. Minna Steele Smith, London: 1908.

Ha-Me'asef [The Collector]. Haskala periodical. Various places: 1783–1811.

Lessing, Gotthold E. *Nathan der Weise*. 1778. English translation: *Nathan the Wise*, tr. Bayard Quincy Morgan. New York: 1955.

Mendelssohn, Moses. *Jerusalem, or On Religious Power and Judaism*. Tr. Allan Arkush. Hanover and London: 1983.

———. *Moses Mendelssohns gesammelte Schriften*. Ed. G. B. Mendelssohn. 7 vols. Leipzig: 1843–44.

Schudt, Johann Jakob. *Jüdische Merkwürdigkeiten*. Frankfurt am Main: 1714–18. Reprinted, Berlin: 1922.

Sulamith. German-language Haskala periodical. Leipzig: 1806–33.
Wessely, Naphtali Herz (Hartwig). *Divrei Shalom ve-Emet* [Words of Peace and Truth]. Berlin: 1782. Over the next three years, Wessely wrote three further pamphlets in defense of his program; all four are now included under the general title.

e. Secondary Sources

Abrahams, Israel. *Jewish Life in the Middle Ages.* London: 1896. Katz refers to this edition, which was recently reprinted and widely distributed in paperback form, New York: 1969. A second enlarged edition, ed. Cecil Roth, London: 1932.
Agus, Irving A. *Rabbi Meir of Rothenburg. His Life and His Works. . . .* 2nd edition. New York: Ktav, 1970.
Albeck, S. "Rabenu Tam's Attitude to the Problems of his Time" [in Hebrew]. *Zion* 19 (1953–54): pp. 104–41.
Altmann, Berthold. "The Autonomous Federation of Jewish Communities in Paderborn." *Jewish Social Studies* 3 (1941): pp. 159–88.
———. "Jews and the Rise of Capitalism: Economic Theory and Practice in a Westphalian Community." *Jewish Social Studies* 5 (1943): pp. 163–86.
Aptowitzer, Victor [Avigdor], ed. *Mavo le-Sefer RaAViYaH* [Introduction to the Book of Ra'AViYAH] of Eliezer ben Joel ha-Levi. Jerusalem: 1938.
Aronstein, Raphael E. "The Jews' Hat" [in Hebrew]. *Zion* 13–14 (1948–49): pp. 33–42.
Assaf, Simḥa. *Batei ha-Din ve-Sidreihem Aḥarei Ḥatimat ha-Talmud* [Jewish Courts and Their Procedures after the Talmudic Period]. Jerusalem: 1923–24.
———. *Ha-Onshin Aḥarei Ḥatimat ha-Talmud* [Criminal Jurisdiction since the Conclusion of the Talmud]. Jerusalem: 1922.
———. "Toward a History of the Rabbinate in Germany, Poland, and Lithuania" [In Hebrew]. Reprinted in *Be-Ohalei Yaakov.* Jerusalem: 1946–47: pp. 27–65.
Auerbach, B. H. *Geschichte der israelitischen Gemeinde in Halberstadt.* Halberstadt: 1886.
Baer, Yitzhak F. *Galut.* Berlin: 1936. English edition: *Galut.* New York: 1947. Hebrew edition: *Galut.* Jerusalem, 1980.
———. *A History of the Jews in Christian Spain.* Philadelphia: Jewish Publication Society, 1966.
———. "Gemeinde und Landjudenschaft." *Korrespondenzblatt des Vereins zur Gründung und Erhaltung einer Akademie für die Wissenschaft des Judentums* 2 (1921): pp. 16–29.
———. "The Origins of the Organization of the Jewish Community in the Middle Ages" [in Hebrew]. *Zion* 15 (1949–50): pp. 1–41.

———. "RaSHI and the Historical Conditions of His Time" [in Hebrew]. *Tarbiẓ* 20 (1949–50): pp. 320–32.

———. "The Unity of the History of the Jewish People and Problems in Its Organic Development" [in Hebrew]. *[First] World Congress of Jewish Studies (5707 [1946–47])*. Jerusalem: 5712 [1951–52]. Pp. 337–43.

Balaban, Meir. *Le-Toldot ha-Tnu'a ha-Frankit* [Toward a History of the Frankist Movement]. 2 vols. Tel Aviv: 1933–34 to 1934–35.

———. "The Legal Status of the Jews and Their Communal Organization" [in Hebrew]. In I. Halperin, ed., *Beit Yisra'el be-Folin* (Jerusalem: 1948) I, pp. 44–65.

———. "Medieval Jewish History" [in Hebrew]. In I. Halperin, ed., *Beit Yisra'el be-Folin* Jerusalem: 1948. I, pp. 1–16.

Baron, Salo W. *The Jewish Community*. Philadelphia: 1942.

———. *Die Judenfrage auf dem Wiener Kongress auf Grund von zum Teil ungedruckten Quellen dargestellt*. Vienna and Berlin: 1920.

Ben-David, J. "Beginnings of Modern Jewish Society in Hungary During the First Half of the Nineteenth Century" [in Hebrew]. *Zion* 17 (1952): pp. 101–28.

Ben-Sasson, Ḥ. H. "Statutes for the Enforcement of the Observance of the Sabbath in Poland" [in Hebrew]. *Zion* 21 (1956): pp. 183–206.

———. "Wealth and Poverty in the Teaching of the Preacher, Reb Ephraim of Lenczyca" [in Hebrew]. *Zion* 19 (1954): pp. 142–66.

Berliner, Abraham. *Religionsgesprach*. Berlin: 1914.

Birnbaum, Solomon. "Jiddisch." *Encyclopaedia Judaica* (1932), IX, pp. 112–18.

Bloch, Ph. *Die Generalprivilegien der polnischen Judenschaft*. Posen: 1892.

Breger, Marcus. *Zur Handelsgeschichte der Juden in Polen während des 17. Jahrhunderts, mit besonderer Berücksichtigung der Judenschaft Posens*. Breslau: 1932.

Brunschwig, H. *La crise de l'état prussien à la fin du XVIIIe siècle, et la genèse de la mentalité romantique*. Paris: 1947. English translation: *Enlightenment and Romanticism in Eighteenth-Century Prussia*. Chicago: 1974.

Cahen, Abraham. "Le rabbinat de Metz pendant la période française (1567–1871)." *Révue des Etudes Juives* 7 (1883): pp. 103–16, 204–26; 8 (1884): pp. 255–74; 12 (1886): pp. 283–97; 13 (1886): pp. 105–26.

Caro, Georg. *Sozial- und Wirtschaftsgeschichte der Juden im Mittelalter und der Neuzeit*. Leipzig: 1908 and 1920.

Dinaburg [Dinur], Ben-Zion. *Be-Mifne ha-Dorot* [Historical Writings]. Jerusalem, 1955.

———. *Israel and the Diaspora*. Philadelphia: Jewish Publication Society, 1969.

———. *Yisra'el ba-Gola* [The Jews in the Diaspora]. Tel-Aviv and Jersualem: 1926. Corrected and expanded 2nd edition, Tel-Aviv: 1961.

———. "The Beginnings of Ḥasidism and Its Social and Messianic Foundations" [in Hebrew]. Reprinted in *Be-Mifne ha-Dorot*, pp. 81–227.

Dinur. See Dinaburg.

Drory, Moshe. See Frank, Moshe.

Dubnov, Semen Markovich. See Dubnow, Simon.

Dubnow, Simon. *Jewish History. An Essay in the Philosophy of History*. Tr. Henrietta Szold. Phildelphia: Jewish Publication Society, 1903. Reprinted in Koppel Pinson, ed., *Nationalism and History*, pp. 253–324. Philadelphia: Jewish Publication Society, 1958.

———. *Toldot ha-Ḥasidut* [History of Hasidism]. Tel-Aviv: 1930–32.

Ehrentreu, H. "Über den 'Pilpul' in den alten Jeschibot." *Jahrbuch der Jüdisch-Literarischen Gesellschaft* 3 (1905): pp. 206–19.

Eliav, Mordekhai. *Ha-Ḥinukh ha-Yehudi be-Germanya* [Jewish Education in Germany]. Jerusalem: 1960–61.

Enẓiklopediya Talmudit. Jerusalem, 1947–.

Finkelstein, L. *Jewish Self-Government in the Middle Ages*. 2nd revised edition, New York: 1964.

Fishman, Isidore. *The History of Jewish Education in Central Europe from the End of the Sixteenth to the End of the Eighteenth Century*. London: 1944.

Frank [Drory], Moshe. *Kehilot Ashkenaz u-Vatei ha-Din Shelahen* [Ashkenazic Communities and their Courts]. Tel-Aviv: 1937.

Freimann, Abraham H. *Seder Kidushin ve-Nisu'in aḥarei Ḥatimat ha-Talmud. Meḥkar Histori-Dogmati be-Dinei Yisra'el* [Post-Talmudic Betrothal and Marriage. A Historico-Dogmatic Investigation of Jewish Law]. Jerusalem: 1944–45. Reprint, 1964.

Freund, Ismar. *Die Emanzipation der Juden in Preussen unter besonder Berücksichtigung des Gesetzes vom 11 März 1812*. Berlin: 1912.

Gelber, N. M. *Toldot Yehudei Brodyde*. [History of the Jews of Brody] [=*Arim ve-Imahot be-Yisrael*, ed. J. L. Maimon, vol. VI]. Jerusalem: 1955.

Gold, H. *Die Juden und Judengemeinden Mährens in Vergangenheit und Gegenwart*. Brünn: 1929.

Graetz, Heinrich. *Geschichte der Juden von den ältesten Zeiten bis auf die Gegenwart*. Leipzig: 1853–76. Many subsequent complete or partial editions. [Professor Katz refers to the 3rd and 4th editions, and no attempt has been made to harmonize the references. For a complete listing, see M. Brann, ed., *Heinrich Graetz: Abhandlungen zu seinem 100. Geburtstage* (Vienna and Berlin: 1917), pp. 124–71. There have been three editions of a partial translation into English as *A History of the Jews*, of which the most complete is Philadelphia: 1891–98.]

———. *The Structure of Jewish History and Other Essays*. Ed. Ismar Schorsch. New York: Jewish Theological Seminary of America, 1975.

Grunwald, M. *Samuel Oppenheimer und sein Kreis*. Vienna: 1913.

———. "Die Statuten der 'Hamburg-Altonaer Gemeinde' von 1726." *Mitteilungen der Gesellschaft für Jüdische Volkskunde* 11 (1903): pp. 1–64.

Halperin, I. *Yehudim ve-Yahadut be-Mizraḥ Eyropa. Meḥkarim be-Toldoteyhem.* English title: *Eastern European Jewry. Historical Studies.* Jerusalem: 1968.

———. "The Beginnings of the Lithuanian Jewish Council and Its Relations with the Council of the Four Lands" [in Hebrew]. *Zion* 3 (1937–38): pp. 51–57. Reprinted in his *Yehudim ve-Yahadut be-Mizraḥ Eyropa,* pp. 48–54.

———. "*Imprimaturs* of the Council of the Four Lands" [in Hebrew]. *Kiryat Sefer* 11 (1934–35): pp. 105–10. Reprinted in his *Yehudim ve-Yahadut be-Mizraḥ Eyropa,* pp. 87–92.

———. "The Minute Book of the 'Havura' of Craftsmen in Luboml" [in Hebrew]. *Yedi'ot ha-Arkhiyon ve-ha-Muze'on shel Tnu'at ha-Avoda* [Newsletter of the Archive and Museum of the Labor Movement] (5695 [1934–35]). Reprinted in his *Yehudim ve-Yahadut be-Mizraḥ Eyropa,* pp. 181–84.

———. "On the Danger of Expulsion of all Polish Jews during the Second Half of the Seventeenth Century." *Zion* 17 (1951–52). Reprinted in his *Yehudim ve-Yahadut be-Mizraḥ Eyropa,* pp. 266–76.

———, ed. *Beit Yisrael be-Folin mi-Yamim Rishonim ve-ad li-Ymot ha-Ḥurban.* 2 vols. Jerusalem: 1948 and 1953.

Heine, Heinrich. *Sämtliche Werke* [Collected Works]. Leipzig and Vienna: 1898. [English translation drawn from F. Ewen, ed., *Poetry and Prose of Heinrich Heine,* New York: 1948.]

Heinemann, Isaac. "The Dispute over Nationality in the Aggada and in Philosophy during the Middle Ages" [in Hebrew]. *Sefer Dinaburg,* ed. Yitzhak Baer, et al. Jerusalem: 1949, pp. 132–50.

———. "Unity in Moses Mendelssohn's Philosophy of Religion" [in Hebrew]. In *Meẓuda* [English title: *Metsudah*], ed. Simon Rawidowicz (London and Waltham: 1954), VII, pp. 197–219.

Hendel, M. *Mlakha u-Vaalei Mlakha be-Am Yisra'el* [Crafts and Craftsmen among the Jewish People]. Tel Aviv: 1955–56.

Hildesheimer, E. E. *Das jüdische Gesellschaftsrecht.* Leipzig: 1930.

Hirsch, Samson Raphael. *Igrot Ẓafon. Neunzehn Briefe über Judenthum.* First edition, Altona: 1836. English translation: *The Nineteen Letters of Ben Uziel.* New York: 1899.

Hoffmann, David. *Der Schulchan-Aruch und die Rabbinen über das Verhältniss der Juden zu Andersgläubigen.* 2nd enlarged edition, Berlin: 1894.

Horodezky, Samuel Abba. Shemi mi-Shmuel. Drohobycz: 1895.

Horovitz, Markus. *Frankfurter Rabbinen: Ein beitrag zur geschichte der israelitischen gemeinde in Frankfurt a. M.* 4 vols. Frankfurt am Main: 1882–85. Expanded edition ed. Josef Unna, Jerusalem: 1969. Hebrew edition tr. Joshua Amir under the title *Rabanei Frankfurt.* Jerusalem: 1972.

———. *Die Frankfurter Rabbinerversammlung von 1603 (Beilage zur Ein-*

ladungsschrift der israelitischen Religionsschule). Frankfurt am Main: 1897.

———. "Die Wohltätigkeit bei den Juden im alten Frankfurt." *Israelitische Monatsschrift* (supplement to *Jüdische Presse*) 27 (1896): pp. 17–27.

Katz, Jacob. *Die Entstehung der Judenassimilation in Deutschland und deren Ideologie*. Ph.D. dissertation. Frankfurt am Main: 1935. Published in *Nach'lat Z'wi* 5–7 (135–37). Reprinted in Katz, *Emancipation and Assimilation: Studies in Modern Jewish History*, pp. 195–293. Westmead, England: 1972. References are to the latter edition.

———. *Exclusiveness and Tolerance. Studies in Jewish-Gentile Relations in Medieval and Modern Times*. Oxford: 1961.

———. *Le'umiyut Yehudit. Masot u-Meḥkarim* [Jewish Nationalism. Essays and Studies]. Collected essays, including a number of papers mentioned in this work. Jerusalem: 1983.

———. "The Concept of Social History and Its Possible Use in Jewish Historical Research." *Scripta Hierosolymitana* 3 (1955): pp. 292–312.

———. "Marriage and Sexual Life among the Jews at the End of the Middle Ages" [in Hebrew]. *Zion* 10 (1944–45): pp. 22–54.

———. "Religious Tolerance in the Halakhic and Philosophical System of R. Menaḥem ha-Meiri" [in Hebrew]. *Zion* 18 (1953): pp. 15–30.

———. [Review of] Ephraim E. Urbach, *Baalei ha-Tosafot. Toldoteihem, Ḥibureihem ve-Shitatam* [The Tosaphists: Their Biographies, Writings, and Methodology] [in Hebrew]. *Kiryat Sefer* [*Kirjath Sefer*] 31 (5716 [1955–56]): pp. 9–16.

Kaufmann, David. *R. Jair Chajjim Bacharach (1638–1702) und seine Ahnen. Zur Geschichte jüdischer Familien*, no. 2. Trier: 1894.

Kestenberg-Gladstein, R. "Differences of Estates within Pre-Emancipation Jewry." *Journal of Jewish Studies* 5 (1954): pp. 156–66; 6 (1955): pp. 35–49.

———. "The Economic History of the Jews in Non-Metropolitan Bohemia in the Seventeenth and Eighteenth Centuries" [in Hebrew]. *Zion* 12 (1947): pp. 49–65, 160–85.

Kisch, Guido. *The Jews in Medieval Germany*. Chicago: 1949.

———. "Der erste Deutschland promovierte Jude." *Monatsschrift für Geschichte und Wissenschaft des Judentums* 78 (1934): pp. 350–63.

———. "The Yellow Badge in History." *Historia Judaica* 4 (1942): pp. 95–144.

Klausner, Israel. *Toldot ha-Kehila ha-Ivrit be-Vilna* [History of the Jewish Community of Wilno]. I. Environment and Communal Organization. Wilno: 1938.

———. *Vilna bi-Tkufat ha-Gaon. Ha-Milḥama ha-Ruḥanit ve-ha-Ḥevratit be-Vilna bi-Tkufat ha-GRA'* [The Jewish Community of Wilno in the Days of the "Gaon"]. Jerusalem: 1942.

Kracauer, Isidor. *Geschichte der Juden in Frankfurt an Main. 1150–1824*. 2 vols. Frankfurt am Main: 1925–27.

Lachower, F., and Isaiah Tishby. *Mishnat ha-Zohar* [The Wisdom of the Zohar]. 2nd edition, Jerusalem: 1957.

Landsberg, H. *Henrietta Herz, ihr Leben und ihre Zeit.* Weimar: 1913.

Lesser, Ludwig. *Chronik der Gesellschaft der Freunde in Berlin.* Berlin: 1842.

Lewin, Louis. *Geschichte der Juden in Lissa.* Pinne: 1904.

———. *Die Landessynode der grosspolnischen Judenschaft.* Frankfurt am Main: 1926.

———. "Aus dem jüdischen Kulturkampfe." *Jahrbuch der Jüdisch-Literarischen Gesellschaft (sitz Frankfurt am Main)* 12 (1918): 1, pp. 165–98.

———. "Jüdische Ärzte in Grosspolen." *Jahrbuch der Jüdisch-Literarischen Gesellschaft (sitz Frankfurt am Main)* 9 (1911): 1, pp. 367–420.

———. "Der Schtadlan im Posener Ghetto." *Festschrift zum achtzigsten Geburtstage . . . Wolf Feilchenfeld.* Ed. Bernhard Koenigsberger and Moritz Silberberg, pp. 31–39. Pleschen-Schrimm: 1907.

Löw, Immanuel, and Solomon Klein. *A Szegedi Chevra 1787 töl 1887.* Szegedin: 1887.

Löw, Leopold. *Gesammelte Schriften.* Ed. Immanuel Löw. Szegedin: 1889–1900.

———. *Die Lebensalter in der jüdischen Literatur.* Szegedin: 1875.

Löwenstein, Leopold. *Geschichte der Juden in der Kurpfalz.* Frankfurt: 1895.

Lütge, F. *Deutsche Sozial- und Wirtschaftsgeschichte.* Berlin: 1952. 3rd edition, Berlin and New York: 1966.

Margalioth, Ḥayim Ze'ev. *Dubno Rabati. Toldot ha-Ir Dubno ve-Haatakot mi-Pinkas ha-Kahal shelah mi-Shnat [5]475 va-Hal'a u-me-Maẓevot she-al Kivrei Gdolei ha-Ir ha-Zot ve-Nikhbadehah* [Greater Dubno. The History of (the Jewish Community of) the City of Dubno, Excerpts from its Communal Register from 1714–15 on, and Epitaphs of this City's Great (Rabbis) and Honored (Leaders)]. Warsaw: 1910.

Mieses, M. *Die Enstehungsursache der jüdischen Dialekte.* Vienna: 1915.

Nadav, M. "The *Pinkas* of the Jewish Community of Frankfort-on-the Main" [in Hebrew]. *Kiryat Sefer* [*Kirjath Sepher*] 31 (1955–56): pp. 507–16.

Netter, N. *Vingt siècles d'histoire d'une communauté juive.* Paris: 1938.

Parkes, James. *The Jew in the Medieval Community.* London: 1938.

Parson, T. Review of *The Rise of Economic Individualism. A Criticism of M. Weber and His School,* by H. H. Robertson. *The Journal of Political Economy* (1935): pp. 688ff.

Perles, J. *Geschichte der Juden in Posen.* Reprinted from *Monatsschrift für Geschichte und Wissenschaft des Judentums* 13 and 14. Breslau: 1865.

Priebatsch, E. "Die Judenpolitik des fürstlichen Absolutismus im 17 und 18 Jahrhundert." *Festschrift Dietrich Schäffer* (1915): pp. 608ff.; chapter 23, n. 7.

Ruppin, Arthur. *Ha-Soẓiologiya shel ha-Yehudim* [The Sociology of the Jews]. Tel-Aviv: 1931.

Schechter, Solomon. "The Chassidim." *Studies in Judaism.* First series. Philadelphia: 1896. pp. 1–45.

Schipper, Isaac. *Toldot ha-Kalkala ha-Yehudit* [History of the Jewish Economy]. Tel-Aviv: 1935 and 1936.

———. "The Economic History of the Jews of Poland and Lithuania from Ancient Times to the Division of the State" [in Hebrew]. In I. Halperin, ed., *Beit Yisra'el be-Folin* (Jerusalem: 1948), I, pp. 155–99.

Schnee, H. *Die Hoffinanz und der moderne Staat*. Berlin: 1952–55.

Scholem, Gershom. *Dvarim be-Go* [Explications and Implications. Writings on Jewish Heritage and Renaissance]. Tel-Aviv: 1975–76.

———. *Major Trends in Jewish Mysticism*. 3rd revised edition. New York: Schocken, 1954.

———. *Reshit ha-Kabala* [The Beginnings of the Kabbala]. Jerusalem: 1948. A much-expanded German version was re-edited and updated as *Origins of the Kabbalah*, tr. Allan Arkush, ed. R. J. Z. Werblowsky. Philadelphia: 1987.

———. *Shabtai Ẓvi ve-ha-Tnu'a ha-Shabta'it bi-Ymei Ḥayav* [Sabbetai Ẓvi and the Sabbatean Movement during his Lifetime] (Tel-Aviv: 1967). English updated translation: *Sabbatai Ṣevi. The Mystical Messiah 1626–1676*, ed. R. J. Z. Werblowski. Bollingen Series, no. 93. Princeton, N.J.: Princeton University Press, 1973.

———. "Devekuth, or Communion with God." *Review of Religion* 14 (1949–50): pp. 115–39. Reprinted in *The Messianic Idea in Judaism* (New York: 1971), pp. 203–27, and (in an edited Hebrew version) in *Dvarim be-Go*, pp. 325–50.

———. "The Historical Figure of R. Israel Baal Shem Tov" [in Hebrew]. *Molad* 144–145 (Av-Elul, 5720). Reprinted in an expanded, corrected version in *Dvarim be-Go*, pp. 287–324.

———. "Redemption through Sin" [in Hebrew]. *Kneset* 2 (1937). English version in *The Messianic Idea in Judaism and Other Essays on Jewish Spirituality*. (New York: 1971), pp. 78–141.

———. "The Sabbatean Movement in Poland" [in Hebrew]. In I. Halperin, ed., *Beit Yisrael be-Folin* (Jerusalem: 1954), II, pp. 36–76.

———. "Thoughts on *Wissenschaft des Judentums*" [in Hebrew]. *Luaḥ ha-Areẓ (5705)*, pp. 94–112. Tel-Aviv: 1944. Reprinted in *Dvarim be-Go*, pp. 385–403.

———. "Tradition und Neuschöpfung im Ritus der Kabbalisten." *Eranos Jahrbuch* 19 (1950): pp. 121–80. English translation: "Tradition and New Creation in the Ritual of the Kabbalists." Chapter 4 of Gershom G. Scholem, *On the Kabbalah and Its Symbolism*. New York: 1965.

———. "The Two First Testimonies on the Relations between Ḥasidic Groups and the Baal Shem Tov" [in Hebrew]. *Tarbiẓ* 20 (1948–49): pp. 228–40.

———. See also Wilhelm, Y. D.

Schorr, Moses. *Rechtsstellung und innere Verfassung der Juden in Polen; ein geschichtlicher Rundblick*. Berlin and Vienna: 1917.

Shmeruk (Szmeruk), Chone. "The Social Implications of Ḥasidic Slaughter" [in Hebrew]. *Zion* 20 (1955): pp. 47–72.

Shoḥet, Azriel. *Im Ḥilufei ha-Tkufot. Reshit ha-Haskala bi-Yahadut Germanya* [Beginnings of the Haskala among German Jewry]. Jerusalem: 1960.

———. "The German Jews' Integration within Their Non-Jewish Environment in the First Half of the Eighteenth Century" [in Hebrew]. *Zion* 21 (1956): pp. 207–35.

———. "Study Societies in Palestine, Poland-Lithuania, and Germany during the Sixteenth through Eighteenth Centuries" [in Hebrew]. *Ha-Ḥinukh* (5716 [1955–56]): pp. 404–18.

Simon, Akiva E. "Pedagogic Philanthropism and Jewish Education" [in Hebrew]. *Mordecai M. Kaplan Jubilee Volume on the Occasion of His Seventieth Birthday*, pp. 147–87. New York: 1953.

Sombart, Werner. *Die Juden und das Wirtschaftsleben.* Leipzig: 1911. English translation: *The Jews and Modern Capitalism.* London: 1913. Reprinted with an introduction by Bert Hoselitz, Glencoe: 1951.

———. *Der moderne Kapitalismus.* Leipzig: 1902.

Stern, M. 'Der Hochverratsprozess gegen die deutschen Juden im Anfange des 17. Jahrhunderts." *Monatsblätter für Vergangenheit und Gegenwart des Judentums*, ed. Bernhard Koenigsberger, pp. 24–39, 80–90, 115–28, 154–62. Berlin: 1890–91.

Stern, Selma. *The Court Jew.* Philadelphia: 1950.

———. *Jud Süss.* Berlin: 1929.

———. *Der preussische Staat und die Juden.* Berlin: 1925. Reprinted, Tübingen: 1962.

———. "The Jews in the Economic Policy of Frederick the Great." *Jewish Social Studies* 11 (1949): pp. 129–52.

Straus, Raphael. "The 'Jewish Hat' as an Aspect of Social History." *Jewish Social Studies* 4 (1942): pp. 59–72.

Sulzbach, A. "Ein alter Frankfurter Wohltätigkeitsverein." *Jahrbuch der Jüdisch-Literarischen Gesellschaft* 2 (1904): pp. 241–66.

Tchernowitz, Chaim. *Toldot ha-Poskim* [English title:*Toledoth ha-Poskim. History of Jewish Codes*]. New York: 1946–47.

Tishby, Isaiah. *Mishnat ha-Zohar.* See Lachower, F.

———. *Torat ha-Ra ve-ha-Klipa be-Kabalat ha-ARI* [The Doctrine of Evil and the *Kelippah* in Lurianic Kabbalism]. Jerusalem: 1941–42. Reprinted, Jerusalem: 1970–71.

Unna, S. "Statuten-Entwurf eines alten Vereins in Frankfurt a/M aus dem Jahre 1822." *Jahrbuch der Jüdisch-Literarischen Gesellschaft* 21 (1930): pp. 265–71.

Urbach, Ephraim E. *Baalei ha-Tosafot. Toldoteihem, Ḥibureihem ve-Shitatam* [The Tosaphists: Their Biographies, Writings, and Methodology]. Jerusalem: 1955.

Vishnitzer, M. See Wischnitzer, M.

Wachstein, Bernhard. "Die Gründung der Wiener Chewra Kadischa im Jahre

1763." *Mitteilungen zur jüdischen Volkskunde* 32–33. Revised and printed separately, Leipzig: 1910.

Weber, Max. *Gesammelte Aufsätze zur Religionssoziologie.* Tübingen: 1920.

———. *Wirtschaftsgeschichte.* Munich and Leipzig: 1923.

———. *Wirtschaft und Gesellschaft. Grundriss der Sozialoekonomic.* Tübingen: 1922.

Weil, Hans. *Die Entstehung des deutschen Bildungsprinzips.* Bonn: 1930.

Weinryb, Bernard Dov. "Beiträge zur Finanzgeschichte der jüdischen Gemeinden in Polen." Part I: *Monatsschrift für Geschichte und Wissenschaft des Judentums* 82 (1938): pp. 248–63. Part II: *Hebrew Union College Annual* 16 (1941): pp. 187–214.

———. "Outlines of the Economic and Financial History of the Jews in Poland and Lithuania in the Seventeenth and Eighteenth Centuries" [in Hebrew]. *Tarbiz* 10 (1938–39): pp. 90–104, 201–31. Now reprinted in his *Meḥkarim u-Mkorot le-Toldot Yisra'el ba-Et ha-Ḥadasha* [Studies and Documents in Modern Jewish History], pp. 68–120. Jerusalem: 1975.

Weiss, Joseph. "The Beginnings of Hasidism" [in Hebrew]. *Zion* 16 (1950–51): pp. 46–105.

Wiener, Max. *Jüdische Religion im Zeitalter der Emanzipation.* Berlin: 1933.

Weisner, J. *Der Bann in seiner geschichtlichen Entwickelung auf dem Bodem des Judenthumes.* Leipzig: 1864.

Wilhelm, Y.D., and Gershom Scholem. "The 'Ḥavaya de-Rabanan' Circulars Against the Sect of Sabbetai Ẓvi" [in Hebrew]. *Kiryat Sefer [Kirjath Sepher]* 30 (1954–55): pp. 99–104.

Wischnitzer, M. "Die jüdische Zunftverfassung in Polen und Litauen im 17. und 18. Jahrhundert." *Vierteljahrschrift für Sozial- und Wirtschaftsgeschichte* 20 (1928): pp. 433–51.

Yaari, Abraham. *Shluḥei Ereẓ Yisra'el* [Palestinian Emissaries]. Jerusalem: 5711 [1951–52].

Zevin, R. Shlomo Yosef. *Ha-Mo'adim ba-Halakha.* 3rd revised edition, Jerusalem: 1953–54. Partial English translation by Sh. Fox-Ashrei, *The Festivals in Halacha.* Brooklyn and Jerusalem: 1982.

Index